Concepts of International Politics in Global Perspective

Fourth Edition

Concepts of International Politics in Global Perspective

Abdul Aziz Said
The American University

Charles O. Lerche, Jr.
Late, The American University

Charles O. Lerche III
Boston University

Prentice Hall, Englewood Cliffs, New Jersey 07632

Library of Congress Cataloging-in-Publication Data

Said, Abdul Aziz.
Concepts of international politics in global perspective / Abdul Aziz Said, Charles O. Lerche, Jr., Charles O. Lerche, III.—4th ed.
p. cm.
Rev. ed. of: Concepts of international politics in global perspective / Charles O. Lerche, Jr., Abdul Aziz Said. 3rd ed. © 1979.
Includes bibliographical references and index.
ISBN 0–13–174640–5
1. International relations. I. Lerche, Charles O. II. Lerche, Charles O., III. III. Lerche, Charles O. Concepts of international politics in global perspective. IV. Title.
JX1308.S25 1995 94–24776
327—dc20 CIP

Acquisitions editor: Charlyce Jones Owen
Editorial assistant: Nicole Signoretti
Editorial/production supervision and
interior design: P. M. Gordon Associates, Inc.
Copy editor: Peter Reinhart
Cover design: Marjory Dressler
Buyer: Bob Anderson

A Simon & Schuster Company
Englewood Cliffs, New Jersey 07632

Printed in the United States of America
10 9 8 7 6 5 4 3 2 1

ISBN 0-13-174640-5

Prentice-Hall International (UK) Limited, *London*
Prentice-Hall of Australia Pty. Limited, *Sydney*
Prentice-Hall Canada Inc., *Toronto*
Prentice-Hall Hispanoamericana, S.A., *Mexico*
Prentice-Hall of India Private Limited, *New Delhi*
Prentice-Hall of Japan, Inc., *Tokyo*
Simon & Schuster Asia Pte. Ltd., *Singapore*
Editora Prentice-Hall do Brasil, Ltda., *Rio de Janeiro*

To the search for solidarity in a global perspective.
To the discovery that the whole of existence is reflected in the parts, and from the parts comes the greater whole.
To the travelers on the marvelous journey of learning.

Contents

Preface

World politics has changed in major ways in recent years. The objective situations, the underlying forces and circumstances, distributions of power, economic influence, and prominent issues are certainly different. But in addition to these differences, the subjective situation, the frame of reference that people bring to the understanding of world events, has also changed—probably for everyone.

The biggest changes have been in values and ideas. We are leaving—have really left—a world in which participants in the global game of international politics could play their roles on the world stage without the self-conscious awareness that they were playing roles. We have entered a world in which the principal actors—from the president of the United States to a student demonstrator in Beirut—are as much concerned with how their actions will appear on television as they are with the direct impact they will have on the events of world politics.

Recently, the first truly global political community has begun to emerge around us. What we in the international relations field called the interpenetration of states in recent decades has not occurred only in the Western world. It has probably evolved so far as to be irreversible, short of global catastrophe. We have moved from a humanity that lived its collective life as fragments of the whole into a new context of humanity as a whole.

In fact, not only is it inaccurate to speak of the West as distinct from the East, but it is also not accurate even to speak of the North as opposed to the South. These distinctions are more appropriate as generalizations for popular mythology than as descriptions for actual international politics. For example, the gross value of manufactured goods exported by the Global South, formerly called the Third World, equaled the value of the manufactured goods exported by the United

States. Other examples abound: Japan is losing market share in steel and electronic home appliances to South Korea. Truly global industries are emerging and, along with them, the foundations for a world economic system.

The recent manifestations of neoconservatism in the West and religious fundamentalism in many parts of the world, for example, are masking the scale of global transformation now under way. Political rhetoric is essentially backward-looking—it translates contemporary issues into political distinctions of the past. This reactionary bias of political rhetoric is not the monopoly of practitioners of world politics. Media pundits and professional analysts are as much—if not more—the victims of rhetorical anachronisms.

If we in the field of international relations have been guilty of a single error during the recent years, it has been to overemphasize the traditional rituals of the world political game and underestimate the impact of the emergence of the first global civilization. Today's emerging global civilization has a far larger relative sway than Rome, the most extensive of its predecessors. For unlike Rome—which knew only dimly of the civilizations of China and India, and nothing at all of American Indian civilizations in the western hemisphere—the global culture now coalescing excludes no one. The remotest jungle village and the most isolated igloo in the arctic are coming to feel the grip and penetrating power of the first planetary culture.

This edition of *Concepts of International Politics in Global Perspective* emphasizes the kinds of new actors and issues now present within the context of emerging global civilization. The Introduction of this fourth edition updates our brief survey of the study of international relations, reflecting and explaining the changing treatment of the subject matter. Part I, "The Actors in Global Politics," underscores the expanding role of nonstate actors in the global system. Concepts are updated to accommodate the broadening environment of decision making and the new requirements of security. Part II, "The Global Political System: Actors and Their Relations," places emphasis on the expanding diversity of global relations. The treatment reflects greater sensitivity to nonstate actors. Part III, "The Substance of Global Politics: Major Issues of Our Age," has undergone major revision reflecting present challenges of world politics.

The new Conclusion develops the concept of cooperative global politics. The recommended readings for the Introduction, for each of the fifteen chapters, and for the Conclusion have all been updated to include essential works published recently. Yet, the concise nature of the previous three editions remains intact.

Acknowledgments

The generous assistance of our many friends and our two families enabled us to complete the fourth edition of *Concepts of International Politics in Global Perspective.* Professor Ivan Volgyes of The University of Nebraska, Professor Thomas O. Schlesinger of Plymouth State College, and Professor James S. Pacy of the University of Vermont reviewed the manuscript and provided thoughtful criticism. Their contributions have been invaluable. Brian Thoka, Ramin Tabib, Seira Tamang, Anita Roper, Oussama Safa, Amir B. Izadyar, Eric Everson, and Gregory Gugel, teaching assistants and graduate students at The School of International Service, The American University, helped us in researching new material. Sean C. Day, Suzanne Wopperer, Ben M. Rose, Valerie Baker, IngJye Cheng, Greta Gard, Gretchen M. Bossert, and Robyn LeBoeuf, undergraduate students at The School of International Service, The American University, helped us with the tedious labor of reading and commenting on the manuscript. Rita Homsieh, constant friend and invaluable research assistant, helped with all aspects of preparation of this edition with great efficiency and good humor.

Our sons Riyad and Jamil, and Carl and Jacob, respectively, inspired us to see and try to find the possibility of something new in the uncertainty of our times.

The boundless love of my soulmate Elena is a source and a mirror of vision and faith. Her radiant mind made me see this new edition, and her generous heart gave me confidence to do it.

A. A. S.

My wife Loni gave me unfailing and generous support. Her patience and encouragement sustained my effort.

C. O. L. III

Introduction

CHANGING FRAME OF ANALYSIS

International relations resists precise definition. It is conventional to suggest that our field involves the description, explanation, and prediction of the behavior of states and other prominent international and transnational actors. However, after several decades of theory and research, no consensus has emerged among scholars about some basic issues as the scope of the discipline (for example, to what extent should economic relations be considered part of our subject?); the actors (who/what, besides states, contributes to important outcomes in the global arena?); and the "stuff" of the field of study (is international politics ultimately about power, ideas, resources, or something else?).[1]

Furthermore, we do not have a body of formal scientific propositions to pass on to a beginning student. What we do have is a set of questions about the world, some of which are very old and some of which are more contemporary, and a variety of approaches to answering these questions from among which a student can develop a viewpoint that may assist him/her to come to terms with this dynamic field of study.

The value of choosing a particular frame of reference for any inquiry is not that it guarantees our ultimate arrival at the truth. Rather, the "meaning" of world politics, like the meaning of the broader currents of history of which it forms a

[1]In this book we use the terms "international relations" and "international politics" interchangeably. As explained in Chapter 1, we are primarily concerned with that which we define as political. Some writers in the field make a distinction between international politics, the uniquely political relations among states, and international relations, other contacts among states and citizens.

part, is necessarily rediscovered and recast by each succeeding generation. A frame of analysis should be chosen for its *utility* to the observer, defined in terms of the insight it provides through highlighting certain aspects of the subject, downplaying others, and thereby revealing patterns.

The contemporary study of international relations has been profoundly influenced by the behavioral revolution in the social sciences, which took place during the 1950s. As a result, the field has incorporated the logic and methodology of positivism, a (Western) scientific empiricism that defines knowledge primarily as that which can be observed through the senses. This approach has had many benefits deriving mainly from its emphasis on valid and precise research procedures, its demand for proof of generalizations, and its cross-fertilization of the field with concepts from other disciplines. However, to the extent that explanations of human behavior emphasize the external material causes of human action, goals and values have at times received inadequate treatment.

The Western scientific approach to knowledge has, traditionally, been *analytical,* that is, it has broken a subject down into its component simple elements, each of which is studied as thoroughly as possible. The knowledge of the whole is then gained by summing what is known about the parts. Though quite valid, this approach is incomplete and if taken to an extreme may distort our understanding of social conditions. The effort to construct such cause-and-effect analyses may also exclude human motives and the moral significance of human behavior, as well as the historical context of events. We would suggest that any explanation of human behavior in general, and international relations in particular, should be at least as concerned with how *goals* and values are selected and pursued as it is with the influence of external *causes* on these activities.

Additionally, much of this academic study of international relations seems to deny a more personal, existential interpretation of experience by forcing theorists into the role of detached observers. Accordingly, to a large extent the contemporary study of our field does not explain the flow of world events from the standpoint of someone actually participating in the process. Yet, only by acting as conscious participants can we connect international relations to the reality of our experience in the world. We can then see our social milieu for what it is—the product of experience and choices—a drama in which we define and change ourselves and our world by pursuing goals of our own choosing. To this end we should try to develop a total view of world politics in which the objective and subjective dimensions of the field complement each other.

DEVELOPMENT OF THE STUDY OF INTERNATIONAL RELATIONS

The study of international relations as an academic discipline is largely a product of the twentieth century. In earlier times, its subject matter was dealt with by scholars of international law, diplomats and policymakers, and political philosophers. It was only as humanity became more able to envision the world as one interrelated system that questions of world politics, per se, began to attract serious attention.

Several major trends can be discerned in the development of the field. Prominent among these are the traditional, or classical, approach of political philosophy, which goes back to ancient times; the study of diplomatic history, which started shortly before World War I; the "idealist" perspective embodied in the promotion of international law and organization, which was another interwar trend; the "realist" viewpoint that emerged from the experience of World War II; the empirical/behavioral approach referred to previously; the analysis of global interdependence and more specifically of international political economy; and the study of world order. These approaches do not represent clear demarcations, because they have run parallel to each other or have arisen in response to a preceding trend. They differ in the kinds of questions that are posed about the field, the nature and priorities of issues highlighted by each one, and the way events and trends are explained. Contemporary writing incorporates the ideas expressed in all of them, and each one continues to contribute in some degree to the advancement of the field.

The traditional, classical approach can be thought of as that part of the broader study of political philosophy which deals with normative aspects of the relations between states. Many of the great figures in the history of (Western) political thought, such as Aristotle, Augustine, Machiavelli, Hobbes, Locke, Montesquieu, Kant, and Hegel, had something to say on the subject. What is perhaps most interesting is how little attention many of them gave to international politics because they tended to view it as a sort of "wasteland" between the sovereign states in which real political communities were developing. Today, many of the "classic" questions of political philosophy are posed in regard to the international political system as a whole—that is, is it fair, democratic, improving, or decaying?

Diplomatic history also has ancient roots. Since classical times scholars and statesmen have attempted to learn from the past in order to better deal with the present. Modern diplomatic history sought, through detailed accounts of particular periods of significant diplomatic events, to demonstrate the truth of such concepts as national purpose and the balance of power in the historical practice of states. Though an essential stage in the evolution of the field, a historical orientation by itself could not fully develop an adequate conceptual framework for the study of world politics.

Yet another approach focused primarily on problems of international law and international organization. Its exponents felt that the task of the scholar was to work toward the transformation of the states system and the creation of international institutions. This activist position was largely inspired by the establishment of the League of Nations, by the hopes associated with its inception, and by the goal of communicating the ideas of the League to the world—particularly the isolationist-inclined United States. These scholars were motivated by the strongly held belief that establishment of a strong international organization would resolve many of the perplexing issues of international politics.

Thus, the scholarship of the early interwar period was optimistic. However, certain events called this optimism more and more into question, and by 1939 a thorough reconsideration was under way. The political turmoil in Europe and the Far East in the 1930s, the rise of fascist dictators, and the impotence of the League of Nations in the face of these events contributed to feelings of despair and cynicism among scholars and the world at large.

This disappointment was particularly acute among American thinkers, and the reformist approach to the study of international relations was in large measure jettisoned. The prevailing academic judgment was that the faith of the reformers had been misplaced; individuals were neither perfect nor perfectible; reason and morality had no role to play in the study or practice of international relations; institutions could never be reformed, nor war eliminated. Power—usually identified with military strength—was considered the only absolute in the affairs of nation-states, and power politics was thought to be neither immoral nor irrational, only inevitable.

This verdict received intellectual support with the appearance in 1948 of an outstanding contribution toward a more conceptual approach to international relations. *Politics Among Nations* by Professor Hans J. Morgenthau emphasized the primacy of a drive to power in human behavior and, by extension, in the explanation of the behavior of states. This view was promoted as the "realist" approach to international politics, as opposed to the "idealist" outlook of the interwar years.

However, when students took a second look at his work, they came to appreciate that Morgenthau's "realism" was simply pessimism and cynicism about human motivations. Furthermore, they discovered that Morgenthau's explanation and use of key concepts such as power and national interest were too imprecise to really help in further study. Today the "realist-idealist" debate, though by no means laid to rest, is far less significant, and even Professor Morgenthau toward the end of his career became less insistent on the importance of the concept of power. Classical realism, however, found an apparently permanent niche in the subfield of strategic studies, which is concerned with the problem of national security in the context of superpower and other conflicts.

Some credit Morgenthau with another more profound contribution to the discipline. A new generation of scholars, using the example of his analytic method, began to think systematically about international politics—in other words, to think by means of *concepts* rather than in terms of institutions or events. From this beginning emerged a new *social science* of international relations concerned with the discovery of the *causes* of state *behavior* that looked less to the traditional subjects of history, law, and philosophy for insight, and more toward other social sciences such as sociology, psychology, and economics.

In the 1970s, students of international relations began to take note of the emergence and acceleration of global interdependence and to assess its impact on world politics. The result has been a reconsideration of many basic issues in the field such as the role of the state, the nature of international cooperation, and, most dramatically, the relative priorities of economic and social as opposed to military and diplomatic issues on the so-called global agenda. This new thinking, in turn, has led to a reassessment of the relationship between politics and economics in world affairs and a renaissance of "international political economy" as a subfield in which the two spheres are seen as two facets of an indivisible whole.

Integral to these developments was the application of general systems theory to the field, which generated the concept of an *international system*—that is, the composite of all the interacting actors in world politics. A *system* can be defined as a whole made up of interrelated parts, and at least in some respects this definition fits the collectivity of states. Such a construct enabled scholars to begin to think in terms of *systemic* properties of world politics. These would include characteristics of the international political system as a whole, such as the amount of conflict at a particular time, the degree to which the principal actors tend to be grouped in blocs, or the overall distribution of wealth and resources.

There remains, however, widespread disagreement about the nature of the international system: What does it encompass and how does it work? We will briefly consider the ideas of three contemporary approaches: neorealism, which is often but not exclusively conservative in outlook; the Marxist-informed world system analysis on the opposite side of the spectrum; and liberal institutionalism, which falls somewhere in between. The differences among these outlooks arise primarily from diverging views about the relative importance of economic and political factors in determining the distribution of rewards in the international system.

Neorealists[2] overcame a number of the limitations of classical realism by focusing on *the distribution of power in the system* and by exploring how the system's overall structure, defined in terms of this distribution of power, influences political outcomes. What emerges from their work is that power has always been distributed unequally, and that the interaction of the most powerful states, each trying to maximize its national interests within the system, determines the general characteristics of international relations at a particular time. When the power distribution changes, the system changes. The most important historical force in international relations is the drive by the most powerful state to establish, maintain, and defend its political dominance over the entire system—a form of primacy referred to as *hegemony.*

The neorealists acknowledge the increasing importance of interdependence and economic questions in world politics, but they argue that each state's policies in all areas continue to be determined by a desire to maximize its relative power. This kind of analysis has produced many important insights, but has also led to some counterintuitive conclusions. For instance, one scholar has argued that the efforts of members of the Global South to change some practices and institutions of the world economy was not motivated by poverty but rather by a concern to exercise more power in international decision making.[3]

World system theory reverses the causal link between politics and economics promoted by the neorealists. Using a Marxist conception of economic determinism, this perspective depicts the state as an actor not primarily in an

[2]Prominent writers include Kenneth Waltz and Robert Gilpin.

[3]See Stephen Krasner, *Structural Conflict: The Third World Against Global Liberalism* (Berkeley, CA: University of California Press, 1985).

international political system, but rather in a world capitalist economy whose dynamics accounts for the fluctuations of world politics. In this context, a state's most important goals are to promote the accumulation of capital in its national economy and to maintain its own legitimacy, and the various aspects of power are seen as means to these ends.

Despite conceptual differences, there are several parallels between neorealism and world system theory. World systems theorists also emphasize the idea of hegemony, but their hegemony first establishes dominance economically in agriculture, industry, and commerce. Furthermore, the two approaches agree that hegemony has been very short-lived historically and that conflict and instability are inherent in an anarchical international system.

Liberal institutionalists emphasize the need for states to coordinate their policies if they wish to truly maximize their national interests in an international system that is becoming increasingly interdependent. Though early institutionalists promoted formal international organization as the best approach to policy coordination, more recent work has revealed that the issues on the global agenda are very diverse, with each one involving a different set of actors in a unique way. Rather than all issues being dealt with in one policy forum, institutionalists now emphasize that there are a variety of "international regimes." These are cooperative arrangements which involve principles, norms, rules, and decision-making procedures for collective action in regard to particular issue areas such as the oceans or monetary affairs. Some may be fully institutionalized, and some may be little more than "gentlemen's agreements" between states.

In contrast to both neorealists and world systems theorists, institutionalists argue that interdependence compels states to work together to promote their individual interests more efficiently, and that where there is increased interdependence in an issue area, more developed procedures for collective decision making among states should follow. Neorealists have responded to this proposition by arguing that an efficient network of international regimes can be established only through the efforts of an effective hegemon in the international system, and that the regime systems will reflect the hegemon's interest and decline when the leading power's influence in the system declines.

Another approach, known as world order studies, developed simultaneously with those just mentioned. In response to the continuing series of crises, whether political, social, or environmental, in our era, a number of scholars in the early and mid-1970s began to question whether the international political system as we know it is really capable of serving humankind's present and foreseeable needs. These "world order" theorists[4] started with certain values, considered to be minimal prerequisites for the promotion of individual well-being, such as the reduction of violence, ecologically sound development, participation in authoritative decision making, and self-realization in the broadest sense. They assessed the degree to which the current world order promoted or frustrated the realization of

[4]Examples would include Richard Falk, Robert C. Johansen, Samuel S. Kim, and Saul H. Mendlovitz.

these values, as well as ways in which the present system could be creatively modified to maximize them.

Though not taken seriously at first by the mainstream of the field, the end of the Cold War and other contemporary developments have focused many people's attention on the quality of world order. The kinds of values suggested by world order thinkers more than twenty years ago now figure more and more prominently on the global agenda as exemplified by the United Nations Conference on Environment and Development (the so-called Earth Summit) in Rio de Janeiro in 1992.

PEACE AND CONFLICT RESOLUTION STUDIES

The post–Cold War era has also seen the acceleration of the development of peace and conflict resolution (PCR) studies. Academic fields are developed in response to major social problems. The disaster of World War I was the impetus for the creation of the field of international relations. Peace and conflict resolution studies emerged in response to critical social problems in the immediate World War II era[5] and surged in the wake of the Vietnam War when there was a need to present new perspectives on the global problematique.[6] As such, PCR studies complement the study of international relations (IR). However, there are important distinctions between PCR and the more traditional power and national security studies approach to international relations.

> Although there is no single definition of PCR, a commonly accepted view suggests it is: an interdisciplinary academic field that analyzes the causes of war, violence, and systemic oppression, and explores processes by which conflict and change can be managed so as to maximize justice while minimizing violence. It encompasses the study of economic, political, and social systems at the local, national, and global levels, and ideology, culture, and technology as they relate to conflict and change.[7]

Peace and conflict resolution builds upon and moves beyond the traditional concept of power and national security studies. While acknowledging that the need for defense against military threats is legitimate for national security concerns, PCR recognizes that hunger, poverty, and exploitation are also breeding grounds for violence and therefore pose a significant challenge to national as well as global security. Generally, PCR focuses on the security of the whole global system. The present interdependent global system carries the promise of security that is

[5]Ron Pagnucco, "CAPS: Part of National Trend in Peace Studies," *Capital Area Association for Peace Studies Chronicle,* vol. 1 (April 1990).

[6]Carol Rank, "The Interdisciplinary Challenge of Peace Studies," In Daniel C. Thomas and Michael T. Klare (eds.), *Peace and World Order Studies: A Curriculum Guide* (Boulder: Westview Press, 1989), p. 87.

[7]D. C. Thomas (1987) quoted in Ian M. Harris, "Peace Studies in the United States at the University and College Levels," in Ake Bjerstedt (ed.), *Peace, Environment and Education* (Malmö, Sweden: Peace Education Commission, International Peace Research Association, Spring 1992), p. 5.

durable—not the elusive security with which we have been familiar. Enhanced security for one state requires improved security for all states. Hence, the concept of common security—which postulates the existence of common interests—results in increased security for all states. The maintenance of the system as a whole thus becomes a priority of national policy.

Peace and conflict resolution studies cover the full continuum of violent versus peaceful activity (from the individual to the group to the global level), with the primary emphasis on the group and global levels, rather than on relations between specific states. The PCR approach sees the connectedness and continuity of time and space and encompasses a wider span of both geography and history than does a more traditional approach to IR, which generally covers the period since the creation of the nation-state system in 1648. Not only does PCR provide greater historical depth, but it also moves further forward through a systematic normative study of the future. Both PCR and IR are interdisciplinary, yet PCR examines a broader variety of potential alternative world order systems. Whereas IR sees politics and culture as separate, PCR sees politics as a cultural activity and world politics as cultural communication. The PCR viewpoint incorporates greater diversity within the social sciences, humanities, and natural and physical sciences, while IR tends to be more limited to the social sciences, especially when constituted as political science. Whereas IR tends to privilege description and explanation, PCR seeks more explicitly to incorporate prediction, the confluence of which is intentionally relevant to policy. Finally, and more often most controversial, PCR is value-explicit—it favors peace (nonviolent conflict resolution) over violence and war, and more readily includes social and economic justice and environmental balance as goals.[8]

EPISTEMOLOGY OR THE NATURE OF WORLD POLITICS

We should reemphasize that behind this diversity of approach to the field lies a serious debate over epistemology—that is, a debate over the true nature of world politics, how we best study it, and what really constitute its "facts." It is a debate between positivists and postpositivists. Positivists, as mentioned earlier, believe in an objective, value-free reality and accept the dominant Western approach to knowledge rooted in rationalism and materialism. Perhaps most importantly, positivists make a distinction between the subject and the object of study. That is, the "facts" of IR are thought of as "out there" in the "real" world waiting to be discovered by objectively minded scientists, who can then use them to formulate unambiguously true scientific statements about how the world works. Positivists thus believe that the language they use can accurately represent the world they are describing to us.

[8]Carol M. Stephenson, "The Evolution of Peace Studies," in Daniel C. Thomas and Michael T. Klare (eds.), *Peace and World Order Studies* (Boulder: Westview Press, 1989), pp. 11–12.

Postpositivists refute the dominance of Western empirical science and argue that there are many logics and ways of deriving knowledge. They maintain that the social world is not objectively "there," but rather constructed by those who act in it, and subject to a variety of interpretations depending on the viewpoints of those involved. Accordingly, an international crisis could *mean* different things to the various parties involved, though the events are the same for everyone.

Furthermore, postpositivists argue that there are political considerations—that is, questions of power—involved in every social question. Even within the discipline of IR itself, for instance, one finds that the theories of scholars who are white, male, and from a superpower are more influential than the views of those who are nonwhite, female, and from the Global South (formerly the Third World). Finally, from this perspective, language is not viewed as representing reality, but rather as creating what we perceive as reality. There are many ways to represent experience in language, many different possible *discourses* on the same subject; and all of them have political overtones.[9]

FEMINIST PERSPECTIVES ON INTERNATIONAL RELATIONS

One important contribution of the debate over the nature of world politics is that other "voices" are beginning to be heard in the study of IR, and prominent among these is the voice of feminist scholars. An increasing body of feminist writing[10] challenges mainstream thinkers to appreciate the extent to which the conventional practice and scholarship of international relations highlight traditionally male conceptions and priorities, ignore the main concerns of women, and contribute to their continuing oppression.

Feminist perspectives in the field of international relations ("perspectives" meaning how we interpret reality around us) are just beginning to gain saliency.[11] The literature on international relations and feminism reveals three significant perspectives, sometimes called frameworks or theoretical accounts: *liberalism, radical feminism,* and *social construction.* The presence of these various perspectives reflects the absence of a unified grand theory.

Liberalism is the oldest of the perspectives. Its origins can be traced back as far as 1792 in a text by Mary Wollstonecraft entitled *A Vindication of the Rights of Women.* The primary concern of liberal feminists is the attainment of equal rights

[9]A good discussion of this topic is Yosef Lapid's "The Third Debate: On the Prospects of International Theory in a Post-Positivist Era," *International Studies* Vol. 33, No. 3 (Sept. 1989).

[10]See the work of V. Spike Peterson, Christine Sylvester, J. Ann Tickner, Rebecca Grant, and Kathleen Newland.

[11]See Enloe, C. *Bananas, Beaches, and Bases: Making Feminist Sense of International Politics* (Berkeley: University of California Press, 1989); Enloe, C. *The Morning After: Sexual Politics at the End of the Cold War* (Berkeley: University of California Press, 1993); Grant, K. and Newland, R. *Gender and International Relations* (Bloomington: Indiana University Press, 1991); Tickner, J. A. *Gender in International Relations* (New York: Columbia University Press, 1992).

and opportunities for women in a male-dominated society.[12] Radical feminism gained prominence in Western societies during the 1960s. It grew out of the climate of student radicalism in Europe, and in the United States it was part of the civil rights movement. Radical feminism has been conventionally divided into two main currents. One, typified as a reform movement, is chiefly concerned with obtaining equal rights and removing discrimination against women. The other, characterized as the women's liberation tendency, is concerned with achieving a more radical program of social change, and contains radical and revolutionary currents. The third feminist perspective, social construction, incorporates the ideas of postmodernism and poststructuralism. The relationship of feminist thought to the theoretical currents of postmodernism and poststructuralism is, however, complex. Yet this complexity has not deterred feminist theorists who have accepted what they believe to be significant contributions offered by poststructuralism and postmodernism. This particular approach is concerned with identity. It seeks to understand not only the confict that occurs between women and men or between groups but the conflict that takes place within a particular group as well. This approach has had tremendous appeal to feminists from the Global South as well as women of color in the Western world. Unlike the previous perspectives, the third perspective addresses the inseparability of oppression based not only on sex but also on race and class.[13]

METHODS OF STUDY

To more fully appreciate the variety of approaches to international relations and the epistemological debate, students need to understand something about the methodology of the field, its *process of research.* The many questions asked about the action and interaction of states required data to be answered convincingly, and this search for different sorts of information led to the development of a variety of techniques of research and the adaptation of others drawn from other social sciences. The behavioralists, in particular, assumed that if scientific knowledge could only be acquired by the observation and classification of quantitative (i.e., numerical) data, then the study of international relations should in some way make use of quantification.

The purpose of quantification is to achieve more precision in analysis. To this end, concepts must be measurable, and they are referred to as *variables:* capable of varying, like gross domestic product, across a set of *cases* (such as a particular group of states). When quantitative data of this kind are collected about international politics, they can be analyzed using a wide variety of statistical techniques to answer very complex questions. There is no doubt that data thus orga-

[12] Jagger, Allison, and Rothenburg, Paula. *Feminist Frameworks: Alternative Theoretical Accounts of Relations between Women and Men* (New York: McGraw-Hill Book Company, 1984); Enloe, C. *Bananas, Beaches, and Bases: Making Feminist Sense of International Politics* (Berkeley: University of California Press, 1989).

[13] Hooks, Bell. *Feminist Theory—From Margin to Center* (Boston, MA: South End Press, 1984).

nized and analyzed have enhanced explanations of national and international events, though they have not yielded the kind of predictive knowledge characteristic of certain of the natural sciences.

A few of the more significant quantitative approaches should be mentioned. One of the most important sources of data has been the study of *national attributes,* and these include any characteristic of a national society considered to be relevant to international politics. The list of such attributes is potentially endless, but most emphasis has been put on such characteristics as geographical size, per capita gross national product, size of population, amount of energy used, kilometers of paved roads, distribution of income, and so on, and so on. A common research orientation has been to try to link specific internal characteristics of states with particular patterns of foreign policy behavior. This technique has certain advantages in that many statistical data from which national attribute measures can be derived are available, and there is a global effort through the United Nations and other organizations to ensure that they are continually improved.

Another innovative area of quantitative research is the study of international *events.* In answer to the question we posed earlier about the "stuff" of international relations, some scholars have argued that the subject of the field is really the events that take place among international actors. Recording and classifying these events produces a data base that can be used to study many questions about world affairs, such as the following: Which actors are most active in what types of events? Is the international system predominantly peaceful or violent during a particular period? How prominent are transnational organizations in the day-to-day activity of world politics?

Finally, we should mention the area of *simulation.* It has often been observed that much of the subject matter of the social sciences cannot be isolated and manipulated under laboratory conditions, and this statement is certainly true of international relations. No scholar would be permitted to provoke conflict among nations simply to observe the results! However, contemporary computer technology has made it possible to construct very sophisticated models of important international political, social, economic, and environmental processes that scholars can manipulate in any way they desire. Though one should never make the error of believing that a model ever fully represents reality, sophisticated modeling techniques are nevertheless capable of providing us with insights into international relations of great theoretical and practical benefit. For instance, contemporary world modeling projects have given us an idea of how dangerous would be the consequences of continuing current rates of environmental degradation and resource exploitation very far into the future.

As useful as the various efforts at empirical research have been, the entire enterprise also encountered certain difficulties and has demonstrated certain shortcomings. First, after some decades of quantitative research, prominent scholars noticed that there had been little accumulation of knowledge in the field, that is, studies did not build on the conceptual frameworks and findings of previous research as is done in the natural sciences to promote a more or less steady advance of knowledge. They came to realize that, though it may be possible to be very precise about certain data relevant to world affairs, it is quite another thing to come to agreement about what those data mean. As discussed previously, social "facts" can be interpreted in a variety of ways, and two different scholars may evaluate the same trends in world politics and draw entirely different conclusions.

Second, it has often been pointed out that the behavioral/positivist study of the field tends to be conservative in that it identifies a certain status quo as "reality" and analyzes the particular characteristics of that status quo, rather than considering the possibilities for change. Though this shortcoming can be overcome by using dynamic, rather than static, models and studying processes of change in the international system over time, there remains an even more serious problem. Behavioralism and positivism focus on the explanation of what "is," at the expense of the equally important questions of what "ought" to be or what could potentially be. A standard reply is that such matters are left to philosophers, but this obscures the fact that, as we argue later, the selection and promotion of values is at the basis of all social life. Normative judgments are implicated in descriptions and explanations of what "is."

Third, until recently the positivist and behavioral approaches have been very "actor oriented" and have tended to overlook structural questions in international relations. This statement means that much of the literature in the field has concentrated on the actions, roles, and qualities of individual states (and other actors) as if they were largely self-determined and autonomous and has failed to appreciate the influence that the pattern of distribution of benefits in the international system has on its members. For example, an emphasis on actors would bring out the fact that some states are wealthy and some are poor, while a more structurally-oriented view would highlight the historical processes whereby certain states become rich and others poor, as well as those aspects of the contemporary system that serve to maintain such a stratification. In social science, one learns from studying both actors and structures, and some of the more recent approaches to the field, such as the world systems approach, are finding ways to marry aspects of both.

In summary, we would say that the cultivation of technical and quantitative competence and the incorporation of psychological, economic, and sociological factors into the study of international relations have been valuable. The emphasis on method rather than substance that dominated the field from the 1950s to the mid-1970s, however, was counterproductive in that those aspects of the field amenable to quantitative analysis received more attention than other dimensions of world affairs that were more difficult to observe yet nevertheless essential.

More recently even, economists and psychologists seem to have reappraised their earlier scientifically inclined aspirations: The effort to interpret all interactions in terms of behavioral determinism has confounded the best efforts of the social scientists. As we have seen, students of international relations have also come to reconsider approaches to their subject, and it seems that the task of discovering and classifying regularities, stable relationships, and uniform sequences could not be performed without having some overall appreciation of the creative disorder of human interventions and strategies. Certainly we can abandon neither the search for new explanations nor the effort to construct new research tools, but it should be remembered that their value lies not in their complexity and sophistication but in their contribution to knowledge.

THE NEED FOR NEW THINKING

We would also argue that to come to grips with and eliminate such contemporary threats to human survival as war, structural violence, and environmental degradation, a fundamental transformation in the way we think about world politics is required. For example, we might wish that pressing a magical button would eliminate all weapons of mass destruction. But, if we cannot change those habits in our thinking about international relations that gave birth to such weapons in the first place, the weapons will be re-created in short order. By habit we think of national security in terms of military forces and capabilities. By habit we think that one people's interests can only be served at the expense of another's. Such habits of thought become deeply embedded in our everyday life in what we call common sense.

The thought forms we predominantly use in international relations are modeled on Aristotelian logic. We need forms of thought that are structured in the same way that our world is structured. For example, looking at a chart of the body's metabolic pathways, one would see an immensely complex network of loops that represent interconnected, interdependent chemical reactions whose products all feed back upon each other—what is called a homeostatic circuit. There are no straight lines in such a chart, and to think in terms of causes and effects makes sense only if we cut out a portion of a circuit and treat it as though it were a whole entity.

We complicate problems of international relations because of our inability to perceive context and long-range consequences. Our information is always incomplete. Natural, biological systems are always more complex and circuitous than our ideas about them. Using linear, cause-and-effect thinking to map a world that is a complex, interdependent network of feedback circuits frequently leads to inappropriate actions that return to haunt us all. Such thinking leads us to falsely regard the world as an object that can be manipulated rather than a home within which we reside.

For instance, it is still conventional to think that ecological values are somehow in conflict with economic values—that we are faced with an "either/or" choice. This is linear thinking. The words *ecology* and *economy* share a common root meaning. They refer to managing a household (Greek). The physiology of the human body, the complexities of family life and community, the realms of domestic and international politics, the network of global trade, and the infinitely varied and delicate interdependencies of the totality of life on Earth share many structural similarities. Yet Aristotelian logic would treat these concepts as distinct, even to the point that they are studied in compartmentalized and separate departments of the university.[14]

There is also a need for new thinking across the full continuum of violent versus peaceful activity, with emphasis on the group and global levels, not only on relations between specific states. It should encompass a wider span of both space and time than do the more traditional approaches to international relations, which generally cover the period since the creation of the nation-state system in 1648. New thinking should provide greater historical depth while moving forward through a systematic normative study of the future and examining a wider variety of potential alternative world order systems. To do so, new thinking should incorporate greater diversity not only within the social sciences and humanities, but in the natural and physical sciences as well. Then, we would suggest, the sort of macro understanding of world affairs sought by scholars of international relations for decades may become possible.

THE APPROACH OF THIS STUDY

Politics can be analyzed usefully and instinctively from any of three points of view. First, we can inquire into the motivations and tactics of individual political actors as they move within the political system. Second, we can examine the political system itself in order to understand the processes of political action and the opportunities and limitations affecting its members. Last, we can focus on the substance of political action to discover what the actors are concerned with and the possible social consequences of what they actually do.

In this book we shall look at global politics from each of these points of view. Part I is a discussion of the nation-state as an individual political actor. This will include a study of the problem a state faces in relating the ends it seeks to the means at its disposal.

We then go on to examine foreign policy decision making and the various factors that influence it. This examination leads in turn to a discussion of the processes through which policymakers discover the range of choice open to them at any given time. Here we focus on the concept of *capability* and divide it into two more precise dimensions: *influence,* which refers to the ability of the state to gain approval for its policies through persuasive means short of force, and *coercion,* the province of force pure and simple, as one state attempts to bend another to its will. Finally, we study the various means employed by policymakers to implement foreign policy decisions in a constantly changing environment.

Part II centers on the global political system, both in theory and in practice. Our effort here is devoted to study of the patterns of interaction among states and other actors, together with the assumptions underlying them. We begin by examining (at times critically) the concepts of sovereignty, independence, power poli-

[14]Stephen Nachmanovitch and Abdul Aziz Said, "Global Thinking: A Call for Reinvestment in Sacred Values," *Acorn* (March 1987), p. 14.

tics, the balance of power, and the regulating mechanisms of international politics and their implications for *transnational* relations—that is, international relations involving actors other than states.

Rather than analyze the interaction of states strictly in terms of the traditional notion of "balance of power," we argue that the proper focus for analysis of state interaction is, as indicated in the previous section, the study of *values,* because all politics is a struggle for the maximization of competing value systems. Because it clashes with the "value-free" orientation of behavioralists and positivists, this approach has relatively few supporters among those who study the interaction of states (although many more among analysts of foreign policy).

We examine next the variety of changing conditions and emerging directions in the present global system. Prominent here is the consideration of the sources and changing nature of international conflict, the restraints on conflict, and the methods of conflict resolution. In this context we analyze a states system in transition from an outmoded past to an uncertain future.

Part III deals with the substance of global politics and is organized as a discussion of actors and issues affecting the entire system and its members. War and peace, ideology and fundamentalism, technology, ecology, interdependence, integration, North-South relations, poverty, development, the world economy, multinational corporations, ethnicity and terrorism, human rights, and cooperative global politics are all studied in depth.

The following pages will provide you with a map to identify the main features of international and transnational relations. You will be exposed to many of the concepts that are in daily use among academic analysts and practitioners of this great drama. You will be initiated into some of the important hypotheses of the field, and have now been alerted to the widespread lack of consensus among us. It is certainly appropriate to ask what relevance all of this abstract system has for you.

We would answer by first explaining that one cannot know the world directly, that is, facts do not speak for themselves, no matter who may argue at times that they do. They require a theory or, at least, a set of concepts to give them meaning. Thus it follows that one cannot make sense of world affairs without the aid of conceptual tools. Becoming conscious of the theoretical underpinnings of knowledge in a discipline also has the advantage of helping one discover that the generalizations that one held previously about the world may in fact be inconsistent, incomplete, or just simply wrong. The student does not start as a blank slate, but brings to the study these previously held ideas. There is always the possibility that a reconsideration of one's own personal concepts and of concepts widely held in society about world politics might result in their clarification, strengthening, or elaboration.

We have already pointed out the determination of many contemporary thinkers to avoid normative judgments and all questions of "good or bad" and "right and wrong." Speaking personally, this is a tendency we understand but find ultimately untenable. We exercise judgment by the mere act of selecting one question instead of another for analysis. Only when we focus on the world's substantive problems and not just the problems induced by one's own method of collecting and evaluating information, and only when we approach these problems not merely with the tools of a laboratory but also with a heightened sense of the values at stake, will we be able to see the resemblance among all of us. In the last analysis, we are all—whether white or black, female or male, upper- or lower-class, nationals of the United States or any other country, stateless persons striving for self-determination or citizens accorded full rights—human, and we should appreciate our common fate. Once we realize this need, we can achieve a better appreciation of the forces that unite us and those that set us apart. We will also come to realize that our most common and basic value in the world today—our survival—is threatened at present by a lack of a sense of community; by racism, sexism, and religious fanaticism; and by poverty, environmental pollution, and weapons of mass destruction. This volume points the way toward solidarity in global perspective.

As we deal with the problems of global politics, we should not forget that we are engaged in something that matters in the here and now, as well as in the awful scales of truth. We should be logical, scientific, rigorous, objective, and honest, but further we should be compassionate. We should think in terms of concepts, but we should never forget that we are a part of the subject.

RECOMMENDED READINGS

BROWN, CHRIS. *International Relations Theory: New Normative Approaches.* New York: Columbia University Press, 1992.

BULL, HEDELEY. *The Anarchical Society: A Study of Order in World Politics.* New York: Columbia University Press, 1977.

DAHL, ROBERT. *A Modern Political Analysis.* 3rd ed. Englewood Cliffs, NJ: Prentice-Hall, 1976.

DEUTSCH, KARL W. *The Analysis of International Relations.* 2nd ed. Englewood Cliffs, NJ: Prentice-Hall, 1978.

DOUGHERTY, JAMES E., and ROBERT L. PFALTZGRAFF, JR. *Contending Theories of International Relations: A Comprehensive Survey.* 3rd ed. New York: Harper and Row, 1990.

ENLOE, CYNTHIA. *Bananas, Beaches, and Bases: Making Feminist Sense of International Politics.* Berkeley: University of California Press, 1989.

GILPIN, ROBERT. *War and Change in World Politics.* Cambridge: Cambridge University Press, 1981.

HOLSTI, K. J. *The Dividing Discipline: Hegemony and Diversity in International Theory.* Boston: Allen and Unwin, 1985.

JOHNSON, LAURIE M. *Thucydides, Hobbes, and the Interpretation of Realism.* Dekalb: Northern Illinois University Press, 1993.

KAPLAN, MORTON. *System and Process in International Politics.* New York: John Wiley and Sons, 1957.

MANSBACH, RICHARD W., and JOHN A. VASQUEZ. *In Search of Theory: A New Paradigm for Global Politics.* New York: Columbia University Press, 1981.

MORGENTHAU, HANS J. *Politics Among Nations: The Struggle for Power and Peace.* 5th ed. New York: Alfred A. Knopf, 1973.

PETERSON, SPIKE V., ed. *Gendered States: Feminist (Re)Visions of International Relations Theory.* Boulder, CO: Lynne Rienner, 1992.

SAID, ABDUL AZIZ, ed. *Theory of International Relations: The Crisis of Relevance.* Englewood Cliffs, NJ: Prentice-Hall, 1968.

THOMAS, DANIEL C., and MICHAEL T. KLARE, eds. *Peace and World Order Studies: A Curriculum Guide*. Boulder, CO: Westview Press, 1989.

TICKNER, J. ANN. *Gender in International Relations: Feminist Perspectives on Achieving Global Security*. New York: Columbia University Press, 1992.

WALTZ, KENNETH. *Theory of International Relations.* New York: McGraw Hill, 1979.

WRIGHT, QUINCY. *The Study of International Relations.* New York: Appleton-Century-Crofts, 1955.

PART I

THE ACTORS IN GLOBAL POLITICS

Chapter 1

THE NATURE OF FOREIGN POLICY

This book is a guide to the ideas we use in the discussion, study, and practice of global politics. Our subject matter is first international and transnational, dealing with relationships among states, those among states and nonstate actors, and those exclusively among nonstate actors. It is also a "political" study; the relationships in which we are principally interested are those we define as political. We acknowledge, however, that there are other kinds of international relations besides the political—for example, economic, cultural, and interpersonal—but we shall consider these primarily in terms of their impact on the political behavior of peoples, governments, states, and other actors.

POLITICS: THE MAXIMIZATION OF VALUES

Politics is a common word in the English language that refers to an equally familiar phenomenon. However, precise definition of the word is rather difficult. Individuals have strong emotional responses to the concept; any definition cannot help but reflect the definer's viewpoint to some extent. Since the words *politics* and *political* appear repeatedly throughout the book, it is important that we make our meaning clear at the outset. We will first present our definition of *politics* and then go on to demonstrate how political concepts are expressed in a state's foreign policy.

The Nature of Politics

We have already argued that values are at the heart of human action and social life, and we would argue further that *politics* is most usefully conceived as the organized activity of individuals seeking to put into practice their convictions about social values. More specifically, through political action individuals attempt to realize their various notions of the "public good," by which we mean their conceptions of how society should be organized and whose interests should be promoted. Thus, to us politics is essentially a *process*—a means to a valued end—that is meaningless except in terms of the values that give rise to it.

Admittedly, certain issues may so predominate in a political system or a particular era as to seem to represent the totality of politics. In this regard, one might think of the struggle among various interest groups in most contemporary states over the allocation of government revenue. However, we are suggesting that the political in fact originates in the personal and collective aspirations, social and economic expectations, and conceptions of justice characteristic of the culture in which the aforementioned struggle occurs.

Such a definition of *politics* covers a wide range of activities—as it must, since political acts can include virtually the entire spectrum of human activity. Our definition is, however, quite explicit in emphasizing *social values* as the roots of politics. Since these shared ideas of the public good are what make political action unique, almost any properly motivated and organized activity could be termed *political*. Without the values and the organizational context, the same action would be *apolitical*. You, the reader, certainly have views that are directly and indirectly relevant to politics, but you would not be actually engaged in politics unless and until you took action to promote your views.

Even the most casual observation of the contemporary world reveals that human beings do not agree on any single set of social values. Struggles arising from incompatible value judgments and commitments have been prominent in the political processes of most societies, insofar as achievement of a political goal by one individual or group frequently can take place only at the expense of other actors with their own, different, goals and aspirations. In contrast, there are historical examples of societies in which a high degree of value consensus was achieved, which in turn contributed to social harmony and progress.

Thus the range of political action may extend from agreement and cooperation between political actors to the various zones of partial agreement or total opposition and conflict. An experienced participant in this process, after carefully assessing the environment in which she/he must act, would, ideally, employ a variety of strategies and tactics in order to attain the highest feasible level of value satisfaction. From the outset, it is instructive to think of any given climate of political action as unstable, since this approach helps us to appreciate that all strategies must be pragmatic and prudent if they are to succeed. One of the classic errors in politics is the failure to adequately appreciate how the environment of action has changed from one moment to the next.

These two ingredients of politics—the value-rooted ends of action and a changing political climate fluctuating between conflict and cooperation—are as clearly demonstrated in world politics as they are in the more familiar environment of electoral politics in a democracy. Foreign policy can be thought of as a state's attempt at realizing, in the external environment, ends derived from conceptions of the public good prevalent in its national society. Because, as we will see, these collective ends have frequently been defined in narrow nationalistic terms, taking only limited account of broader concerns, the resolution of international conflict has at times proved to be very difficult, and world politics has often been characterized by a climate of disagreement and conflict. The fact that some of these conflicts have resulted in major and minor wars has also given a particular slant to our perceptions of politics at the global level. However, we would argue that in its key aspects global politics is the same sort of social process as politics at any other level; and with some conceptual adjustments, insights derived from domestic politics can help us to understand international relations.

We can think of a political *system* as any set of interacting political actors, and for a political system even to exist there must be some minimal value consensus among the participants—that is, certain "rules of the game." It is this agreement on certain fundamentals that creates at least some coherence in the system at all times, except during periods of crisis, and makes political action possible, even if it is largely contentious in nature. We shall see later that the global system is based on such a consensus, although it may have been only imperfectly grasped by some states and only partially supported by others, and that political action on the global plane has been feasible only because of this consensus. Furthermore, we will go on to suggest that for the system to avoid serious breakdown in the face of contemporary challenges to its survival, this consensus may well need to be broadened and strengthened.

Social Values and Foreign Policy

Certain aspirations, needs, and wants are widely shared in any society. These prevalent social values play a major role in shaping the goals of national policy and are thereby central to the integration and progress of states. Though a state is also defined by its people, territory, and institutions, the abstract element of purpose provided by its values, or social code, is perhaps the most important aspect of its self-image and the image of it held by others. The images of America as the land of opportunity, France as the promoter of a particular culture, and the former Soviet Union (historically) as the exporter of revolution come to mind.

In the contemporary world, many social aspirations require governmental action to attain even partial fulfillment, and individuals have come to expect political leaders to act on their behalf. One area in which public agencies have for several centuries been regarded as the only legitimate actors is international relations, and only officials endowed with the state's authority and capabilities may deal formally with extrasocietal problems. That is to say, the international society we have inherited is conceived in such a way that foreign policy is the exclusive prerogative of government, because only government is empowered to act on behalf of all the people individually and of the national society collectively.

Though this ethos remains dominant and states continue to fulfill this function, in today's world, official diplomatic channels are certainly not the only medium through which the value concerns of one society impinge on another. As we have mentioned, our world is also characterized by an increasing volume of *transnational* relations, indicating that world politics is conducted through private as well as public channels. We will treat this theme at greater length later.

When the states system was younger, and still largely European, citizens' aspirations for identity, prosperity, and justice were largely irrelevant to international relations because they could be fulfilled within the local political or religious community. During this early period, before the spread of democracy, international politics was mainly the business of kings; mass attitudes and preferences did not greatly encroach on the sovereign's foreign adventures. However, since the Industrial Revolution and the dawn of modern nationalism, collective goals, wants, and needs have come to influence and be influenced by the outside world to a much greater extent. Increasing nationalism contributed to the democratization of foreign policy—in the sense that governments became obliged to structure their international efforts, to some degree at least, to reflect the value preferences of their peoples.

Over the years, social values have unavoidably become more closely connected with questions of foreign policy. The contemporary practice of foreign policy, therefore, requires some procedure to translate the value prefrences of a society into a workable framework for governmental action. How this transformation is generally achieved will be discussed under "Interests, Goals, and Objectives," but we first highlight the variety of origins of foreign policy in the contemporary international system.

Cultural Diversity

From our perspective, political activity derives from values and therefore should be seen in the context of the larger culture in which it exists. Depending on the culture in which it is studied, it can be intensely rationalistic and competitive, or it can be hierarchical and passive. We would suggest that this cultural diversity must always be kept in view when analyzing the actions of states.

In order to impose some kind of order on our understanding of world politics, the study of international relations has often given the impression that, in spite of the differences that characterize the internal politics and cultures of states, the external politics of these states can be conceptualized by certain common norms and attitudes. Though at times useful for analytical purposes, such assumptions may incline us to ignore the broad spectrum of human cultures. World order does not require a world that is in any sense or at any level culturally uniform.

As discussed earlier, certain behavioral studies of international politics concentrated on discovering the common denominators of relations among states from which a calculus of war and peace could emerge. The quantitative study of foreign policy proceeded from the assumption that all states shared a common agenda in world politics, the only difference being their respective capacity to achieve their ends. Presumably the Bahamas would like to exercise the power of Russia, but is constrained by size, population, resources, and industry. This emphasis on common denominators tended to obscure the multifaceted nature of political phenomena. For instance, are all states really motivated by the desire to maximize military power and accumulate wealth, or is it only the imperial and acquisitive states that act in this way?

Thus we can see the difficulties that arise from attempting to reduce the external behavior of states to a formula without examining states' internal environments. Furthermore, such an approach would tend to reinforce the notion that external politics is governed by one set of rules and internal politics by another, when the real situation is quite different. It is true that the kinds of demands made by states upon the environment share certain common themes, as we shall explore later, but one should always bear in mind that these demands arise from a specific sociopolitical culture—that is to say, from the collective life of people whose historical antecedents, present condition, and prospects for development are unique. In this context, every general goal of state action in international relations, such as protecting national security, acquires a particular connotation.

The recognition that politics is *ascriptive* (i.e., culture specific) in nature makes us attentive to basic differences in worldview among peoples, and protects us from the fallacy of believing that "they" think precisely as "we" do. Perhaps an example will make the point more clear. The United States underestimated the will of the North Vietnamese to resist aerial bombardment. This tragic miscalculation, it now seems, was a logical outgrowth of the belief that the North Vietnamese, as a state, shared certain common objectives with the United States. American policymakers determined that since the United States would have responded to the threat of bombing to save its industries, so too would the North Vietnamese. This was not a casual miscalculation, but the logical outcome of the belief that all states have a breaking point that can be methodically determined. Emphasis on the common denominators, which the North Vietnamese presumably shared with other states, obscured the context of their demands, the nature of their conflict, and the tenacity of their resistance.

Value Content of Foreign Policy

Our discussion so far suggests that one cannot be overly specific about the social values that underlie foreign policy, because values are seldom self-evident and the desired ends that a government chooses to pursue always stem from a variety of sources within the national society. As recent headines tell us, national societies may be influenced by a variety of ideologies, religious systems, economic goals, and cultural inclinations, all and any of which serve to provide individuals and groups with identity and direction in life. However, we can suggest five different dimensions of the "public good," each of which is involved, at least to some extent, in a country's foreign policy.

1. *The Good of the Individual Citizens.* The most frequent justification for the state in Western political thought is that, in exchange for a monopoly on coercive force in society, it provides internal and external security. The anarchic international political environment is perceived as a source of particular threat, and national security, in the sense of protection of persons, beliefs, and property, is a main concern of most foreign policies. Furthermore, in recent times, citizens have come to expect that the state, besides protecting them from harm, should also promote their personal prosperity and fulfillment, and contemporary foreign policies are necessarily as concerned with economic growth as they traditionally have been with military security.

2. *The Good of "Special Interest" Groups in the State/Society.* The state is responsible for the authoritative allocation of values, and all national societies have interest groups that try to influence this process in preferred directions. Foreign policy is as much a target of interest groups as is domestic policy, particularly in regard to trade issues and arms spending, but other issues such as human rights and the environment also come into play. The groups best known are private, such as labor unions, or activist such as Greenpeace and Amnesty International, but there are also more informal groups within the governmental bureaucracy that seek to be heard in the policy process.

3. *The Good of the Society at Large.* Leaders in the United States have talked often and forcefully about preserving "the American way of life," and many other states use similar notions in justifying particular foreign policy initiatives. In some cases, ideology (secular or religious) may figure prominently; in others, such concerns as ethnic identity or technological skills are important. This dimension highlights the extent to which foreign policy helps a people define various aspects of its national identity in contrast to others. No people wishes to feel its social institutions and culture under attack or even undervalued by others, and governments are at times obliged to defend and promote the inherent value of the nation's collective life.

4. *The "Good" of the Government/Administration.* We mentioned earlier that foreign policy was originally the sole concern of the king, and it still remains the aspect of government policy that is most fully under the control of the executive branch of government. Because, in most states, other branches have only limited powers to monitor foreign activities, a group in power, or an administration or political party, is relatively free to use foreign policy to promote its own political goals—that is, to reinforce and perpetuate its hold on state power. This fact should not be understood to mean that foreign policy is primarily aimed at this goal, but rather that such considerations are frequently involved when deciding the style and substance of policy. For instance, if certain actions can be timed to most enhance a political party's prospects of reelection, they may well be implemented with this purpose in mind.

5. *The Good of the State* (as a political entity among other states). Here we are referring to abstractions that often arise in official discourse on foreign policy, that

is, sovereignty, self-preservation, and independence. These are the fundamental principles of the state system, and every recognized member of that system is "entitled" to the benefits conferred by these principles. However, the system is also based on self-help, and each state must act to protect its own sovereignty, independence, and self-preservation. Since few peoples would remain indifferent when convinced that the sovereignty of their nation is endangered, governments often invoke threats to the integrity of the state as justifications for various policies.

We would suggest that these are commonly occurring *elements,* but that states vary widely in the relative weights they consciously or tacitly assign to each one. Different weightings would result in both varying style and diverse substantive content in foreign policy. A few examples will help illustrate this point.

Consider a hypothetical state with a right-wing authoritarian government, which has to deal with rising discontent and which requires substantial foreign investment to guarantee its hold on power. Such a government might be particularly inclined to and capable of using foreign policy to enhance its domestic position (item 4 in the list on the preceding page), through rhetorical means if nothing else, and may find itself obliged to curry favor with those special interest groups most closely linked to sources of foreign capital. Of course, if one seeks out the origins of the social values underpinning such states and their foreign policies, one might discover that authoritarianism is frequently rooted in widespread patriarchal attitudes that have fostered particular expectations about the style of political leadership.

On the other hand, many Western democracies put relatively more rhetorical and real emphasis on the promotion of the personal well-being of their citizens, and the good of the society (i.e., their "way of life"). They have often done so by seeking to spread their form of democracy and their "liberal," market-oriented approach to the organization of the world economy. This effort has the effect of satisfying interest groups involved in export-oriented industries and services, and it promotes citizens' economic well-being. To reiterate, all these concerns go into the formulation of most states' foreign policies, but they find expression in a multitude of ways and with varying emphases.

Furthermore, we can see from the list that the values promoted by the state in foreign policy are varied in origin and substance, and not necessarily mutually compatible. One can conceive of the policymaker's tasks as shaping this broad spectrum of needs and wants into some internally consistent *value synthesis* to be applied to international politics. However, at times domestic social tensions and external pressures render this demanding goal unattainable, and the exigencies of the real world require compromise among competing values, the acceptance of some and the rejection of others, or some other rationalizing device.

Foreign Policy and International Politics

From the perspective of the individual state, the essence of its foreign policy is to pursue and, hopefully, fulfill the composite of its needs and aspirations—what we have called its value synthesis. However, once it interacts with the external environment, it encounters other states and actors seeking accomplishment of their own goals. The constant threat of conflict and the limits on cooperation that characterize contemporary world politics result, in large measure, from the heterogeneity of values animating the more than 160 nation-states, each having its own political culture and material needs. Despite their fundamental similarities, there are also significant differences between global and domestic politics. In the majority of states, domestic politics goes on within a set of fairly well-understood rules that specify the range of permissible action and are enforced by social and governmental mechanisms. World politics is a much cruder form of the political process in that the restraints on state action are partial, diffuse, and backed by only limited means of institutionalized enforcement. Rightly or wrongly, many powerful states have sought to pursue their purposes as far as their wishes and strength would permit. This statement implies that heretofore the most effective external check on state action has been the opposing strength of other states. In summary, because the values that go into foreign policy are most frequently nationalistic and deeply held, and because formal international restraints on it are few and of limited scope, world politics is potentially explosive.

INTERESTS, GOALS, AND OBJECTIVES

Our discussion so far has established that foreign policy is purposeful and that value judgments are the basis upon which a state proceeds in world politics. A state, however, must act in the real world, and it cannot function effectively if its values remain abstract, absolute, or undefined. No foreign policy can really achieve "freedom," "power," "justice," "honor," or even "peace"—to mention a few of the more common values ascribed to foreign policy—except in concrete terms and in relation to specific situations. The policymaker must translate values into *objectives* before he/she can act.

From "Social Values" to "National Interest"

The concept of "national interest" has traditionally been considered as the means through which a policymaker applies value judgments to the realities of political action, but this idea has always been and remains a notoriously vague one. We would suggest that what is usually intended by the term "national interest" is a general, long-term, and continuing purpose that the state, the nation, and the regime would all, ideally, see themselves as serving at any given time. It would be rooted in the social consciousness and cultural identity of a people and include aspects of all the disparate elements of the public "good" that we have noted. In practice, it is the decision makers, the official link between the national society and the external environment, who formulate and articulate the state's national interest; so national interest necessarily reflects their assessments of the public good and of the state's material circumstances—its size, population, wealth, internal divisions, geography, major economic activities, and so on.

We cannot be more precise in defining the national interest because in each case its content and the process through which it is formulated are peculiar to the history and institutions of a given society. As an expression of the broad purpose governing the state's relations with the outside world, national interest can be said to fulfill two important functions: (1) it gives policy a general orientation toward the international political environment, and (2) more importantly, it serves as a basis for choosing among alternative actions when the state is faced with a situation demanding an immediate response. In other words, a coherent conception of the national interest can both guide the state's long-term effort in foreign policy and govern what it does in a short-term context.

National interest thus manifests itself as an application of a state's values to its place in world politics. The national interest is normally slow to change, and the change it does undergo is, except in special circumstances, evolutionary rather than revolutionary. Thus it is intended to provide a measure of consistency to national policy, and, according to traditional political wisdom, a state consciously adhering to a conception of national interest in a rapidly changing situation is more likely to progress toward its goals than it would if its interest were redefined in light of each new situation.

Ends and Means in Foreign Policy

Defining national interest is the first step in formulating a foreign policy, even if it remains an abstract concept. Before the national interest can serve as an actual guide to action, policymakers must grapple with a classic problem: reconciling ends and means. Effective policy requires that those responsible mesh the facts of a problem, including whatever means are available, with a set of desirable ends. In specific policy situations, the determination of an appropriate relationship between abstract ends and concrete means is frequently one of the more difficult problems decision makers must solve.

Ends, in theory, determine means. In a situation permitting several possible courses of action, the one chosen should most directly advance the national interest. In practice, however, there is a temptation to allow means to determine ends, to decide that the objective most easily attained is the one the state should seek. Another related problem is the tendency to allow intermediate ends—ends that, if achieved, are only supposed to serve as means to still further ends—to become final ends in themselves.

Perhaps more important is the ethical dimension to the means/ends aspect of policy, best summarized by the classic question "Do the ends justify the means?" A great many actions that are repulsive in themselves, such as subversion, bribery, or political manipulation, have been considered acceptable means to promote the national interest under certain circumstances. Though officials sometimes argue that every means should be at the disposition of the decision maker to guarantee national security, public opinion has rarely, if ever, been prepared to accept the justification of all actions on the basis of *raison d'état.* Still, when a climate of conflict and competition characterizes international politics, even states whose national values include "freedom," "justice," and "democracy" may feel compelled to consider policy initiatives that seem to be the very antithesis of these values, and such dilemmas are not easily resolved.

Not being clear about questions of ends and means almost inevitably has a negative effect on a state's prospects in the international system. Such states may find themselves largely at the mercy of others who know more precisely what they are trying to accomplish and how they intend to do it. There is no substitute for a clearly understood purpose in foreign policy, especially in the contemporary period of great change in the global milieu.

The Nature of an Objective

Ideally, all foreign actions of a state are in pursuit of an *objective*—the state of affairs that the state feels is most in its national interest in a particular *situation.* An objective may call for some change in the existing situation or for the protection and preservation of a desirable set of existing relationships. The link between objectives and national interest may not be direct, in that before an objective is selected, an intermediate judgment is often made concerning a *goal.* We would define a goal as the most desirable future state of affairs regarding a particular *issue.* Issues that involve questions of value conflict or consensus are central to international politics. Adoption of a goal, since it is based on relatively fixed factors, helps policymakers establish parameters within which they can arrive at a specific objective.

We should alert beginning students in the field that they will encounter the terms "national interests," "goals," and "objectives" used as if they were interchangeable. However, to us they refer to different time frames. National interest is a long-range factor: A national society that believes in and promotes "democracy" will presumably continue to try to do so in some form for as long as the political system lasts in its contemporary form. A goal is usually considered operational for the *foreseeable* future: As long as the situation remains fairly constant, the goal will remain relevant. Any drastic change, however, would require selection of a new goal more in harmony with the nature of the problem. Objectives are immediate or short-term. An objective should represent a state of affairs potentially attainable at the moment of decision.

The relationship between ends and means is central in the choice of an objective. While the goal represents the best conceivable state of affairs, the objective is usually the closest approximation to the goal that decision makers believe feasible. The postulated end of state action in most situations does no more than point out the direction in which the state should move. The distance it actually proceeds along this course depends on the means the state has available for use in the situation.

Another example can be taken from the Global South context. During its bloody civil war in the late 1960s, Nigeria's military government came to believe that France, through recognizing the rebel government of Biafra and other actions, sought to reduce Nigeria's influence in West Africa, where the majority of states were francophone and highly dependent on France for aid and trade. After the war, the Nigerian government adopted a goal of diminishing French influence in the subregion and seeking a role for Nigeria as the predominant power in the area. Achieving this goal would have helped to insure the self-preservation of the state, a central element in the predominant conception of national interest in the wake of the civil war, and done much to increase the state's prestige in Africa and abroad. One objective derived from this general goal was the establishment of the Economic Community of West African states, plans for which were put into action in the mid-1970s. Through this initiative, Nigeria hoped, at least to some extent, to replace France in the economic and political life of Nigeria's francophonic neighbors by offering access to its more industrialized and productive economy.

As this example illustrates, goals grow out of decision makers' perceptions of the state's purpose and its material circumstances at a given point in time. For instance, if a state is very poor, objectives related to the goal of promoting economic development would be likely to predominate, whether such efforts involved negotiating a loan with the International Monetary Fund, seeking technical assistance from the United States, the European community, or Japan, or something else. In the case of Iran, the goal of promoting Islamic fundamentalism is pursued through a variety of specific initiatives such as aiding Shiite groups in Lebanon and supporting Shiite separatists in Iraq.

POLICY AND DECISION

The tension between ends and means can be great when a state's policymakers are deciding whether to act and determining what steps, if any, should be taken first. An objective must be selected and a course (or courses) of action launched. Officials are committed to serve the interests and goals already formulated, and yet they may find themselves compelled to act in situations that permit only a limited range of means. The choices involved are extremely difficult because they may involve huge sums of money, the future of the political system, and at times the lives and property of millions of people. Unable to accomplish everything they wish, states often must weigh the competing claims on their resources and capabilities and decide not only which of their goals they can hope to achieve within a given period, but also the relative importance of different areas of action.

The Meaning of "Policy"

A *policy* is here understood to be a course of action designed to attain an objective. Although we shall put off a detailed analysis of policymaking until the next chapter, certain more general aspects of the concept are appropriately considered here.

We should first note a problem in terminology. The *foreign policy* of a state usually refers to the general principles by which a state governs its relationship with the international political environment. Such catchwords as *isolationism, bal-*

ance of power, and *imperialism* have been used, if somewhat inaccurately, to characterize particular foreign policies. On the other hand, if a policy is defined as a course of action oriented to a single objective, a state has as many policies as it has objectives. Thus *foreign policy* and *foreign policies* may have completely different meanings. Probably the best way to avoid confusion is to keep in mind that *foreign policy* (singular) is usually phrased in terms of goals, whereas *foreign policies* (plural) are formulated in terms of objectives.

One may say that the U.S. foreign policy after the fall of the Soviet Union will be that of undisputed leader of the world. The foreign policies of the United States, as leader, can include helping former communist states convert to capitalist economies; reevaluating foreign aid criteria to emphasize economic and social development rather than security concerns; reducing the tension and conflict in the Global South; and providing the motive force and initiative for solving global concerns like the degradation of the environment and nuclear proliferation.

Second, a policy always involves both *decision* and *action,* with decision perhaps the more important ingredient. Action on behalf of an objective can result from policy only if the decision itself indicates clearly what the policymaker had in mind both as to objective and procedure. As a result, the formalized decision (the "policy paper") normally includes at least three elements of clarification and guidance for anyone concerned with its implementation: (1) formulation of the objective in the most precise terms possible; (2) the nature of the action to be undertaken, stated with sufficient clarity to guide and direct the state's other officials; and (3) the forms and perhaps the amounts of national resources to be applied in pursuit of the objective.

A third factor bearing on policy is reflected in the final point in this list. A policy decision normally calls for the commitment of resources, the assumption of risk, or both. This is what we call the "cost/risk" factor in policymaking, which we shall examine in more detail later. Here we only wish to indicate that in foreign policy as in life everything has its price. Often the most demanding problem in policy formulation is deciding how much effort should be exerted in pursuit of an objective in view of competing claims of other goals and limitations on the state's resources.

The Need for Priorities

No state has ever accomplished everything it wished in its foreign policy. As we have seen, goals tend to be formulated in absolute terms—a government speaks of "security," "peace," "freedom," or "growth," never of "partial security," "relative peace," "a measure of freedom," or "limited growth." Thus the ends of policy are unlimited, but the means are sharply limited, both in theory and in practice.

Most states, even the large and powerful, have priorities that help to guide policy choices. Some questions are simply more important than others when considered in light of a state's underlying social values. Certain priorities are literally absolute, such as self-preservation; unless the state exists, any other purposes are really beside the point. Others, though important, must take second place to those of the highest priority. As a scale of priorities is worked out, each objective finds a place in relation to others.

Priority ranking of goals and objectives is crucial in determining the relative claim that each will have on the attention of the state's decision makers and on the resources of the state. It follows that a state might be willing to give in on a low-priority goal in order to gain ground on a higher-priority one. Overall strategies are established on the basis of relative priorities; long-term commitments of resources can be made intelligently only according to the principle of "first things first."

Conversely, a state attempting to conduct foreign policy without having established priorities, or with priorities that are vague, rapidly discovers priorities imposed upon it by force of circumstance. When there is no real sense of the relative importance of different problems, all issues tend to become equally significant. Furthermore, top priority tends to be assigned to what is happening at the moment rather than referring to the state's longer-range pattern of goals.

So far, we have been using the concept of "importance" as if it were itself an absolute and as if priorities flow automatically from a single unified system of values. In practice, however, many different kinds of concerns are important to a state, and selecting an appropriate basis for determining priorities is in itself a serious problem in policymaking.

One of the more common conflicts of policy is between a *functional* or *procedural* ("means") priority and a *substantive* ("ends") priority. Priorities of means and priorities of ends, in other words, often apply in different ways and impose hard choices. A state may be vitally interested in preserving the principle and practice of peaceful change in world affairs in general (a procedural priority) and yet may at the same time be under great pressure to use force to make an important gain in its level of security (a substantive priority). There is, unfortunately, no easy or simple answer to this dilemma; governments must resolve it again and again on an ad hoc basis.

Time pressures alone may lead to a confusion of priorities. Leaders frequently find themselves in situations where a particular move must be made immediately; even though the issue concerned might be minor and the action could in some way have a negative effect on other longer-term policy initiatives. Competent officials would make every effort to avoid real setbacks to their long-range and higher-priority concerns while dealing with immediate issues.

A final consequence of an unclear priority system should be noted. If a government faces a priority choice without really being sure of the relative importance of the issues involved, it may refuse to make any choice at all. Its policy objective will therefore be to put off making a decision—"buying time"—which, if successful, may allow the state to deal effectively when the issue arises again. However, in a dynamic situation, such an effort to stall may only lead to even more unfavorable conditions of choice.

For example, the call for a ban on the production of chlorofluorocarbons (CFCs) has been issued since the mid-1970s. Scientists have repeatedly warned of the adverse effects that the use of CFCs may have on the ozone layer. Yet, national governments have consistently refused to recognize the dangers involved in their allowance for the use and production of CFCs. It was not until a hole in the ozone layer appeared over Antarctica that national governments realized the severe consequences of their inaction and issued a global ban on the production of CFCs. As of this writing, there is an enormous ozone hole appearing over much of Canada and the northern parts of Europe and Asia, threatening to kill phytoplankton, the basis of all food chains, and cause skin cancer.

The Classic Compromise

The role of the policymaker, as the cliché puts it, is to "reconcile the desirability of the possible with the possibility of the desirable." Though somewhat glib, this assessment of foreign policy does epitomize the task of the responsible policymaker.

Much of our preceding discussion has been leading up to this point. On the one hand, in any (given) policy situation, a hypothetical state would have a range of ends, all desirable in terms of its national interest, that could be arranged in order of preferability. Some would be attainable with relative ease, some only by great effort and expenditure, and others would be simply beyond the range of (present) attainability. On the other hand, the state would also have a certain range of action open to it; that is, it would have the capacity to produce a number of different outcomes. Some of these might be highly desirable, others neutral, and still others inherently undesirable. If one could plot these factors on a "graph of priorities," an optimal decision would be found where the two "curves" formed by the range of desirable ends and possible actions cross.

Ideological rhetoric aside, foreign policy normally consists of enterprises involving partial commitments of resources for the accomplishment of partial purposes. As a rule, a state would not count on obtaining either all it wants or all it can get in any one situation. We would suggest, and emphasize, that the policy decision is almost always a compromise among these diverse factors.

Initiatives and Responses

The fact that civilization as we know it has so far survived the nuclear age indicates that strategic decision in most states is characterized, at least to some extent, by prudence and restraint. We would suggest that whatever a state's goals and values may be, strategy should be a cautious enterprise because of the potentially devastating consequences of failure in statecraft. The recent historical record shows some disastrous exceptions to this premise, but these have only served to underline its veracity. In fact, for the majority of states, policy is more responsive than it is initiatory because, in an environment containing so many dangers, policymakers are frequently obliged to give first priority to threats from outside before seeking to launch enterprises of their own. Responding to challenges, therefore, characteristically takes precedence in allocating a state's resources.

Some states possess relatively extensive capabilities to undertake policy initiatives. States that lead in scientific achievement, technological innovations, and military power have traditionally had great freedom to assert themselves against lesser states. If powerful states have an interest in changing some aspects of the international political environment, they are better able to get more of what they want. Other states commit a larger proportion of their capability to a range of responses, leaving only a modest surplus for initiatives. Modern democratic states have been criticized for exercising so much caution in foreign policy that their actions are almost purely responsive. Such fundamental differences in policy arise from decision makers' varying interpretations of their state's status and role in the international system. We shall examine these variations and their implications in the next section.

TYPES OF FOREIGN POLICIES

Throughout this chapter we have stressed the impact on foreign policy of social values and a conception of national purpose derived from these values. Now we consider viewpoints that help to lend overall coherence to the application of values and the determination of purpose in foreign policy.

One of the most basic judgments the leaders of a state must make concerns the relationship between their society and the rest of the world. The verdict can be affirmative; that is, the regime and society may be basically satisfied with its share of benefits and prestige and seek no major changes in the international system. On the other hand, the conclusion may be negative: status and benefits are inadequate. We would argue that either decision determines *all* subsequent discussion of foreign policy.

If the policymakers are willing to accept indefinitely their state's place in the system, their approach to foreign policy will be a *conserving* (not necessarily *conservative*) one. If, however, they decide to reject the role played at the moment, they may choose to try and bring about favorable change in the global order. Every state in the world, at some time and in varying ways, has made such a choice and then based its foreign policy on it. The bases for a state's satisfaction or dissatisfaction with its role in the system are diverse. For some states, the judgment is determined largely by economic factors—whether it belongs to the "center" or the "periphery." For others, it has to do with the level of prestige accorded by other states, or the progress of their ideology. All we can say is that a given regime would be satisfied with the existing pattern of relations in the international system if its critical, or *core,* values are receiving adequate fulfillment. Dissatisfaction means that certain core values are not being adequately addressed.

The Policy of the Status Quo

We would suggest further that from this basic decision about the environment derive two general types of foreign policy. The first of these we call the policy of the *status quo,* and it gives expression to a basic satisfaction and wish to conserve the contemporary pattern of international relations and the state's place in it. States that assume this role develop policies with a number of distinguishing traits.

Before examining the content of a policy of the status quo, we must define the sense in which we are using this common but often misunderstood term. A status quo posture does not necessarily imply enthusiasm for the details of the existing state of affairs, but rather a judgment by policymakers that the level of satisfaction received from the system is the most favorable it can hope for by any reasonable expenditure of effort. Thus a status quo policy does not compel a state to defend all the details of the established order. In fact, an enlightened status quo position—particularly when held by a major power during a period of flux—leaves ample room for change and initiative, while at the same time preserving the state's favorable position in the evolving structure of the system.

Status quo policies, therefore, are defensive in orientation. The national interest of status quo states is usually expressed in such terms as *defense, stability, preservation,* and *neutralization,* rather than *offense, change,* and *advantage.* Status quo policies seek the stabilization of relationships rather than their modification. To reduce threats to their positions, status quo states may advocate the adoption of institutional and procedural restraints on state action.

A state following a status quo policy accepts conflict as a condition of existence in the system but seldom initiates it. When caught in an overt struggle, it consciously attempts to avoid escalation of the conflict, works for resolution of the dispute at as low a level of tension as possible, and is normally willing to view an inconclusive outcome as a victory—because it is left in possession of all or most of what it had at the beginning. Historically, status quo states have not been the initiators of major wars.

The policy of the status quo, whether followed by a large or a small state, seeks to maintain a stabilized set of international relationships that include the relatively advantageous situation the state currently enjoys. As a result, status quo policies tend to be marked by restraint in conception, caution in execution, and acceptance of only a limited amount of risk. When status quo policies are prevalent in the global system, conflict is limited and change is incremental.

The Policy of Revisionism

The second type of foreign policy—which flows from either a rejection of the current status and role of the state in the system or a rejection of the structure and dominant values of the system itself—is known as *revisionism.* In many respects it is the polar opposite of the policy of the status quo. However, one should note that, though status quo policies are usually similar in value content, there can be any number of alternative revisionist outlooks, varying in the scope of their demands from reformist to revolutionary.

Revisionism aims at favorable modification of the state's overall position in the global system. It does not necessarily operate on the assumption that all international relationships are fluid and subject to change, but only those that it feels are crucial. It will accept no solutions except those that give it the measure of fulfillment it demands.

A policy of revisionism is strategically offensive: Stability is the problem, not the solution. National interest demands major environmental change in the state's favor, and policy is directed toward the discovery or creation, and complete exploitation, of opportunities for effective action. A revisionist state will not seek or agree to a stabilization of international relationships until it achieves what it wants. Revisionist states, therefore, are normally cool to proposals for the organization of world politics that might in any way inhibit their freedom of action to seek change.

Revisionist states not only accept conflict; they may actively seek it if it offers hope for the attainment of an objective. They may accept a higher level of tension in a dispute, be less adverse to escalation (at least up to a point), and be much more resistant to accepting a stalemate or a draw than are status quo states. In a struggle between the two types of actors, it is typically the revisionist state that begins the conflict and sets its terms; in any such controversy short of all-out war, it is usually the revisionist state that also decides how long the dispute will continue. Major wars have generally been begun by states that were revisionist in orientation, at least at the time the critical decision was made.

Revisionist policy is generally characterized by relative daring in conception, an optimistic calculation of factors of cost, and a willingness to take risks. A historic period dominated by revisionist policies would be marked by a high level of tension and rapid and extensive change.

The most current and obvious example of revisionist states is Iraq. In the aftermath of World War II, colonial powers like Great Britain still wielded enough power to set international boundaries for their soon-to-be former colonies. In its pursuit of easy access to crude oil, Great Britain created the kingdom of Kuwait and designated its ruler. In its dissatisfaction (or greed), Iraq sought to obtain control over the rich oil fields of Kuwait through war and conquest. Though it met its objective for a short period of time, the combined forces of status quo powers forced Iraq to withdraw with heavy casualties.

RECOMMENDED READINGS

ALMOND, GABRIEL A. *The American People and Foreign Policy.* New York: Praeger Press, 1960.

BELOFF, MAX. *Foreign Policy and the Democratic Process.* Baltimore: Johns Hopkins University Press, 1965.

BLOOMFIELD, LINCOLN P. *The Foreign Policy Process: A Modern Primer.* Englewood Cliffs, NJ: Prentice-Hall, 1982.

CHASE, JAMES. *The Consequences of The Peace: The New Internationalism and American Foreign Policy.* New York: Oxford University Press, 1992.

CINGRANELLI, DAVID L. *Ethics, American Foreign Policy, and the Third World.* New York: St. Martin's Press, 1993.

DAHL, ROBERT A. *Who Governs? Democracy and Power in an American City.* New Haven, CT: Yale University Press, 1961.

DECONDE, ALEXANDER. *Ethnicity, Race, and American Foreign Policy: A History.* Boston: Northeastern University Press, 1992.

DEESE, DAVID A. *The New Politics of American Foreign Policy.* New York: St. Martin's Press, 1994.

DEUTSCH, KARL. *The Nerves of Government: Models of Political Communication and Control.* London: Free Press of Glencoe, 1963.

GEORGE, ALEXANDER. *Bridging the Gap: Theory and Practice in Foreign Policy.* Washington, DC: United States Institute of Peace Press, 1993.

GOLDSTEIN, JUDITH, and ROBERT O. KEOHANE. *Ideas and Foreign Policy: Beliefs, Institutions, and Political Change.* Ithaca, NY: Cornell University Press, 1993.

LASKI, HAROLD J. *An Introduction to Politics.* New York: Barnes and Noble, 1962.

LASWELL, HAROLD D. *Politics: Who Gets What, When, and How.* New York: Meridian Books, 1961.

MCELROY, ROBERT W. *Morality and American Foreign Policy: The Role of Ethics in International Affairs.* Princeton, NJ: Princeton University Press, 1992.

NINCIC, MIROSLAV. *Democracy and Foreign Policy: The Fall of Political Realism.* New York: Columbia University Press, 1992.

ROSENAU, JAMES N. *The Scientific Study of Foreign Policy.* rev. ed. New York: Nichols, 1980.

SKIDMORE, DAVID, and VALERIE M. HUDSON. *The Limits of State Autonomy: Societal Groups and Foreign Policy Formulation.* Boulder, CO: Westview Press, 1993.

Chapter 2

GOVERNMENT AND POLICYMAKING

We have argued that states act purposefully in world politics, and that the making and implementing of decisions lies at the heart of the foreign policy process. Our next inquiry is into the ways states organize themselves for their international and transnational contacts and the considerations that influence their decisions. We will depict the state as an actor continually adapting to an evolving environment.

STATE ORGANIZATION FOR INTERNATIONAL ACTION

Government and Foreign Affairs

In the increasingly interconnected world of today, foreign affairs are unavoidably one of the principal concerns of all governments. For a state with limited resources, the basic issue of foreign policy may be no more (or less) than survival, while those more powerful pursue a variety of positive goals and objectives. Each state's purpose in the system is unique, but all consider foreign policy a matter of high priority and major impact. As might be expected, governments organize themselves to conduct international relations with considerable care, and the foreign policy "establishment" of a state often reflects the best that its civil service has to offer in terms of training and competence.

States resemble each other much more in their *organization* for external affairs than they do in their domestic institutions. Atop the organizational pyramid is the head of government, whose preeminent role in international relations dates from a time when the states system was largely run by absolute monarchs. The head of government is directly assisted by whatever close advisory and administrative institution exists in the government, whether a cabinet of the British or American type, a revolutionary or military council as found in some authoritarian systems, or a presidium such as in the former Soviet Union. The principal foreign affairs specialist in the government is the foreign minister (minister for external affairs, secretary of state), who heads the administrative department concerned with foreign policy and is usually the principal official adviser to the head of government. In all states, other departments participate directly in foreign policy decisions, and prominent among these are financial and military experts, economic ministers (on questions of trade or development), and, depending on their constitutionally defined role, legislative bodies. In a few states, such as the United States and Israel in recent history, legislatures play significant important influence upon world events. However, we would still suggest that foreign policy remains primarily an executive prerogative only occasionally inhibited by legislative interference.

Another distinct role in policymaking and implementation is played by the representatives a state maintains abroad, and the number of economic, cultural, and military representatives is increasing worldwide. Information they relay to their home governments influences policy, and they are at times called upon to conduct negotiations on behalf of the state. We will discuss each of these elements in more depth.

The Head of Government

The head of government—president, prime minister, or dictator—is formally the key figure in all foreign policy decisions. According to international law and practice, the head of government, as the political leader of the people, officially speaks for the state in international relations and exercises ultimate authority in the area of foreign policy.

The head of government may structure her/his role in foreign policy in a variety of ways. Though leaders seek advice and information to guide their foreign policy decisions, they differ greatly in the degree to which they rely on the opinions of subordinates or ultimately put trust in their own personal judgments and intuition. Much depends on whether the head of government has experience in and knowledge of foreign affairs—characteristics that do not always figure prominently in the selection of leaders. It is a cliché of contemporary political analysis that elections are not (usually) won or lost on foreign policy issues, so the foreign policy competence of the head of government is often unknown before he/she takes office.

Furthermore, a head of government may function entirely within the official channels of decision making or may rely more on informal and unofficial sources of recommendations—for example, the Communist Party in the former U.S.S.R., the National Security Council in the United States, or the "Establishment" in

Great Britain. Finally, heads of government may confine their personal attention only to issues of major and general importance, leaving detailed implementation to subordinates, or they may choose to involve themselves in decisions of more limited scope and significance—an involvement that is sometimes referred to as micromanaging.

Above all, the head of government is looked to for political leadership. Whatever the specific characteristics of the regime, she/he is ultimately responsible for translating the prevailing values of the society and state into a coherent foreign policy—for formulating national purpose and giving it expression through goals and concrete objectives. As the pace of global change has quickened and certain assumptions of statecraft are increasingly called into question, heads of government have been required to expend more effort in maintaining the link between an evolving environment and the political community they lead. Their policy decisions, therefore, have tended to become more general, symbolic, and direction setting, and necessarily less concerned with immediate practical choices.

The Foreign Minister and the Foreign Office

Foreign ministers in most states have a very demanding role. Ideally they should be specialists and technicians concerned with the complexities of day-to-day decisions as well as have an appreciation of the larger internal and external political problems with which the head of government is faced. Simultaneously, they are required to be administrators (as each is the head of a foreign office and a foreign service), decision makers (insofar as permitted by their superiors), and advisers.

In many cases another task is added to this already long list of responsibilities: high-level negotiation. Modern transportation and communication, coupled with the frequent need for quick decisions, have given the foreign ministers of leading powers and of many smaller ones a roving commission to travel widely and conduct important negotiations among themselves, either bilaterally, before the United Nations, or in some form of conference. As a result, foreign ministers' meetings (as well as "summit" meetings among heads of governments) have become a regular feature of international political life.

The foreign office of a state constitutes the primary grouping of expertise on international affairs within the government. Traditionally its domestic staff have been relatively fewer than the diplomatic corps abroad, but the number of personnel at home has tended to increase in recent years. Usually it is organized into subsections that reflect the priorities and capabilities of the state in foreign policy. There is often a breakdown by geographic areas corresponding to the state's involvement in various parts of the world and a number of "functional bureaus," each of which focuses on a special function or a particular issue in a global context.

Within the context of formal interstate relations a foreign office has a dual mission: to communicate with its own personnel abroad and with foreign diplomatic missions in its own country. In performing this dual role, foreign office personnel necessarily make a vast number of policy decisions at all but the highest level of importance. The foreign office also acts as a source of policy recommendations that flow upward to the higher decisional levels: the foreign minister, the cabinet (or equivalent), the head of government, and various staff members. In this respect, by defining alternatives and channeling information, foreign policy bureaucrats often significantly influence final policy decisions.

In most states, senior foreign office personnel have traditionally formed a part of the inner bureaucratic elite within the government. However, in recent times foreign policy responsibilities have tended to diffuse more widely through the governmental structure, and the foreign office has found itself increasingly in competition for resources and attention with other agencies and departments.

The Diplomatic Service

Every state maintains at least some diplomatic missions abroad. In principle a state should have a mission in every country with which it conducts diplomatic relations, but in practice having so many missions is too expensive for all but the richest. Once states have exchanged missions, official diplomatic communications can flow between them in a dual channel: A message can go directly from the foreign ministry of one state to the resident ambassador of a second state, or it may go to the first state's ambassador in the second state and then go to the second state's foreign minister.

Each mission abroad is led by a "chief of mission," usually titled "ambassador." An ambassador has several distinct but related responsibilities: representation before the host government, acting as a channel of communications, reporting information, performing a public relations task before the people of the host country, maintaining contact with nationals of his/her country who are subject to the jurisdiction of the host country, and (sometimes) conducting negotiations. The twentieth century has seen a great magnification of the public relations and representational roles of ambassadors, along with a corresponding reduction of their importance as negotiators. Though in some respects regrettable, substantial elimination of the ambassador as an important decision maker was inevitable as soon as instantaneous communication and rapid transportation made it possible for higher officials to conduct negotiations themselves. Another contemporary development in light of the expansion of world trade is the role of the ambassador and her/his staff in the promotion of their country's commerce with the host state.

Diplomatic missions vary in size and structure according to state resources, the importance of the states to each other and the image each wishes to project. Regardless of size or detailed organization, some degree of functional specialization among embassy personnel is the rule. For purposes of reporting and representation, different officers concentrate on political, economic, cultural, and labor matters; while specialized (non–foreign office) representatives for military, scientific, commercial, agricultural, intelligence, and various other affairs are also frequently found, at least in the embassies of larger and more prosperous states.

Most governments rotate diplomatic personnel between assignments abroad and tours of duty in the foreign office. There is much to be gained by this practice, because policymakers at home gain an appreciation of the problems faced by diplomats abroad, while the missions themselves gain insight into the larger dimensions of national policy and into the difficulties of decision making that confront their own governments. Also, if diplomats remain for an extended period in any one foreign country, they may become so attuned to the host country's perspective on major bilateral issues as to be unable to represent and promote the interests of their own state effectively.

Other Departments

The importance of foreign affairs to most governments is further demonstrated by the wide involvement of other departments besides the foreign office in the matters. Two departments in particular participate in nearly all states: the agency charged with raising and allocating public funds (the Treasury Department in the United States, the Exchequer in Britain, finance ministries in many other states) and the military establishment. Each has its own distinct orientation to foreign policy matters, and we will consider both in more detail.

Questions of national survival, security, and interest receive top priority in the allocation of a state's resources, and, generally speaking, foreign policy for both large and small states is expensive. Therefore, any major foreign policy decision (and most minor ones) involves some demand on public finance and requires the active or tacit approval of the appropriate department. Furthermore, the government revenues expended come from taxes, and matters of taxation are politically sensitive in that they influence the popularity of the regime in power. Such considerations are unavoidably involved in decisions to commit public funds for international purposes.

For the major powers, as well as for many less influential states, the largest share of foreign policy expenditure has traditionally gone for military purposes, and, despite the various signs of reduction in international tensions, most governments are still committed to the maintenance of substantial military forces. Security is the most obvious motivation in this regard, but such a commitment may also arise from a desire for prestige as well or from domestic politics as embodied in Eisenhower's military-industrial complex. In some states, the military are responsible for internal as well as external security, or they govern, and in such cases it is hardly surprising that government expenditures on military hardware, facilities, and training are relatively high, regardless of whether the state is facing any immediate external threat. For whatever reason, military leadership and the armed forces are actively involved in foreign policymaking in nearly all states. It is frequently argued that the military characteristically distrust bargaining and negotiation in foreign policy, have a strong preference for more direct methods, and demand the freedom to act decisively when force is deemed to be necessary. Such attitudes may put the military somewhat at odds with the foreign office, whose approach is often characterized by gradualism, restraint, and bargaining.

Increasingly important also are those departments and ministries that deal with international trade and monetary matters. Every government is necessarily concerned with the interrelated problems of trade, foreign reserves, aid, and investment. In the richer states, the relevant government agencies do what they can to promote an increase in the overseas activities of domestic firms (whether state owned or private) to insure that the currency remains strong and that a positive balance of trade is achieved. In the poorer states of the Global South, the accent is on fostering modernization and development by attracting beneficial foreign investment, fostering industries, and gaining access to foreign markets. In short, in our era economic issues have taken on higher priority for all states, and government institutions concerned with them are more central to the making and execution of foreign policy.

There are other agencies that play secondary or more irregular roles in foreign policy. Special mention should be made here of the organization a government maintains for what would be most correctly called propaganda. Modern mass communciations are a powerful tool, and potentially an effective instrument of policy. Other departments with foreign policy responsibility, including the intelligence services, tend to be called into the decisional process if and when a particular problem demands.

THE POLICY PROCESS

We now turn our attention to a more detailed discussion of the process of foreign policymaking—that is, how the national interest is applied to the external environment. We treat the subject generally because there are many aspects of the policy process shared by all (or nearly all) foreign policy bureaucracies, but the reader should bear in mind that what follows is an ideal type and that policymaking in any particular state would be influenced by all the ascriptive factors mentioned earlier.

The Process of Decision

When we focus on decision making we are focusing on decision makers, and foreign policy flows directly from their understanding of a fluid and only imperfectly perceived external environment. In carrying out their task, they apply conceptions of national interest and purpose that derive, generally, from their societies and, specifically, from their professional background and the institutional setting in which they work.

If we return to the conception of the state as a system in an environment, it is the decision makers who process "inputs" from the environment. Inputs take the form of a constant stream of information about international events that officials analyze and evaluate so as to determine which events affect the national interest in such a way as to require decision or action. For most states the bulk of data is simply noted and disregarded as peripheral to the national interest. Thus only those matters judged to have policy relevance actually give rise to an occasion for decision.

Foreign policy is essentially the application of the internal goals of a national society or the dominant groups within the society to a dynamic external environment. We may conceptualize the process as, ideally, consisting of the following steps: (1) determining the goals of the state; (2) determining the most important aspects of a particular situation in the environment; (3) evaluating the situation in terms of the state's goals; (4) selecting an objective; (5) working out a strategy to reach the objective; (6) the decision to act; (7) the action itself; and (8) evaluation of the results of the action in terms of the original goals.

One should appreciate that this series of steps is in fact an ideal type of a highly rational decision process, and as stated is applicable only to a single problem. Real decision making is never so clear-cut. Usually many decisions must be made simultaneously, and each analysis has its own peculiarities that affect all the others and are affected by them. Very few decisions go to completion without being modified by changing circumstances, and many enterprises are dropped before completion because time and new concerns have rendered them obsolete.

Furthermore, a large organization such as a foreign office should not be thought of as single-mindedly pursuing a goal in the same way as an individual. In the first place, it is difficult to innovate in a bureaucratic context: Innovation requires the mobilization and coordination of many departments in doing something with which few, if any, have experience. It is far easier to do what the organization already "knows" how to do. Hence, there is at times a tendency to recommend types of action with which the organization is already familiar and experienced, rather than seeking a truly suitable approach. Also, there are always "bureaucratic" factors, such as the interests of certain individuals and departments, which come between the original conception of the national interest and its concrete expression in policy decisions and actions.

The Analysis of Foreign Policy Situations

Having decided that a situation demands a decision, officials would in most cases analyze it further with two purposes in mind. First, they would wish to know the manner and extent of their state's involvement in the area or issue under scrutiny in order to determine the most advantageous objective. Second, they would want to know what courses of action the situation makes possible, independent of their desirability.

This kind of analysis ordinarily involves the consideration of three distinct sets of factors: (1) the general characteristics of the event or issue that are beyond the control of any single state; (2) the pertinent policies being followed by other states—at least the important ones—in the given context; and (3) one's own state's capabilities for action in light of the first two factors. For policy to be maximally effective, this analysis should be as precise and objective as professional skill can make it, but so many intangible factors must be weighed and evaluated that in practice no government can be more than approximately accurate.

A situation that demands a foreign policy decision would, optimally, be analyzed three times. The first analysis would stress long-term factors in order to arrive at relevant goals. The second would focus on middle-range aspects in order to suggest objectives. The third analysis would concentrate on short-run and immediate aspects of the problem. This process is a logical way to arrive at objectives, and it is only after objectives are selected that one should consider courses of action. Again, the degree to which this optimally rational and efficient procedure can be applied to any given situation is a function of capacity, time, and the experience and style of the officials involved.

The Choice Among Alternatives

A decision maker would usually like to preserve, at any stage of the policy process, the maximum range of choice. To this end, opportunities and imperatives are most frequently formulated as a set of alternatives for action. Statespersons and militarists are often counseled never to put themselves in a situation in which they have only one possible course of action. As long as a state retains a range of policy choices, it is better equipped to attain a favorable outcome in either conflictive or cooperative situations. A lack of alternatives, however, may limit a state to a response that other actors can easily anticipate and perhaps turn to their advantage.

Thus a truly optimal decision would benefit from a prior assessment of all the alternatives open to the state in the particular context, together with estimates of the probable outcome of each one. This range of choice would then be considered by the "decisional unit," whether a single policymaker or a group. The alternative ultimately selected should, logically, be the one that promised the greatest gain or the least loss as measured against the state's goals.

In the real world a range of policy alternatives for a state rarely comprises several clearly inappropriate actions and one "right" one. Rather, the real differences among various alternatives may be relatively small or difficult to determine. Selection of one can be difficult, especially when pressures of time or administrative necessity rush the decision-making process. When pressed, decision makers often accept the first alternative found that meets their minimum criteria for acceptability. Still, no state would dispense entirely with alternatives, however obscure their differences may be in a particular situation, because effective policy cannot be made for long on an ad hoc basic.

Furthermore, alternatives help provide a measure of flexibility in foreign policy. Basing a decision on a choice among alternatives, especially if the courses of action are not mutually exclusive, facilitates adaptation to the consequences of errors or unforeseen circumstances. If a selected course of action fails to evoke a desired response, it would be possible to follow an alternative course without going through the entire decision-making process again. However, such policy flexibility depends on available resources, and it may be beyond the capability of some states.

The usual method of testing the validity of a choice is to take initial steps tentatively and provide means to withdraw if the judgment proves to have been faulty. In such a case, a state can hold its losses to a minimum while preserving the freedom to undertake different policy initiatives later. Only after the correctness of its assumptions and the accuracy of its analysis of the situation have been reasonably confirmed would a government take further steps to become fully committed to its initial choice of action.

Evaluating and Revising Decisions

The discussion to this point indicates that the effectiveness of state action depends on the extent to which that action is responsive to the actual situation that gave rise to it. Given the fact that decisions are made on the basis of incomplete and inaccurate information, prudence demands constant evaluation of the results of decisions and, if possible, immediate revision of policies that are not producing desired effects.

In this regard, modern communications are of great utility to the policymaker. Policymakers in the past waited weeks or even months to learn of responses to their moves. Today, information is received within a much shorter period—sometimes instantly—and in this sense the process of policy evaluation and revision is much simpler. But in another way modern conditions complicate the task of making decisions. Events today move even more rapidly than decisions, which are, after all, made by human beings subject to fatigue and bad temper. Furthermore, the very complexity of foreign policy causes major states to implement their decisions through relatively fixed commitments and long-term "programs"—both extremely difficult to change even in circumstances of stress. A third factor that makes evaluation difficult is pressure caused by the simple volume of foreign policy business. When new problems crowd the decision maker, it is more likely that these problems will be dealt with before those associated with the sometimes agonizing reappraisal of earlier decisions.

It is, therefore, not uncommon today for a particular policy to be utterly invalidated by an unexpected train of events that could have been anticipated by adequate evaluation and revision. States with extensive and complicated networks of commitments are particularly prone to this danger. Although they have the greatest need for constant evaluation, they tend to find it the most difficult to implement. Smaller states with less margin for error and with a narrower range of concerns have proved much more adept at adjusting their policies to even modest change in situations.

FACTORS INFLUENCING DECISIONS

Despite the information revolution, foreign policy is not made by computer. Rather it is formulated by individuals who possess and exercise judgment. We have seen that a policy decision incorporates a major element of choice, and we will now consider some further influences on the selection of one course of action over others.

The Appreciation of the Problem

No policy can be chosen without an appreciation of the problem the decision is to affect. To begin with, no two officials in any government would see the same set of problem-related facts in the same terms. Each brings a distinct personality, professional and organizational outlook, moral code, and intuitive skill to bear on the task, and each may have personal sources of information. Policymaking, particularly in democracies, can resemble a Tower of Babel in that officials experience great difficulty agreeing on the meaning of the events that have provided them with an occasion for a decision. Ideally, good leadership, whether political or professional, should insure that all subordinate decision makers follow standard criteria of problem identification; but in practice the degree to which this idea is realized is inversely related to the size of the policymaking bureaucracy.

The word *problem* sometimes causes some confusion in this regard. There is a natural tendency (at least in Western languages) to think of "problems" as obstacles to be overcome and pressures to be resisted. In our discussion, however, a "problem" is an element in a foreign policy situation that demands a solution, and it can be as much an opportunity as an obstacle. It is, in this sense, just as "problematic" to determine ways of capitalizing on an unexpected advantage as it is to develop a strategy to lessen the effect of some misfortune.

The Calculation of Costs and Risks

A second major factor that affects foreign policy decisions is the estimation of costs and risks associated with a given action. All political action requires the expenditure of some of the actor's resources, and this statement is certainly true for foreign policy, which, as we have mentioned, can be very expensive in both material and human terms. We would suggest that any policy carries with it some risks—generally of failure and the particular negative consequences that would result from failure. To the extent that they are accurately appraised and seriously considered, the twin cautions of cost and risk will tend to limit the real range of choice of the statesperson.

In establishing possible costs and risks, prudent decision makers often assume the worst possible consequences of any possible move. Of course, the "worst-case scenario" they envision is that which is foreseeable in the light of available information. Cost factors are actually estimated in terms of the range of probabilities open at any time, combined with the costs of each of the probable outcomes. In other words, a decision to act indicates that the policymakers feel the objective sought is worth the highest price the state conceivably might have to pay for it.

Evaluating risk can also be thought of as calculating the relative odds in favor of the success of a particular policy initiative. Such assessments try to allow for some measure of influence of the unforeseen events, and not infrequently risk assessments have had a significant impact on the direction of international relations. Thus the evaluation of risk is an acknowledgment of the element of uncertainty and guesswork inherent in all foreign policy. One device sometimes used in this regard is to postulate an "acceptable" degree of risk: the amount of failure that can be tolerated. The acceptability of such a "calculated" risk is determined by two sets of interrelated factors: the importance of the objective being sought (a value judgment) and the seriousness of the consequences of failure (an analytical conclusion).

We should reemphasize, in light of our previous discussion of ascriptive politics, that although the process of policy planning is similar in most capitals, the actual level of acceptable risk is a product of the particular political culture of a national society. For instance, we mentioned in Chapter 1 that states with a revisionist orientation toward the international system would generally be willing to incur higher risks than those supporting the status quo.

The Problem of Domestic Consensus

Another limit upon the decision maker originates in the domestic politics of the state. Regardless of forms of government or political ideology, any state's foreign policy is to some degree bound by popular consensus and limited to what mass attitudes may allow. This is not to suggest that foreign policies always reflect the true "will of the people." In fact, the consensus that restricts decision makers may in certain cases be the mainly synthetic result of a deceptive campaign of misinformation. But regardless of its origin or degree of sophistication, consensus plays a role in determining the latitude of decision a statesperson enjoys at any given time. Mass identification with foreign policy issues, though potentially an important source of support to a regime, can also be a debilitating factor that at times prevents officials from following their best professional judgment.

In practice, popular consensus imposes varying degrees of constraint. For instance, when a regime is very popular or when it is dealing with matters of secondary importance, its decision makers often may act without much concern for mass reactions. However, the more narrow and specific popular concern is, the more officials feel its impact.

There is an interesting relationship between the breadth and the intensity of domestic foreign policy consensus. A broad grant of discretion to government usually implies that there is a relatively low level of identification with policies among the populace. When a government increases the intensity of its popular support on an issue, it may see the number of acceptable alternative policies narrowed. This phenomenon can have particularly negative consequences in situations of intense international conflict: Generally, the closer to war the situation drifts, the more public attitudes become inflamed, and the less control policymakers exercise over events. In gaining popular support to deal with the worst contingencies, governments may sacrifice their ability to capitalize upon more favorable circumstances.

Consensus is most obvious when it is most specific. Particularly in moments of crisis, mass attitudes will seize upon a specific issue or problem of policy and insist on a (frequently oversimplified) position. If the mass response does not take into account enough relevant data or a practical range of choice, such manifestations can be quite problematic for decision makers. Officials in democratic and dictatorial states alike dread such developments and try to keep popular attitudes excited but safely below the boiling point. When public opinion does get out of control, policymakers may ignore or defy it only at their own risk, and even then only for a limited time.

On the other hand, consensus may develop in the domestic population for a particular course of policy or range of policy options over a long period, as a result of widespread public involvement, activism, and education. A recent example is the consistent two-thirds or more of the U.S. public that opposed military support to the contras in Nicaragua for many years. When these deeply rooted instances of consensus are treated by policymakers as merely troublesome meddling in the affairs of state, the success of official policy choices may be seriously curtailed by a lack of public support.

The Incompleteness of Information

Most foreign policy decisions are made in a context of incomplete information because the time lag between event and decision makes it futile for policymakers to wait until they have complete facts. They are obliged instead to act on the information available to them and arrange their decisions so as to reduce the risk factor to a minimum.

The inadequacy of information available to policymakers manifests itself in either of two ways: They may not have enough data, or they may have too much. In the first instance, they lack the crucial information that would have enabled them to construct a meaningful and valid decision. If data are unavailable or if policymakers cannot wait for more complete information, they must fill the gaps with estimates, extrapolations, or assumptions and go ahead anyway. In the second situation, the decision maker in fact has the information he/she needs, but it lies buried under mountains of extraneous or only mildly relevant data. Because of time pressures or because they lack clear priorities to aid in separating the important from the trivial, officials find themselves little better off than they would have been without the accumulation of unsifted information.

The constant effort of governments to improve both the quantity and usefulness of the information upon which it must base decisions is what we normally call "intelligence." As more areas of human life and action become relevant to foreign policy, more kinds of information are gathered and funneled into the decision-making apparatus of each government. Once gathered and "fed" into the policy bureaucracy, the information is digested, evaluated, correlated, and distributed to decision makers whose responsibilities make these data useful and necessary to them.

The purpose of this emphasis on information is to reduce the risk associated with decisions—that is, to minimize the extent to which the outcomes of any action are unknown and to amplify what is known of the probability of their occurrence. Though certainty may be the idealized goal, *any* effective substitution of knowledge or informed insight for pure guesswork in foreign policy decisions is a net gain.

The Pressure of Time

Another influence on foreign policy decisions, which we have so far only mentioned in passing, is the limited time available in which to decide. With improvements in transportation and communication, events now occur much more rapidly than in the past, and their outcomes reach the decision maker in a much shorter time. This acceleration of forces greatly complicates the policymaker's task, because officials often lack the time needed to analyze situations, compare alternatives, and make choices. They can deal with most issues only in a summary, routine, and, frequently, unimaginative, fashion. At best they manage to make a more thorough analysis of the questions of far-reaching importance, but even this task is difficult. They may be so pressed for time that a crucial issue, if it is in any way difficult to identify, could well slip by as "just another problem."

In an attempt to cope with a larger and more rapidly moving flow of business, many governments have expanded their policymaking organizations. Such expedients have often proved to be self-defeating because the increased rigidity and complexity of bureaucracy have more than offset any gain in administrative capacity. Communication patterns within the bureaucratic structure and the need for a variety of clearances and approvals slow down decision making and deprive it of focus and force.

One particularly unfortunate consequence of the pace at which most foreign policy decision makers drive themselves (or are driven) is the tendency for reflective thought to disappear in a climate of tension. When there is no time to "waste in just thinking," officials may lose a quality of perceptiveness and flexibility ordinarily considered an advantage for a policymaker. This tendency is most exaggerated during periods of "crisis" when researchers have shown that leaders' ability to deal with ambiguity, to think ahead, and even simply to behave rationally are at times sharply reduced.

In effect, individuals under pressure tend to make decisions that will clear their desks for the next problem. If they are prudent, they will prefer to make minimum commitments and extremely cautious responses, to follow precedent closely, and to interpret directives as narrowly as possible. A harried official always prefers giving a "no" answer rather than a "yes," for the former not only spares the individual responsibility for a decision that might later prove unwise, but also avoids the necessity of opening up entirely new areas of analysis and decision for which there is little time.

National Style

One of the direct manifestations of ascriptive politics in foreign policy is the degree to which decision makers in any state are affected by what is called "national style"—the prevailing tradition and self-image of a society that predisposes its officials to perform their duties and make their decisions in ways considered unique and peculiarly appropriate. "Style" as a concept is much more useful, as well as being easier to defend, than the once-popular idea of "national character." Although it is unreasonable to expect an entire people to conform to a given character, the majority of the members of any coherent society will tend to share at least some characteristics.

National style is important in shaping decisions because of its influence on decision makers' general perceptions of the international environment and their analyses of specific threats and opportunities before their state. Officials may well be unaware of the extent to which they share and draw upon a larger code of appropriate and socially sanctioned behavior when they grapple with their special problems, but only hopelessly alienated (and therefore largely ineffective) public servants could dissociate themselves completely from their societies. A common style of analysis and decision forms one of the real elements of cohesiveness in all reasonably well-integrated government structures.

The relevance of notions of style to decisions may be suggested by some examples. In Great Britain, for instance, the idea of "muddling through"—a conspicuous reluctance to relate immediate choices overtly to long-range purposes—has given British policy a certain resilience and adaptability not enjoyed by other states. Russia is known for its concern for secrecy, and China's proclivity for suspicion is revealed in a policy style of centrism and maintenance of distance from others. Countries in the Global South, particularly those that have actively promoted the demand for a new international economic order, have developed a style of protest. The French have demonstrated a particular concern with "honor" and "glory" far in excess of the norm among states. The style of the United States has long involved casting international issues in moral terms and viewing foreign policy as a series of crises broken by random intervals of relaxation.

These dimensions of national style cannot help but modify the decision-making process in each government concerned. Considerations of style help also to explain both deep animosities and close associations between pairs of states, as well as many otherwise perplexing patterns of interaction. For instance, the differences between the styles of the United States and the former Soviet Union during the Cold War, quite apart from any differences of ideology and governmental system, help us to understand the depth and complexity of their conflict in the postwar era.

Commitments and Precedents

Last on our list of factors influencing decision, but arguably one of the most important to a policymaker, is the structure of already-existing commitments and precedents within which she/he must act. No policy decision is ever made in a vacuum at a given moment in time. Rather, each is affected to a great extent by many earlier decisions, the state as a whole, the policy bureaucracy, and the individual decision maker are all bound in different ways by the remote or immediate past.

One important type of commitment that affects decisions is that made to a state's own public opinion, and we have noted its effects in our discussion of consensus. A second includes all the understandings, arrangements, alliances, and other fixed relationships a state has developed with other states. A decision violating any of these, or even changing one to any significant degree, would almost certainly cause a perceptible response and might cause many new problems. Therefore, such initiatives are usually avoided whenever possible. A third type of commitment is perhaps less obvious: Long-standing hostilities and disagreements with other states may also function as fixed factors and may materially affect decisions.

This third category merits a final word. Since major policy undertakings today require extensive preparation and long-term implementation, deep-seated conflicts among states have on occasion assumed a quasi-institutional character. Any radical improvements in relations would, when viewed in decisional terms only, present almost as serious a problem as would a major crisis. Once such a confict has become one of the "givens" of a state's international position, the government's foreign policy officials might feel that its prolongation would be preferable to almost any modification in its conditions, because, despite the danger and possible costs of the conflict, at least its scope and intensity are already known, and one can plan accordingly.

RECOMMENDED READINGS

ALLISON, GRAHAM T. *Essence of Decision: Explaining the Cuban Missile Crisis.* Boston: Little, Brown, 1971.

ALLISON, GRAHAM T., and GREGORY F. TREVERTON. *Rethinking America's Security: Beyond Cold War to New World Order.* New York: Norton, 1992.

ART, ROBERT J., and SEYOM BROWN, eds. *U.S. Foreign Policy: The Search for a New Role.* New York: Macmillan, 1993.

AXELROD, ROBERT. *The Structure of Decision: The Cognitive Maps of Political Elites.* Princeton, NJ: Princeton University Press, 1976.

BELOFF, MAX. *Foreign Policy and the Democratic Process.* Baltimore: Johns Hopkins University Press, 1965.

DESTLER, I. M. *Presidents, Bureaucrats, and Foreign Policy: The Politics of Organizational Reform.* Princeton, NJ: Princeton University Press, 1972.

DYE, THOMAS R. *Policy Analysis: What Governments Do, Why They Do It, and What Difference It Makes.* New York: Wiley Interscience, 1984.

HALPERIN, MORTON, PRISCILLA CLAPP, and ARNOLD KANTER. *Bureaucratic Politics and Foreign Policy.* 2nd ed. Washington, DC: Brookings Institution, 1974.

HUNT, MICHAEL. *Ideology and U.S. Foreign Policy.* 2nd ed. New Haven, CT: Yale University Press, 1987.

KEGLEY, CHARLES, JR., and EUGENE WITKOPF. *American Foreign Policy: Pattern and Process.* New York: St. Martin's Press, 1991.

LANDAU, SAUL. *The Dangerous Doctrine: National Security and U.S. Foreign Policy.* Boulder, CO: Westview Press, 1988.

NATHAN, JAMES A., and JAMES O. OLIVER. *Foreign Policy Making and the American Political System.* Boston: Little, Brown, 1987.

NOLAN, CATHAL J. *Principled Diplomacy: Security and Rights in U.S. Foreign Policy.* Westport, CT: Greenwood Press, 1993.

NYE, JOSEPH, JR. *Bound to Lead: The Changing Nature of American Power.* New York: Basic Books, 1990.

ROSENAU, JAMES. *International Politics and Foreign Policy.* New York: Free Press of Glencoe, 1961.

SAID, ABDUL AZIZ, ed. *Ethnicity and U.S. Foreign Policy.* rev. ed. New York: Praeger Press, 1981.

SIMON, HERBERT. *Models of Bounded Rationality.* Cambridge, MA: MIT Press, 1982.

Chapter 3

CAPABILITY IN ACTION

In this chapter we are interested in how states estimate what can be achieved in a given context, how these estimates find their way into policy decisions, and what factors contribute positively and negatively to their realization. Central to this discussion is the concept of capability.

CAPABILITY

Definition

The broadest and most useful definition describes a state's *capability* as the capacity to effect changes in the global environment in its own interest. This definition does not include all the actions a state may be in a position to take, but only those deemed advantageous to itself. Any particular state's capability is therefore assessed in light of and derives its meaning from the state's foreign policy goals.

By means of its capability a state acts to alter the environment in desired directions; and under circumstances beyond its capability to alter it must accept externally imposed outcomes. Environmental "change" is to be understood in the broadest sense—in terms of relationships and situations that are different than they would have been without application of the state's capability. The concept therefore includes, again, avoiding negative outcomes as well as achieving positive results. Thus a state makes its intentions effective in the international system by means of its capability. Capability pertains to the "means" aspect of the ends-means continuum in foreign policy. However generally the notion may be conceived and discussed in the abstract, capability judgments in foreign policy are useful to policymakers only when made in highly concrete, specific, and immediate terms.

The Function of Capability

Capability has a very particular role in the pursuit of state objectives. In the international political environment a state can achieve its purposes only by gaining either the voluntary or the forced acquiescence of other states. This largely informal and at times crude approach to politics prevails in the absence of an effective international governing body. The assent of other states may be stated or tacit, voluntary or grudging. It may be extended after a relatively simple process of explanation or persuasion, or only after a struggle of will and might. Regardless of its source, nature, extent, or durability, this gaining of assent alone makes possible the state's accomplishment of a national objective.

Influence and Coercion in Capability

A state's ability to persuade other states to agree to its designs is demonstrated in two different ways. A policymaker may be able to obtain the acceptance of another government in an atmosphere of agreement and cooperation. Consent may be given freely for any of a variety of reasons: The other state may approve of the projected action on its own merits (i.e., in this situation the policies of the two states are in *harmony*); it may be neutral or uninvolved in the question; or its disagreements may be so small as to be negligible. More commonly, there may be limited bases of disagreement that are resolvable after some measure of positive inducement: the promise of direct benefit, a modification of policy in another area, or some other quid pro quo. In any of these instances, the low level of conflict and the willingness to adjust or coordinate policies is the significant dimension. These are instances when the state's ability to *influence* is central. The state is able to gain adequate consensus through persuasion or policy coordination without directly calling into question issues of force.

When acquiescence must be gained in a context of more intense conflict and disagreement among states, one or more actors may attempt to *coerce* others to accept their wishes. There are many forms of coercion, ranging from the mildest allusion to negative repercussions, through a long continuum of increasingly hostile threats and forms of pressure, culminating finally in the use of military force—traditionally regarded as the ultimate coercive method. At whatever level coercion is employed, its purpose is always the same: to overcome other states' opposition to one's goals. Influence and coercion are equally important instruments of state capability. Since intense conflict has figured more prominently in both academic and popular writing on the subject than has effective policy coordination and cooperation, the coercive dimension attracts greater attention and is often mistaken for the dominant aspect of capability. Yet, in practice, policymakers spend the majority of their time and effort manipulating such influence as they possess and resort to coercion only as a last resort. It costs less to win assent by influence, fewer undesirable aftereffects are produced, and the results tend to be longer-lasting. Policymakers with only coercive forms of capability available to them find that their choice of policies is sharply limited by the relatively high cost any coercive procedure would entail.

Furthermore, increasing interdependence in the international system has further reduced the utility of coercive military capability. We will discuss this topic in more detail later, but in this context we simply note that, given a high level of interdependence among states, coercive policies may produce negative consequences for the initiator as well as the targeted state. In these circumstances the process of policy coordination through negotiation becomes even more important as a means of conflict resolution because it offers at least some positive outcomes for all involved in a situation, whereas coercive measures might be almost wholly counterproductive.

Capability and "Power"

Although it is possible to define and use the term *power* much as we are using *capability* in this chapter, *power* has come to symbolize the capacity of a state to coerce others or to avoid coercion by them. Such an emphasis on coercion has often led to a concentration on the most obvious form of coercive capacity—military force. A conception of world politics founded on "power" runs the risk of overemphasizing a victor and a vanquished in every international confrontation. World poiltics is thus often conceived as a "zero-sum" game: One player can win only to the extent that other players lose.

As discussed earlier, a coercive, zero-sum approach is simply not the way contemporary world politics usually proceeds. Although the values that states seek are in some respects incompatible and their prosecution creates at times an atmosphere of conflict, this fact does not make all relationships coercive. In many cases values overlap or coincide, and more importantly the fact of value "conflict" does not in any way directly imply the use of coercive means of action. Thus a simplistic "power theory" of world politics ignores far too many aspects of the actual relations of states to be a reliable guide.

The concept of "power" has yet another significant shortcoming. Capability is always the ability to *do* something—to act purposefully in an actual situation. Power should have the same meaning; popular political discourse frequently portrays "power" as a status to which states aspire and which a chosen few achieve. One often hears a state described as powerful in the abstract, regardless of how effectively it might pursue its foreign policy objectives. As we are using it, the concept of capability preserves the necessary connection with specific goals and objectives that the prevalent emphasis on "power" has often tended to obscure.

CAPABILITY JUDGMENTS IN FOREIGN POLICY

What Is a Capability Judgment?

A *capability judgment* is an analysis of the real opportunities and limitations on a state in a given policy context. Ideally, it should result in the formulation of a range of possible actions by the state, as discussed in Chapter 2, with the emphasis here being on *possibility*. Capability provides the state with the resources of action, but it should in no way predispose the state toward any of the possible alternatives. The choice among alternatives is a value choice; capability judgments do no more than clarify the viable alternatives. Finally, though our discussion will present the analysis of capability as an essentially rational decision-making process, the reader should bear in mind that this description represents an ideal and that the application of the process is influenced, sometimes decisively, by the bureaucratic and organizational factors we mentioned earlier.

Capability judgments have a special role in analysis of foreign policy situations. The policy context should dictate the specific elements of capability that enter into the analysis, while the capability judgment establishes the parameters within which the operational decision will eventually be made. No realistic policymakers would knowingly attempt a policy that requires an effort beyond their state's capability.

Judging the State's Own Capability

Besides being fully informed about alternatives, policymakers also need to know what part of their state's total resources is available to them in a given situation. They may be (and frequently are) restricted by the fact that much of the state's capability is already invested in other commitments and also by previous policy decisions that limit them to certain forms of action. For example, military power may not be available or suitable, but they may have recourse to large measures of propaganda or economic inducements. They may also be obliged to predict the consequences of applying any of the available forms of capability, or they may consider it wise to make this attempt.

This process, carried out to the level of detail that is necessary and appropriate, leads to a fuller appreciation of the policymakers' span of meaningful choices. On the basis of this judgment they proceed to assess the desirability of each of the several courses of action they have formulated and to select one of them as policy, as outlined in Chapter 2.

The major actors in the system are acutely concerned about capability and characteristically expend so much effort keeping up-to-date on available options that policymakers rarely find it necessary to go through the entire analytical operation that we have sketched. Yet the essentials of the process remain the same regardless of how extensively it may become institutionalized.

Taking the October War of 1973 as an example, after the United States had decided that helping Israel best served its goals in the region, the United States had to decide which resources it could mobilize for assistance. In this instance, the sum of the possible alternatives for the United States were direct military involvement, military and economic aid, appealing to the Arab states and the former Soviet Union for peace, supporting the UN's efforts at negotiating a cease-fire, or any combination of these alternatives. Direct military involvement was out of the question because it might have provoked a direct major-power confrontation. The United States sought to sustain Israel by providing it with military and economic assistance, while negotiating for peace with the Soviets and the Arab leaders after Israel had gained the upper hand. Finally, the United States and the former Soviet Union made a cease-fire proposal to the Security Council of the United Nations.

Capability Judgments of Other States

Capability judgments are really exercises in the determination of relationships. No capability judgment is of real use except in comparison with judgments of the capabilities of other states. To have an effective foreign policy, therefore, governments must spend at least as much time and effort in attempting to judge the capabilities of other states as in assessing their own.

It is critical to strategists to have an appreciation of the range of action open to other states, particularly those with which they are directly involved at the moment. If they can sense the parameters of action accepted by their opposite numbers in the other governments, they will have a great advantage in developing their own policy. As a result, the major focus of contemporary intelligence work is the assessment of the capabilities of other states.

The method of reaching a capability judgment about another state is not radically different in nature from that used on one's own, but its application is much more difficult. Information on which the judgment is based is even more fragmentary and difficult to obtain, because no state is eager to have any other gain complete insight into its own capabilities. Even more perplexing is the problem posed by differences in analytical points of view. Capability analysis, in spite of its total emphasis on possibilities, still requires interpretation and evaluation of data, and decision makers from no two states are likely to interpret facts in quite the same way. For capability judgments to be of maximum use in devising strategy and tactics, a state's officials must somehow also determine how other states' policymakers interpret their relationships with the environment.

Research has shown, however, that this last recommendation is more easily prescribed than realized. Many studies have demonstrated just how limited is the ability of most decision makers to empathize with the outlook of their opposite numbers. Furthermore, beliefs, and predispositions are very slow to change and resist all but the most unambiguous contradictory information. Since much information encountered in policymaking is ambiguous to some degree, it seems that policymakers often find ways to make new data agree with their preconceptions rather than remaining truly open to new inputs from the international political environment.

FACTORS IN CAPABILITY ANALYSIS

Capability analysis, we have concluded, is a crucial step in policymaking. We have also sketched out the essentials of the approach to reaching capability judgments. We will now review the factors that enter into these analyses.

Analytical Point of View

Perhaps the most important influence on the analysis of capability is the point of view of the analyst. Because a capability judgment is an estimate of the opportunities and limitations in any situation that demands a foreign policy decision, there is inevitably a gap between the environment as the analyst interprets it and as it exists in reality. Policymakers, subject to all human perceptual and behavioral limitations, must act on the "milieu" as they perceive it, in full knowledge that many factors of the situation are unknown to them and will serve to modify and possibly upset whatever capability judgments they may make. We have noted that this condition of uncertainty tends to make policymakers more cautious, tentative, and closed-minded in their commitments.

The Situational Base

As we have said, capability is only a useful concept, and meaningful capability judgments can be made only in terms of a specific set of policies under analysis and evaluation. Furthermore, it is also true that the concept is useful only in a particular context. A state never has more than a fraction of its total theoretical or actual capability available for its immediate purpose. What may seem to be an overall "high" or "favorable" level of capability may not translate into an equivalently high range of capability in a particular situation. In fact, a small and ordinarily "weak" state may, in certain contexts, have greater capability not only to influence a larger "stronger" one, but also to coerce it.

Certain forms of capability, whether influential or coercive, are appropriate in a given situation, but others are not. The actual capability a state enjoys in a situation is determined by which of its available modes of action would be effective in dealing with that situation in view of the state's policy at the moment. The actual outcome of most international conflicts tends to be less a reflection of any generalized "power" relationship than a function of time, place, and the policies being carried out by the respective states.

This concept is easily illustrated with the Soviet invasion of Hungary in 1956. Despite the desire of the United States and its NATO allies to see the liberation of Eastern European countries, they were essentially helpless to assist the Hungarian nationalists' struggle to assert their independence.

> President Eisenhower concluded that nothing short of US intervention would cause the Soviets to reverse their course of action, and that geography made it out of the question for such a response to be made either alone or through NATO.[1]

[1]Max Harelson, *Fires All Around the Horizon* (New York: Praeger, 1989), p. 82.

Relativity of Capability

There is only one rational answer to the question "How much capability does a state need?": "Enough." The goal of any contingency planning is adequacy—sufficient capability to fulfill the anticipated needs of policy. There is no real advantage in increasing the state's capacity to act beyond what it is likely to need, with a generous allowance for analytical error and unpredictable quirks of fate. Of course, in times of great international tension and uncertainty, adequacy may be difficult to determine with any degree of precision.

Regardless of what a state may be able to do in a situation, its net capability is zero if other states can neutralize each of its moves. However, even a narrow range of action may be enough to give the state absolute capability if other states are relatively less well-off. Thus capability analysis focuses not so much on absolute levels of environmental change as on the margin of operational superiority one state may enjoy over another. This consideration is particularly pertinent in questions of military confrontation today. Several states have the capacity to severely damage or destroy each other with thermonuclear weapons. Since none is able to focus its absolute military strength to gain a strategic advantage, the massive military machines of contemporary superpowers are frequently of limited utility or even irrelevant as elements of functional capability.

The Dynamic Nature of Capability

Capability is a highly dynamic factor in policymaking. Judging capability involves correlating a broad variety of factors within a state with an international situation, all elements of which are moving at different speeds. Any final conclusion about relative capabilities, no matter how up-to-date the information on which it is based, is obsolete by the time of its formulation. To make such an analysis applicable to an existing situation, it is necessary for a policymaker to predict future trends and variables, both in his/her own state and with regard to all others involved.

It should not be surprising to see that almost all countries of the world have agencies that make daily reports on the current status as well as future projections to the policymakers. The individual governments realize that in order to make timely and appropriate policies, they will have to be informed of not only how their country's resources are and will be utilized, but what other countries are and will be doing as well.

In theory, any single capability analysis should serve as the basis for only one decision to act, in that any later consideration of the same situation would require a new calculation of the relative status of all the states concerned. However, literal adherence to this principle would render decision making almost impossible; most governments merely adjust a previous capability analysis with whatever additional data they have available and then proceed to make a new decision. The need for even such partial recalculations illustrates the transitory character of the ingredients of a capability comparison and the constant necessity of keeping it up-to-date.

ELEMENTS AND FACTORS OF CAPABILITY

Though we have stressed that capability is a relative concept, we would still suggest it is possible to catalog certain elements in a state's makeup and objective position that contribute directly and indirectly to its capacity to act. What follows may be thought of as a checklist that indicates the disparate sources from which a state may, in a particular situation, draw resources with which to support its policy. It should not be thought of as a basis for conclusions about the absolute strength or power of any state.

The Major Categories

The "elements and factors" of capability are usually broken down into two broad categories for convenience of discussion, although the classification is a rough one. Keeping this uncertainty in mind, we may generalize that the capability of a state derives from both tangible and intangible sources.

Tangible factors are listed in various ways. Here we include five categories: (1) geographic position; (2) population and workforce; (3) resource endowment; (4) industrial and agricultural productive capacity; and (5) the armed forces. Each of these could be further subdivided, and when actually used to analyze the capability of a state, they would be broken down in greater detail.

The intangible factors we use here are three in number: (1) political, economic, and social institutions; (2) educational and technical levels; and (3) national morale. As with the tangible factors, these three as listed are broad and necessarily somewhat vague because they must be given specific content and applicability if they are to be used meaningfully.

A quick comparison of the two lists leads to the conclusion that each of the so-called tangibles has a measure of intangibility about it, while the intangibles all have certain aspects of tangibility. Tangible factors are analyzed in terms of *quantity*—as modified by such concerns as availability, convertibility, and substitutability. The significant dimension for the intangibles is *quality*—estimated not only in terms of "excellence," but also by such criteria as appropriateness and relevance. The analyst *measures* the tangible factors but *evaluates* the intangibles. For a given state, the quality of the intangibles would influence the effectiveness with which the tangible elements could be employed.

Thus a capability analysis would logically begin with the most obvious physical factors of a state, such as geography, that not only are the most easily measured, but also usually have the slowest rates of change. It would proceed through the less obviously concrete (and thus more dynamic) factors, and ultimately come to rest, so to speak, at the opposite pole of intangibility, where there are fewer empirical data on which to rely but a potentially rapid rate of change and evolution with which to cope.

The Tangibles

1. *Geography.* Geographic factors enter into state capability in a number of ways. Among the more apparent are such characteristics as a state's size (which is either an advantage, a handicap, or a neutral factor, depending on the policy being pursued), shape, topography, location, and climate. More subtle geographic influences include the nature of the state's frontiers; its neighbors; its insular, peninsular, littoral, or landlocked condition; its internal penetrability; and the distribution of its population over the landscape. None of these factors affects any two states in the same way, yet any capability analysis, either overall or specific, must take into account such geographic factors, which are relatively fixed conditions of state existence.

Both the practice and the study of international relations have been influenced, sometimes decisively, by theories of geographic determinism. However, the effects of geography on foreign policy have always been mediated by decision makers' perceptions of the features and significance of geographical "givens" and by contemporary communication and transportation technology. These influences are most obvious in regard to the military realm, where strategies giving primacy to sea-, land-, air-, and space-based forces have succeeded one another, but it is equally applicable to questions of international economic relations where the time required to move currency across oceans and continents has accelerated nearly to the speed of light. In summary, we would suggest that matters of spatial organization will always be relevant to foreign policy but that they are essentially neutral and subjectively (rather than objectively) perceived and interpreted by decision makers.

2. *Population and Workforce.* A second tangible factor is population and workforce. The relevant base figure is the total size of the population. On the assumption that other things are equal, greater population means greater capability to perform more tasks at a higher level of effectiveness. But other things are seldom equal; population data must be qualified by such factors as age distribution, sex distribution, and spatial dispersion. For military purposes, as an example, a population clustering heavily in the upper age groups may be capable of making less of a contribution than might be estimated from its size alone.

Population is perhaps a less meaningful notion for purposes of capability analysis than is "manpower," that portion of the population available for broadly defined foreign policy purposes. All individuals who are politically marginal, as well as those needed simply to keep the society functional (such as the producers of food), must be subtracted from the gross total. The result is the workforce that, with appropriate direction, leadership, and administration, can be used to contribute to the military, productive, and political capability of the state.

Capability estimates involving workforce, especially when any but the briefest time spans are concerned, must take into account trends of evolution and development within the population. A comparison of birth and death rates, for example, will suggest such insights as the net growth rate and trends in age levels and life expectancy. It is possible, over a fairly long period, for government action to bring about perceptible change in population trends by the encouragement of early marriage and large families. France did so early in the twentieth century, and a number of other countries are trying to accomplish the same thing today.

3. *Natural Resources.* The third more or less quantifiable element of capability is natural resources, which include the state's natural endowment and the additional reserves that it can control. Natural resources are both agricultural (food and fiber) and mineral. The latter category has been crucial since the Industrial Revolution, as industrial processes have contributed many new forms of capability to states. In this sense, mineral resources include energy sources (coal, petroleum, wood), the metals of ferrous metallurgy (iron ore and the various metals involved in steelmaking), nonferrous metals, and metallic minerals.

Resource endowments clearly are limiting factors on capability; no state can function at a level beyond that permitted by its resources. But the resource endowment of a state does not determine its foreign policy, either. Development of synthetics and other new industrial processes, the ability of some resource-poor societies, such as Japan, to establish and maintain lines of external supply, the elaboration of stockpiling techniques, and, in conditions of intense conflict, the capacity of embattled populations to endure chronic shortages all indicate that there are many "intervening variables" that can alter the influence of resource endowments on foreign policy.

4. *Industrial and Agricultural Productivity.* In one sense, industrial and agricultural productivity is a function of the two preceding factors of workforce and resources. That is, production is the application of human effort to the transformation of resources from raw material into finished products. Thus the level of industrial and agricultural production is determined in part by the initial resource endowment and in part by the amount and quality of the workforce committed to the task.

Production levels are obviously of more immediate relevance to capability than are resource potentials; whatever is produced is then available for utilization. Production, however, takes many forms, and only a portion of the total output has any significance for the foreign policy of the state. The capability dimensions of production are suggested by the question "How much is being produced of what is needed at the moment?" Once again we see that this question can only be answered in reference to specific policies and priorities.

Particularly relevant in dealing with productivity are such considerations as availability, convertibility of facilities, and "lead time." Since capability judgments normally involve some attempt to estimate future requirements and capacities, these sorts of estimates assist the policymaker in anticipating what the state might be doing, or be obliged to do, at some point in the future. Estimates of the ability of the state to increase its politically significant production must take into account the willingness of the population to undergo deprivation because increased productive capability frequently involves reductions in the consumer-oriented sector of the economy.

5. *The Armed Forces.* The most obvious—and the most relativistic—of the tangible factors of capability is the military. The analysis of capability has tradi-

tionally given high priority to military factors because it is by military means that states have taken overt action at the highest level of intensity. Thus the military element in capability has necessarily been central to all estimates of a state's capacity to act.

Such being the case, it is no wonder that considerably more effort has been expanded on the development of doctrines and techniques for estimating military factors than has been spent on other elements of capability. As with other tangible factors, the initial consideration is one of size: How large is the military establishment in terms of troop force? A second criterion is that of equipment and arms: How up-to-date and sophisticated are they, and what is the state's capacity to produce more? Third, inquiry is made into deployment—involving (1) the relative allocation of personnel and matériel among the various services; and (2) the pattern of their placement within the state's territory and (sometimes) its overseas bases. Finally, the full military capability of a state is comprehensible only in terms of the strategic and tactical doctrines that are in control at the time of the analysis, because these principles govern the way in which the armed forces are actually used in support of state purposes.

As we shall see in later chapters, in no area is there a greater danger of making absolute capability judgments. There is a consoling but deceptive objectivity and clarity about aggregate troop force and equipment figures that has at times led analysts to unsound conclusions. Historically, what has been important is the military margin of superiority that existed among states, not the absolute level of military power each may have mobilized. In this sense, Switzerland is a "David" to France, but a giant to Liechtenstein.

The Intangibles

1. *Political, Economic, and Social Institutions.* We have pointed out that the tangible elements of capability tend to be measured, whereas the intangibles are evaluated. In approaching the intangibles, the analyst is not seeking a quantitative finding so much as trying to establish the extent to which the phenomena being studied contribute to or detract from the state's effectiveness in a specific situation.

This proposition becomes obvious when we examine the first in our list of intangibles—the political, economic, and social institutions of a state. Any official charged with assessing the capability of another state should, optimally, be free from prejudices concerning any one political, economic, or social system. Instead, the analyst should apply the yardstick of efficiency. Considering the mission that the state has set for itself, do these patterns of social organization represent the best possible way of mobilizing the state's capacity to act? Does the political system, for example, provide for both efficient administration and a workable rapport with mass consensus, or is there sufficient disaffection to constitute a drag on governmental effectiveness? Does the economic system reduce waste and inefficiency to a practical minimum, or are many opportunities for rational production lost? Is the society integrated and coordinated and thus capable of unified effort, or are there chronic internal tensions that distract its decision makers from foreign policy concerns? These and similar questions contribute to an overall verdict on the national society's pattern of organization.

2. *Educational and Technological Levels.* In an era of ever-changing technology, another societal characteristic that bears directly upon capability is the educational and technological levels of the national society. Industrial productivity and military effectiveness are in large measure functions of the extent to which education and technical facility are dispersed within the society; this relationship suggests further that the level of education is a major factor influencing the potential of a workforce.

A second element is what we might call *tool skill,* which means orientation toward and facility in the employment of the tools and techniques of modern industrial civilization. Tool skill involves emotional adjustment and acculturation as much as the actual learning of skills and procedures. Unless people are familiar with the subtle ramifications of an industrial system, they will waste considerable effort in making the machinery work. Extensive training and inculcation of the necessary discipline are prerequisites to effective tool skill.

The factors of general education and tool skill are characteristics of the mass of a population. A third factor—and in many ways an equally crucial element in a state's educational and technological levels—is the quality of the higher stratum of educated specialists. Does the state have enough specialists of the right sorts? Are their training and level of performance adequate to the demands the state will make on them? Is the overall standard of scholarly, scientific, and technological effort advancing, declining, or merely static? These and related questions may, even in the short run, be the real determinants of the state's range of capability.

3. *National Morale.* Among the difficult factors to measure, yet one of the few constant determinants of capability, is the elusive notion of national morale. We use this term to describe the mass state of mind or mood in a country, with particular reference to how far the society feels itself committed to the government's policy.

A state has high morale when the regime in power feels itself supported by an active and involved consensus. Such a condition requires that the politically salient elites are convinced that the government's foreign policy is derived from the prevailing values of the society, and that they have confidence in the capacity of the policymakers to meet and overcome challenges implicit in the policy.

Thus national morale has a direct effect on the ways in which officials can mobilize and employ the tangible factors in capability. Widespread apathy toward foreign policy can place certain limitations on foreign policy decision making, and active disagreement within the body politic may virtually paralyze the government. Morale involves not only the positive characteristics of loyalty and confidence but also such negative elements as the capacity to endure stress, disappointment, or temporary failure.

If consensus is weak or lacking, decision makers may try to improve the state of national morale. The approach a given regime might take to this task would depend on its judgment of the dynamics of the society and its needs at the moment. It may choose to frighten its people or try to encourage them; it may become more generous with information and explanation; or it may tightly control the flow of communciation to the public. Whatever the devices adopted, extensive policy initiatives may have to be suspended until the level of support for the regime increases.

In order for the reader to get a better grasp of the application of these various elements of capability, each of these elements will be considered in a historical scenario of America at war in World War II.

I. The Tangibles:

1. *Geography.* Prior to the beginning of World War II, the geographically isolated United States had sought to stay out of the European and Asiatic theaters. Nicely sheltered by the great oceans of the Pacific and the Atlantic, its focus had been on the domestic front where the Great Depression was affecting all aspects of society. When advancements in technology made the attack on Pearl Harbor a relatively easy task, the American public was jolted out of its complacency and well-being to take part in the war.

2. *Population and Workforce.* The U.S. population was large enough that it could afford to participate in both the European and the Pacific theaters of operation. It enacted the draft requiring men to participate in the war effort overseas. At home, it also called upon the rest of its population to work in factories and other productive services in participating in the war effort.

3. *Natural Resources.* The United States was in a unique situation where its continental territories were comparatively untouched by the ravages of war. As a result, it was able to mobilize its vast human and natural resources in the production of goods for the war effort.

4. *Industrial and Agricultural Productivity.* The Depression administration of Franklin Roosevelt had been trying to revive the U.S. economy through the use of public works as well as subsidies for farmers. Once the United States was propelled into the war, the Roosevelt administration quickly called forth the participation of the population in converting many industries for the production of war matériel. Farmers were given incentives to increase production for domestic consumption as well as aid to allies in need.

5. *The Armed Forces.* Having essentially relied on volunteers for peacetime defense, the United States legislated the draft to obtain as many able men as possible to fight abroad. With this large force, combined with vast production in armaments and other goods, the United States was able to "outman and outgun" the opposition.

II. The Intangibles:

1. *Political, Economic, and Social Institutions.* Prior to America's involvement in World War II, the Roosevelt administration already enjoyed wide support for its programs of creating jobs for Americans. Massive public projects, such as building dams and bolstering infrastructure, gave the administration experience in mobilizing immense amounts of human and natural resources. After the declaration of war, the administration was able to draw upon its experiences to provide a relatively effective mobilization of resources for war.

2. *Educational and Technological Levels.* Though the technological level of the United States was not considered to be the front-runner of the world, it was able to galvanize the development of new technologies and products. Furthermore, with the influx of refugees from Europe, the United States was able to utilize its technological know-how to develop improved weapons. These, combined with the industrial capability to mass-produce armaments, would ultimately prove to be one of the deciding factors in the winning of the war against the fascist states.

3. *National Morale.* Perhaps paramount over all other concerns, the national morale of the American people was at a very high level. Traditionally, the American public believed in the principles of justice, democracy, and morality. The attack on Pearl Harbor only further proved that these principles would have to be upheld by an armed struggle against the totalitarian states of Germany, Japan, and Italy. The government needed and got the support of the people of the United States.

RECOMMENDED READINGS

BOULDING, KENNETH. *Three Faces of Power.* Newbury Park, CA: Sage, 1989.

CAPORASO, JAMES A. *The Elusive State: International and Comparative Perspectives.* Newbury Park, CA: Sage, 1989.

COHEN, RONALD, and JUDITH D. TOLAND. *State Formation and Political Legitimacy.* New Brunswick, NJ: Transition Books, 1988.

COLLINGWOOD, R. G., and DAVID BOUCHER. *The New Leviathan, or Man, Society, Civilization, and Barbarism.* rev. ed. New York: Oxford University Press, 1992.

DEJOUVENEL, BERTRAND. *Power: Its Nature and History of Its Growth.* Boston: Beacon Press, 1962.

GIDDENS, ANTHONY. *Durkheim on Politics and the State.* Stanford, CA: Stanford University Press, 1986.

HUMBOLDT, WILHELM VON. *The Limits of State Action.* Indianapolis: Liberty Fund, 1993.

JOB, BRIAN. *The Insecurity Dilemma: National Security of the Third World.* Boulder, CO: Lynne Rienner, 1992.

KENNEDY, PAUL M. *Grand Strategies in War and Peace.* New Haven, CT: Yale University Press, 1991.

LEVINE, ANDREW. *The End of the State.* London: Verso, 1987.

MCNIEL, WILLIAM H. *The Pursuit of Power: Technology, Armed Force, and Society Since A.D. 1000.* Chicago: University of Chicago Press, 1984.

MANN, MICHAEL. *The Sources of Social Power, Vol. 1: A History of Power from the Beginning to A.D. 1760.* Cambridge, UK: Cambridge University Press, 1986.

NISBET, ROBERT A. *Making of Modern Society.* Brighton, England: Wheatsheaf Books, 1986.

NORTH, DOUGLASS. *Structure and Change in Economic History*. New York: Norton: 1981.
PFALTZGRAFF, ROBERT L., and URI RA'ANAN. *National Security: The Decision-Making Process*. Hamden, CT: Archon Books, 1984.
RUSSELL, BERTRAND R. *Power: A New Social Analysis*. New York: Barnes and Noble, 1962.
TUCK, RICHARD, ed. *Leviathan*. New York: Cambridge University Press, 1991.
WERTHEIMER, ALAN. *Coercion*. Princeton, NJ: Princeton University Press, 1987.

Chapter 4

THE IMPLEMENTATION OF DECISIONS

After policymakers have stipulated their objectives and determined their capabilities, they usually select means to implement their decisions. We have suggested that they have a considerable range of choice, and that well-informed and rational decision makers develop courses of action designed to carry them to their chosen goals. In this chapter we will examine four categories of techniques on which the policymaker may draw in world politics. This outline, however, is certainly not comprehensive, because the avenues of policy implementation are many and varied, and they are largely dependent upon the characteristics of any particular occasion for decision.

First, we ought to make one basic point that will be implicit in all our subsequent discussions. Although this chapter concentrates on the various ways states may act, action of any sort is not a necessary consequence of a policy decision. The net result of the elaborate analytical process outlined in Chapter 2 may be a decision to refrain from action. Though it is true that inaction is a form of action and should proceed from the same intellectual process that action does, the strategy of inaction obviously raises fewer questions of implementation.

If a state decides to act, the states system provides four possible channels for the application of its resources. The first is political in nature, and its most conspicuous manifestation is diplomacy. The second, the economic approach, is probably the most varied and complex of the four. Third on the list are psychological techniques, of which propaganda is an example. Finally, military techniques may range from symbolic nonviolent use of armed force to open warfare.

Theoretically, in a particular situation, a state could place its entire reliance upon any one of these generalized techniques. More commonly, however, states develop an approach based on a mix of techniques designed to produce the greatest effect. Officials often attempt to preserve flexibility in the implementation of policy, and, to this end, it is important that any commitments considered permit intensification, reduction, modification, or even abandonment if circumstances should so dictate. The need for flexibility is even greater in the contemporary era when, as we have noted, technology has radically curtailed the time available for decision.

POLITICAL TECHNIQUES: DIPLOMACY

In one sense all foreign policy techniques are, or ought to be, political. No matter what a state may do in the execution of its purposes, its orientation and goals are always political in that they seek the maximization of its national values. However, in practice the word *political* is applied more narrowly to those methods that involve direct government-to-government relations. The contacts that governments have with each other and the manner in which this intercourse is carried on are generally referred to as the practice of *diplomacy*.

The Nature of Diplomacy

Diplomacy, as a technique of state action, is essentially a process whereby communications from one government go directly to the decision-making apparatus of another. It is the most direct technique of state action, in that the policymakers of one state exert their influence (or their ability to coerce) directly upon the key personnel of another government. If, as we argued earlier, the purpose of a state's policy is to secure the agreement of other states to its designs, then it is only by diplomatic means that such assent can be formally registered and communicated. In this sense, diplomacy is the central technique of foreign policy.

Besides being a technique in its own right, diplomacy is also an instrument in the utilization of other techniques. A state may act politically in a purely political context, using only the methods and resources of diplomacy, or it may implement economic, psychological, or even military action by diplomatic maneuvering. Although the operating requirements of pure diplomacy and what we might call "mixed" diplomacy differ to some extent, their fundamental rationale remains essentially the same.

The actual procedures of diplomacy are many, ranging from such highly formal devices as notes, memoirs, and communiqués to more informal and almost casual conversations. Fundamentally, diplomacy is a method of negotiating between sovereignties, and, although the elaborate ritual and protocol that surround the practice may sometimes seem pretentious and time-consuming, their roots lie in the nature of the task. By diplomatic means a state transmits its position on an issue to another state and receives the other state's response. Changes in the respective positions are registered diplomatically, and the eventual elaboration of the relationship that develops also lies in the hands of diplomats.

The Functions of Diplomacy

We can distinguish several distinct functions of diplomacy. Which of these the working diplomat may be called upon to perform depends on the nature of the policy her/his government is following.

First, diplomacy may serve as an instrument of *coercion.* Coercive moves made by other means are communicated diplomatically, and diplomacy itself can be used to exert pressure. Breaking diplomatic relations with another state or excluding a target state from international organizations or conferences can be done for coercive purposes. Coercion may also be applied in negotiation by an ultimatum, by the establishment of a rigid time limit for conclusion of an arrangement, or by the registration of a formal or informal protest or complaint. In the twentieth century, certain revolutionary or authoritarian governments have added an element of psychological coercion to diplomacy by eliminating the courtesy and good manners of traditional diplomatic practice and conducting relationships in an atmosphere of vilification and intense emotion. This policy seems to have produced some short-term advantages, but its effect on states' external relations over a longer period is likely to be negative.

Second, diplomacy is a technique of *persuasion.* Advancing arguments and suggesting mutual concessions, both persuasive devices, are central to the practice of diplomacy. This kind of diplomacy is the most frequently used and the best suited of all techniques for the application of influence. The distinction between coercion and persuasion is often vague, and the two approaches frequently blend into one another; but there is a real difference in both motivation and atmosphere, and most diplomatic initiatives are at least initially cast in a persuasive form.

Third, diplomacy is a procedure of *adjustment.* It is well suited to the task of enabling two states to modify their positions on an issue in order to reach a stable relationship. Its directness of communication and its potential for subtlety and flexibility contribute to its usefulness. States may prosecute their differences and intensify their conflicts by a great variety of methods, but tensions between them are most effectively managed and reduced through diplomatic means.

Finally, diplomacy is a technique for reaching *agreement;* indeed, it has been said that diplomacy is the art of negotiating written agreements. Formal written agreements embody the most binding commitments in the contemporary states system, and they can be brought into existence only by diplomatic procedures. Agreements may involve some degree of coercion, as well as persuasion or adjustment, but a formal agreement is possible only if both parties wish it. On the other hand, even a strong interest in formalizing an understanding would be pointless if instruments and procedures for reaching one were not available. Here is where diplomacy fulfills an essential function in international relations.

Success and Failure in Diplomacy

There is little disagreement about the requirements for success in diplomacy. The essentials of the diplomatic art have been well known for centuries, and the actual practice of its "past masters" furnishes us with some clear guidelines. The following list is an attempt to reduce the vast literature on diplomacy to four basic principles, which, again, represent an ideal type.

1. *The diplomat should have a clear understanding of the situation.* A diplomat must possess sensitivity to the forces at work in the problem area, clarity of one's own purposes, and an understanding of the ultimate implications of one's policy with respect to long-range goals. An accomplished diplomat would also try to have a clear understanding of the points of view, interests, and goals of other states, because without such empathy he/she would not be able to negotiate effectively.
2. *The diplomat should be fully aware of the state's real capability.* This awareness requires the diplomat to appreciate how much coercive capability the regime is actually ready to commit and how much influence the state may enjoy at the particular moment. Under normal conditions, an experienced diplomat would not attempt initiatives that lie beyond the state's capability, nor be content with less than full exploitation of the resources appropriate to the state's objectives.
3. *The diplomat's approach must be flexible.* Diplomats have to be prepared for unforeseen developments or for withstanding the consequences of analytical error by having some alternative policies or "fall-back" positions in reserve. This characteristic depends on the diplomat's ability to distinguish between abstract principle and concrete interest, and on her/his ability to remain firmly committed to the latter while being quite flexible with regard to the former.
4. *The diplomat is frequently ready to compromise on nonessentials.* A diplomat requires a clear set of policy priorities, because only in this way can it be determined which issues are subject to bargaining and which are not. Priorities also assist a diplomat in devising compromises without giving away matters of importance in return for lesser concessions. In theory, a good diplomat should always be willing to give up a position of lower priority to secure one of higher rank.

During the Cold War, diplomacy was frequently ineffective in coming to grips with the dilemmas of politics. Its inadequacy was so obvious that some critics suggested we were witnessing the end of "traditional" diplomacy. From the end of World War II until approximately 1985, the four principles we have outlined were honored more often in the breach than in the observance. Situations were often analyzed in ideological and nationalistic terms, and too seldom realistically. It was often difficult or impossible to admit that one's opponent had any point of view, let alone one meriting consideration. Capability factors were frequently misinterpreted, especially in the military realm. Because of ideology and nationalism, flexibility was in short supply, and as a result compromise was often impossible.

In such circumstances, diplomacy clearly could not flourish, and what most often occurred were either ill-concealed and blatant attempts at coercion or non-purposive propaganda. Real negotiation, persuasion, and adjustment of positions culminating in agreement were sporadic phenomena instead of the normal procedures of statecraft. Furthermore, deep popular involvement in foreign policy by means of emotional sloganizing, common in both large and small states, seriously impeded the force of diplomacy by depriving it of the necessary flexibility to maneuver.

With the decline and proclaimed end of the Cold War, diplomacy has been reinvigorated as an effective instrument of state action, and the ideal that we have outlined has been more fully reflected in actual negotiations. Absolutist positions are advanced much less often, and responsible and increasingly prudent governments are willing to entertain the possibility of partial solutions: the current watchword in many regions is "pragmatism." With this attitude becoming more widespread, the prospects for diplomacy to work its adjusting effect become brighter. In light of this trend, there is reason to believe that the future will see greater reliance on diplomacy, and there have already been noteworthy successes in areas as diverse as decolonization, arms control, and the environment.

One has only to scan the headlines of a major newspaper or watch television news to be able to gauge, at least superficially, the quickened pace of contemporary diplomatic activity. The travels of the U.S. secretary of state provide a good indicator of this trend. Characteristically, we see him arriving at a foreign capital, being officially greeted at the airport by a delegation sufficiently prestigious for his rank, holding a press conference to state the objectives of his visit and being answered by his opposite number in the host country, having a "photo op" before formal negotiations, emerging from negotiations to make a brief statement about the talks, and then speaking to the press before getting back on his airplane. This pattern is similar for most other major foreign secretaries, as well as other envoys. You will also notice that, except in conditions of grave crisis like the war against Iraq in the Persian Gulf, most of this activity is oriented toward persuasion and adjustment rather than (overt) coercion.

ECONOMIC TECHNIQUES: THE CARROT AND THE STICK

Economic techniques of state action are as old as the states system itself, but their full development dates only from the Industrial Revolution. The increasing complexity of modern economic and industrial life has made the states of the world to a large degree mutually interdependent, and this reciprocal involvement has in turn created new possibilities for state action. In recent times a variety of states have either initiated international economic action in pursuit of foreign policy goals or have been the targets of such initiatives.

The Rationale of Economic Methods

Perhaps the most obvious characteristic of economic techniques is their diversity. Almost any aspect of economic life can, with sufficient ingenuity on the part of policymakers, be turned into a tool of state action. Still, certain generalizations are possible about the rationale of economic methods in foreign policy.

First, economic techniques are indirect in their application, in contrast to the directness of diplomacy. Their immediate target is not the decision makers of the other state, but rather the totality of the state's society. The consent sought is supposed to flow from internal pressures of that society upon the regime in power rather than from any direct action by the initiating state. Thus economic techniques are designed to force the hand of the other government and to urge or coerce it to accede to the wishes of the first state.

Second, as the title of this section indicates, economic methods are two-sided, in that they may be either coercive or persuasive in intent. A coercive economic move is one that, in general or specific terms, threatens the target state with deprivation or impoverishment unless it submits. A persuasive move holds out the possibility of economic reward or advantage in return for satisfactory modification of a target state's behavior. A single economic maneuver may reflect both dimensions, threatening economic damage if no agreement is forthcoming but simultaneously promising rewards for acquiescence.

Third, economic techniques develop directly out of a particular foreign policy situation because the effectiveness of any action is completely dependent upon the nature of economic relations between the states involved. A state with no economic leverage on another is in no position to threaten economic reprisal in response to an unacceptable policy. Therefore, maximum use of economic instruments is reserved to those few states with widespread economic influence or to those controlling crucial economic goods or services. An otherwise weak state controlling an important mineral resource, such as oil, may have a considerable range of capability made possible by this atypical and accidental economic fact.

Fourth, economic techniques tend to produce resentment, resistance, and retaliation by the target state. Coercive economic moves obviously create hostility, because few peoples are prepared to passively accept either the threat or fact of economic deprivation. Even persuasive policies that are advantageous to the target state can engender enmity on the grounds that it is humiliating to submit to "bribery" or "blackmail" for policy reasons. Much of the call in the Global South for "foreign aid without strings" reflects this point of view.

Fifth, as a result of the points we have already discussed, economic techniques have a limited range of effectiveness. Policymakers take account of resistance to economic pressures and discount accordingly the return expected from their use. As a rule, in bilateral relations, economic techniques are rarely used alone. A persuasive economic policy is usually linked with extensive propaganda and diplomatic initiatives, whereas coercive programs are accompanied by a strong diplomatic line and frequently by military pressures of various sorts. We should mention that the broadening network of interdependence has further restricted the utility of coercive economic techniques because in many cases an effort to pressure a target state might have the effect of harming the initiating state's own economy.

Persuasive Economic Techniques

Under the conditions of contemporary world politics, certain persuasive economic techniques have proved useful and appropriate. Probably the best known is "foreign aid": the direct grant or favorable loan of either cash, credits, or goods to other countries. These may be "economic" in nature and consist of foodstuffs, capital goods, or consumer products. However, the early years of the Cold War placed a high premium on military aid, including all types of military matériel and what the United States called "defense support" in the form of economic aid committed to military purposes.

A second technique is development assistance, through which developed states attempt to assist less-developed countries in constructing infrastructure and industry, and generally fostering a higher standard of living for their people. Originally undertaken in a Cold War context, development assistance has proved to be so expensive, of such long duration, and so unproductive of political advantage that the leading donor states have experienced "donor fatigue" and reduced it to a minimum. In fact, the results of bilateral development assistance have not been altogether positive for the Global South, either.

Third, much effort has gone into the use of trade and investment policy as a technique of state action. Bilateral trade agreements and international investment are familiar features of world politics today, and they have taken on greater significance as the utility of certain types of military force has declined. Most of them have clear political overtones, and some—particularly those between a large and powerful state and a smaller one—formalize the exchange of economic advantage for political rewards and investment. In the postwar period, another aspect of trade policy has appeared: the creation of trading blocs of various kinds and the extending of invitations to join such groups as enticements to induce political cooperation.

Illustrative in this regard is the influence the major industrialized market-economy countries have had on the course of events in the new democracies of Eastern Europe, as well as in the former Soviet Union, because of what they can offer in terms of aid and technical assistance. Also, France, in particular, has been able to use the economic dependence of its former colonies in Africa to discourage them from publicly criticizing controversial French foreign policy initiatives.

Coercive Economic Techniques

Coercive economic techniques are limited in number and variety only by the resources and imagination of the implementing state. Here we do no more than attempt a rough classification.

The first type we may call restrictions on economic relations, which include the whole range of currency control, export licenses and quotas, tariffs and nontariff barriers, foreign exchange blocking and control, and freezing of credits. The intent of all of these is to insure that economic relations continue in a way favorable to the dominant state. The implication of these restrictions is that an improvement in political relations would have immediate economic consequences.

More overtly coercive is the outright interruption of economic relations, notably trade and investment. If the target state is sufficently dependent on trade and investment with the dominant state, interruption will cause serious hardship and compel the victim toward reestablishment of normal patterns at a political price. Interruption of relations may be effective when the powerful state is a critical supplier of certain categories of capital and goods or when it is a major market for the products of a single-commodity agricultural economy. Such a boycott is perhaps the most infuriating of all economic practices, and because it usually leads to strong pressures for retaliation it is seldom employed.

A special type of coercion stems from the cancellation or suspension of a program of capital investment or economic aid. Recipient states, specifically the poiltically relevant elites, may become accustomed to a steady flow of assistance once such a program is established. Their dependence upon continuation of capital flow or aid thus makes them vulnerable to the pressures that develop if the regular supply is interrupted. Again, this technique is most valuable when the coerced state is almost completely dependent on the state that is extending aid. If the former can actually do without the assistance, or if it should develop another source of capital or aid, then the results of the former donor state's action may be limited or even counterproductive.

Also, a coerced state's willingness to endure the hardship of sanctions is directly related to the importance of the concession it is asked to make. Cuba, for instance, has been willing to endure the economic deprivation imposed by the West for decades because this strategy was aimed at reversing the effects of its revolution and reintegrating the country into the Western, and specifically American, sphere of political and economic influence.

There remains a collection of coercive economic steps that do not readily lend themselves to classification. They include such trading practices as dumping (selling at large volume and low price in a foreign market in order to gain an advantage on domestic producers), preemptive purchases of raw materials (intended to deprive another country of these supplies), unilateral currency devaluation (to make one's own exports more attractive at the expense of a rival's), and nationalization of foreign property (to try to break a dependency relationship).

It should be mentioned that the UN Charter allows for coercive economic measures to be taken against states deemed to be responsible for threats to international peace and security, and there have been several examples of such actions. However, the results of even multilateral boycotts have been ambivalent, and opinion also remains divided on their effectiveness. Two divergent cases are illustrative: international sanctions against South Africa and the sanctions against Iraq.

There is little doubt that the increasingly stiff sanctions brought to bear against apartheid South Africa during the 1970s and 1980s contributed to the dismantling of that system of institutionalized racism. At the time, however, the issue was hotly contested, with the conservative prime minister of Great Britain, Margaret Thatcher, insisting that sanctions simply would not work. In fact, the effectiveness of the sanctions did not lie in the deprivation they caused the ordinary citizen, but rather in their ultimately cutting off the flow of foreign investment that was the lifeblood of South African economic growth. Thus, given time and adequate multilateral support, sanctions can work.

Time was precisely the key issue in regard to the sanctions strictly enforced against Iraq after the invasion of Kuwait in 1990. Though the sanctions were hurting the Iraqi people, it was not clear how long it would take to cause enough deprivation either to force Saddam Hussein to withdraw his forces from Kuwait or to precipitate an overthrow of his regime. Given the mobilization of troops, which was expensive, and the harsh climatic conditions during the summer months, the allied governments found themselves facing a difficult decision about the capacity of economic sanctions alone to achieve their objectives in the region. Ultimately, the Allies decided that military action was necessary.

Conclusions on Economic Techniques

Our conclusions in regard to economic techniques may appear somewhat contradictory. As we have said, because of both the unpredictability of their results and their detrimental effect on relations, they are of only limited and special usefulness by themselves. Still, under appropriate circumstances they may be very effective. Coercion in economic terms will undoubtedly cause hostility, but it may also move the target to rapid and extensive policy revision. At the persuasive end of the spectrum, an imaginatively conceived and skillfully presented program has on occasion yielded political benefits in a noncontroversial way. Discrimination in the use of economic techniques, adequate understanding of the relevant circumstances, and a refusal to adhere to a particular technique all contribute to their effectiveness as tools of foreign policy.

Third, economic techniques are of less value in short-term situations than over a longer period. To expect to extract short-run political gain from the application of a single economic device is unrealistic; seldom is a target state so vulnerable as to be obliged to respond politically under such circumstances. Over longer time spans, however, the correct economic policies may well begin to reduce the barriers of disagreement between states, and thus they may be of value.

PSYCHOLOGICAL TECHNIQUES: PROPAGANDA AND CULTURE

Psychological techniques, aimed at the mass psyches of relatively large bodies of people, are also indirect means of state action. Thanks to improvement in the art and science of mass communication, propaganda and culture have become major elements in state capability and constitute in themselves a significant area of political action.

The Nature of Propaganda

Propaganda has been defined in many ways, but all definitions agree that, operationally, it consists of messages in a context of action; that is, the purpose of communication is to inspire the audience to act in a particular way. In practice, propaganda breaks down into two dimensions. Some is basically a problem in audience conditioning, designed to increase both the audience's size and its sympathetic receptivity, while the remainder is directly action centered, with the goal of persuading the audience to act in certain specified ways. Both forms have had a place in policy implementation.

Propaganda as a Foreign Policy Tool

We should distinguish among the four distinct "audiences" to which the foreign policy propagandist speaks. The first audience is the citizens of a state, whose morale and support require that they at least believe they are being kept adequately informed, as well as inspired and ideologically motivated. The second consists of the populations of those states associated with or friendly and cooperative toward the initiating state. These also need to have policy explained in such a way as to impress them with the necessity of remaining true to their allegiance. The third is the audience formed by those who are neutral toward the propagandist's policy. They may be won to the state, or at least prevented from active opposition, by a well-conceived program of information. Finally, there is an audience composed of the people of states in opposition to the initiating state. The flow of information in this context seeks to reduce their support for the official policy of their state and perhaps to loosen their bonds of loyalty.

We have spoken of "audiences" in terms of "people" because propaganda is largely a mass phenomenon. Decision-making personnel are normally too committed and too sophisticated to be significantly influenced by such information from abroad. Most mass communicators believe that they obtain the greatest results for a given effort by aiming at the broadest possible audience, and, to some extent at least, the record confirms this judgment.

The great bulk of the propaganda messages put out by states are aimed at audience conditioning and sympathy building, a focus that is today called image projection. The state's goal is to be viewed in a favorable light by its various audiences. Direct calls to action are relatively few, partly because of the remote likelihood of their being heeded except in special circumstances, and partly because of the ease with which they can usually be neutralized by domestic counterpropaganda.

Therefore, most foreign policy propaganda is auxiliary to diplomatic efforts, and propaganda is seldom the only dimension in which a state acts. Effective use of information may increase the policy impact of diplomatic, economic, or even military moves, but it can rarely accomplish policy objectives by itself. Also, unless the goal of policy is to confuse, it is crucial that there be consistency between words and action.

A factor seriously inhibiting propaganda today is the fact that virtually everybody is using it. With each audience bombarded by messages and appeals from every part of the globe, and with almost every policy point of view receiving eloquent and repeated expression, the listener has difficulty in formulating a clear impression by which to be guided. The listeners thus tend to select from the variety of information at their disposal those messages and appeals that are already familiar and to which they are predisposed, and simply ignore the rest. For this reason, propaganda has relatively little influence on established patterns of behavior and response, and therefore its policy impact is limited. This pattern helps explain the great emphasis on audience building displayed by so many propagandizing states.

The most direct way to sample various states' efforts at image projection is with a shortwave radio. One can, for instance, compare the content and emphases of news broadcasts, the variety of national achievements that are highlighted, and the efforts made to promote a country's culture through language instruction. The Voice of America, for instance, has frequently-broadcast programs that emphasize American achievements in science and technology and the country's democratic tradition, two subjects that foster a positive image of the United States in most foreign populations.

The promotion of certain nations' cultures has in some cases been so forceful as to amount to cultural imperialism toward newer and weaker states. Cultural imperialism is an attitude of cultural superiority and of insensitivity to other cultures and worldviews, characteristically allied to superior political, economic, and military power and superior technology. It favors and reinforces one set of cultural values and styles over others and produces a displacement of the cultures of weaker communities by the values selected and imposed by the dominant culture. The French have consciously promoted their language and literature, and the United States has perhaps somewhat more guilelessly put forth the American way of life as an example worth emulating.

The Role of Subversion

When international relations are characterized by an atmosphere of intense conflict, states have seen fit to resort to subversion. Although subversion—by which we mean the attempt of a state to overthrow or weaken another by means of internal agitation and conspiracy—is a direct-action technique in its own right, we include it in this discussion of psychological techniques for a special reason. Crucial to a state's establishment and implementation of a subversive activity has been the psychological problem of undermining the loyalty that binds citizens to their government.

Subversion is an old technique, but it has been developed and used with greater frequency and intensity in the contemporary era. This trend has been due in part to the development of modern ideologies—nationalism, imperialism, communism, anticommunism, fascism, and anticolonialism—and in part to the improvements in communication that have made it possible for a government to control a subversive movement (or many subversive movements) from a great distance. However, more important than either of these in explaining the rise of subversion as a technique is the fact that the present age has been one of great social disaffection, change, and revolution. When a state has or develops substantial internal divisions and deep animosities, the vulnerability to subversion is heightened. Protagonists of change have capitalized on such internal cleavages by enlisting key leaders and groups to prosecute their own purposes under the sponsorship of a foreign government.

In theory, subversion is a technique of revolution, the ultimate purpose of which has been the complete overthrow of the government and its replacement by the revolutionary group. As a technique of foreign policy, however, it has been employed in pursuit of more restrained ends. Organized subversion can deepen divisions within a society to the extent that the government's integrity is compromised, its vitality weakened, and the course of its foreign policy altered in favor of the intervening state.

Subversion is a technique of opportunity, usable only in those special circumstances when the target is vulnerable. Societies in which disaffection is minimal may be inconvenienced but not inhibited by subversion, and the hostility engendered toward the initiating state is likely to have a negative influence on relations between the two countries for an extended period. States with a revolutionary policy have on occasion exploited popular discontent successfully because they have appealed to individuals and groups seeking self-determination or liberation, while states pursuing a stabilizing status quo policy have utilized subversion to insure the existence of regimes favorable toward their goals.

MILITARY TECHNIQUES: WAR AND ITS APPROXIMATIONS

We now come to the fourth and final set of techniques of state action—military capability and the role of force. In logic and practice, there is no substantive difference between military techniques and any others. Thus war is not abnormal in interstate relations. Yet policymakers have always recognized that the use of military techniques is predictably more costly and more dangerous than other ways of acting and have in most cases considered military techniques a last resort, to be used only if lesser measures prove inadequate for attaining a necessary objective. The great technological revolution in warfare has sharpened the impact of this dilemma. Today, one of the most pressing practical problems of policymaking is that of the utility of military power—offensive, defensive, and deterrent—in foreign policy.

War in Foreign Policy Calculations

The phrase *military techniques* really refers to a variety of applications of military power, the ultimate being the actual conduct of war. Reconciling policy considerations with the threat, initiation, conduct, or avoidance of war has long been one of the major concerns of the policymaker.

It is important to keep in mind that military action is a means to a policy end and not an end in itself; that is, "victory" is a technique and not a goal. The object of the exercise of military power is exactly the same as that of any other type of state action: attaining a preselected objective through acquiring the acquiescence of other states. The extent to which military power is used in pursuit of policy goals is determined by the value placed on the objective and by the amount of resistance policymakers expect to meet. The object of combat, which we define as the manipulation and application of military force, is to break the enemy's will to resist—not necessarily, it should be noted, the *capacity* to resist (understood in physical terms).

Resort to military techniques is in principle derived from the same type of cost/risk calculation that precedes any policy decision. Although there is a significant difference in an ultimate decision for war, the difference is less one of quality than of quantity. Costs in war are obviously much higher, since they must be measured to a great extent in human lives. Given this special context, most policy officials would require greater odds in favor of success because the price of failure in war is much higher than in any other policy enterprise. Thus cost factors demand that war be reserved for purposes great enough to justify the inevitable expenditures.

In principle, therefore, the use of military techniques that may culminate in war demands that the magnitude of the force and violence be directly in proportion to the worth of the objective and the extent and nature of the resistance to be met. It is this concept of the role of force—expressed by the French political philosopher Montesquieu as doing no more damage to the enemy than is absolutely necessary to the attainment of one's purposes—which has prevailed through most of the states system's history, and it is in this way that war has traditionally figured in foreign policy.

Technology, Nationalism, and War

Two of the great historical forces of modern times have seriously complicated the role of war in statecraft. The first is technology, which has made possible new horizons in weaponry and expanded incalculably the ability of states to inflict damage on each other. The second is modern nationalism, which has involved entire populations in warfare and thereby reduced the control of governments over their military effort. In short, technology and nationalism have made war a struggle between peoples rather than between states.

During the twentieth century, the world entered an era of "total war," which is divorced from single-policy objectives and which is instead a simple, if desperate, matter of survival. Under contemporary combat conditions, it is difficult to think of total war as a rational application of capability to foreign policy (although conflicts on levels below that of total nuclear war may be). Instead, some commentators have suggested that total war represents a catastrophic breakdown in the international political process, whereas limited wars, internal wars, proxy wars, and the use of threat and bluff, though destructive and disruptive, indicate that the system is operating with some prospect of conflict resolution short of annihilation. It could be argued, for instance, that the reduction of ideological tensions between East and West greatly facilitated the limited war against Iraq by removing the possibility of escalation to a total global confrontation.

The Appropriateness of War

The policymakers of today, knowing that the use of military techniques may stir up extreme nationalist emotions in their people and possibly provoke attacks by the most horrible of modern weapons (both conventional and nuclear), are inhibited in their policy choices if they wish to keep a given situation within controllable limits. Although in theory policymakers are as free as ever to resort to techniques leading to war, the logic of the cost/risk continuum is inexorable and, at times, frustrating to them. Furthermore, with war certain to cost far more than it ever has before, the number of objectives for which such an expenditure is justifiable has shrunk dramatically. In fact, few besides national survival and removal of serious threats to international peace and security would be worth the price.

Nevertheless, war, total or otherwise, has not become impossible, because either an irrational outlook or a serious analytical error could lead a government to take the risk. What has happened is that aggressive war, particularly if it could escalate to total war, has become largely inappropriate to a foreign policy conceived and implemented in a climate of calculation, prudence, and rationality. This situation, which undermines many previous operating assumptions of world politics, has engaged the attention of scholars and policymakers since the dawn of the nuclear era. A considerable body of speculation and doctrine has been concerned with the implications of modern warfare for the future of foreign policy and world politics. We shall be examining these contentions in some detail in Chapter 9, but we may anticipate the conclusions reached there, at least in general terms. There is a persuasive case to be made for the continued relevance of military considerations to world politics, but the ubiquitous factors of cost and risk have served to deter states, particularly nuclear powers, from venturing too far into the dangerous waters of open warfare.

Military Techniques Short of War

The role of military techniques in policy implementation has not been confined to open warfare. In fact, military factors short of combat have long been an ingredient in the normal conduct of foreign policy by all states.

The military "ranking" of states has been one of the fundamental structural elements in the state system. Relations between any two states in time of "peace" have been materially affected and at times dominated by their respective military postures, partly because of the direct impact of military differentials that always involve a subtle or blatant threat to the weaker state. As long as a state retained the right and capability to back its demands by military force, a weaker state was obliged to take this possibility into consideration and to formulate policy in light of the credibility of the threat. The notion of a "sphere of influence," as enjoyed for many years by the United States in the western hemisphere and the former Soviet Union in Eastern Europe, was based on this dynamic.

Even more importantly, military differentials had a crucial status-conferring effect. Something very much like a class system gave form to the global scene, as great military powers, medium military powers, and weak military powers developed standardized relations to one another, with differing rank, role, and status in world affairs.

However, both the elements of threat and of status depended for their effect upon the credibility of the military means. The threat of military power could influence a weaker state only if that government believed that the more powerful state was willing to risk the commitment of force and was also in a position to use that force meaningfully. As soon as smaller states came to realize this paradox—that the more military capability major states acquired in the nuclear age, the less real opportunity they had to use it, and the less willing they were in committing themselves to its use—credibility began to erode. Threats lost much of their compelling character, and clear-cut demarcations of status began to fade.

This reevaluation of the role of military techniques in foreign policy has gone so far that some analysts contend that the world has entered an era of the "tyranny of the weak." Others (including ourselves) argue that we have at least left the era of "monopoly of the strong." If the purpose of high capability is to broaden the area of freedom of choice enjoyed by a state, then the greatest measure of such freedom seems often to be enjoyed by states almost entirely devoid of military power, while those governments with the largest establishments discover that their freedom is drastically circumscribed by the very existence of their military machines. In practice, therefore, the strength of the militarily powerless and the weakness of the traditionally powerful limit the utility and therefore the choice of military techniques. We are not saying that military means are no longer used—obviously, at times they are. It is becoming more and more apparent to all involved, however, that they can only infrequently provide a real and lasting solution to a state's problems in today's world.

The preceding discussion relates primarily to bilateral relations among states. The multilateral use of force to deal with threats to international peace and security, as designated by the UN Security Council, is a different matter. The Gulf

War against Iraq demonstrated that this is, aside from purely defensive action, the only truly legitimate use and one of the few effective uses of the military option in foreign policy. However, prior to far more extensive disarmament than has so far taken place, this method can only be used when all the major powers in the system support it.

Military action not only was historically the final resort of states but also was essential to the orderly operation of the traditional system. However, if our conclusions regarding the place of military techniques are largely accurate and there has been a fundamental change in the nature of state relationships, rather than a temporary distortion of regular patterns, then it would seem that the global political system must inevitably undergo far-reaching modification of its capacity for and means of conflict resolution.

RECOMMENDED READINGS

AGEE, PHILIP. *Inside the Company: CIA Diary.* New York: Stonehill, 1975.

CHAY, JONGSUK. *Culture and International Relations.* New York: Praeger Press, 1990.

CIMBALA, STEPHEN J. *Force and Diplomacy in the Future.* New York: Praeger Press, 1992.

ELLUL, JACQUES. *Propaganda: The Formation of Men's Attitudes.* New York: Vintage Books, 1973.

GEORGE, ALEXANDER. *Propaganda Analysis: A Study of Influences Made from Nazi Propaganda in World War II.* Westport, CT: Greenwood Press, 1973.

GEORGE, ALEXANDER, and GORDON A. CRAIG. *Force and Statecraft: Diplomatic Problems of Our Times.* New York: Oxford University Press, 1983.

JERVIS, ROBERT. *Perception and Misperception in International Politics.* Princeton, NJ: Princeton University Press, 1976.

LAVY, VICTOR, and ELIEZER SHEFFER. *Foreign Aid and Economic Development in the Middle East: Egypt, Syria, and Jordan.* New York: Praeger Press, 1991.

LEE, JOHN D. *The Diplomatic Persuaders: New Role of the Mass Media in International Relations.* New York: John Wiley and Sons, 1968.

MULNOZ, HERALDO. *Environment and Diplomacy in the Americas.* Boulder, CO: Lynne Rienner, 1992.

NEWSOM, DAVID D. *Diplomacy Under a Foreign Flag: When Nations Break Relations.* New York: St. Martin's Press, 1990.

NICHOLSON, HAROLD. *Diplomacy.* 3rd ed. London: Oxford University Press, 1963.

ROTHGEB, JOHN M. *Defining Power: Influence and Force in the Contemporary International System.* New York: St. Martin's Press, 1993.

SHLAPAK, DAVID A., and DAVID E. THALER. *Back to First Principles: U.S. Strategic Forces in the Emerging Environments.* Santa Monica, CA: Rand, 1993.

SMITH, BRIAN H. *More Than Altruism: The Politics of Private Foreign Aid.* Princeton, NJ: Princeton University Press, 1990.

TUCH, HANS N. *Communications with the World: U.S. Public Diplomacy Overseas.* New York: St. Martin's Press, 1990.

WEAVER, R. KENT, and BERT ROCKMAN. *Do Institutions Matter? Government Capabilities in the United States and Abroad.* Washington, DC: Brookings Institution, 1993.

PART II

THE GLOBAL POLITICAL SYSTEM: ACTORS AND THEIR RELATIONS

Chapter 5

TRADITIONAL IDEAS AND PATTERNS OF GLOBAL POLITICS

The second part of this book is devoted to the global system—the more or less regularized patterns of relationships that are formed by the contacts of states and other actors with each other. Our focus will continue to be political, in that we are most concerned with relationships among actors that stem from their respective attempts at value maximization.

We have mentioned several times that the system is in transition, and this inescapable fact renders our task more difficult. In this chapter we describe what have constituted, until quite recently, the basic elements of international relations as conducted by states. In Chapter 6 we will try to demonstrate how contemporary events and global trends have begun to call into question and modify some of these elements. Our hope is that this approach will make the reader better able to appreciate the extent to which contemporary practice in the states system is influenced by both the heritage of the past and the uncertainty of the future.

THE SYSTEM OF STATES

The global system is a special type of social system, and a social system can be defined as an arrangement of actors, individuals, or collectivities among whom interaction has become sufficiently patterned to be in some sense orderly and to some extent predictable. The states of the world have been the principal operating units of the global system, and over three centuries of experience have indeed established a degree of regularity and a kind of "order" in the operation of this system. However, the global system has a number of characteristics that mark it as a distinctive and unique social system, and it is with the consideration of these elements that we begin our discussion.

The Nature of the System

First, we take the position that world politics goes on within a system, as distinguished from a society or a community. Certain writers have argued the existence of a "community of nations" or a "society of states," and we would certainly admit that contemporary international relations possess some elements of "society" and "community." In general, however, we consider such terms as expressive of what the system might become, rather than accurate reflections of what it is and has been. Basic to either a society or a community are acceptance of a common set of goals for collective action and a common value consensus. The global system has, depending on one's point of view, either lacked these collective norms altogether or developed them in a very weak and embryonic form. States traditionally have not manifested a sense of ultimate responsibility or concern for anyone or anything outside of themselves.

More specifically, besides an overall moral consensus, the global system has also lacked a well-developed and firmly enforced code of behavior prohibiting actions destructive of good order and demanding other behavior as socially necessary, as well as an institutional structure to implement a moral consensus and enforce such a behavioral code. Instead, the global system gained its form and dynamics from a far more rudimentary set of controls, often little more than a kind of self-serving prudence exercised by statespersons, and from a consensus among the principal actors in favor of preserving the system in its essentials as preferable to any other basis of organization, either more or less restrictive.

The operating assumptions of the traditional global system may be classified as those of a semiorganized anarchy. Certain anarchic presumptions were paramount—those concerning the free will of the individual state, the right of the state to choose any goal it wishes and to take any appropriate implementing action, and the resolution of conflicts of interest in terms of the relative strengths of the disputing parties. The principle of sovereignty, taken literally, permitted none but an anarchic base for political action among states.

Granted, to a certain extent, a state's policy in the international political environment must make provision for the possible necessity of being thrown entirely upon its own resources, and it is not uncommon for the rhetoric of statecraft to evoke images of the individual state bravely making its way against the active or passive opposition of the remainder of the system. However, the logic of anarchy is in fact a faulty guide to explaining the actual historical patterns of state relations. Policymakers have continually made progress in softening and diverting the more onerous consequences of the minimally organized states system.

This progress is partly due to the tendency of policymakers to prefer pragmatic to absolute formulations of goals and objectives. We have already seen how essential pragmatism and flexibility are to the practice of foreign policy, especially as the consequences of failure become more awesome. But the regularities of world politics have also resulted in large part from habit and inertia; policymakers no less than ordinary people can be imprisoned by their past patterns of action. Nonetheless, despite the theoretical anarchy of world politics, there has been a definite countertendency toward standardization and stabilization, and today the global system is in fact more elaborately and tightly organized than is generally appreciated.

The State in the System

According to the inherited wisdom of the field, an individual state, viewed as a functional unit within the global system, is a solitary, self-contained, and self-justifying entity. It was thought to draw its motivations for acting solely from within itself, to feel itself obliged to no other state, to be prepared to devote its own resources to the satisfaction of its needs, and to be ready to enjoy the rewards or suffer the consequences of its actions. It judged all situations and the actions of all other states by the single criterion of national interest; it acquired enemies or friends and acted in cooperation or in conflict in response to its internal evaluation of the ebb and flow of political action.

This emphasis on the internalized mission and function of the state clearly reflects what was for centuries the dominant concern of policymakers. The state was conceived to be a free agent and attempted to achieve as much real freedom of action as possible for as long a time as possible. It was even argued by Machiavelli, the Renaissance Italian political philosopher, that the state's control over its own international role was so complete that it could, and should, be the architect of its own moral code. In these terms the only "good" the state served—that is, the supreme value of foreign policy—was the accomplishment of its own ends. This is very close to the notion of *raison d'état* developed in France at the time of Louis XIV, which held that whatever the regime decides to do in world politics is transformed by the very fact of decision into a moral goal. Thus success in achieving an objective, regardless of the means used or any other ramifications, was seen as a "good" thing, while failure was intrinsically immoral and therefore reprehensible.

With such dominant conceptions we can see that the motive force of the global system flowed from the individual states and not from any central source. The "climate" or general atmosphere of world politics, within which relations are conducted and which may change over time, was the product of the prevailing conceptions and actions of the dominant states in the system at any particular time.

The Interstate Relationship

The premises described in the preceding paragraphs have governed the approach of states to one another. We have already mentioned that states, lacking a solid consensual base, must develop their relations with each other on an ad hoc basis. Thus the initial stages of any new interstate relationship have tended to be tentative and probing, as each participant tries to discover the nature and extent of the common interests and conflicts among states. Only after each state has outlined an initial profile of the evolving relationship would it feel free to elaborate and exploit more detailed strategies. Broadly speaking, the relations of any two states within any situation can be located along a continuum ranging from harmony (i.e., total agreement) through various forms of cooperation (i.e., conflict that can be resolved through bargaining and policy coordination) to total, irreconcilable conflict and hostility.

Though divergent interests have often led to some form of conflict between states, one should not assume that such an evolution is automatic. Having a conflict of interest is one thing, but what comes out of it is quite another and depends entirely on the values, styles, and capabilities of the states involved. In other words, the degree to which interests clash does not dictate the level of hostility or tension at which the disagreement is prosecuted. The scope of a disagreement merely outlines the arena of conflict; whether the conflict is fought at a high or low level, allowed to lie virtually dormant, or resolved through mutual accommodation depends on further policy decisions by the governments involved.

We have already discovered that the primacy of interest, combined with the anarchy of the system, makes the rational practice of foreign policy necessarily a very cautious business. With no certain foreknowledge of how other states will react to a given stimulus, officials have at times been obliged to assume the worst—that is, that all other states were always potential enemies. For this reason the "realist" school we mentioned earlier considered international politics to resemble the "state of nature" described by the British political philosopher Thomas Hobbes as a "war of all against all."

The Pole of Order and the Pole of Disorder

We prefer the image of a states system oscillating between what we might call symbolically the pole of order and the pole of disorder. In concept and in practice, the system has at times manifested a disorder so complete as to nearly reduce world politics to the law of the jungle. However, though violence has broken out with a certain regularity, it has in fact been relatively infrequent. States have expended a much greater proportion of their energies in prosecuting their ends through means that reflect order and restraint than in any type of open conflict.

The system has varied between order and disorder with a certain regularity. At times, pressures toward disorder overcame the countervailing tendencies, and the system broke down. Historians seem to agree that this kind of breakdown occurred at the time of World War I. However, the closer to open disorder and breakdown the system drifts, the more powerful becomes the urge toward reestablishment of order, and in other instances equilibrium was restored short of the precipice. The Cuban Missile Crisis in 1962 comes to mind in this regard. In the same way, there have been times when there was too much "order" in the system, in that certain states felt that the status quo embodied unfair advantage and privilege for the dominant actors.

EQUALITY AND INEQUALITY IN GLOBAL POLITICS

One of the paradoxical aspects of world politics has been the constant tension between the claims of states to substantial equality and the practical fact of their actual inequality. Both equality and inequality are manifested concretely in the conduct of the relations of states. Both affect the way peoples and governments view the world and the tasks they attempt to accomplish in their foreign policies. States exist and function simultaneously on the planes of conceptual equality and operational inequality, a fact central to the understanding of contemporary international relations.

The Law and Myth of Sovereignty

Equality of states as a characteristic of world politics has its roots in one of the most basic concepts in the study of political science: sovereignty. From both the legal and mythical consequences of sovereignty flow many fundamentals of world politics.

Sovereignty has always been the key characteristic of a state. To be accepted as a state, a political society must have within itself a supreme law-giving authority with the power to issue commands from which there is no rightful appeal. The concept was born during the formative era of the modern state, and today does no more than state a truism. No one would quarrel with the necessity of having a central authority in a political society. Difficulty arose when this internalized idea of considerable utility was applied to interstate relations. What in law and in logic could be the appropriate relationship between two sovereign states, each incorporating an alleged supreme authority that recognized no superior? No relationship except complete legal and status equality was conceivable. It is on this basis that international law, the body of jurisprudence that regulates the relationships of sovereignties, was built.

Accordingly, sovereignty in international relations and law came to stipulate the absolute and perfect equality of all states. None could rightfully dictate to another; each was declared the equal of all others in status, dignity, and honor. All the protocol and procedure of formal international intercourse pay respect to this symbolism of sovereign equality; even the Charter of the UN states that "the Organization is based on the principle of the sovereign equality of all its Members."

Legal sovereignty was given added dimension with the birth of modern nationalism. As popular self-consciousness evolved into intensive nationalist identification, the doctrine of sovereignty, with its insistence that all states were equal and independent, became of great value in molding nation-states. From this process has developed the contemporary myth of sovereignty.

Nationalism demands that the nation-state be at least symbolically free from responsibility to external authority. The "national will" is sacred and not to be tampered with, and the symbols of national identity—the flag, the uniform, the historical monuments—may acquire overtones of almost mystical sanctity. Any impairment of sovereignty is to be resisted as a major patriotic duty.

Thus the myth of sovereignty and the concept of nationalism, both grounded in a formalized concept of state equality, have united to reinforce the anarchistic tendencies of the state system. The insistence that the state cannot be controlled by any larger community has contributed to the instability of world politics. Operationally, the incapacity of the state to accept coercion (for to do so would deny the equality and independence of states) made it necessary for all international arrangements to be ratified by the (free or forced) consent of the participating states. So long as states consent officially, the integrity of sovereign equality is preserved at least in a formal sense.

The Political Inequality of States

The persistence of states in acting as if sovereignty were a reality gives the doctrine great political significance, but the conceptual equality of states exists alongside an absolute inequality in political competence. States are completely equal in their right to develop national goals and adopt strategies, but they are unequal in their competence to fulfill their purposes. Either in absolute terms or with reference to a particular situational setting, no two states are ever equal in capability.

This political inequality, long recognized as dominant within the states system, was most clearly seen in the surprisingly formalized horizontal stratification of states into great powers, medium powers, and small powers. Great powers were the few states whose capabilities were sufficiently large to permit them to assert the political right to interfere in and be consulted with regard to the resolution of any issue anywhere in the world at any time. A medium power was treated with a modest degree of formal deference by great powers, but was in fact expected to confine its concerns to matters geographically or politically close to home. Small powers were permitted to exist but could not ordinarily maintain an interest in opposition to either larger type; the conditions of their political activity were imposed upon them by the decisions of more powerful states.

The Trend Toward Greater Inequality

The gap between the mystique of state equality and the reality of political inequality is not decreasing, but rather growing steadily greater. The increasingly greater capability conferred by modern technology on industrial states, contrasted with the birth of so many new, less-developed, and often unstable states, has vastly extended the spectrum of inequality. The powerful, both absolutely and relatively, are far more powerful, while the weak are relatively much weaker than ever before. In this context, to speak of the "sovereign equality" of the members of the UN seems almost meaningless.

To some extent, however, the growing disparity between equality and inequality has been mitigated by certain factors. As we have mentioned, politically relevant forms of capability have changed drastically since World War II;

that is, military differentials are no longer so absolute an element of inequality. The UN and other international forums have also provided a means for weak states to combine to wield aggregates of strength at times sufficient to offset the political dominance of larger states.

But these factors only retard and cannot stop the advance of inequality in the system. There is ample evidence that contemporary political leaders and professional policymakers are beginning to question the rationale of a political system that assumes equality among states and yet attempts to function with such disparity among its members. Whether, in fact, the states system can continue for long with such an internal contradiction is one of the major issues of the contemporary period.

POWER POLITICS

The basic dynamic of the states system has long been known as *power politics.* This term, brought into the English language as a translation of the German word *Machtpolitik,* has both a pejorative and a purely descriptive use. It may be used to characterize the relationships of states as being governed almost entirely by force or threat, without any consideration of right and justice. This meaning is perhaps closest to the sense of the original German word. We use the term, however, more generally to indicate the way in which the global political process has actually worked from the early modern period until quite recently.

The Assumptions of Power Politics

Our discussion of the states system and the respective roles of equality and inequality in the relations of states has already indicated the bases of the practice of power politics. Given the conceptual foundations of the nation-states (i.e., sovereignty and its implications), a political system including all states could really develop in only one way. Power politics rested on a set of assumptions that were accepted and implemented by most governments most of the time. We can see from what follows the extent to which these organizing and operating assumptions flowed logically from the governing conception of the sovereign nation-state.

1. There were no absolutes of right or justice in the relations of states. Each state was the judge of the correctness of its own actions, and world politics went on in a climate of moral relativism.
2. The only collective value shared by all participants was the desirability of preserving the system. Except for the common concern not to destroy the system and its members, states thought of themselves as being almost entirely on their own.
3. Self-help was the rule of action. Lacking common values, the system could not evolve authoritative institutions and mechanisms of collective action.

Individual states had to enforce their own rights and could count on only limited support from external sources.

4. Each state had only as many rights as it could enforce itself. The individual state was obliged to content itself with such rewards as its strength and the wit of its leaders could extract from the system.

5. The relations of states were determined not by the application of any general principles, but by the expedient interaction of their respective capabilities. This was the crux of "power politics": considerations of "power" (capability) governed the outcome of state contacts.

6. In practice, therefore, factors of power determined questions of right. In this sense, might (broadly interpreted) actually did make right.

Of course, the validity of these assumptions depends ultimately upon the extent to which the phenomenon of power or capability can be meaningfully quantified. Such a relativistic and supposedly value-free system demanded the existence of an objective and universally accepted arbitrating apparatus. Power played this role for centuries. The generally blurred appearance of the global system today is at least partially due to the diminished skill of policymakers in quantifying power. As a result, the continued relevance of several of these assumptions is in question.

Power Status in World Politics

The practice of power politics became formalized as a basis for state interaction only when status configurations reflecting the power and strength (actual, potential, or formal) of states crystallized into a quasi-stable form. The social system of world politics has traditionally been sharply stratified, because the three "classes" of states—great powers, medium powers, and small powers—structured the entire political process. Essential to a working class system is a full appreciation by each class of its relative place in the system and a recognition of the peculiar roles of all other players, and this has generally been the case for the global political system. To continue our analogy, the relatively small group of great powers has, throughout history, insisted on their right to regulate all matters within the system in their individual and group interest. In fact, for many years the study of world politics involved little more than the analysis of relations among a cluster of between four and eight major states. So great was their influence and so complete their collective monopoly over the relevant instruments of coercion that these few states repeatedly demonstrated their capacity to police all international relationships.

Membership in the elite inner circle of states was not the result of any mathematical calculation of power components, but rather a function of international practice and consensus. Certain "qualified" states were taken into the group by joint agreement, frequently registered in a major international conference culminating in a reordering peace treaty—such as the Peace of Westphalia (1648), the Treaty of Utrecht (1713), the work of the Congress of Vienna (1815), and the several peace treaties known as the Peace of Paris at Versailles during the end of World War I (1919). Each of these epoch-making instruments brought erstwhile outsiders into the group of great powers and also temporarily or permanently expelled certain states.

We have already indicated that the chief reward of great power status was the implicit right (deriving from capability) of the state to extend its interest as far as it wished and to act in support of this interest. The fact that the great powers overrode longer-lived and deeper-rooted interests of lesser states was regarded as irrelevant. Some writers tried to formulate principles of an alleged "responsibility of power" that would have authorized formal, universally accepted great power intervention anywhere, which, through legitimizing a special role for the great powers, would have provided some kind of order and security to the system as a whole.

The consensual basis of great-power status is clearly shown by the periodic appearance of states that were given membership in the inner circle for various political reasons but which in fact lacked the requisite capabilities. Spain, for example, was kept in the great-power class long after its effective role had been extinguished in the seventeenth century. Italy was given courtesy membership after its unification in 1870. France and (Nationalist) China were included at U.S. insistence in the immediate aftermath of World War II. Such states certainly enjoyed prestige among lesser powers, but their actual influence on the deliberations of the real great powers was minimal.

The global system has at times given institutional expression to the role of great powers through the mechanism of the "concert of power"—formal assemblies of leading states that attempted to arrange a set of relationships to their mutual satisfaction. In the past this effort has been most apparent at major peace conferences, such as the Congress of Vienna, and at periodic gatherings for the resolution of particular problems, such as the Congress of Verona (1822) and the Congress of Berlin (1878). Since 1945, the "concert of power" has found expression in ad hoc summit meetings of various kinds and through the permanent machinery of the UN Security Council, where the major powers control almost all outcomes through their veto power.

Less need be said of the two lower-status groups, since the values of the great powers have tended to be accepted by the other states. The smaller powers have tried to play as extensive an international role as they could manage, given their capabilities, and characteristically they have tried to augment their limited stores of status and influence. Of course, among both the medium and small powers there were many further gradations, and something like an international pecking order was generally the norm.

Patterns of Power Politics

Among the general characteristics of power politics we can distinguish four clear patterns of relationships that have recurred frequently. Two of these patterns involve only the great powers, two also involve the smaller powers, and all relate to the general state of relations between great powers and small powers.

The first pattern has developed when the great powers are in substantial agreement about the existing shape of their own relationships across the entire spectrum of international political issues. Such a situation has occurred only when the entire group (or all but a fraction of the membership) is committed to a status quo orientation. Great-power agreement has usually resulted in their exercising control over the system through their combined force. A notable historical example of this pattern is provided by the course of affairs in Europe between 1815 and (roughly) 1848. The détente between the United States and the former Soviet Union also approximated this pattern.

The second pattern is the converse of the first in that the great powers, instead of agreeing on the preferable state of relationships, split into hostile and competing camps. This state of affairs has usually appeared when a sizable number of the leading actors were revisionist. When major states fall out, the overall control of the elite group on world affairs inevitably diminishes, because the break in their common front and the dynamism that characterizes a great-power struggle may offer opportunities for small states and divergent coalitions to assert themselves. The neatest example of such a pattern was the early Cold War period that split the great powers between 1947 and the early 1960s.

The third pattern arises when the smaller states of the world (including both medium and small powers) develop a common interest, point of view, and overall strategy to govern their responses to major states. This is a relatively recent development in world politics, made possible by the appearance of the UN, an international actor that has come to derive its motive force from its majority of smaller members. Under appropriate conditions, notably the military balance of terror that inhibited great-power use of armed force, this pattern acquired surprisingly broad scope. Late 1970s developments in world politics, especially the rise in importance of the General Assembly of the UN, the demands of Global South countries for reform of the world economic system, and the related phenomenon of cartelization, were clear demonstrations of this pattern.

The fourth pattern, consisting of small-state disorganization, lack of communication, and incipient or actual mutual hostility, is historically far more common. In this pattern each small state is subject to isolation and pressure from predatory medium or great powers, irrespective of the state of unanimity of the elite group itself. This tendency of the more numerous but less well-organized medium and small powers to break into uncoordinated fragments has facilitated their control and domination by the great powers.

We can use these patterns to go one step further in analysis. Either the first or the second pattern will describe the relations of the great powers, while either the third or the fourth describes the remainder of the states. Whichever pair (one or two, plus three or four) was in effect has given a general shape to international power relations during any historical period.

THE REGULARITIES OF GLOBAL POLITICS

The anarchy of the global system has always had a certain potential for explosion. Managing the affairs of states in an anarchic environment required the development and application of a variety of relatively unstructured but quite pervasive principles of action. These regularities of world politics functioned in such a way as to moderate the use of power in the system and thereby to temper the effects of power differentials among states.

Patterns of Equilibrium of Power

From time to time interstate relations have attained one or another sort of equilibrium, and we would suggest that equilibrium has usually taken one of three basic forms. Our first type is characterized by a widespread dispersal of capability among states. This pattern has long been known as "the multiple balance of power" and was in effect most clearly in the classic European system of the seventeenth through nineteenth centuries. The second pattern is marked by a concentration of power on a bipolar basis around two great powers. This pattern, predominant from 1945 until recently, is usually defined as a "simple balance of power." Finally, there is the pattern of integrated power radiating from a single central point, like spokes of a wheel. Although this has not been realized since the decay of the Roman Empire, some would argue that the UN could eventually evolve into a center for such a global system.

The multiple-balance system, based on a concentration of power in individual states, is decentralized. The simple balance is in one sense a midpoint in that the number of poles of concentration is reduced to two. The integrated system theoretically does away with dispersed power and replaces it with an integrated power structure.

Multiple Balance of Power

As we mentioned in the preceding subsection, a multiple balance characterized interstate relations throughout the seventeenth, eighteenth, nineteenth, and early twentieth centuries. The global system during this period had multiple great powers, at least five at any time, dominating the course of world politics.

In a multiple-balance system, the great powers frequently acted so as to complement each other and maximize the prospects of their survival as individual states and the survival of the system as a whole. This system demanded an implicit agreement to respect each other's existence and spheres of interest, and to confine disagreements to issues considered marginal. Coalition formation was normal, as well as the tendency for these groupings to balance each other. Any reduction or (to a lesser extent) increase in the number of great powers was considered undesirable, because either modification ran the risk of upsetting whatever stability the system may have achieved. It followed that, under these conditions, no great power would plan to eliminate another.

World War I signaled a definite and perhaps final breakdown of the long-standing multiple-balance system. Several profound historical trends, imperfectly understood at the time, had undermined the operative conditions essential to the perpetuation of the tidy world of an earlier period. The emergence of Germany and Italy dramatically increased the number of great powers, and the two new major states energetically pressed for the expansion of the system to include their own interests. The end of imperialist expansion meant that further gains by one great power could only be at the expense of another. Britain lost the freedom of action it had once enjoyed as the self-conscious "holder of the balance" and found itself drifting into opposition with Germany and a blurred but binding affiliation with the Franco-Russian alliance. And the heterogeneous and disparate empire of Austria-Hungary could no longer function meaningfully as a great power. After 1907 the inner political world of the great powers had become almost bipolar as two rigid blocs confronted each other in a situation permitting no real maneuver.

Simple Balance of Power

A bipolarization of power between the United States and the former Soviet Union, partly caused by historical developments during World War II but also the result of a series of policy choices by both sides, characterized world politics from 1945 until the end of the 1980s. This balance was simple in its structure, but difficult and dangerous to operate. Alignments shifted around the "poles" of the two major powers. When the system was "tightly" bipolar, movement and change were minimized because the rationale of great power policy was to reduce world politics to a concentration on the single issue of the bipolar struggle. The simple balance was, therefore, reminiscent of a seesaw, in contrast to the multiple balance, which was more like a chandelier.

Integration of Power

An integration of power in international relations would imply that instead of there being few or many contenders in the system, a single set of goals and institutions would exist. The logical conclusions of a process of power integration would be a world government of some kind that would use power to serve its global (and hopefully benevolent) ends. In a less extensive form the concept of collective security, exemplified today in the UN, also reflects some notion of integration of power in the management of global affairs.

The obligations of collective security are spelled out in Articles 39 through 51 of the Charter of the United Nations. The heart of these provisions is found in Article 42. The Security Council "may take such action by air, sea, or land forces as may be necessary to maintain or restore international peace and security. Such action may include demonstrations, blockade, and other operations by air, sea, or land forces of Members of the United Nations." The "other operations" obviously include military action under UN direction, first implemented in Korea and later (in different form) in the Suez Canal Zone, Congo (now Zaire), Lebanon, and Cyprus.

Collective security has yet to prove really successful in countering threats to international peace and security. Pending the transfer of state sovereignty to a single world government, collective security may function only upon the basis of a massive consensus among the world's leading powers. So long as the international system remained deeply divided (particularly the leading powers), true collective action to protect a common conception of peace and order was out of reach. The logic of collective security suggests that any potential aggressor is an outcast and that every other government should turn against that government the moment the peaceful climate of international relations becomes threatened. Thus collective security is a viable pattern only when the vast preponderance of capability is in the hands of states with a deep interest in the preservation of at least the essentials of the status quo. A significant revisionist faction among the major states can, and has, rendered the idea inapplicable. With the end of the Cold War and the general decline of communism, one of the major revisionist forces of the twentieth century, the prospects for more effective collective security, at least, seem to be greatly enhanced.

Methods of the Balance of Power

In this final subsection, we present a set of seven different techniques of statecraft that have been used either regularly or intermittently to manage the traditional balance-of-power system. This list is not exhaustive but does provide a useful topology of the variety of foreign policy actions witnessed over the course of the system's development.

1. *Intervention.* Intervention refers to interference by one state in the internal affairs of another; it has assumed either "defensive" or offensive forms. (We put "defensive" in quotation marks because it is used here in a sense that, although common, contradicts a commonsense definition of defense as defense from attack and the like.) What is seen as "defensive intervention" normally aims at the preservation of a particular regime or system, whereas offensive intervention is directed at altering such a system. "Defensive intervention" has most frequently been based on the assumption that a state, particularly a great power, cannot permit the distribution of power in the system to be materially changed to its disadvantage by another state's change of government policy. Examples of "defensive intervention" are numerous in contemporary history: Allied intervention in Russia (1918) in an attempt to maintain the pre-Bolshevik regime; Soviet intervention in Hungary (1956) to protect the János Kádár government; U.S. intervention in Lebanon (1958) in support of the Camille Shamoun administration; Indian intervention in Bangladesh (1971) to protect the government; and Syrian intervention in Lebanon (1976) in support of the Lebanese government.

Offensive intervention is expansive and has been used to bring about a change of policy or government in another state or to eliminate its independence completely. The manner in which both Italy and Germany became united in the second half of the nineteenth century represents offensive intervention employed by Piedmont and Prussia, respectively. The establishment of communist governments in Eastern Europe after World War II is another illustration of offensive intervention, and the old American custom of "dollar diplomacy" is still another example of this form of intervention in Latin America.

2. *Compensation.* Compensation involved giving a state the equivalent of the territory of which it was deprived or the equal of what was given to other states. This practice usually applied only to victorious states and their allies; defeated states customarily lost territory without compensation. Peace treaties often encompassed territorial changes that reflected the principle of compensation. The territorial settlements embodied in the peace treaties that followed World War I and World War II were made in this spirit.

The basic assumption underlying compensation was that one state resented seeing another state increase its power without obtaining a compensating aggrandizement of its own. This assumption characterized the approach of the great powers toward the partitioning of Africa and the Far East during the second half of the nineteenth century. It was an insistence on compensation that made Mussolini actively join the side of the Axis after the fall of France; he refused to permit Hitler to settle Europe's future without deriving benefits for Italy. The assignment of mandated areas to France and Great Britain following World War I and the authorization of the UN trust territories after World War II are more recent examples.

3. *A Buffer Zone.* A buffer is a small power situated between two or more great powers. It may also be a relatively weak state located between the spheres of interest of great powers. The assumption underlying this technique is that it is in the interests of each of the great powers to prevent the other from controlling the buffer zone. Each competing power seeks to preserve the integrity of the small state in the middle as preferable to its falling prey to the other. Historically, Switzerland and Belgium played the role of buffer zones between Germany and France. During the latter part of the nineteenth century, Afghanistan was a buffer zone between the British Empire and Russia, and the Spanish colonies in Africa played the same role between the colonial empires of France and Britain. During the Cold War, Austria was a sort of buffer between the Eastern and Western spheres of influence in Europe, and Nepal was a buffer zone between India and the People's Republic of China.

4. *"Divide and Rule."* The phrase "divide and rule" refers to the policy occasionally employed by great powers of dividing opponents and competitors into hostile camps, or at least heightening their disunity. The principal assumption underlying this technique is that disunity and partition will keep the competitor weak. The former Soviet Union was frequently accused of practicing this policy in regard to Western Europe and its role in the North Atlantic Treaty Organization (NATO).

5. *The Sphere of Influence.* The sphere of influence is a device through which competing great powers have at times delineated their areas of hegemony. Each of the great powers concerned undertakes to respect the others' undisputed predominance in specified zones, assuming in this manner that disputes between

great powers can be minimized. North Africa was considered a French sphere of influence from the late nineteenth century until only a few years ago, and Egypt and the Sudan became British spheres of influence after 1882. The Balkans were regarded as belonging to the Soviet sphere of influence during the Cold War, and parts of Latin America have been considered to be in the U.S. sphere of influence.

6. *Armaments.* Armaments, clearly, have been the principal means by which the leading great powers in an era have tried to maintain or reestablish a preferred configuration of power in the system. The underlying assumption is that a greater quality and quantity of armaments maximizes the capability of a state for attack and deterrence. As we note elsewhere, in either a multipolar or bipolar system the general application of this principle leads to a spiraling arms race that tends to consume an ever-greater portion of the budgets of the states involved.

7. *Alliances.* Alliances have until now been the most important means of balancing power in the system. An alliance is an agreement between two or more states for the defensive or aggressive purposes of its members against a state or states outside the alliance. Besides NATO, other historically important recent alliances include the Warsaw Pact and the Rio Pact.

Alliances have assumed such importance because of the general belief that states can increase their own power by linking themselves to others of particular strategic importance. Alliances are dynamic, and their changing patterns have most often been the product of expediency rather than principle. Common interests are the primary considerations in the establishment of alliances between states, with the alliances themselves defining the general policies and concrete measures serving these interests. Although the interests that unite states in an alliance against an opponent are usually explicit, the policies to be pursued and the objectives to be sought have frequently been less precise.

Thus alliances have played a regulatory role in world politics. They are important instruments in the adaptation of the nation-state to the environment and have helped fill the gap between the ideals of organization and the realities of quasi-anarchy in the system. However, alliances have also contributed to divisiveness in world politics by casting interstate relations into rigid groupings and increasing the destructiveness of violent conflicts when they break out.

RECOMMENDED READINGS

BELOFF, MAX. *The Balance of Power*. Montreal: McGill University Press, 1967.

CAPORASO, JAMES A. *The Elusive State: International and Comparative Perspectives.* Newbury Park, CA: Sage, 1989.

CARR, EDWARD. *Twenty Year Crisis 1919–1939: An Introduction to the Study of International Relations* (2nd ed.). New York: St. Martin's Press, 1956.

CIMBALA, STEPHEN. *Force and Diplomacy in the Future.* New York: Praeger Press, 1992.

DAVID, STEVEN R. *Choosing Sides: Alignment and Realignment in the Third World.* Baltimore: Johns Hopkins University Press, 1991.

DEHIO, LUDWIG. *The Precarious Balance: Four Centuries of the European Power Struggle.* New York: Alfred A. Knopf, 1962.

EVANS, PETER, et al. *Bringing the State Back In.* New York: Cambridge University Press, 1985.

GULICK, EDWARD V. *Europe's Classical Balance of Power: A Case History of the Theory and Practice of One of the Greatest Concepts of European Statecraft.* New York: Norton, 1967.

HALL, JOHN A., and G. JOHN IKENBERRY. *The State.* Minneapolis: University of Minnesota Press, 1989.

HERZ, JOHN. *The Nation-State and the Crisis of World Politics: Essays on International Politics in the Twentieth Century.* New York: McKay, 1976.

JACKSON, ROBERT H. *Quasi-States: Sovereignty, International Relations and the Third World.* New York: Cambridge University Press, 1990.

KENNEDY, P. *The Rise and Fall of the Great Powers: Economic Change and Military Conflict, 1500–2000.* New York: Random House, 1987.

MANDELBAUM, M. *The Fate of Nations: The Search for National Security in the Nineteenth and Twentieth Centuries.* New York: Cambridge University Press, 1988.

MERIAM, CHARLES E. *History of the Theory of Sovereignty Since Rousseau.* New York: Scribner's, 1959.

VASQUEZ, JOHN A. *The Power of Power Politics: A Critique.* New Brunswick, NJ: Rutgers University Press, 1983.

WIGHT, MARTIN. *Power Politics.* London: Royal Institute of International Affairs, 1949.

Chapter 6

NEW CONDITIONS OF GLOBAL POLITICS

The international political system, incorporating the historically validated ideas and patterns we have examined, has been decisively influenced by major changes in contemporary world civilization. The several "revolutions" in transportation, communication, energy, production, weapons, information, and space have all had their direct effects on the actors as well as the environment. Thus the conditions of global politics today are radically different from those of even a half century ago. As we will attempt to demonstrate, many of the tensions of present world politics come from the inevitably frustrating attempt to fit the contemporary environment into traditional political categories.

Today the states of the world function within a political system that is both global and interdependent. Every explosion of political, economic, or social force within this system is felt all around the planet. No part of the Earth's surface can any longer be classified as politically remote, and to a greater or lesser extent every state is involved with every other state.

A WORLD OF STATES

One new dimension of world politics is the great change in the number and nature of participants in the process. The environment shapes the actors at least as much as actors shape the environment—in fact, in our era the system's influence may be more important. Thus there is good reason to describe and analyze the characteristics of the overall environment faced by the diverse ensemble of actors in global politics. We will see that political actors, like biological organisms, thrive in certain environments and decline or expire in others.

By stressing the nature of this environment—that is, the breakdown of distance, technological diffusions, expanding communication and information grids, and changing belief systems and forms of human organizations—we can anticipate what kinds of actors we would expect such an environment to support. Furthermore, we can analyze actual and potential patterns of change in the system and the types of new actors such changes might foster.

The international system, though still the arena of relations between states, is also increasingly characterized by *transnational* relations—relations among states and nonstate actors—and the politics of transnational exchange. This new variety of relations among actors has also modified the process of international politics.

The Contemporary Global System

The total number of national actors (states) in world politics has more than tripled since the end of World War II. When the UN was established in 1945, its membership included 51 states; the present membership has risen to 184. This increase in number has been accompanied by a change in the geographic distribution of membership. In 1945 the UN had 19 members from Central and South America, 19 from Europe and other Western areas, 9 from Asia, and 4 from Africa. The number of Central and South American and other American states remained unchanged until the Caribbean states Jamaica, Trinidad-Tobago, Guyana, Barbados, Grenada, and the Bahamas became independent in the 1960s and 1970s. The states of Europe and the West have increased to 34 as a result of the breakup of the Soviet Union and Yugoslavia. In contrast, the number of African and Asian states has increased to more than 100. Together the states of Africa, Asia, and the Caribbean constitute nearly two-thirds of the present UN membership, and the vast majority of these new members were formerly colonies or annexed parts of Western powers and the Soviet Union.

Thus the system that once had a purely Western cultural pattern has been altered by other peoples and their value structures. This great shift in the background and general orientation of the vast majority of participants in world politics has had a number of immediate consequences for the system. Consensus on many issues is more difficult to obtain than it was when states shared a common cultural and historical orientation. The new states arrived in the system with a point of view different from that of the older states, and they apply different criteria of judgment and evaluation.

Communication between old and new states has been marked, at least so far, by a certain degree of suspicion, misunderstanding, and confusion of motivations. A new force—Global South nationalism, expressing itself initially in the form of anticolonialism or anti-imperialism, and more recently in demands for change in the global economy—has come to play a major role in the course of political life. Many of the new states look upon their former colonial masters with (perhaps deserved) mistrust and press their cases against imperialism and for a restructuring of the economic order as matters of principle. The older states—which have a history of rule over alien peoples and which continue to enjoy favorable positions in the world economy, both because of and in spite of their imperialistic pasts—have encountered difficulty in defending themselves against this onslaught.

Entry into the states system of peoples who were formerly peripheral to it has also unveiled to the masses of the less-developed countries the startling contrast between their way of life and the much higher standard long enjoyed by older states. The governments of these new states have pressed for a more just share of resources, wealth, and opportunity for their peoples, or at least for greater assurance of continued survival. Thus the familiar "revolution of rising expectations" was a direct consequence of the broader membership in the global system. In turn, the older and more favorably placed members of the system were obliged to broaden their own political perspectives (not a little grudgingly at times) to take account of the new conditions of world politics. Not only have they been required to extend their interests to include many once-neglected areas of the world, but they have also been constrained to deal with a broad range of substantive problems (e.g., basic human needs, ethnicity, terrorism, human rights, the environment) that were considered to be outside the traditional context of international politics.

Origins of the Nation-State System

To better appreciate the potential significance of the various changes in world politics, we should try to see the current system in a broader perspective. Then we can avoid the common tendency to take it for granted and begin to understand it as a product of a particular set of historical circumstances that are themselves subject to change.

Social behavior is closely related to our basic physical needs. Historical example suggests that, though individuals have organized in a variety of ways, the reasons for grouping together have remained relatively constant—search for food, shelter, and protection. A variety of interrelated personal motives—fear, hunger, anxiety, and drives for recognition, power, material gain, or self-fulfillment, as well as an instinctive need for community—probably explain why individuals organize into larger collectivities.

More importantly, the way individuals organize presupposes a type of value system. Even if our basic needs—food, protection, and shelter—do not change in their essence, our values and belief systems do change, and the prevailing sociopolitical order changes with them. When a political system does not adapt spontaneously to changes in the value system or to a new technology, it is forced finally to adjust or to go into decline. The failure of the former Soviet Union and the communist-bloc states to adopt a more liberal value system based on the discourse of rights is an example. When humanity valued kinship and community most, individuals grouped into tribes; when religion was most important, there existed the universal systems of Christendom or Dar al-Islam[1]; and when we valued land, property, and political freedom, we embraced the nation-state system. In summary, when the system of political organization has not reflected the shared values of the community, the system has changed.

The first form of political organization appears to have been the tribe. In the Middle East, the indispensable conditions for the permanent settlement of the nomadic gatherers and hunters of the Neolithic period—food, water, and building materials—were provided by the Nile Valley and the region between the upper waters of the Tigris and Euphrates rivers in what is now Iraq. Ties based on family and kinship were then formalized. The cohesion in these small bands of people was reinforced by mutually perceived fear: These tribes were nomadic partly because they were confronted periodically by more powerful tribes. The tribe was a small social group that could move with facility and protect itself. In other words, the functions of the tribe—providing security, access to food supplies, and a sense of community—are not dissimilar from the functions of the modern state.

Later, people began to settle in river valleys and other fertile regions, and they subsequently developed agriculture and domesticated animals. Nomadic tribes began to form villages around their cultivated land. Kinship no longer was the singular tie that held human communities together. The village, as a method of organization, reflected increased concern with territory. It was the result, too, of increased population and new technological discoveries. The tribe simply could not serve as an adequate means of organization in this changed environment. Villages began to unite or to associate with one another, especially as labor became more specialized. In Greece, for example, villages would group around a common myth or religion. Thus shared value systems became elements that increasingly contributed to social cohesion. In what became known as the city-state, the society constructed temples for religious worship as well as fortifications for defense against enemies.

We observe a similar macrosocial change in the emergence of the modern world out of the Middle Ages. During the Middle Ages the Christian worldview was dominant: the pope held spiritual dominion over Christendom, and the Holy Roman Empire held secular dominion. However, this worldview was upset by a number of developments, such as the scientific discoveries of Copernicus, Galileo, and Kepler and by the Peace of Westphalia, which we have already mentioned. This shift in values, in shared perceptions of the universe and humankind's individual and collective place in it, resulted in the burial of an antiquated form of political organizations—but only after it fought for hundreds of years to survive.

The nation-state as a sociopolitical construct is the fusion of two separate components, the nation and the state. A nation is a group of people who through common historical experience come to identify themselves as a unique group. These people usually speak a common language, share a common race, culture,

[1]The Abode of Islam, a term designating the Islamic Order.

and historical tradition, and inhabit land that is contiguous. The state, on the other hand, is a system of centralized organization encompassing territory.

The identification of the individual with a larger whole is the basis of national identity. An ideal nation would be made up of people with the same racial characteristics, culture, language, and historical tradition who alone inhabited a distinct part of the globe. The ideal nation, however, has occurred rarely, if ever, in history. One factor (such as language, culture, etc.) has typically played a greater role than others in determining whether people consider themselves part of a particular nation. What is of most importance is the *perception* of the individual that one or another grouping of people is more or less similar to himself/herself and is therefore deserving of allegiance. There are many examples of several smaller nations merging to become a larger nation through common historical experience, and this process further highlights the fact that national identity, though resistant to change, is not immutable.

The state is fundamentally a construct of the human mind, a tool to be used to fulfill basic human needs and aspirations. A state is not just territory and not just people, although without these two components there is no state. The state is the methods, the institutions, and the purpose that give it form, by which land and people are organized to attain certain goals. As we mentioned earlier, a state should be supreme within the territory it encompasses, and this supremacy implies that no other state should impinge upon its dominion.

The ideal state has occurred infrequently in history. The supremacy of the state within the boundaries that delineate its jurisdiction is often called into question through the actions of other states. Intervention by one state in another state's affairs clearly diminishes the supremacy of the state in which the act takes place. The ideal state would have perfect and complete control over all that occurs within its borders and would have a completely free hand in external relations.

Imperfect nations and imperfect states have not combined to produce perfect nation-states. The boundaries of a nation and a state are not necessarily coterminous, and indeed frequently have not been so. States can encompass many nations (for example, China and India). States can cut across nations (for example, Iran and Iraq's border cuts the Kurdish nation in half). States may be a collection of many nations, none of which is exclusively contained within the boundaries of the state (for example, Zaire and Angola). However, despite the ambiguities of the nation and the state and their infrequent coherence, the nation-state has still been *the* organizing concept of the traditional international system until very recently.

THE RISE AND DECLINE OF THE TRADITIONAL INTERNATIONAL SYSTEM

With the background presented in the preceding section, we can return to our central theme. Most of the disruptions in international relations today are due to one fact: The technological and political developments of the past three decades have created a set of new conditions. Policymakers, however, have not yet succeeded in adjusting to this new global system. More precisely, many of the classic doctrines of statecraft have been substantially undermined. The traditional premises of "power politics" and *raison d'état,* though not yet wholly outmoded, have less to say to us today because the world in which they were formulated no longer exists. The state that defines its purposes solely in the old terms and seeks its goals only by the old methods is likely to experience continual and increasing frustration.

The Old International Order

What is the nature of the new global order? We may characterize it as a pluralistic one with a limited but vital form of international democracy, as contrasted with the essentially aristocratic states system it is replacing. "Democracy" in this context refers in some measure to relations between and among *states,* as well as to trends in internal political arrangements. States approach each other differently today than they used to. In the past they pursued their purposes and resolved their differences within a rigid and hierarchical social system. Today they function within a system that, though in some ways very much still stratified, is in other respects more flexible and somewhat more egalitarian. Looking at the world from this orientation results in a drastically different interpretation of trends and events.

We may make fruitful use of historical analogy. At the height of the feudal system during the fifteenth century, society was rigidly stratified. Individuals knew their place, their superiors, and their obligations. The key to the whole society was the status of the nobility. Sharply differentiated by privilege from the other orders, the nobility nevertheless gave the entire system its dominant tone. Acutely sensitive to matters of rank, status, and honor as symbols of their greater intrinsic worth, they guarded their right to defend their own interests and were proud of the status symbol of their class: the sword. Although prone to quarrel among themselves, they were unanimous in denying all protests from the lower orders and stood shoulder to shoulder against threats from below. What doomed feudalism, aristocracy, and the sword was, of course, the invention of the crossbow and the later introduction of gunpowder. Through this new technology, aggressive monarchs were able to force the aristocrats to submit to central authority. The national state that followed feudalism was royal rather than aristocratic and depended for its survival on bourgeois-financed peasant armies.

It was during the era of absolute monarchs that the international system as we know it was given shape at the Peace of Westphalia in 1648. The new generation of royal sovereigns, in subduing their fractious nobility, had transferred to their own persons the personalized authority they had stripped from the barons. We know this today as the "divine right of kings." They carried into their dealings with each other—the primitive form of what became international relations—the identical aristocratic code that had flourished under feudalism, garnished first by the legal paraphernalia of sovereignty and later by the mystique of nationalism.

In some respects, the traditional international system has never departed from its initial orientation to the rules and practices of feudal aristocracy.

The Emerging System

The traditional form of order worked so well for three hundred years that no practitioners thought it really necessary to introduce any modification. Each technological development was incorporated into the system without altering its basic design. Governments practiced the rules of survival within the confines of the status quo. Proposals for change were not well received because policymakers consistently preferred the shortcomings of the familiar to the unknown dangers of a new set of arrangements and techniques. Problems, after all, led to solutions that were at least tolerable; the costs of conducting international relations were kept within limits deemed reasonable; and familiarity with the mechanisms of power bred confidence and skill.

Nevertheless, the events of the twentieth century have contributed to an increasing sense that something is wrong, and as the century draws near its end this feeling has become particularly acute. The old order and its traditional configurations of power have regularly been unable to deal with the issues of the contemporary world, and stalemate has become the usual fate of any problem that becomes entangled in the net of great-power relations. States, apparently no longer able to individually achieve their own fulfillment, have retained the ability to frustrate each other. Although everyone has been trapped in this dilemma, it has been the erstwhile major powers, their dominance increasingly questioned, who have found the situation most trying.

Once again we may usefully turn to the history of feudalism for insight into what happened to international relations. Technological advance, in the form of the crossbow and the musket, ended the reign of the aristocrat's limited resources. At the same time, a dynamic egalitarianism was rising that challenged the static belief structure of the stratified feudal system and prepared the way for the eventual victory of democracy. The historical parallel with the present is striking.

Modern technology has made the terms of combat as heavily disadvantageous to the "aristocrats" of the traditional international system as they have long been to smaller states. Furthermore, the entry of dozens of new and small states into active participation in world politics and the vehement protest that has characterized most of their participation reminds us strongly of the sudden eruption of the bourgeoisie into postfeudal politics. Like their middle-class predecessors, the new states find the long-sanctified aristocratic values of international life (as represented by international law, for example) largely irrelevant to their own concerns. They have demanded recognition, satisfaction, and justice from an order that has long slighted them as virtual nonentities.

We are suggesting that the old international system began to change primarily because of two intersecting and mutually reinforcing historical trends. First, war as traditionally conceived came to be perceived as no longer a useful means of implementing policy, thus contributing to change in the position of the former leaders. Second, a new set of issues has emerged to share, and at times eclipse, the preeminence of great-power strategic rivalry on the agenda of world politics: the egalitarian and transforming urge of the new states toward a drastic reordering in international relations.

Diversity and Integration

As long as power in the international order was confined to a limited number of European and Western states, there was no need for any supranational authority to regulate the relations of states. The balance of power, as practiced by the policymakers of Europe, more or less served to stabilize the traditional international political process.

The new dimensions of global politics have given rise to a drastic modification of the traditional patterns of power distribution. The conditions underlying the old balance have in large measure disappeared, and the devolution of power since the industrial revolution has created an entirely new situation. Besides the enormous increase in the number of national actors mentioned earlier there have been two other particularly noteworthy trends. First, the number of *essential* national actors in the system has decreased. During World War II there were eight essential national actors (i.e., great powers)—the United States, the Soviet Union, the United Kingdom, France, Italy, Germany, China, and Japan. Then the number was reduced to two unmistakable superpowers, the United States and the U.S.S.R., while China, the United Kingdom, France, Japan, and the former West Germany occupied important yet secondary positions. Currently, in the wake of the dissolution of the Soviet Union, some experts argue that the United States is the sole remaining "super" or great power, though the significance of this status itself is currently far from clear. In any event, the number of great powers, in the traditional sense of the term, is the smallest today it has been since the beginning of the nation-state system.

Second, the differentials between categories of national actors are becoming wider, due to differences in industrial, political, and military conditions rooted in the newer aspects of technology. Barring some reversal of trends, many experts fear the indefinite prolongation of this evolution, with important consequences for the future of world politics. In short, the East-West ideological division has given way to a North-South division based on technological and economic indicators.

These trends, operating within the more interdependent global environment created by technology, have had a significant dual effect. First, they have led to a concentration of the visible forms of power within the major actors that dominate contemporary world affairs. Second, to respond to the newer questions facing the system, there has been some integration of power through the UN system and regional actors as exemplified by the European Community. There is also a new dimension to diversity in that there are now a variety of actors whose identity and activity transcend national boundaries. These would include transnational actors such as multinational corporations, ethnic nations, terrorist groups, and nongovernmental organizations such as Amnesty International. The struggle between diversity and integration, although as old as political life itself, has acquired a new salience in our age. The traditional system and the new system as ways of organizing power and defining and pursuing interest stand in direct confrontation.

NONSTATE ACTORS IN GLOBAL POLITICS

Actors and institutions usually develop as responses to compelling societal needs within any given historical period. Hence the compulsion to satisfy unprecedented needs, generated largely by the technological revolution, has given rise to nonstate actors and institutions in world politics whose function has been to deal with systemwide or regionally defined issues. Some of these issues had heretofore been considered only by states acting unilaterally. The experience of two world wars, the increasing vulnerability of the national actor (with the resultant inability to guarantee national security), and the recognition that economic and social instability produces political instability, which may in turn threaten general systemic stability, have combined to produce an accelerated growth in internationalism and transnationalism. The new institutions that manifest the international and transnational trends have at least minimally assumed the role of actors themselves. The bounds of action permitted these actors, however, are determined by the collectivity of national actors comprising each institution in the case of international actors and nongovernmental organizations or the mother country in the case of transnational actors, and these bounds are usually situationally determined. The interests of the members and the issues of the moment determine the extent to which the new institutions can act in the global system.

International Actors

The term *international actors* refers to institutions whose structure, composition, and interests transcend national boundaries but whose membership is composed of states. There are, according to our reckoning, three major types. *Bloc actors* are groups of states that share certain political and security interests, and usually a common orientation in their foreign policy objectives. The *international organizations* are actors that comprise within their respective structures almost all the existing members of the global system. These take the form of general or specialized international organizations. (A general organization incorporates all aspects of international life, whereas a specialized organization is restricted and incorporates only a few.) *Regional actors* are geographically limited associations of states that may share a variety of interests. Like the international organization, regional actors may be either general or specialized in terms of the problems, issues, and interests with which they are concerned. The most common type to date is the regional economic community.

Bloc Actors

Bloc actors are not a new phenomenon in world politics. However, by virtue of such midcentury developments as the technological revolution, ideological competition, and the emergence of a large number of economically and socially underdeveloped and politically incompetent entities as independent states, bloc actors became more prominent and at times more cohesive than ever before. Until a few years ago, many of the essential national actors in world politics were more or less bound through alliances to one of the two main competing blocs. Each of these blocs was led by a dominant national actor (the United States and the former Soviet Union) and comprised a number of middle and small powers that acted in conjunction with their respective leaders on many issues. These alliances did not long remain as monolithic or cohesive as they were in the immediate postwar period; their cohesion was directly proportional to the consensus produced by the situation and issue of the moment. In other words, alliances during the Cold War were much more fluid and, according to some, in a state of decay and increasing irrelevance, as middle and small powers grew reluctant to focus their foreign policies solely within the confines of alliance or bloc policy.

The identity and integrity of each bloc depended on the ability of the dominant essential actor to preserve its capacity as the leading producer of things deemed necessary to the vital interest of all other members of the bloc—such as materials, money, moral stimulus, and leadership. This was not just a simple matter of the bloc leader exercising internal hegemony over its associates. Each of the dominant states made commitments to the other members, but the relationship was reciprocal in that even relatively small and weak bloc members contributed in some measure to the overall viability of the grouping.

The recent breakup of the Eastern bloc and subsequent disintegration of the Soviet Union brought an end to the interbloc rivalry of the Cold War. It can be argued that these events were precipitated by the realization of Soviet leadership that their country no longer benefited from the confrontation between East and West and the realization by the peoples of Eastern Europe that the governing ideology had failed them. In effect, only the Western bloc remains, but its scope and purpose are currently under discussion, and one can safely speculate that it will not remain what it has been for nearly half a century.

Nonalignment was a product of the interaction between decolonization and the Cold War. As the foreign policy tasks of the United States and the former Soviet Union became more complex, their range of interest expanded. Each attempted to extend its span of action worldwide, and interbloc conflict impinged forcibly on the emerging and newly sensitive non-Western world.

Some prominent new states, most of which became active in the system after the major blocs had been institutionalized, reacted by resisting affiliation with either one and by developing a variety of approaches to nonalignment. Although admittedly imprecise, this idea generally implied a desire by new states to articulate their own independently defined interests in foreign policy, apart from the criteria of superpower conflict. This orientation unquestionably reflected both the instinctive leanings of much of the so-called Global South and the practical range of possibilities open to them in the pattern of interbloc relations. Fortuitously, this range increased as the fluidity of the major blocs grew and as opposing factions within the major blocs became more manifest. The frequently used term *non-aligned bloc* somewhat overstated the actual situation because the nonaligned group never displayed either the relatively high degree of integration or the policy consensus that marked the other blocs. However, it is undeniable that on issues separating the United States and the former U.S.S.R., the otherwise incongruous nonaligned states were at times able to form a common front in opposition to the attempt of bloc leaders to universalize their dispute.

Subsequently, these states developed a new pattern of affiliation along a North-South division, the North being the industrialized states, and often at the heart of the lack of agreement and cohesion in the "nonaligned" grouping was the tremendous power and influence of the North in the system, expressed through relationships of dependency and reinforced by debt, military arrangements, and intellectual and ideological influence. Thus, although a Global South country might assert its political independence through its votes at the United Nations, its economic sovereignty was still threatened by northern control of the global economy exercised through stringent debt payments and austerity programs.

The future of the nonaligned movement (NAM) is now uncertain. The elimination of one major bloc and one superpower eliminates the possibility of a middle position between the two. Though this change reduces the likelihood of total war, it also reduces the importance of many poorer states to the great powers, because they are no longer significant in strategic terms. Furthermore, the former communist states in Eastern Europe seem to be embracing capitalism and democracy in one form or another, and this trend puts further pressure on governments of the Global South to conform to the same pattern. Countries with chronic economic problems see no alternative but to embrace the "new pragmatism" of courting foreign investment on terms set by the International Monetary Fund and moving their political systems toward pluralist democracy.

International Organizations

The conditions that have given rise to the evolution of blocs have also contributed to the creation of the most inclusive institutional form: international organizations with both specialized and general competence. International organizations with general competence, defined as having the capacity to consider all aspects of the global system (political, security, economic, social, and humanitarian), have included the League of Nations and the United Nations. International organizations with specialized competence are usually restricted to consideration of selected economic or social concerns. The essence of the international organization in world politics is that it acts in the global system in the name of all members of the system, subject to the authority granted by the membership. It is able to draw on any measure of systemwide consensus that is available and performs restrictive, ameliorative, or affirmative functions as the case may dictate.

The League of Nations. The League of Nations, founded as part of the peace settlement after World War I, was the first serious attempt to create an international organization. Although the total membership ultimately included the majority of national actors then active, significant absences in the membership virtually doomed it to ineffectiveness. The United States never became a member, and the Soviet Union and Germany only became members very late in the League's brief history. After a hectic period of prosperity in the mid-1920s, the League fell apart under the successive shocks of the depression of 1929, the Japanese invasion of Manchuria in 1931, the rise of Hitler, Italy's aggression in Ethiopia, the Spanish Civil War, and the Russo-Finnish War of 1939–1940. It went out of formal existence in 1946 when its property and personnel were transferred to the United Nations.

Though the League was certainly not well equipped to cope with this wave of crises, the member states did not even use the machinery that was available. Despite the effects of World War I, it seems that the major statespersons of the time were not yet convinced of the need for a more integrated and well-defined international order.

The United Nations. World War II stimulated the establishment of the United Nations. The real history of the United Nations began with the London Declaration of January 1941, the Atlantic Charter of 1942, and the Moscow Conference of October 1943. Churchill, Roosevelt, and Stalin, during the Teheran Conference of 1943, strongly supported the movement. In the Dumbarton Oaks Conference between August and October 1944, the governments of the United States, Great Britain, the former Soviet Union, and China drew up the blueprint for what later became the Charter of the United Nations. At the Yalta Conference in February 1945, the same three powers agreed to a conference (the United Nations Conference of International Organization) designed to draft the Charter of the United Nations. The San Francisco Conference met between April and June 1945, with 51 states attending. In October 1945 the United Nations was officially established.

The declared purposes of the UN are to maintain international peace and security; to develop friendly relations among states based on respect, equal rights, and self determination of peoples; to cooperate in solving economic, social, cultural, and humanitarian global problems; and to promote respect for fundamental freedoms and human rights.

The UN has a number of operational principles set forth in its Charter:

1. The sovereign equality of all members is assumed, at least theoretically.
2. Members are to fulfill in good faith the obligations they have assumed under the Charter.
3. Members are to settle their disputes by peaceful means and refrain from the threat or use of force.
4. Members are to give every assistance to the United Nations and refrain from giving assistance to belligerent states.
5. The United Nations is not to intervene in matters essentially within the domestic jurisdiction of member states.

The UN is different from the League of Nations in a number of respects, the most important being that the major powers of the global system are all members. The UN has developed a more elaborate organizational structure and hence is better prepared than the League to carry out its functions. It is composed of six principal organs that operate through a number of committees, commissions, and boards. They are the General Assembly, the Security Council, the Economic and Social Council, the Trusteeship Council, the International Court of Justice, and the Secretariat.

The Specialized Agencies. The development of the UN has stimulated the growth of international actors operating in the form of specialized agencies—multilateral institutions to assist the UN in carrying out the economic and social stipulations of its Charter. The specialized agencies have emerged in functional response to the new technical, economic, social, and humanitarian conditions of the international system. The Economic and Social Council (a "principal" organ of the UN) is responsible for their coordination.

There are now fourteen specialized agencies. Three were established before World War II: the International Telecommunication Union (ITU) and the Universal Postal Union (UPU) were founded in the latter part of the nineteenth century, whereas the International Labor Organization (ILO) developed with the League of Nations. The remaining eleven agencies, products of World War II and the United Nations, include the International Bank for Reconstruction and Development (IBRD—known as the World Bank), the International Monetary Fund (IMF), the International Finance Corporation (IFC), the International Development Association (IDA), the Food and Agricultural Organization (FAO), the United Nations Education, Scientific, and Cultural Organization (UNESCO), the World Health Organization (WHO), the International Civil Aviation Organization (ICAO), the World Meteorological Organization (WMO), the Intergovernmental Maritime Consultative Organization (IMCO), the World Intellectual Property Organization (WIPO), and the International Fund for Agricultural Development (IFAD). There are two semiautonomous authorities that are responsible directly to the UN General Assembly: the International Atomic Energy Agency (IAEA), established in 1957, and the General Agreement on Tariffs and Trade (GATT), established in 1948. The Marrakech Agreement of 1994 would expand GATT to become the World Trade Organization (WTO).

Regional Actors

There are two types of regional actors operating in the global system—general regional actors and specialized regional actors. The latter deal with specific economic and technical matters. The distinction between the two categories is determined by differences in competence or purpose and scope of activities.

General regional actors are more inclusive in membership. Their range of interests tends to be broader and less sharply defined than that of the regional actors for specific technical and economic cooperation. They are associations of states with a community of interest. There are three general regional organizations that have been institutionalized into formal organizations: the Organization of African Unity, the League of Arab States, and the Organization of American States. Such associations as the British Commonwealth of Nations and the French Community, carryovers from colonial pasts, do not have the structure or competence to be considered formal organizations, but may be more akin to bloc actors.

Regional actors for specific technical and economic cooperation are more exclusive in membership. Their interests are limited to economic, social, and technical matters. The European Community provides an interesting example of cooperation that has expanded in the technical domain and has to some degree spilled over into the development of a regional political grouping.

In 1951, France, the former West Germany, Italy, Belgium, the Netherlands, and Luxembourg signed the draft treaty of the European Coal and Steel Community (ECSC), thereby establishing the first European organization with a structure extending beyond the state. Since the launching of European integration by the Coal and Steel Community, the six participating members have formed the European Atomic Energy Community (EURATOM) and the European Economic Community (EEC or Common Market), the latter formed in 1958. These three organizations came to be known as the European Union. There is also a European Parliament and a system of European courts, and there is regular "political cooperation" between member governments in the area of foreign policy—though this process is still more informal than formal. The original membership of the Community has been expanded to include the United Kingdom, Ireland, Denmark, Greece, Spain, and Portugal.

Integration in Europe continues to broaden and deepen. Despite obstacles and entrenched resistance, the unified market with no internal customs or trade barriers was established at the end of 1992. Furthermore, the Maastricht Treaty, signed among the member states in 1991, has strengthened community decision making, laid the foundations for a unified foreign policy, and specified the steps to full economic and monetary union. Though the negative world economic conditions and new political crises (i.e., in the former Yugoslavia) raised serious questions about Europe's role in the post–Cold War world, the process of building the new union continues. In fact, at the time of writing, the membership applications of four states—Norway, Sweden, Finland, and Austria—had recently been approved.

Regional actors have appeared in response to the need for units of action larger than the nation-state but short of some form of superstate. Their usefulness depends in great measure on whether the problems they face can actually be solved on a regional basis. Because of their smaller and generally more cohesive membership, regional actors have proved in some cases to be more efficient than the United Nations.

Transnational Actors

The term *transnational actors* refers to organizations whose structure, composition, and interests transcend national boundaries and whose membership is not composed of states. There are four types that we feel merit special attention: multinational corporations, ethnic nations, terrorist groups, and nongovernmental organizations. Like the other nonstate actors we have discussed, these transnational actors developed in response to the changing conditions of world politics during the third quarter of the twentieth century.

Multinational Corporations. Multinational corporations (MNCs, also known as transnational corporations, TNCs) are commercial enterprises that produce and market in several countries under central direction. The growth of these commercial enterprises is a distinct trend with important implications for contemporary and future world politics (and we will consider these implications in more depth in Chapter 13). At the present time, between one fifth and one fourth of the gross world product is produced by MNCs—and this proportion is forecast to exceed one half by the end of the century. There is no country that is not affected by the capital movement and technological transfer generated by the multinationals. These MNCs are unique instruments of the industrial states, particularly the United States and Japan, and to a lesser extent Germany and France. Most often their interests as actors coincide with those of their home countries, but on occasion they may differ significantly. Such differences were perhaps most dramatically demonstrated during the 1973 oil crisis when the petroleum companies operating in the Middle East generally followed policies detrimental to the overall national interest of the United States.

Investment is an instrument by which allocation of wealth, power, and prestige is determined, hence affecting the pattern of stratification in the global system. In terms of scope, the transactions of the MNCs rival traditional economic exchanges between states because of the size and geographical spread of multinationals and the diversity of their activities and objectives. Furthermore, they are not yet subject to regulation and control by a single authority and are able to profit enormously from the anarchy in the system. One should remember that, though their operations are global, their interests are corporate.

Ethnic Groups. The significance of ethnic groups as transnational actors lies in the growing tendency of individuals to reject identification with their nation-state and seek some sort of separate political status. The transformation of ethnic discontent into ethnic nationalism, as in the case of the Basques and the Kurds, has made its mark on the internal and external policies of states in a persistent and meaningful fashion. Out of an estimated 164 disturbances of significant violence within states between 1958 and May 1966, a mere fifteen were military conflicts involving two or more states. The most significant violence that has taken place since 1945 has been rooted in ethnic and racial disputes that have demonstrated a "spillover" effect in world politics. The legitimacy of the modern nation-state is at stake in the struggle to overcome a challenge to its supremacy rooted in primordial concepts of "blood and land."

Terrorists. Terrorism, because of its diffuse and individualistic nature, does not lend itself to a single definition, but we can say that terrorists use violence or the threat of violence for political objectives. They are generally motivated and sustained by deep feelings of frustration seated in perceptions of profound social, economic, and political inequities. While the exact causes of frustration vary from case to case, these general factors usually are among the causes of terrorism. Not only are terrorists motivated by similar frustrations, but also the methods they use to vent their frustrations are similar. Terrorist groups have been forced because of practical limitations to pursue the strategy of a small group against a larger group. The violent tactics that are employed by terrorists also are limited to a few major classifications: killing, bombing, kidnapping, and sabotage. Some groups that practice terrorism may also employ nonviolent or less violent strategies such as propaganda and various forms of political mobilization and protest.

Nongovernmental Organizations. The term *nongovernmental organization* (NGO) is defined by ECOSOC as any international organization that is not established by intergovernmental agreement and that enjoys a consultative status with ECOSOC. Provided that membership does not interfere with the free expression of views of the organizations, NGOs accept individual members or persons designated by government authorities. International Associations, itself an NGO, has set criteria that have been endorsed by both the UN and ECOSOC. These criteria assert that the aims of NGOs must be genuinely international in character, that membership should include individuals or groups from at least three countries, that the organization must provide for formal structure, that there should be designated intervals of headquarters and officers among the various member states, and that substantial contributions to the budget must come from at least three countries.

Nongovernmental organizations have grown rapidly since World War II, from less than a thousand to more than three thousand at the present time. An NGO such as the International Cooperative Alliance has a membership of over 200 million people; the World Federation of Trade Unions has a membership of over 125 million; and the World Federation of Democratic Youth has over 100 million. The membership of these NGOs as well as others extends to all but a handful of states in the global system. Other important NGOs include Amnesty International, focusing on human rights, and organizations ranging from religious concerns to medical, literary, and a thousand and one other interests, including the International Society for the Protection of Animals.

Nongovernmental organizations perform diverse functions, all of which are nonprofit and service oriented. Accordingly, NGOs enjoy international legal status, in fact if not in theory, and exert influence on the conduct of world politics. However, NGOs do not have the same stature as other actors in the global system. They do not possess the power of national actors, the scope of international organizations, the economic influence of multinational corporations, or the dramatic appeal of ethnics or terrorists. Nevertheless, they have come to play the role of multinational interest groups, and when they band together in blocs they can bring real pressure to bear on host governments.

The number of organizations that are similar in their structure and purpose to NGOs yet not officially recognized as such by the UN is far greater than the number of official NGOs. Some of these are truly international in their makeup and activities and have been called INGOs (international nongovernmental organizations). Others are national or local in character. There are about one thousand nonprofit groups around the world that promote and defend human rights. There are about six thousand organizations in the United States that do work on various aspects of peace. (This number includes national and international groups, individual local chapters of such groups, and local groups.)

RECOMMENDED READINGS

ALTSCHILLER, DONALD. *The United Nations' Role in World Affairs.* New York: H. W. Wilson, 1993.

BOWKER, MIKE, and ROBIN BROWN. *From Cold War to Collapse: Theory and World Politics in the 1980's.* Cambridge, UK: Cambridge University Press, 1993.

BROWN, SEYOM. *International Relations in a Changing Global System: Toward a Theory of the World Polity.* Boulder, CO: Westview Press, 1992.

FERGUSON, YALE H., and RICHARD MANSBACH. *The State, Conceptual Chaos, and the Future of International Relations Theory.* Boulder, CO: Lynne Rienner, 1989.

FUKUYAMA, FRANCIS. *The End of History and the Last Man.* New York: Free Press, 1992.

KENNEDY, PAUL. *The Rise and Fall of Great Powers: Economic Change and Military Conflict from 1500 to 2000.* New York: Random House, 1987.

KEOHANE, ROBERT. *After Hegemony: Cooperation and Discord in the World Political Economy.* Princeton, NJ: Princeton University Press, 1984.

LUNDESTAD, GEIR, and ODD ARNE WESTAD. *Beyond the Cold War: New Dimensions in International Relations.* Oslo: Scandinavia University Press, 1993.

MILLER, LYNN H. *Global Order: Values and Power in International Politics.* 3rd ed. Boulder, CO: Westview Press, 1994.

NORTHEDGE, F., and M. GRIEVE. *A Hundred Years of International Relations.* New York: Praeger Press, 1971.

POLANYI, KARL. *The Great Transformation.* Boston: Beacon Press, 1957.

ROSENAU, JAMES N. *Turbulence in World Politics: A Theory of Change and Continuity.* Princeton, NJ: Princeton University Press, 1990.

SPIEGEL, STEVEN L., and DAVID J. PERVIN. *At Issue: Politics in the World Arena* (7th ed.). New York: St. Martin's Press, 1994.

STRANGE, SUSAN, and ROGER MORGAN. *New Diplomacy in the Post–Cold War World: Essays for Susan Strange.* New York: St. Martin's Press, 1993.

YODER, AMOS. *The Evolution of the United Nations System* (2nd ed.). Washington, DC: Taylor & Francis, 1993.

Chapter 7

CONFLICT AND CONFLICT RESOLUTION

We have argued that international politics fluctuates between "poles" of conflict and cooperation, and that there are structural and dynamic elements in international relations that create tendencies in both directions. The lack of a strong central authority, the variety of political cultures, and the enormous disparities of wealth in the international system are among the most obvious sources of conflict. In this chapter we will examine in some depth the phenomenon of international conflict and explore traditional and more contemporary approaches to its moderation and resolution.

THE NATURE OF CONFLICT

It is a realist truism to say that the states system is inherently competitive. Insofar as states seek to preserve and increase their power and stature relative to each other, rather than to cooperate and coexist, they come inexorably into conflict. Many conflicts are rooted in the state's never-ending (and probably quixotic) search for security in an anarchic environment. National security has often been understood as controlling more power than one's principal competitors, but when one state makes even slight progress toward this objective, its rivals feel less secure and seek some corresponding advantage. Furthermore, conflict is more prevalent when states articulate and pursue their policy objectives in absolute terms. Although states can generally achieve limited objectives that are spelled out in concrete terms, pursuit of an absolute objective tends to involve the state in continuous struggle. Enhancement of prestige, aggrandizement of power, and promotion of ideology are examples of objectives that have attracted opposition and conflict because of their lack of specific content and clearly defined limits. Even objectives that can be clearly specified in concrete terms, such as territorial integrity or political independence, may be so entwined with nationalistic feelings as to greatly intensify conflicts resulting from their pursuit.

Types of Conflict

There are two broad categories of international conflict: armed and unarmed. In armed conflict, some type of military means, from low-intensity or guerrilla tactics to full-scale international war, is used, whereas unarmed conflict may involve diplomacy, pacific methods of conflict resolution, or forcible procedures short of war to pursue objectives in a climate of disagreement.

Armed Conflict in World Politics. War, a condition in which two or more states carry on a conflict by armed force, is a common form of armed international conflict. War is, of course, a legal status as well as a means of executing policy, but its policy relevance is much greater.

Since the sixteenth century, the devastation of war has grown as weapons increased in effectiveness and new theories of warfare were developed. Today, entire populations are personally involved and identified with military operations as combatants, targets, or producers. The objectives of war are now usually formulated in terms of one state's gaining an absolute triumph over another. The once limited conduct of warfare has become universal in scale, and great powers, forces, and ideas are caught up in it.

Wars do not usually arise out of disputes concerning the respective rights of the belligerents, but spring instead from conflicts of interest. States' motives in war are almost entirely political, even though a legal discussion of "rights" and "justice" often furnishes the pretext for violence. Many causes of war have been isolated by scholars, but rather than enumerate them here we will simply state a generalization: Insofar as the anarchic global system fosters competition and offers only limited means of conflict resolution, any specific war is as much a product of the general dynamics of the system as it is of the unique circumstances out of which the conflict grows.

Unarmed Conflict in World Politics. The difference between unarmed and armed conflict is of degree rather than kind. Unarmed conflict has the same rationale as war, with the single exception that the states involved conclude that costs and risks associated with the disputed objectives indicate that the struggle should be carried on at a lower level of intensity and commitment. Otherwise, both the purpose and conduct of the conflict are conceived using the same principles of strategy and tactics employed in the most violent warfare.

As a rule, states accept unarmed conflict as routine but look on armed conflict as exceptional. The overall costs of unarmed conflict are always less than those of a war, at least within similar time spans. By the same token, the penalty for defeat in a unarmed struggle is almost always less than that demanded by a military victor.

Armed and Unarmed Conflict: The Problem of Distinction. Before the advent of twentieth-century military technology, the distinction between armed and unarmed forms of conflict was relatively clear and unambiguous. A state of war was recognizable militarily, politically, and legally. The devastating nature of modern military technology is blurring the traditional contrast between the two types of conflict, which had formerly been marked by qualitative and quantitative distinctions of a legal and military character. In part, this blurring is a result of what has been termed the "technical surprise" of modern weaponry (initially experienced in World War I), in which the means of warfare have far outdistanced rationally-conceived ends. Military means, once they are employed, tend to force a reappraisal of ends: The warring parties want to insure that the objectives of conflict appear justifiable and proportional to their physical and emotional commitment.

Thus the traditional view of means and ends in conflict has been transcended through the threat of escalation into mutually destructive nuclear war. Total warfare has been discarded as an acceptable option (at least among nuclear powers), and more ambiguous and less overtly provocative forms have taken its place. In this sense, unconventional warfare and limited warfare represent a return to the view of the nineteenth-century Prussian general Carl von Clausewitz that war should be the continuation of diplomacy by other means. Although the post–World War II experience with conflicts of this order would seem to validate such a conclusion, it is equally clear that conflict and war have taken on special meanings unknown to eighteenth- or nineteenth-century strategic thinkers.

The difference lies in part in the more modest nature of political objectives (as distinct from goals) for which states are apparently willing to commit military forces, and in the reduced (relative) number of forces actually employed in support of these objectives. Thus armed conflict is limited (both as to means and ends) in a way unknown even to the eighteenth century. Such an assertion does not imply that escalation could not occur through miscalculation, desperation, or reckless aggression. However, the post–World War II experience of international violence, actual and potential, has created an awareness of the inescapable dangers of nuclear conflict, with a general if tacit willingness to limit the means and ends (objectives) of military and political policy.

This return to modified traditional forms of armed conflict is largely dependent upon the continuing credibility of the threat of nuclear destruction. Should this threat subside markedly—a process perhaps already under way—or should peoples and decision makers become conditioned to its presence and immune to its demands, it is possible that the level of permissible conflict might rise. Such a development, in turn, might close the gap between limited warfare as a *condition* and nuclear warfare as only a remote *possibility* in the spectrum of armed conflict.

Objectives of Conflict

We can distinguish analytically between two major categories of conflict objectives. The first, *balancing-objective* conflict, is typical in a multipolar international system characterized by a wide dispersal of power. Under such circumstances, the participants in an interstate conflict seek primarily to restore the disturbed equilibrium in the system. The range of choice open to all is narrow, and the conflict is centered on one or a few points of controversy that are largely independent of relations in other policy areas. *Hegemonic-objective* conflict, however, has a goal of domination rather than balance. The disputing parties are less concerned with specific objectives than with who will be *primer inter pares* among the great powers.

Balancing-objective conflicts may assume many forms: the clash of expansionist policies; confrontations between revisionist and status quo powers; disputes between aroused nationalisms; conflicts growing out of history; and a variety of racial, religious, social, and cultural involvements. In short, any aspect of historical change, whether at the systemic level or within states, that challenges either the ideological or strategic basis of the prevailing status quo may give rise to a balancing-objective conflict. Hegemonic-objective conflict has only one real source—the determination by a powerful state to dominate, reorganize, and control the international system in its own interest and efforts by other powers to prevent or challenge this dominance.

Balancing-Objective Conflict

Expansionist Policies. The form of conflict that arises from a collision between two or more states that are following policies of expansion or revision is the most dynamic and potentially dangerous. Such states are usually driven by strong motives like prestige, acquisition of raw materials, new markets, cheap labor, military bases, or various internal pressures. When a revisionist policy encounters resistance, the government's initial response is usually to increase pressure on the opposition. When two such states conflict, the dispute is marked by a rapid increase in each side's commitment to its objectives and the rapid development of crises. Furthermore, in the face of mounting internal and international pressure, revisionist states often find it difficult to reverse their policies short of their ultimate objectives. This form of conflict was most characteristic of the era of European colonial expansion.

Revisionism Versus Status Quo. A frequently recurring form of conflict arises when a policy of expansion collides with the interests of a passive, status quo state. In contrast to the first category, in this type of conflict the objectives of the contending states are complementary: The revisionist state seeks to take away from the passive state a particular object or advantage. The latter, seeking nothing new, tries to retain what it already has. The dynamics of this kind of confrontation follows the pattern described in Chapter 1.

Conflict of Nationalism. Many of the areas of tension in contemporary world politics are characterized by a clash of embittered or exaggerated nationalist attitudes. An aroused nationalistic group may turn a routine disagreement between its own country and another state into full-scale conflict or war by exaggerating affronts to "national honor." When mass emotions are aroused in this way, great pressures may be brought upon the government to take forceful measures against the offender. If similar pressures exist in the other state, it may happen that trivial incidents, such as misunderstandings at borders or breeches in diplomatic protocol, lead to full-blown international incidents or violence.

Another example of nationalist conflict is furnished by colonial revolutions and their aftermath. Subject peoples could not become free of alien control without first developing a sense of national identity and adopting independence as a primary objective. After independence, the hatreds that evolved through the struggle for self-determination have often continued to form a significant part of the policy of the new state toward the former colonial master.

Conflict of Historical Experience. The foreign policies of many states are characterized by nationalist animosities nourished by a long history. Even though the origins of these hatreds are often veiled in obscurity, the concerned peoples may come to see them as a familiar and expected part of the way their government formulates its foreign policy. These animosities may lie dormant for long periods, but they often flare up at critical moments. Familiar examples of such historical animosities are the Russo-German, Franco-German, and Greco-Turkish nationalist hatreds. Some of these, of course, slowly recede in the face of changed circumstances, but it is difficult to know when they have lost all political relevance.

Conflict of Racial, Religious, Social, and Cultural Issues. In racial, religious, social, and cultural forms of conflict, the specific contentious issues may seem to have limited importance, but they have come to symbolize deeper, even primordial, differences between the parties. Compromise is usually difficult because in the minds of the people it would involve making concessions upon points of fundamental moral significance. Examples of such conflicts are apartheid in South Africa and the religious split between Muslims and Hindus in India and Pakistan.

Hegemonic-Objective Conflict

Though hegemonic-objective conflict was synonymous with the Cold War struggle between the United States and the former Soviet Union, world system theorists and neorealists have demonstrated that it is in fact a recurring phenomenon in international politics. It grows out of the constant competition of the center states to achieve effective hegemony over the rest of the system and to gain the economic and political benefits that accompany that position.

Specific conflicts and wars have occurred either when one state's bid to dominate is blocked by a major coalition or when a hegemon's "reign" is challenged by a rising state. An example of the former case was the successful frustration of France's attempt, under Louis XIV, to attain hegemony over Europe in the eighteenth century, and the latter is exemplified by Germany's military buildup and colonial expansion to challenge Great Britain in the late nineteenth and early twentieth centuries. Seen from this perspective, the Cold War can be understood as a successful defense of American hegemony against a major strategic and ideological challenge from the former Soviet Union.

From the time of the French Revolution, and particularly during the Cold War, hegemonic-objective struggle has, at times, resembled a crusade by zealots and has given rise to widespread subversion, with the mobilization of minds and psychological warfare supporting political-military efforts. This form of tension has also led to the centralization of governmental power in the major states involved, in response to a generally high level of mass emotional stress. Characteristic of these conflicts are spirals of insecurity, arms races, and series of crises that may or may not escalate to open warfare.

Recent Views of Systemic Conflict

Though it is informative to classify conflicts as we have in the preceding subsections, any specific conflict is, as noted earlier, as much a product of the general dynamics of the global system as it is of the unique circumstances of the actors directly involved. Starting from this premise, some recent theorists have challenged the philosophical bases of our understanding of global conflicts. The core issue of war and peace is being scrutinized, and the categories of conflict are being recast to reflect an appreciation of the role of the environment in shaping and creating conflicts.[1]

Legitimacy Conflict. The various new approaches share in common a concern for the perceived legitimacy of the authority wielded by the state. One school of thought grounds the legitimacy of a political system in the perceptions of individuals. When individual psychological and material needs are not met by the state or are decidedly thwarted by state actions, theorists endorsing this perspective predict that conflict will emerge. People's perceptions explain minority and ethnic protests as well as mass popular protests in many states. Thus reasons for conflict lie in questions of legitimacy, but its forms and means of expression are culturally determined and influenced, and can be manipulated by political elites. International conflict is, therefore, no longer easily separated from racial, class, or religious problems within the state. These phenomena are now seen to have an important impact on international relations because their repercussions spread beyond one nation-state.

Structural Conflict. It is evident that, on a global scale, there exists a maldistribution of resources among states and people. Structural elements, such as uneven exchange relationships between states, are believed by some theorists to be at the

[1]Here we are referring to J. W. Burton, A.V. S. de Reuck, David Mitrany, Kenneth Boulding, and the participants in the World Order Models Project, among others.

root of international conflicts. Structure is understood as a process whereby benefits in the system are distributed unequally, and its general patterns and features can be predicted based upon the amounts and types of interactive transactions that occur within a system. The structure involves most obviously political and economic exchanges but also cultural and social interaction. From this perspective, war is seen as an effect of unequal exchanges.

Functional Conflict. Functional theorists have proposed that the state system does not adequately fulfill necessary global functions. This judgment is based on the premise that an efficient world order must accomplish certain tasks to provide a minimum of services to the world's population. These might include such things as an effective communications network, adequate institutions for economic cooperation, and basic social welfare. Inefficiency in these areas results in human needs exceeding the capacity of the existing structures available to address them; this disparity, in turn, precipitates crises of legitimacy and conflict on both the intrastate and interstate levels. The creation of new institutions, at both the regional and global levels, to address these concerns more adequately is proposed as a solution by some functionalist writers.

The Tactics of Conflict

Certain conceptual elements in the process of international conflict can usefully be reviewed here. Fundamentally, there are three sorts of decisions required of a policymaker in the course of a struggle with another state: (1) when to begin the active phase of the conflict; (2) how to conduct her/his own part of the dispute; and (3) when to break off the controversy and resume normal relations.

The decision to begin active contention is usually made by the state whose interests are most involved or the one that experiences the greatest internal political pressure to act. Once the first overt step has been taken, a certain power of decision remains with the second state because it is not obliged to respond unless it wishes to. If the original provocation is perceived to be intolerable in the normal course of relations, some conflict-oriented response is almost automatic. Lesser initiatives may often be ignored unless intensified or repeated. This principle is more applicable to nonviolent moves than to military attack because modern nation-states normally react without hesitation to direct violence. Nonviolent actions usually leave more options open, whereas an actor's alternatives are more limited once the military threshold has been crossed.

Once launched, open conflict requires further tactical decisions from each side, depending on whether its approach is basically balancing or hegemonic. Both sides must decide how intense a conflict they will accept—that is, how deeply they are willing to commit themselves. Next, various operational decisions must be made. Each participant has to decide whether it will initially adopt an offensive or a defensive posture, and whether or not this posture will be retained throughout the struggle. For instance, an initially defensive state may, in the wake of success, decide to magnify its objectives and take the offensive. Each state's decisions are, as we have been arguing, inevitably colored by the biases of a particular political culture, recent and long-past historical experiences, and, at times, emotional attachments to particular policies and positions.

Ending a conflict is frequently more difficult than beginning one. In principle, a state may escape from a dispute on any of four grounds: (1) achievement of its objective; (2) negotiation of an acceptable compromise that gives it adequate if incomplete satisfaction in return for the human and material resources expended; (3) abandonment of the conflict as inconclusive; or (4) defeat. If the objectives of both sides are clear, then it should be obvious when they have won or lost. An acceptable compromise is often the most useful avenue of escape, but it is feasible only if both sides are clear about what they will accept and if these minimum requirements can be made to coincide. An inconclusive breakoff, usually occurring only if both sides decide that their objectives are beyond reach at a bearable cost and risk, most often happens quietly without formal acknowledgment.

THE RESOLUTION OF CONFLICT

The existence of conflict in the global system has obliged states to develop techniques for the resolution of their disputes. The choice of a particular method and its ultimate success or failure depends upon the purpose, skill, and interests of the contending parties. As each conflict grows out of environmental factors and the nature of international relations, its resolution may depend upon a long history of preventive or ameliorative activities, such as cross-cultural exchanges and joint endeavors, good trade relations, and friendly diplomatic relations. A history of any of these will greatly enhance the effectiveness in resolving the conflict of each of the methods described in the rest of this chapter.

Not every conflict or disagreement between states needs to be formally resolved. Many disputes resolve themselves. However, when popular passions become increasingly inflamed, especially when the object of the conflict is a matter of great importance to the disputing states, a formal resolution may become the only viable alternative to violence. Acceptable solutions to the more pressing and important disputes are usually the most difficult to find, because of the danger that both sides may have hopelessly involved their prestige. Unless both sides are able to preserve their self-respect, the substantive core of the problem may be beyond reach.

The methods developed over the centuries for the resolution of international conflict may be classified into three general categories: methods of pacific conflict resolution, coercive procedures short of war, and forcible procedures through war. Each of these has its strengths and weaknesses.

Pacific Methods

The methods of pacific resolution make available a variety of peaceful substitutes for violence. In general terms, they may be classified as diplomatic-political or judicial.

Diplomatic and Political Methods. Diplomatic and political methods of resolving conflict do not result in final judgments that the disputing states are obligated to accept. Hence they are described as nondecisional or nonbinding. Resolution rests on mutual agreement, usually based on substantive compromise. Political disputes involving value judgments of environmental factors are particularly susceptible to diplomatic procedures.

Diplomatic methods of resolving conflict can be attempted through direct negotiations, good offices, mediation, inquiry, and conciliation.

Direct negotiations may take the form of bilateral or multilateral diplomacy. Such negotiations may be conducted between heads of state (as in the currently common personal or summit diplomacy), directly through ambassadors and other accredited diplomats of the concerned parties, or through an international conference.

Good offices is the name given to a semidiplomatic contact through the intervention of a third party (a state, an international organization, or a prominent individual). It is frequently resorted to when the disputing parties have become deadlocked in their diplomatic negotiations. A third state offers its services as a go-between to expedite contacts between the disputants. Although negotiations proceed through the third party, the party is not empowered to suggest a solution, nor does it participate directly in the negotiations. Good offices, once accepted, usually lead to mediation. A famous example of good offices was the role played by President Theodore Roosevelt at the conclusion of the Russo-Japanese War in 1905.

In addition, not-so-well-known private individuals and groups have been known to play key roles in resolving international conflict. "Track two" diplomacy refers to these informal, often unplanned connections that have been and continue to be of great aid when official channels are clogged or rigidly inflexible.

Mediation is a procedure by which, in addition to providing good offices, a third party participates actively in the negotiations. It tries to reconcile the opposite claims and to appease mutual resentments developed by the contending parties. The mediator may not impose its own solutions on the dispute but is expected to take a strong initiative in proposing formulas.

Inquiry designates the resolution of conflict through establishment of a commission of inquiry. Such a group, consisting of an equal number of members from each of the disputing parties plus one or more from other states, acts to facilitate a solution of the conflict. Article 33 of the Charter of the United Nations authorizes the organization to create such a commission when appropriate.

The commission of inquiry does no more than determine the facts of a dispute by means of impartial investigation. The theory of inquiry is based upon two assumptions. The first is that a basic obstacle to peaceful conflict resolution is the difficulty of establishing a statement of facts to which both parties agree. Second, this difficulty perpetuates itself by allowing passions to be aroused that obstruct agreement between the parties on points of principle.

Conciliation is a procedure that combines inquiry and mediation. An individual or a commission (structured much like a commission of inquiry) may perform the functions of conciliation. Its functions thus extend to both determination of facts and presentation of formal recommendations for resolving conflict.

Conciliation multiplies the pacifying effects of both mediation and inquiry in the resolution of troublesome disputes. It is the most formalized of the diplomatic and political methods of settling international conflicts. It is particularly useful for serious political disputes because its flexibility makes it more adaptable to varying circumstances than more rigid judicial or legislative procedures. Its object is always peace by compromise, not justice by law. The UN has used several conciliation commissions since its inception in 1945.

It must be pointed out that neither inquiry nor conciliation provides a means of settling conflict unless the solution worked out is acceptable to the disputing parties. Usually the contending parties will agree to such a solution only when they are persuaded that it offers them enough to justify breaking off the struggle.

Judicial Methods. Judicial methods of resolving conflict are an attempt to regularize the terms and procedures that form the basis of the disposal of disputes. The two judicial procedures are arbitration and adjudication. Solutions are reached on the basis of law—and in some cases, equity—but they explicitly exclude political compromise because only legal disputes can be judicially resolved. The awards of arbitration and the decisions of an international court are binding on the disputing parties, and hence these procedures are described as decisional or binding.

Arbitration is accomplished either by an ad hoc tribunal or by the Permanent Court of Arbitration at The Hague. Adjudication today is the exclusive province of the International Court of Justice (or the World Court, as it is popularly known), an organ of the UN. Except for a few relatively unimportant exceptions, submission of a dispute to either judicial procedure is a voluntary act of the states involved.

Judicial methods of resolving conflict have certain advantages over any diplomatic method. Probably most important is that the conflict is taken almost entirely out of the hands of the disputing parties, thus avoiding prestige problems that might impede a resolution. The conflict is disposed of by reference to standards common to both parties and external to the dispute. Judicial resolution may depoliticize a dispute more completely than diplomatic methods of conflict resolution because it implies voluntary renunciation by the parties of their individual powers of decision and submission to the impersonal criteria of law.

Judicial resolution of conflict, however, presents some disadvantages. Relatively few of the important issues of world politics have, to date, been cast in terms of controversies that could be resolved in a court of law. The more crucial the conflict has been to the parties, the less they have been willing to accept a resolution by outside agencies.

Arbitration may be defined as the resolution of conflict through judges chosen by the parties. The first Hague Conference in 1899 established the Permanent Court of Arbitration. Since then, this court has become the principal instrument of international arbitration. The Permanent Court consists of a panel of judges, four appointed for six-year terms by each member state.

Disputing parties wishing to use the Permanent Court of Arbitration must first negotiate an instrument called the *compromis d'arbitrage.* This agreement spells out the procedures the tribunal will follow and the rules of law to be applied. Each party then selects two judges from the panel, only one of whom can be its own national. These four judges choose a fifth member, called the umpire. In their deliberations, the arbitrators can utilize only the rules of law that the contending states have agreed on in the *compromis.*

Adjudication has come to designate the resolution of conflict by the International Court of Justice of the United Nations. The court, established in 1945 as a successor to the Permanent Court of International Justice set up by the League of Nations, is also headquartered at The Hague. It consists of fifteen judges elected concurrently by the Security Council and the General Assembly of the United Nations for a term of nine years. Decisions of the court can be based on either law or the principle of *ex aequo et bono* (equity and justice).

All members of the UN are automatically parties to the statute of the International Court of Justice. In practice, however, states are not compelled to submit their disputes to the court, particularly since each state may qualify its adherence to the court's statute. A state not belonging to the UN may adhere to the court on conditions to be determined by the General Assembly on recommendation of the Security Council.

States that are parties to the court's statute may at any time declare that they recognize its compulsory jurisdiction, ipso facto and without special agreement, in relation to any other state accepting the same obligation, in all legal disputes concerning (1) interpretations of a treaty; (2) any question of international law; (3) the existence of any fact that, if established, would constitute a breach of international obligation; and (4) the nature or extent of the reparation to be made for breach of an international obligation. States that choose to accept this compulsory jurisdiction may do so either unconditionally, on a basis of reciprocity, or for only a certain time.

The functions of arbitration and adjudication as methods of resolving conflict are narrow. Obstacles to the broadening of these functions spring directly from the nature of the states system and the intensity of the political relations within it. In this sense, resolution of conflict between states is not fully comparable to resolution of conflict between individual people.

For individuals, judicial resolution is the impersonal application of law, an expression of inculcated discipline embracing virtually the whole of social relations. As a result, individuals are predisposed to formulate their claims on society in terms of legal rights and obligations, and to seek redress for wrongs through legal process. The global system incorporates neither a hierarchic order embracing the interests of all states nor a strong central power that could regulate competing forces. Under these conditions, therefore, law can have only a limited influence on the resolution of interstate conflict.

Coercive Procedures Short of War

States turn to coercive but nonviolent methods of settling a dispute if pacific procedures fail to produce satisfaction. Among the leading nonviolent coercive techniques are the recall of diplomats, expulsion of opposing states' diplomats, denial of recognition of a regime, breaking off diplomatic relations, and suspension of treaty obligations. More obviously "unfriendly" (in both a diplomatic and legal sense) is the class of actions involving *force short of war:* blockade, boycott, embargo, reprisal, and retorsion (a form of reprisal sanctioned by international law).

Forcible Procedures: The Role of War

As we have argued, for most of its existence the anarchic states system has had no final arbiter of conflict except violence, and war has become an integral part of states' foreign policy. Until the nuclear era, force was viewed as creative in the right circumstances because it could be employed to resolve outstanding political issues. The scope and function of wars lent credence to the assumption that force and politics complemented each other.

Wars, like other forms of conflict, may be either balancing-objective or hegemonic-objective. In other words, a war may either be fought "according to the rules" and seek to restore the status quo, or it may threaten to destroy the system by altering relationships drastically and permanently. The balancing-objective form of war is known today as limited war, and the hegemonic-objective type is total war.

Limited war—the form of war made classic by centuries of examples—is a familiar policy technique: a single enterprise aimed at achieving a single objective. The amount of violence employed is calculated to inflict no more damage than is necessary to gain "victory" in the form of that objective. The end of such a war is theoretically marked by reestablishment of normal relations between the former enemies after political readjustments have been made. Such wars are supposed to culminate in a negotiated peace. The participants, having committed only part of their resources to the contest, are left with a basis for bargaining when the struggle ends. The terms of peace reflect the new relationship between the contending parties as modified by the battlefield.

The Changing Nature of Force

Discrimination in the use of force in total war has become extremely difficult because the only possible outcomes are absolute dominance or submission. Since international politics involves many conflicts of less magnitude, policymakers have faced the dilemma of finding a clear political (i.e., dispute-settling or objective-gaining) role for modern warfare.

It would be incorrect to argue that total war can never render a political decision; decisions are possible even in a thermonuclear war. But total war cannot provide the broad spectrum of possible outcomes that simpler warfare made available. It is inconceivable, for example, that anything resembling the traditional form of negotiated peace could emerge from a war initiated by a massive nuclear exchange. Solutions by total war are inevitably extreme. Such a war will either run its full course and result in the collapse, capitulation, or obliteration of one belligerent and a claim of victory for the other, or it will be abandoned by both as inconclusive and mutually devastating. Such an expensive and dangerous method that can produce only absolute answers, or none at all, retains only very limited political usefulness today.

Recent Trends in Conflict Resolution

Processes of change in international relations, particularly the changed conditions surrounding international conflict, have spurred new thinking about conflict resolution. In the last subsection of this chapter, we will summarize some of the important elements in this reappraisal.

As a new century approaches, we see the global system as pluralistic with a crude but vital form of egalitarianism. In this system, few of the conflicts will have ideological roots; rather, most conflicts now derive from clashes of communal identity, whether on the basis of race, ethnicity, nationality, or religion. These conflicts are proving to be intractable to the dominant methods of conflict resolution.

Traditional techniques of conflict resolution using engineering, mechanistic, isolated approaches to problem solving, including the often manipulative signaling of positions, are suitable for dealing with conflicts that relate to tangible material interests for which it is usually possible to forge some sort of compromise. In contrast, nonmaterial, identity-based conflicts are often not well understood by diplomats accustomed to operating in a Western, state-centered, culturally homogeneous system. In the new international environment, viable conflict resolution requires an understanding of the beliefs, values, and behavior of conflicting parties.

Western Cultural Dominance. Issues of Western cultural dominance are rooted in the basic premises of international relations. International political culture—to the extent that it exists—is the product of the conquest and acculturation into Western values of non-Western peoples. Beginning in the eighteenth century, non-Western peoples were reduced to passivity in world politics and were, in large measure, excluded from history as their destinies were determined by the West. Thus the rules and practice of contemporary world politics, including methods of conflict resolution, reflect eighteenth- and nineteenth-century Western experience and interests—not the experience of the people of the Global South.

This historical legacy is a source of deep-seated political, economic, and cultural conflict and instability for the Global South and the world. Western civilization is, in many respects, characterized by a *cultural triumphalism,* which asserts that what is right, true, and real, here and now, is the same for everyone else, past, present, and future.[2] This attitude generates Western approaches to international issues that are, at times, arrogant and insensitive, in the face of

[2]This attitude is attributed to the combined influences of Hebraic messianism and Hellenic rationalism in the Western experience.

which non-Western peoples feel defensive and insecure, fearing continued discrimination, deprivation, and domination.

An alternative view suggests that there is something in traditional cultures worth preserving. This premise places much more emphasis on *humane* values. Fritz Schumacher, in *A Guide for the Perplexed*,[3] emphasized the principle of *adequatio:* Our thinking has to be adequate to the nature of the problem. Thinking adequate to the multifaceted problem of domestic and international conflict has to be diverse and symbiotic, pointing not to cultural superiority but to cultural *eclecticism.*

Alternative Views. We can identify five emerging trends in conflict resolution, which can best be expressed in contrast to traditional approaches:

1. Where traditional methods of conflict resolution emphasize *position,* there is a new emphasis on *interests.*
2. Where traditional methods of conflict resolution emphasize *issues,* there is a new emphasis on *attitudes.*
3. Where traditional methods of conflict resolution emphasize *states,* there is a new emphasis on *individuals.*
4. Where traditional methods of conflict resolution highlight *demands,* there is a new emphasis on *needs.*
5. Where traditional methods of conflict resolution are primarily *competitive,* there is a new emphasis on developing *cooperative nonadversarial* processes of conflict resolution.

Two of these recent trends deserve further elaboration: the trend toward needs and the trend toward cooperative process.

The Trend Toward Needs. Though research in the area of needs is still expanding, an initial list of human needs related to conflict would include those in the following list[4]:

The Need for Security. Security is safety from violent attack. Security also includes the psychic safety from being engulfed. When individuals or groups feel secure, they experience an independence.

The Need for Identity. Individual identity includes both a sense of "I know who I am" and "you know who you are." Group identity is similar: "we know who we are" and "you know who we are." Connected with this sense of identity is the feeling of self- and group worth. In other words, "who I am/who we are matters to you."

The Need for Bonding. A human needs to feel connected to others. There is a

[3]Ernst Frederick Schumacher. *A Guide for the Perplexed* (New York: Harper & Row, 1977).

[4]For more on needs and conflict, see John Burton, *Conflict: Human Needs Theory* (New York: St. Martin's Press, 1990).

desire to belong, a need for sacred meaning, for the experience of a connection with that which is greater and beyond the immediate.[5]

The Need for Control. Humans need power to effect change in their external environment. This is political power in its most basic and existentially relevant form. Choice, and the freedom to exercise it, also require some degree of predictability and order in the external world to be meaningful.

The Need for Development. Freedom to grow, to explore and develop one's potential, and to experience beauty are also among humankind's most fundamental needs.

Having identified the needs, one can look at conflict resolution as a process of finding adequate *satisfiers* to meet these needs. When a party to a conflict takes a position, that party has usually identified a chosen satisfier, which in fact may be only one of a number of adequate satisfiers. The process of conflict resolution requires the development of a *range of options.* From these options, the parties work together to identify and implement authentic and adequate satisfiers for each party's needs. This is a process that takes time, and therapy may even be necessary if the identified needs have a pathological base. It is, however, quite predictable that if the human needs of the parties are not met, the conflict will not be resolved, and it should be expected to erupt again at a future time, though perhaps in a different form.

The Trend Toward Cooperative Conflict Resolution Processes. The traditional competitive process of conflict resolution does little or nothing to improve the future relationship of contending parties. In fact, it often perpetuates a relationship in which control over the other party is rewarded, and it severely limits the way "power" is perceived and utilized, usually promoting the "negative" power of dominating and trying to weaken the other party. It becomes more difficult to bring about the creative changes a relationship may need because such an approach tends to perpetuate the status quo. And finally, the traditional competitive process polarizes positions and greatly restricts options for resolving conflict.

An alternative, cooperative paradigm for conflict resolution is based on the concept of *conflict partnership.*[6] Conflict partnership requires an understanding of the role culture plays in conflict resolution and identifies a set of skills. These skills include creating a partnership atmosphere, clarifying perceptions, focusing on individual and shared needs, developing shared positive power, focusing on the present and future and learning from the past, generating "do-ables," and developing mutually beneficial proposals and agreements.

In summary, cooperative conflict resolution combines three components: first, settling the atmosphere, which gives the participant a feeling of comfort; sec-

[5]Mary Clark, *Ariadne's Thread: The Search for New Modes of Thinking* (New York: St. Martin's Press, 1989).

[6]Dudley Weeks, *Eight Essential Steps to Conflict Resolution* (Los Angeles: Jeremy P. Tarcher, 1992).

ond, developing effective conflict resolution power, which gives the participant a sense of safety; and, finally, moving toward effective conflict resolution steps, which creates a coordinated pace.

A cooperative process of conflict resolution also challenges the assumption that power is a static quality. By identifying the role of actors involved in a conflict, such a process makes it apparent that power is shared by both. When actors are encouraged to define their roles and reveal the power available to them, new options for resolution may become apparent to both parties.

These methods are more relevant to the kinds of conflicts produced by the new conditions of world politics we described earlier. Even though the international system is still far from completely egalitarian, more and more issue areas are characterized by complex interdependence. Solutions to contemporary world problems require both an acute sense of human needs and effective means to move from conflict to policy coordination and cooperation at all levels.

RECOMMENDED READINGS

BONDURANT, JOAN V. *Conquest of Violence: The Gandhian Philosophy of Conflict* (rev. ed.). Princeton, NJ: Princeton University Press, 1988.

BOULDING, KENNETH. *Conflict and Defense: A General Theory.* New York: Harper & Row, 1962.

BURTON, JOHN. *Conflict: Resolution and Provention.* New York: St. Martin's Press, 1990.

———. *Conflict: Human Needs Theory.* New York: St. Martin's Press, 1990.

CASHMAN, GREG. *What Causes War: An Introduction to Theories of International Conflict.* New York: Maxwell Macmillan International, 1993.

COHEN, RAYMOND. *Negotiating Across Cultures: Communication Obstacles in International Diplomacy.* Washington, DC: United States Institute of Peace, 1991.

FAURE, G. O., and J. Z. RUBIN. *Culture and Negotiation.* Newbury Park, CA: Sage, 1993.

FISHER, ROGER, ELIZABETH KOPELMAN, and ANDREA KUPFER SCHNEIDER. *Beyond Machiavelli: Tools for Coping with Conflict.* Cambridge, MA: Harvard University Press, 1994.

FISHER, R., WILLIAM URY, and BRUCE PATTON. *Getting to Yes.* 2nd ed. New York: Penguin, 1991.

GALTUNG, JOHAN. *Solving Conflicts: A Peace Research Perspective.* Honolulu: University of Hawaii Press, 1989.

KRIESBURG, LOUIS, et al. *Intractable Conflicts and Their Transformations.* Honolulu: University of Hawaii Press, 1979.

LAKEY, GEORGE. *Powerful Peacemaking: A Strategy for a Living Revolution.* Philadelphia: New Society, 1987.

LOCKHART, C. *Bargaining in International Conflicts.* New York: Columbia University Press, 1979.

NICHOLSON, MICHAEL. *Rationality and the Analysis of International Conflict.* New York: Cambridge University Press, 1992.

RUBIN, J. Z., B. R. BROWN, and S. H. KIM. *Social Conflict: Escalation, Stalemate and Settlement.* New York: McGraw-Hill, 1993.

SANDOLE, DENNIS J. D., and HUGO VAN DER MERWE. *Conflict Resolution Theory and Practice: Integration and Application.* New York: Manchester University Press, 1993.

SCHELLING, THOMAS C. *The Strategy of Conflict.* Cambridge, MA: Harvard University Press, 1960.

WEEKS, DUDLEY. *The Eight Essential Steps to Conflict Resolution: Preserving Relationships at Work, at Home, and in the Community.* Los Angeles: J. P. Tarcher, 1992.

Chapter 8

LIMITATIONS ON STATE ACTION

Despite the primacy of a conception of unrestricted national sovereignty, the global system would not long have survived unless states actually accepted and acted upon a set of well-understood, though limited and conditional, restraints. These limitations on state action, acknowledged by all (or at least most) governments as the price they pay for the continued viability of the global system, are only partially formalized. They rest to a large extent upon tacit agreement and the force of practice.

In this chapter we shall examine three categories of restraints that in some measure inhibit the choices that states make. Initially, we shall consider the extent to which states are restrained by concepts of morality. We shall next examine the role of international law in narrowing human choice in foreign policy. Finally, we shall briefly review the effects of policymakers' own sense of prudence on outcomes in world politics. Although this three-category list is by no means exhaustive, each restraint acts in its own fashion to reduce the effective range of state action beyond the implications of pure theory.

MORALITY AS A LIMITATION: WHAT IS MORAL CONSENSUS?

The state is composed of human beings, the vast majority of whom accept and act upon a set of moral principles, by which we mean aspects of a general code for distinguishing right and wrong. All human action may be judged, with varying accuracy and relevance, in moral terms. Accordingly, in this section we will examine the nature and extent of the role of morality in the atypical context of planning and executing foreign policy.

The Moral Problem in International Politics

Central to this complex issue is the intrinsic morality of the state and the relative claims that public purpose and private morality make on the consciences of individuals. The classic conception, derived directly from the doctrine of national sovereignty, is that the foreign policy of any state has no necessary connection with any absolute or universal moral code. Whether the state is viewed as an amoral agent destined to function in an order beyond conventional moral codes or as the architect of moral principles that are higher and more binding on individuals than private ethics, the result is the same.

As long as politics and private morality are kept separate, such a duality raises few problems other than abstract ones. The moral issue becomes pertinent, however, when commands of the state to the individual represent a direct contradiction of what that individual has been taught to regard as right and good. The classic instance is the taking of human life. The Ten Commandments, as well as other world scriptures, stipulate that killing is forbidden on moral grounds, but killing enemies of the state on command of one's government is still considered an act of the highest patriotism.

Regrettably perhaps, states have not yet been seriously inhibited by this contradiction. Nationalist codes either emphasize that ordinary moral scruples do not apply to public purposes, or else assert that killing, stealing, and lying on behalf of the state are in themselves moral acts. In other words, the national interest becomes the highest moral value and the criterion against which the rightness or wrongness of action should be judged. Somewhat more sophisticated versions of these arguments suggest that moral principles might apply in ordinary circumstances, but the demonic nature of the enemy and the special sacredness of the national mission are reason enough to suppress any personal qualms.

Theologians, philosophers, and psychologists of all kinds have grappled with the problem of reconciling the requirements of foreign policy with the absolutes of personal morality, or at least reducing the clash between them. Publics have been told that, because the human being is inherently sinful, we should not worry about committing what we might consider immoral acts for public reasons—a sufficiently worthy end justifies any expedient means. Another argument suggests that morality and conscience are not more than semisuppressed guilt feelings, and "mental health" is attained by cheerful support of political leadership and performance of any tasks assigned to the citizen.

The ingenuity of these arguments has not relieved us from our essential dilemma. Widespread moral attitudes continue to contradict the pretensions of the state at many points, and no completely satisfying rationale of reconciliation can be found. Furthermore, states (in some cases not infrequently) take actions that, if they become public, create general feelings of outrage and further deepen the sense of moral crisis in public affairs.

The Rupture of the Moral Consensus

The problem of moral consensus, always inherent in world politics, has been exaggerated by certain trends in the development of the states system in the past two centuries. Modern world politics was born in Europe at a time when the moral consensus of the Middle Ages, though in decline, was still prevalent. The monarchs who shaped the system in its early stages thus shared a moral outlook that provided them with some common parameters for action. But by 1815, Czar Alexander's "Holy Alliance," which proposed joint action by the rulers of Europe in a spirit of Christian brotherhood, was clearly an anachronism.

The moral consensus that served to restrain world politics in the seventeenth and eighteenth centuries no longer exists because of two related historic forces—nationalism and universal ideology. Modern nationalism, born in the era of the French Revolution, replaced "Christendom" as the supreme *moral* unit with the concept of the "nation." This atomization of a once-universal moral order produced a variety of differing political moralities, all phrased in absolute terms but each incorporating a distinct national point of view on questions of good and evil.

No state admits publicly that its policy has any but a moral base. Political conflict between mature states has an inescapable, if totally futile, moral dimension, insofar as both sets of participants insist that their goals represent the highest good. However, only rarely does a moral argument advanced by one side receive even a hearing, let alone acceptance, by the other. World order today is suffering both from too few universal moral referents and from too many particular ones.

Morality and Foreign Policy

The pervasiveness of moral issues has an immediate effect on the choices made by states. Decision making goes on in a social context, which reflects the moral orientation of the society, and the objectives of policy are derived from social values with a self-evident moral basis. Furthermore, a moral code generates a worldview, a way of observing, classifying, and giving meaning to phenomena in the real world. Thus what we have earlier called situational analysis is limited by the prevailing moral predisposition of the society. The tactics of policy are clearly affected (though by no means determined) by considerations of what public actions are right/permissible and wrong/prohibited. At every turn the policymaker must take account of the morality of his/her society.

If policy is developed by individuals who take note of the consensus and if it is consistent with public interpretations of absolute good, its implementation can be greatly strengthened. Any contradiction of mass moral expectations raises the prospect of internal divisions or reduced enthusiasm. Such matters as nuclear testing, espionage, strategic bombardment, and compromise bargaining with official state enemies have spawned serious moral problems for Americans in the recent past.

Furthermore, the changing nature of warfare has led to increased conflicts between state policy and public morality. The overwhelming majority of casualties in contemporary wars are civilian. Even in limited war, including its modern variant "low-intensity conflict," civilian casualties may be extensive, and total war strategies have on occasion resulted in the destruction of health clinics, schools, and irrigation projects. Such affronts to public morality, whatever their military justification, have provoked negative public reations that serve to limit future policy options.

Morality, Interest, and Power

Two conceptual distinctions have plagued the discussion and analysis of moral issues in world politics. The first is the distinction between morality and national interest; the second, between morality and power. Although these conflicts are too complex to detail or resolve here, an overview of the issues involved is pertinent to our theme.

The alleged clash between morality and national interest would appear to be false, because there is no *a priori* reason why the teachings of any moral code and the formulation of any state's national interest should conflict. National interest is based on a dominant value system and if a state makes promotion of moral principles its highest political value, this choice does not make its national interest any less valid. Those who profess to discover such a contradiction are often in reality pressing a particular policy in the face of opposition and are usually convinced that they can strengthen their case by discrediting "idealists" who advance moral principles in support of different policy prescriptions than their own. The promotion of certain values even at the expense of national survival is certainly an extreme to be avoided, but very few (if any) of the so-called idealists have ever gone this far in their prescriptions.

Morality and power present a more formidable contrast. Power in this sense is understood to be coercive force, the prevalence of which in world affairs is alleged by some to reflect humankind's inherent tendencies toward aggression and domination. This formulation deprives force of its moral neutrality and instrumental character and views it as a determining factor in a moral equation. A state, it is alleged, either can be moral and therefore ineffective in a world in which the most important questions are settled by force, or it can maximize its coercive capabilities and be effective. Such emphasis on coercion contradicts conventional morality and can be justified only through arguments such as the following: Absolute moral solutions cannot be found in an amoral (often immoral) system; therefore, individuals should agree, even if sometimes regretfully, to set aside moral principles in the interest of effective application of force.

Though possessed of a certain plausibility, this position in fact is illogical and indefensible, because there is no reason to equate foreign policy capability exclusively with force or to strip it of moral content. A state is ultimately concerned with winning the acquiescence of other states to its initiatives, and there are many examples of cases in which moral principles have proved important to the achievement of that aim. In this sense, morality can become an important dimension of foreign policy capability. The role of morality in strengthening or weakening a state's international competence is therefore a function of particular circumstances and outlooks and not really subject to generalization.

The Rise of International Morality

A vision that has inspired the efforts of many promoters of reform in world politics is that of a rebirth of international moral consensus. If some way could be found to recreate and broaden the common moral ground rules that governed the course of world politics prior to the birth of modern nationalism, the political system and humankind itself might well be better off. The danger that differing but equally passionate moral outlooks could precipitate catastrophe would be sharply reduced, and the possibilities for finding common ground for mutually acceptable solutions to important problems would be correspondingly increased. Such ideas motivated much of the effort that culminated first in the League of Nations and later in the United Nations.

We would suggest that an international moral consensus is a prerequisite to a more orderly and stable world order. The development of more efficient international organizations and safer world politics cannot progress very far so long as the human species, bound into a constricted political space, remains divided into quarrelsome and mutually exclusive factions on moral issues. Some agreement on basic moral terms of reference—that is, our values and priorities—is an essential prerequisite to any significant improvement in the climate of tension in world affairs.

Put this way, the proposition has traditionally been regarded as self-canceling. A world divided into a set of sovereign states, each busily perfecting and promoting its own nationalistic morality, has long been considered incapable of mustering adequate agreement to permit formulation of "international morality." Ideologies, cutting across national and ethical lines, provided a broader base of moral action than state morality, but ideological conflict represented movement away from consensus rather than toward it. The failure of Woodrow Wilson's dream of the "Parliament of Man" as epitomized in the League of Nations, along with the deep and bitter divisions of the Cold War era, seemed conclusive proof of the unattainability of international moral consensus.

But recent developments throw doubt on this long-standing generalization. The technology that has made war so destructive has also brought states into closer physical contact with each other. Especially in the United Nations, but also in all manner of conferences, meetings, and assemblies, individuals and governments are jointly exploring the larger issues of the age and discovering, often to their surprise, that their moral judgments are astonishingly similar. The calling into question of our survival as a species seems to have contributed to the emergence of the first signs of a true international morality. The genocidal actions of the Nazis during World War II and various other atrocities of this century have contributed to an international consensus on human rights that led to the Universal Declaration of Human Rights in 1948 and numerous conventions on human rights since then.

The root of this emerging international morality is expediency—the urge to survive on a planet increasingly perceived to be in danger. No moral code makes a senseless death morally justifiable, and sanity argues that the continued existence of humankind is a desirable goal. Sheer biological survival is not, however, the crux of this moral outlook. If individuals are to die, they usually would insist that they die for a *cause* that is in some way advanced or defended by their deaths. This would certainly not be the case if the international system were to erupt in all its potential fury—no cause would be promoted by such a cataclysm. The new morality is slowly redefining the ends and means of rational state behavior in terms of the new logic of interdependence in the late twentieth century.

Any international morality must inevitably weaken the narrow bonds of nationalism. Although this is still a highly nationalistic age, the character of mass national identifications is perceptibly changing. In some areas, a clear decline has set in; in others nationalism is seeking new directions, and, in still others, it continues to seek larger units of loyalty. However, only a few states espouse the old, militant, integrating brand of nationalism. Similarly, the decline in the impact of ideologies on the behavior pattern of average citizens, a very recent phenomenon, is a hopeful sign.

The Restraining Effect of Moral Consensus

The new force of international morality is given form by means of an international consensus. Whether expressed formally in the resolutions of the General Assembly of the United Nations or informally by a rather amorphous "world public opinion" shaped and directed by global broadcast media, collective moral judgment is now a factor that policymakers cannot avoid taking into account. The global concern over human rights, discussed later in detail, is a prime example.

However, until such time as authoritative institutions enforce it, international moral restraint is powerless to prevent a great power from taking any overt step or even from launching a particular policy. Its role up to the present has been to help condition the climate of decision for both large and small states by developing clearer and more restrictive limits within which the state system can evolve. It is not likely to go beyond this role in its present form. Morality may define the permissible for states, but not yet the mandatory.

Nonetheless, advances in technology and the evolving mutual awareness of individuals and regimes have combined to make moral judgments again relevant to the course of world politics. Their usefulness so far, although admittedly limited, argues for their continued and more extensive application. Morality, international as well as internal, will continue to be a limitation on state action, difficult to define but impossible to ignore.

INTERNATIONAL LAW

Whether international law is "law" in the true sense has been a subject of constant debate among jurists. Certain aspects of legal theory must be understood in order to grasp the significance of this problem.

Law in the abstract suggests a fixed relationship between or among certain things. Two types of law may be distinguished in terms of their subjects: natural law (in the sense of law of nature) and human law. Natural law is the law of natural causes of human or nonhuman phenomena and thus contains no element of volition. In human relations, however, volition is the key element. Human law covers the relations among persons or groups governed by rules to which the subjects have explicitly or tacitly agreed to conform, subject to official demands for obedience. Human law rests ultimately on agreement.

International law is a branch of human law. National sovereignty notwithstanding, the global system is generally regarded by all its members as having a legal base resting on the (theoretical) consent of all states bound by the law. International law is essentially a product of the operation of the global system. Its growth has been at times accidental in that it is often not the result of deliberate planning, but instead developed slowly from international practice. A rule often attained near-maturity before policymakers realized that there had been an addition to the body of the law. On the other hand, in the contemporary era there have been more and more occasions when the international community has come together to draft law in particular areas, such as the 1982 Law of the Sea Conference. Though much of the resulting treaty merely codified past international practice, some new international law was created in an organized manner. States have increasingly become aware of the role that their actions and the actions of others play in establishing legal precedents, and often voice their agreement or disagreement with particular interpretations.

Probably the greatest inspiration for the continued historical growth of international law has been the demands of states for reciprocity, uniformity, and equality of treatment. These conditions are what "justice" means in international law. Thus the legal rights a state may enjoy depend upon the willingness of other states to recognize these rights in practice.

The Subject Matter of International Law

The various aspects of international law can be reduced to four general areas: the acquisition and meaning of statehood, the rules and procedures of peaceful international intercourse, the rules and procedures of war, and the law of human rights.

The Law of Statehood. The law of statehood deals with the legal personality of the state and its rights, duties, and privileges. It covers such subjects as assumption of statehood through recognition, state succession, and loss of international personality. It delineates the methods of acquiring and losing territory, and it defines the status of equality of states and the responsibility of a state for events on its territory and actions by its nationals abroad. It defines national territorial jurisdiction over air, land, and sea; it also covers state jurisdiction over persons, including the broad ground of nationality, citizenship, and the rights of resident or transitory aliens on its territory.

The Rules and Procedures of Peaceful International Intercourse. Rules and procedures of international intercourse include the law of diplomacy, the law of treaties, and the law of pacific settlement of international disputes. The law of diplomacy prescribes the powers and privileges of diplomacy and establishes the protocol affecting the conduct of diplomatic business. The law of treaties, one of the most important aspects of international law, designates the methods of negotiation, tests of validity, rules of interpretation, and processes of termination of a treaty. Treaties themselves, covering a tremendous variety of topics, are considered a key component of international law. The law regulating the pacific settlement of disputes controls the various procedures utilized to settle international conflicts short of war and the rights of the parties in such procedures.

The Law of War. The law of war deals initially with the legal concepts of belligerency and neutrality. In traditional international law, belligerency grants a state many legal rights it does not enjoy when at peace, while depriving it of others. It also requires a state to obey the laws governing the conduct of warfare. Neutrality confers certain special rights upon a neutral state, such as the maximum immunity practicable from the effects of the war. In return, it imposes certain obligations on the neutral state, such as abstention from specific nonneutral acts and preservation of strict impartiality. In addition, the law of war covers rules for the conduct of warfare relating to attacks on general populations and treatment of prisoners of war, prohibition of certain weapons, and similar matters.

Human Rights Law. Unlike the rest of international law, which has a history of several hundred years, the codification of international human rights law dates only from the years following World War II (although some of the provisions of the Geneva Conventions of 1899 and 1907 can be classified as human rights law). The discovery of the mass killing of millions of civilians, Jews and others, by the Nazi regime during World War II prompted the international community of states to codify into international law restrictions on their own freedom of action vis-à-vis their citizens, specifying unacceptable forms of treatment of human beings by the state. Human rights law covers such issues as the treatment of prisoners; the prohibition of genocide, torture, "disappearance," and political assassination; and the guarantees of civil and political liberties. While honored often more in the breach than the practice, these laws nonetheless place some limitations upon the actions of states. Chapter 15 discusses issues of human rights in more depth.

The Political Conception of International Law

International law reveals most sharply the contrast between domestic and global political systems. The legal order in the global system is decentralized, resting upon the reciprocal discharge of functions by national states that are theoretically equal. In a national system, the legal order includes a centralized hierarchy of institutionalized decision makers, ranging from the minor political official to the head of state. Thus the differences between them are extensive and, some would argue, fundamental.

State officials acknowledge the obligatory character of international law as a body of rules, but reserve to themselves determination of the rules, how they apply to specific situations, and the nature of their administration. Such a decentralized system is not utterly chaotic, and state officials do not have unlimited discretion to act arbitrarily. They are deterred from doing so by a number of considerations: the general need for order and stability, the reciprocal advantage of many rules, and the desire not to offend other states for a variety of reasons, including the possibility of incurring various sanctions. In addition, because international law evolves from the consensus of state actors on laws that are in their respective interests, it serves as a useful guide for government officials, both to international opinion and potential reactions to various policy options, and to long-standing judgments by experienced policymakers about what kinds of actions are in the interests of a state. In some cases, the international law that a policymaker is considering whether to violate (or "reinterpret") is one that his or her state played an active role in creating. The United States's mining of Nicaraguan harbors is one example of a state's choosing to arbitrarily violate the rules of international law in pursuit of its own goals.

International law undoubtedly functions as a regulatory and limited mechanism in world politics, but only in an intermittent and partially effective fashion. In large measure, this incomplete effect is due to certain key characteristics of international law as a legal system.

First, its exact content has been, and remains, difficult to determine because states define their legal rights and duties themselves with a sharp eye to their own interests. Second, international law is still predominantly a self-help system and is thus not enforced in the fashion of municipal law by a socially sanctioned international institution. Third, obedience to law is in legal theory a voluntary act on the part of any state, for any stronger doctrine is incompatible with the dominant conception of national sovereignty. Fourth, international law is still an incomplete system, with many aspects of interstate life clearly beyond the scope of the law. Most importantly, the political judgments of states remain in large measure beyond legal restraint.

In spite of these limitations, however, the great bulk of normal and routine international and transnational relations take place within the framework of principles of international law. In general, we may conclude that *procedural* law is very well established in the relations of states but that *substantive* law (that part of law that gives concrete content to abstract matters of right) is still amorphous. It is in this second area that international law in its contemporary form most obviously fails as a regulatory technique.

As mentioned earlier, international law emphasizes self-help and the unilateral enforcement of legal rights. The global order does not provide automatic and effective social sanctions for the principles of law that it identifies. Yet it is a mistake to conclude that there are no sanctions at all to contribute to the enforcement of the legal rights of states. The greatest sanction of all, the one that led to the birth of the legal order in the first place and has constantly stimulated its growth, is inefficiency. An international legal code exists because states find it more expedient to develop and apply generalized legal rules to their relations than to live always in a condition of unregulated anarchy. States, in other words, are impelled toward obedience to the law because the positive advantages of obedience are usually considered to be relatively greater than those arising from disobedience.

A second category of sanction is disruption. Long-standing legal procedures have become so well established in state practice that conformity to them is usually a matter of conditioned response and ingrained expectation. The possibility of disobedience is simply not one of the realistic alternatives considered by the policymaker, except in the most extreme circumstances.

Finally, as at least a semicoercive sanction today we may cite the means of generating international consensus discussed earlier. We do not wish to overestimate the effect of world public opinion, but we also should be careful not to undervalue it. As we have suggested, the global media diffuse information and shape attitudes on a scale unimaginable in the past, and leaders have learned to be careful of the image they cultivate for themselves and their states. A legal sanction, after all, is primarily a method of securing obedience to law rather than of punishing disobedience, and it is undeniable today that the demand of much of humankind for greater order in world affairs, accentuated by striking visual images of disorder from various parts of the world, has made many governments pay more attention to international law. State decisions to bow to world opinion on legal issues may be based on expediency rather than principle, but the effect is the same: a greater conformity of state behavior with the rule of law.

Global South Attitudes Toward International Law

Newly independent states have had an undeniable, though not easily measured, impact on international law. Their interpretation of international legal norms differs from traditional Western views and expresses the need for change. Basically, they consider many of the rules of international law inconsistent with their conditions, concerns, and aspirations.

Newer states generally acknowledge the binding force of international law, most if not all of them having invoked its norms in disputes with other states and in debates in international organizations. However, their leaders have stressed the need for further development of international law to reflect non-Western values and interests in such areas as nationalization, investment, resources, territorial rights, the law of the sea, and treaties.

For example, a generally accepted "international standard" in traditional international law governs state responsibility for the treatment of aliens, as regards both their persons and their property. In the case of a state's expropriation or nationalization of alien property on its soil, the international standard has required payment of "prompt, adequate, and effective" compensation. The Western states uphold this traditional standard, whereas poorer and excolonial states favor the doctrine of "equality of treatment," providing for compensation to aliens in accordance with the local laws of the expropriating state.

With regard to the law of the sea, most of these states were against the traditional doctrine of the three-mile offshore territorial sea boundary, though the great powers continued to favor it. At the 1958 and 1960 Geneva Conferences on the Law of the Sea, coalitions of most of the non-Western states with the Soviet bloc frustrated the prospects for reaffirmation of the three-mile limit. The territorial sea was eventually extended during the prolonged Third United Nations Conference on the Law of the Sea, and this aspect of the new oceans order represented a victory for the smaller powers. During the same conference the new states demanded that an international authority under the aegis of the UN be the exclusive agency allowed to exploit mineral resources on the deep seabed. The United States, however, wanted to create a dual- or parallel-access system that would allow any state or private corporation access to deep seabed minerals.

The Law of the Sea Treaty, which was first proposed in 1967, is an example of the role of general consensus, as opposed to unanimity, in the creation of international law and of the problems such a system engenders. Although the treaty was signed by 155 countries and ratified by the necessary 60 members of the United Nations to go into effect, the United States delayed signing until 1994. The U.S. State Department has acknowledged that the treaty is, for most issues, the best source of current international law of the sea. While the deep seabed mining issue was resolved in favor of the less-developed states, through calling for unprecedented global cooperation in exploiting ocean minerals for the benefit of all humanity, the United States has signed an amendment to the treaty incorporating changes in provisions related to seabed mining that the United Nations has insisted upon.

Assertions that underdeveloped and non-Western states are not bound by old norms does not imply wholesale rejection of traditional international law. Rather, these assertions must be regarded as an expression of the resentment still felt by these states over their colonial past, as well as an affirmation of their sovereignty and equality. They also serve to remind the older states that the views of the newcomers are not to be disregarded in the formulation and further development of international law. There is resentment among leaders of Global South countries against what appears to them a double standard—reliance by the developed states on the arrangements obtained by force or pressure during the colonial era and their simultaneous denial of the lawfulness of the use of force by excolonies to right the wrongs of past aggression. In an attempt to provide legal justification for their efforts to change the status quo, newer states rely increasingly on the argument that "unequal" treaties imposed by duress are invalid. It should be added, however, that concern for equality is not limited to newer and weaker states. This principle has been enshrined in such documents as the UN Charter and the final act of the Conference on Security and Cooperation in Europe—the Helsinki Agreement of August 1975 (Articles 1 and 8).

Not unlike some of the developed states, smaller powers are cautious about the compulsory jurisdiction of the International Court of Justice under the optional clause of Article 35 of the court's statute. This caution may stem from fear that the court might apply norms of international law rejected by states of the Global South or that it might uphold the legal rights of developed states against attempts to change the status quo inherited from the colonial era.

Recent Trends in International Law

Contemporary trends in international law demonstrate a closer link with world politics. It has proved impossible to adjust life to law, so the new emphasis is upon the adjustment of law to life. International law of the nineteenth and earlier centuries assumed above all the sovereignty of states. Its object was not to eliminate war but to restrict it in time, place, and method, and hence establish an equilibrium of power. Late-twentieth-century international law has acquired the goal of establishing an equilibrium of justice and assumes the interdependence of states and some degree of power integration.

The technological revolution has produced both positive and negative effects on international law. On one hand, the development of new and increasingly destructive weapons initially tended to further emphasize the role of coercive force in world politics at the expense of legal principle. However, as the problems and dangers inherent in the technological revolution have become more evident, states have begun to seek a better balance between law and politics in order to form a more cohesive, and thereby safer, global system. This trend is already apparent in such areas as the law of telecommunications and the law of outer space. In this way the international legal order will almost inevitably become more effective in response to increases in global interconnectedness and interdependence.

THE CALCULUS OF PRUDENCE IN STATECRAFT

We now shift our attention to a constraint on state action that is central to the dynamics of foreign policy decision making. Our analysis of the foreign policy process in Part I suggested that rational policymaking in an intrinsically unstable environment should be a cautious enterprise. Limitations on time and information as well as problems of misperception all indicate that effective policy over the long run requires a healthy measure of what we call prudence, by which we mean discretion informed by a deep appreciation of the potential impact of unknowns on the success or failure of policy. The historical record presents a sorry chronology of human and political disasters resulting from a superficial or overly confident analysis of a state's chances of success in a given situation. Our premise is simply that given the stakes, it is better to err on the side of discretion.

Rationality and Prudence in Statecraft

Theoretically, there is no reason why all policymakers should be sane. A lunatic, if capable of issuing coherent orders, would be as qualified to operate the controls of government as a philosopher-king. But sanity and rationality are assumed to be requisite qualities in a foreign policy official because only individuals marked by these traits can anticipate the probable results of their actions and govern their decisions in response to these calculations. The rational policymaker is the prudent one.

An analytical and rational approach to foreign policy must be marked by caution because of a number of factors already discussed, including incompleteness of information, possibility of accident or pure chance, and perverseness of the human personality. If every decision took account of these limitations on the accuracy and validity of choice, a generous margin of error would be built into policy. Game theory, for instance, teaches that the primary responsibility of the player is to insure her/his continued participation in the game. No more graphic summary could be made of the task of the policymaker, the very survival of whose state depends on an ability to create and implement coherent strategies.

The Role of Probability

Policymaking requires the application of probability theory. Every policymaker accepts that nothing in world politics is *a priori* either inevitable or impossible—or, more accurately, that the determination of inevitabilities or impossibilities is often beyond the scope of his analysis. A prudent policymaker would therefore try to estimate the relative probability of the various possible outcomes of each problem faced. Action decisions are based upon the greater probability of one outcome, with the necessary margin for error provided by a conclusion about how much more probable one alternative is than others.

One psychiatric interpretation of this situation asserts that to ignore relative *probabilities* and instead become fixated on *possibilities* is a mark of paranoia. A policymaker may on occasion conclude that a certain eventuality is cosmically inevitable (as Adolf Hitler did in trusting to his "intuition" that the Nazi armies would defeat the Soviet forces in World War II)—and pay very dearly for an error. Much more common, however, is the opposite error: to conclude that a desired result is impossible, and thereby miss a real opportunity. Regardless of whether policymakers who commit these blunders are actually paranoid, they are certainly performing at a level far below the optimum.

The Virtues of Half a Loaf

Prudence is also demonstrated in a policymaker's preference for partial successes achieved at minimum risk rather than all-or-nothing choices at extremely high risk. With continued survival as the prime consideration in statecraft, rational policymakers strive to gain such prizes as can be won without endangering their self-preservation or security. This approach has contributed to what we have noticed as a characteristic pattern of interstate conflict under "normal" conditions: the struggle for small victories with only partial commitments of capability. Each state involved in such a contest can accept defeat with only minimum disturbance because it knows in advance that even the most unfavorable outcome will leave it in a viable position for further action.

The prudent cost/risk calculation requires that analysts never give themselves the benefit of any major doubts and that they be prepared to pay the maximum probable cost for their objectives. Since the individual decision maker has only a limited ability to reduce cost factors in a situation over which there is only minimal control, the only way of avoiding an unfavorable cost/risk ratio is by scaling down one's objective to an affordable level. Once again, prudence dictates restraint on decision.

If all policymakers were equally prudent, world politics would never reach the boiling point. But history also points out many overoptimistic leaders who misread the probabilities of a situation, as well as some who were persuaded that they had the key to the final significance of history and could reshape human destiny. The global system could, to some extent, tolerate such leaders in an earlier, simpler era, when failure was more confined to the offending state. Today, however, humankind in its entirety may be the loser any time imprudence takes command of the policy machine of a state. The stakes are too high to permit any but the cautious to play the game of survival in an age of unimaginably destructive nuclear, biological, and chemical weapons.

RECOMMENDED READINGS

BENNET, JOHN. *Foreign Policy in Christian Perspective.* New York: Scribner's, 1966.

BUTTERFIELD, HERBERT. *Christianity, Diplomacy, and War.* New York: Abingdon-Cokesbury, 1953.

CINGRANELLI, DAVID L. *Ethics, American Foreign Policy, and the Third World.* New York: St. Martin's Press, 1993.

CROMARTIE, MICHAEL. *Might and Right After the Cold War: Can Foreign Policy be Moral?* Washington, DC: Ethics and Public Policy Center, 1993.

DEUTSCH, K., and STANLEY HOFFMAN, eds. *The Relevance of International Law.* Garden City, NY: Anchor Books, 1971.

FALK, RICHARD. *Revitalizing International Law.* Ames: Iowa State Press, 1989.

HENKIN, L., ed. *Right Versus Might: International Law and the Use of Force.* New York: Council on Foreign Relations Press, 1989.

HOFFMAN, STANLEY. *Duties Beyond Borders: On the Limits and Possibilities of Ethical International Politics.* Syracuse, NY: Syracuse University Press, 1981.

JENSEN, KENNETH M., and ELIZABETH P. FAULKNER. *Morality and Foreign Policy: Realpolitik Revisited.* Washington, DC: United States Institute of Peace, 1991.

KAVAK, G. *Hobbesian Moral and Political Theory.* Princeton, NJ: Princeton University Press, 1986.

MCELROY, ROBERT W. *Morality and American Foreign Policy: The Role of Ethics in International Affairs.* Princeton, NJ: Princeton University Press, 1992.

NIEBUHR, REINHOLD. *Moral Man and Immoral Society.* New York: Scribner's, 1960.

OVERVOLD, MARK C. *Rationality, Morality, and Self-Interest: Essays Honoring Mark Carl Overvold.* Savage, MD: Rowman & Littlefield, 1993.

SCHMOOKLER, ANDREW BARD. *Out of Weakness: Healing the Wounds That Drive Us to War.* New York: Bantam, 1988.

THOMPSON, KENNETH W. *Traditions and Values in Politics and Diplomacy: Theory and Practice.* Baton Rouge, LA: LSU Press, 1992.

PART III

THE SUBSTANCE OF GLOBAL POLITICS: MAJOR ISSUES OF OUR AGE

Chapter 9

WAR AND ARMS CONTROL

Heretofore we have analyzed the rationale of foreign policy as conceived and executed by individual states, and we have examined the general characteristics of the global political system within which actors move. One primary consideration has affected everything said so far: Violence and, more particularly, war have had an integral place in the foreign policy of the individual state and in the overall operation of the international system. Therefore, we cannot minimize the importance of military judgments. The system has been postulated on the right and capacity of states to attempt to work their will by force if they so desire. This right of resort to force is even provided for in the UN Charter under limited circumstances and is maintained by states as the ultimate defense of their national security.

This condition is counterbalanced by the fact that world politics has undergone a dramatic transition. Foreign policies, particularly those of major powers, are not always implemented with the degree of force one might expect, and interstate disputes do not always reach the resolution through force that the logic of the system would seem to demand. Paradoxically, small states have often enjoyed relatively greater choice of action, while great powers have sometimes cast about (with indifferent success) for ways to make their apparent dominance a reality.

As indicated earlier, the major reason for this unprecedented state of affairs is that new theories of warfare and the weapons that have given rise to these theories have radically altered the traditional conceptions of interstate political relations. Policymakers wrestle with the problem of fitting modern military doctrines and techniques within the framework of foreign policy and world politics, and there are numerous indications that they have not yet succeeded. The old ways of war are outmoded, and the new warfare has not yet found a political niche.

Paralleling the difficulty in defining the relationship between military power and political consequence has been the increasing incidence of conflict used to achieve change within states. In recent years, force has fulfilled its traditional role as a coercive agent of change more within states than across international boundaries. However, these internal conflicts have placed greater emphasis upon the political effects of military action than upon military outcomes per se, thereby further obscuring the conventional relationship between military and political objectives.

In this chapter we shall examine the nature of the military dilemma, in terms of both its own components and its impact on the political process. Recent years have seen a great increase in emphasis given to military matters in the study and teaching of world politics. While this chapter can only skim the surface of the vast subject of military science, it is designed to acquaint the reader with at least the basic vocabulary of contemporary military discussion and to relate these concepts to the larger context of world political affairs.

TOTAL WAR AND THE STATES SYSTEM

What have been the specific effects of total war upon the states system? How has the possibility of general nuclear warfare affected the general pattern of world politics? We have already answered both questions in general terms, but certain basic considerations merit further attention.

The Possibility of Catastrophe

When other means for settling disputes were tried and gave the appearance of failure, war became a normal aspect of world politics because it seemed to provide a final answer to certain kinds of problems within the system. However, as humankind's ability to wage war became more technologically advanced, war began to change the structure of the political system. As weaponry became more advanced and expensive, war demanded more resources, both human and industrial, and the consequences of either winning or losing became much more far-reaching. For instance, in the wake of World War II, Great Britain no longer had the resources to maintain the empire, causing a fundamental change in the character of the international system. Also, in an earlier era war could serve as an instrument for balancing the political process without endangering it. Even World War II, with all its destructive and disruptive results, nevertheless ended with a recognizable political system still in existence. During the Cold War era, however, the specter of general nuclear war raised the grim possibility of destruction of the political system itself, and threatens the very physical survival of much of the human race.

Advocating resolution of an international dispute using a technique that might completely destroy humanity is like recommending decapitation as a cure for headaches; that is, no purely political goal is important enough to justify risking survival. Considerations of risk—even assuming an optimistic cost calculation—thus seem absolutely to rule out a decision for total war. This factor has restrained all policymakers who have faced choices of this kind since the dawn of the nuclear era.

During the early stages of the nuclear era, when today's massive nuclear arsenals did not yet exist, analysts speculated that total war might not obliterate humanity or the monuments to our civilization, but rather that industrial society could achieve relatively rapid recovery from a thermonuclear holocaust. More recently, in light of the destructive power associated with modern nuclear weapons and the effects that such weapons would have on organized societies and the global ecological system, no government has been willing to gamble its existence (and that of the entire world) on the validity of these hypotheses. The possibility of catastrophe and the inestimable costs of general nuclear war loom large in all strategic military calculations today.

The Invalidation of "Victory"

With the constant possibility of a fiery holocaust, and with the certainty of monumental devastation no matter what the course of the war, the classic military objective of "victory" has been substantially stripped of meaning. Victory in battle has always meant submission of the enemy; victory in war has always meant achievement of the positive or negative goal for which war was fought. These classifications are almost meaningless with respect to present-day total war.

The destructiveness of thermonuclear war is beyond belief. That such an experience defies conventional political analysis is portrayed by such hypothetical questions as this: If one state loses 75 percent of its people and 90 percent of its productive capacity, would the survivors be consoled by realizing that the enemy lost 85 percent of its people and all its productive capacity? Would victory in such a case be sweet, or—in the words of a leading theorist of nuclear war—"Will the living envy the dead"? Contemporary American strategy in fact has incorporated the belief that nuclear war would not and could not be waged because of the utter chaos and destruction that would result. Thus the basis of the relatively stable deterrence system that evolved between the United States and the former Soviet Union was known as the principle of mutual assured destruction (or MAD). A related concept, known as "counterforce strategy," emphasized targeting enemy military facilities and forces with even greater nuclear firepower while attempting to minimize civilian losses. There would still be millions of civilian casualties, however, and the number of nuclear weapons required to destroy the military targets was substantially higher than in a strategy that targeted cities and populations.

Victory in total war is, therefore, a notion without content, and this fact has exercised an inhibiting effect. The development of secure, invulnerable strategic weapons systems all but eliminated the prospect of destroying in one blow an enemy's capacity to retaliate. Since even a retaliatory blow would wreak havoc on the attacker's society, there was no advantage in launching a surprise first nuclear strike (and hence no incentive to do so). With no likelihood of bringing about a real triumph, a policymaker's enthusiasm to begin combat would at best be limited. Total war was, in this context, unthinkable for any rational decision maker; without victory to give it point, there was no political justification.

The situation has, however, continued to evolve, and in recent years we have witnessed investment in the Strategic Defense Initiative (SDI), often referred to as Star Wars after the well-known film. Many saw an arms race in space as being the next logical extension of the ground-based arms race. Some argued that this new arms race began with the first introduction of military satellites into space, but regardless of where one defines the start of this new arms race, the result was, initially, a new dimension in superpower confrontation. The former Soviet Union and the United States were the primary competitors in space, with the rest of the developed world following closely behind. Both took steps to militarize space—the U.S. space-based SDI and the Soviet Antisatellite (ASAT) programs.

Though the official rationale for this new arms race was to render nuclear weapons obsolete by making a target state invulnerable, the program rekindled the controversy that surrounds the deployment of any antiballistic missile system in the context of deterrence. Simply put, if you have coexistence or "peace" based on deterrence, any effective antimissile defense on one side at least appears to endow that side with a capacity to launch an effective first strike against its opponent because the system, though nominally intended to defend against an incoming first strike, could equally be used to render ineffective a retaliatory second strike. Thus the strategic advantage would inevitably be seen as shifting toward the side that was able to first deploy an effective space-based defensive system. This shift clearly would undermine the principle of mutual assured destruction and thus lead to greater instability in superpower relations. In addition, advocates of a more limited space-based defense, such as kinetic energy rather than laser beams and more esoteric antiballistic missile systems, claim that such a defense can seriously impair a potential first strike, thereby enhancing the stability of a nuclear deterrent. Opponents argue that by providing a better defense such systems reduce enemy deterrent capability and therefore foster instability.

Few believe now that any such system can provide real invulnerability to nuclear attack; but even if the point of total invulnerability was not reached, being able to destroy most incoming missiles could mean that after you strike first, very few of your opponent's remaining missiles will successfully strike you back. Thus even a partially successful strategic defense might make a first strike more feasible.

Substantial progress on such systems has been made. The former Soviet Union successfully tested and began to deploy ASAT weaponry, and the United States continued to develop SDI for the stated purpose of rendering nuclear weapons obsolete. However, another positive effect of the improvement in East-West relations is that both sides have seen fit to reassess their commitments to such programs, which in an era of reduced tensions no longer seem to merit the enormous expenditures necessary for their successful implementation. Also, SDI was hampered by technical difficulties and greater economic cost than anticipated.

The Rethinking of Political Values

Historically, citizens have been expected to support their state's policies no matter how great the cost to themselves, even to the point of sacrificing their lives. Now that total war may have lost its point, the justification for patriotic death also loses much of its meaning. Giving one's life in defense of the homeland had a far different connotation than did being killed in the pursuit of national interests. The former Soviet Union sought to overcome this obstacle by stressing one's "international" duty, whereas the U.S. approach has been cloaked in less stirring rhetoric. In recent decades both great powers experienced a lessening of support by the general public and the military establishment for the pursuit of what were at times unclearly defined political goals against motivated and dedicated Global South adversaries.

Additionally, as we have already discussed, the traditional concept of victory is hardly applicable anymore. To be sure, there are levels of conflict below total war that might be waged, but they would be limited wars, fought for limited objectives. It will be increasingly difficult for states to inspire their citizens to make the ultimate sacrifice for "limited" results.

Re-evaluation of the conditions under which such demands might be made has led to a serious rethinking of political views. Many once self-evident truths about the purpose of foreign policy are undergoing reanalysis, and drastically different answers are being advanced to old questions. Some observers are suggesting that the content of political life needs overhauling in order to make it more directly responsible to individual needs and aspirations. This was the concept of our nation's founders, but after securing independence Americans viewed Europe and its wars as far removed from concerns of the day, and the new concept was restricted to domestic affairs. In today's world, such a trend could conceivably sweep away many of the underpinnings of traditional world politics. Civil wars, terrorism, and well-circumscribed wars between smaller powers employing conventional weapons remain exceptions to this evolution of political values. In these conflicts, patriotic death has not yet totally lost its meaning or allure.

There are still peoples and some states willing to make sacrifices for political, religious, or social goals. Conflicts of this kind, usually labeled "limited wars," are limited only in the eyes of the major nuclear powers; to small states and to countries in the throes of revolution, these wars are absolute. In this sense, such low-level conflicts and their persistence in the nuclear age have restored the efficacy of war as an instrument of political policy, even if only as a mutation of the pre–World War II variety. But the invalidation of "victory" in total war between major powers has led inevitably to a rethinking of the political values that underlie considering the use of force as a legitimate and viable policy alternative, and even in regional conflicts there is a newfound willingness to talk rather than fight. Of course, there is no inevitability to this trend, as the fragmentation of the former Soviet Union and the states of Eastern Europe, as well as the internecine conflicts of Africa, constantly reminds us.

The Disappearance of Decision

With war no longer a profitable foreign policy investment, the states system is deprived of a definitive method of reaching decisions in direct confrontations between states. Smaller states, although not risking nuclear incineration if they fight, have operated in an environment severely constrained by the probability of great power intervention and the fear of conflict escalation, perhaps to the level of total war. States repeatedly become involved in positions from which a successful war might extricate them, but inhibitions on warfare prevent them from taking the critical step. Unable to go forward and unwilling to retreat, twentieth-century contestants have at times remained locked in an uneasy stalemate, unable to resolve the issues that divide them. In "microwars" between or within small states, great powers, spurred by fears of the ultimate confrontation, have on occasion intervened prior to the achievement of a permanent political or military resolution. Although the small states have fought, the issues have tended to remain undecided.

During the Cold War period, world politics witnessed a succession of great power issues strained to the breaking point without a clear resolution. Many states persisted in embarking on policies whose full fruition might have required war, and they expressed baffled annoyance when they found themselves trapped. Some smaller states, recognizing both the opportunities and limitations inherent in such an era, had great success in pursuing active policies cast in a frame of implementation that excluded high probability of war. With increasing frequency, they have enlarged that frame of execution to include war itself.

Decision by Consensus

With war stripped of its role as last resort, some effective substitute is necessary if the global political system is to maintain stability. The most broadly applicable alternative to war has been the institutionalization of consensus. Speaking primarily through the Security Council and General Assembly of the United Nations, but on occasion through special conferences or other ad hoc instrumentalities, a cohesive and articulate body of supranational consensus has come to exert more and more influence on crisis situations. If international consensus continues to develop and increasingly displace military power as final arbiter, the global political system will be vastly different then it has been for three centuries.

POLITICAL EFFECTS OF THE NEW WARFARE

We have considered some of the effects of total war on the operation of the states system. Equally important to an understanding of the impact of military technology are its influences on policymakers.

The "Balance of Terror"

The most important consideration affecting foreign policy decisions during the Cold War, by both large and small states, was the so-called balance of terror. This situation stemmed from the distribution of military capability in the world: Two great states had built up arsenals of new weapons that far outclassed all other states, yet each remained incapable of achieving superiority over the other. Since neither of the great powers was able to contemplate unleashing war on the other, both the United States and the former U.S.S.R. had a vested interest in avoiding war. There was little philanthropy or charity in this self-restraint, only elementary calculations of the prospects for survival.

If the nuclear giants were inhibited by the balance of terror, so were the smaller states. Neither nuclear leader could view calmly an outbreak of war anywhere, so both denied smaller powers the capability to reach decisions using the violence that they themselves were denied. Their reasons for preferring peace were the same as those governing their direct confrontation: A war that could not be won, or one in which the prospects of real victory were remote and difficult to visualize, was of no value to them. A small war could spread and involve either or both in massive risk for small possible profit. Even here the influence of the nuclear standoff was paradoxical because control of a conflict might have required the active great-power intervention the nuclear nations sought to avoid.

Small-war belligerents often exploited the freedom afforded by this dilemma. When the superpowers chose restraint, combat was at times pursued to exhaustion or completion. When some intervention was carried out, the small states skillfully manipulated their bargaining position between the powers. Thus it may be said that, even during the Cold War, modern weaponry, as long as it remained narrowly distributed, showed itself to be a poor way to fight a war but an effective, if rather risky, device for preventing one.

The continuing proliferation of nuclear weapons, however, promises to upset commonly accepted views about their deterrent effects. New nuclear states such as Great Britain, the People's Republic of China, and France, although attaining only a marginal degree of military "power" vis-à-vis the United States and the former Soviet Union, have greatly enhanced their prestige and created serious political repercussions within their military blocs and geographic regions. This lesson is not lost upon other states with the means of purchasing nuclear technology, and it is a variable in recent trends in nuclear proliferation.

Such nonnuclear states as the former West Germany and Japan, potentially facing an intransigent nuclear-armed opponent, deliberately retained the technological options necessary to achieve nuclear capability at manageable cost within a relatively short period of time. The acquisition of nuclear capability by India demonstrates that the allure of becoming a nuclear power is strong among the less-developed countries of the world. A number of these states—Pakistan, India, and Israel—are generally credited with having developed a substantial nuclear arsenal. Brazil, South Korea, Egypt, and Iran, among others, seem capable of producing nuclear weapons without undue economic dislocations.

Whatever may be the reasons for which states seek nuclear arms, the uncertainties of nuclear proliferation and its strategic consequences loom large on the contemporary horizon. As ownership of nuclear weapons expands, the mathematical probability of their use increases. The political and military pressures demanding their use are not as great but are still quite as predictable. Whether these influences will be balanced by the deterrent effect of some new balance of terror and an awareness of the responsibility of nuclear weapons remains a major uncertainty in the late-twentieth-century nuclear environment.

The Declining Credibility of Military Force

The balance of terror not only makes war irrelevant to policy, but also deprives military power of much of its credibility as a coercive or persuasive technique in the course of ordinary political confrontation between nations that command equivalent levels of military strength. The credibility of the threat of violence as a tool of policy is no more than a partial function of the threat. Of even greater importance today is the likelihood of its being made a reality. The sheer enormity of contemporary threats, especially threats mounted by nuclear states, is greater than at any earlier period of history. Their impact on outcomes, however, is almost negligible because it has become quite unlikely that the threatening state will make good its menace.

We have seen the consequences of this development at every turn. The fear of escalation to nuclear war influenced the United States and the former Soviet Union to make every effort to avoid direct confrontation; even in the event of confrontations, the nuclear giants searched for conventional military forces to implement a "nuclear" strategy that they were not prepared on any level to use.

Among nonnuclear powers, where more traditional calculations might be expected to hold sway, a variety of restraints have also called into question traditional military calculations of force. Ironically, however, stability on the nuclear level may have led to some measure of instability on the conventional level. As the nuclear powers and their proxies became accustomed to the environment of possible mutual annihilation, they edged with increasing temerity away from the view that the use of military force was restricted to either total war or complete abstinence, and they began to think once again in terms of the gradations of force.

The End of Status

The declining credibility of military power has threatened to erode (but not eliminate) the status system that regulates the relations of states. The old classification of states into categories of rank and privilege based upon their respective military capabilities has been substantially invalidated. Great powers could not receive deference if they could not act in the way expected of great powers.

States of all military levels approach each other on a basis of theoretical status equality. The deference and privilege enjoyed by each in a particular relationship are a function of the specific situation and each state's respective range of capabilities, and cannot be inferred in advance from any generalized characteristics or self-image. The essence of a status or class system is a fixed stratification of groups, and military capacity long functioned as the determinant of a state's position. No universally accepted criterion of rank has arisen to replace military power, although economic power may be a more relevant measure of influence than traditional calculations of military might. Militarily inferior states such as Japan and certain Persian Gulf countries wield much more international influence than their limited military forces would indicate. The burgeoning number of newly independent states in the past two decades has rendered the global social system more fluid and less structured today than it has been since its inception. The ability of habitual "leaders" or an "inner circle" of dominant powers to shape the agenda of world politics has been muted (though by no means eclipsed) by the number and increasing nationalism of states in the system.

The Utility of Military Force Today

Are we arguing that military force and the institution of organized armed conflict have lost all relevance to contemporary world politics? In strict conceptual terms, the temptation to adopt that position is strong, but a glance at the real world suggests that military power has retained significant capacity to render a decision in an increasing number of special cases. A brief catalog of these instances will not only measure the relevance of war today, but also highlight some salient characteristics of the contemporary political world.

The Cold War era witnessed situations in which a leader of a major bloc used armed force to subdue a rebellious or recalcitrant military dependency. Classic instances were the Soviet interventions in Hungary in 1956 and Czechoslovakia in 1968, and the failed attempt in Afghanistan in 1980. With the threat of violent intervention thus made credible, armed forces could be used by the bloc leaders to coerce maverick satellites, with the contingent mission of reinforcing indigenous bloc forces if violence flared. The rigidity of the bloc's international position effectively inhibited the likelihood of an attempt at interference from any outside source, specifically from the other bloc.

The worldwide competition between the superpowers led to the development of "proxy" relationships whereby a smaller state was supported in its efforts by one of the major powers. Consequently, a new range of "proxy wars" materialized. Proxy-patron relationships assumed a surprising degree of complexity and unpredictability on all levels. Probably the most conspicuous example of one form of this device was the extensive Chinese and Soviet support given North Korea during the Korean War of 1950–1953. The pattern there of proxy versus great-power multilateral force was altered by the appearance of mainland Chinese "volunteers" who fought a large part of the battle.

The Indo-Pakistani Wars of 1965 and 1971 also demonstrated the complex and confusing nature of proxy relationships. The United States was caught in a conflict where both combatants were to some degree its proxies, while the former U.S.S.R. was supporting a friendly state, India, against a strategically important neighbor, Pakistan, which was backed by the Chinese. Under such confusing circumstances, the haste of the great powers to achieve some kind of peace is understandable.

The Arab-Israeli conflicts of 1967 and 1973 illustrate yet another kind of proxy war, but one on three levels, where one bloc leader, the United States, played patron to segments of both sides. The United States resisted the Soviet drive to polarize the region into Arab-U.S.S.R. and American-Israeli blocs by keeping a foot in both camps—supporting moderate Arabs while also sending massive amounts of aid to Israel. The increasingly close relationship between the United States and Egypt in the mid-1970s indicated that the United States would become even more committed to both sides because it could not lend support to Egypt without corresponding assurances of Israeli security. The peril inherent in assisting two proxy states that were themselves antagonists was demonstrated in 1977 when Somalia expelled the Soviets because of continuing Soviet support of Ethiopia, with whom Somalia was in conflict over the Ogaden region.

The emergence of wars of national liberation in the less-developed states lent still another aspect to the texture of proxy wars in this decade. They provided ideological justification as well as practical opportunities to play out the great-power conflicts through proxies in the Global South. Vietnam, in particular, illustrated the dynamic quality of such conflicts. It was not uncommon for the confrontation to evolve as one or another of the proxy states found itself unable to continue the fight. At that point, the supporting power found itself in the position of either assuming greater responsibility for the conduct of operations or of losing the effort invested up to that point. Domestic political pressure built to prevent the supporting power from discontinuing the fight. From its origins as an internal or civil guerrilla war with outside support from both blocs, the Vietnam War evolved into an international war much like the Korean War. Thus the conflict moved from the guerrilla-internal war side of the spectrum toward conventional war with direct great-power involvement, a development that illustrated that great powers could and would engage in "limited" conventional military actions in the nuclear age.

In a more recent example, the former Soviet Union invaded neighboring Afghanistan at the end of 1979 to prevent a satellite government from losing control and to reestablish a leadership more amenable to Soviet desires. Islamic fundamentalist Afghans rose up in rebellion, and the Soviets ultimately committed more than 100,000 troops in an unsuccessful effort to gain control. With substantial assistance from the United States, the rebels inflicted heavy casualties on the Soviet and Afghan soldiers.

Another military scenario that may become more prevalent, especially if major-power intervention in "small wars" persists in being as unsatisfactory as the U.S. experience in Vietnam and the Soviet experience in Afghanistan, is conventional combat between small states. Wars in sub-Saharan Africa or Latin America have not seen the degree of superpower participation that was evident during the 1950s and 1960s because the costs of involvement outweighed the benefits. Mutual indifference will also deter interference, although political and military developments, possibly instigated by a third power, may change the calculations of the major powers. Intervention in these cases would not be unlike proxy war situations. Great powers may also refrain from intervening in small-state wars because they fear escalation to the nuclear level, although this constraint seems less compelling now than a decade ago.

Significantly, modern experience has indicated that military power may be used to obtain political decisions by groups of small states acting under authority given by the United Nations or regional organizations. For example, UN troops have been used successfully in the Sinai after the 1973 Middle East War and on Cyprus following the Greek-Turkish dispute in 1974. However, a realistic appraisal of UN peacekeeping during the Cold War would conclude that little can be done in the face of great power intransigence. Although the nonaligned movement (NAM) may have been able to set the agenda of the UN for some years without superpower acquiescence, this or any other movement had little ability to influence events positively.

Despite the instances we have mentioned, however, the range of effective military action to influence behavior in the interestate system is quite narrow. At the superpower level, the problem of relating contemporary military capability to foreign policy objectives will continue to defy solution until military specialists and political leaders learn more about the implications of modern technology as applied to complex political warfare in Global South countries. Smaller powers are also faced with the problem of understanding and handling the use of military force within an uncertain and dynamic great power milieu that provides no safe or predictable frame of reference for their operations.

Arms Transfers

Arms transfers between supplier and recipient governments have become a major contentious issue within the present global system. By any reasonable standard of measurement, the great powers, particularly the United States, are the leading suppliers of military equipment to less-developed countries. In 1990 the United States exported $8.9 billion of such equipment.[1] Developing countries received $16.5 billion of the $21.8 billion in officially recorded arms imports worldwide during 1991.

Most independent states have some kind of armed forces to insure internal order, territorial integrity, and national dignity. Whether new or old, superpower or ministate, few states judge themselves able to maintain only a constabulary rather than a military establishment. In 1991 the military expenditures of 140 countries amounted to approximately $676 billion. Most of these countries have no arms industry, or at best a rudimentary one, and must acquire military equipment from other more industrialized states on a cash, credit, or grant basis. Basic questions for a great power such as the United States are where it should supply

[1]The statistics in this section are all taken from Ruth Leger Sivard, *World Military and Social Expenditures, 1993,* 15th ed. (Washington, DC: World Priorities, 1993).

military equipment, the type of equipment it should supply, and in which instances it should exercise restraint in selling weapons of war. One issue that has received very little attention in public discussions within the United States is the transfer of antipersonnel weapons and the tools or implements of torture. While various efforts both within the U.S. Congress and by public activists have attempted to shed light on and limit such transfers, information on the supply of such weapons is often not readily available or is misleading. In late 1986 the Reagan administration was severely criticized for selling arms to Iran as a precondition for the release of U.S. hostages held in Lebanon and possibly Iran by Islamic extremists loyal to the Ayatollah Khomeini. Profits from the sale were funneled illegally to the Nicaraguan contras by arms dealers and midlevel National Security Council officials. While subsequent investigations attempted, with uncertain success, to prove that the president and senior officials of the administration were not aware of the contra link, they were criticized for not exercising oversight and control to prevent such incidents from occurring. In spite of legal guidelines, government officials and associated private citizens in the United States and abroad have sometimes been able to use foreign military sales programs to further their personal perceptions of national interest or to further their own enrichment.

Arms transfers occur through the provision of training, the sharing of technology, and gifts of, loans for, or sales of military equipment. The United States provides economic support in order to reduce the budgetary burden associated with purchases of new arms or training of military personnel. Arms transfers are motivated by profit, high arms research and development costs, and both internal and external security considerations. Of the 112 developing countries, which imported $16.5 billion in military equipment during 1991 (as noted previously), 94 countries practiced official violence against their citizens in 1992 (torture, brutality, disappearances, or political killings).

NEW DOCTRINES AND THE MILITARY DILEMMA

We must not suppose that military experts have remained suspended in bemusement at the massive effect of the new technology of warfare on their profession. On the contrary, military and civilian analysts in all countries have been devoting great effort to coming to terms with the changed conditions of war. Out of this enterprise have come a great number of new doctrines and concepts that cover a broad gamut of situations but are analogous in their attempt to develop an intellectual base for warfare in the modern world.

The Importance of Military Doctrine

The scope of modern warfare is so vast and its instruments so complex that it would be impossible to conduct a campaign without a doctrine governing the military process. A military doctrine spells out a series of assumptions about the nature and conditions of combat and the calculations defining its initiation, prosecution, and termination. Military doctrines also resolve in advance the dilemmas inherent in battlefield operations: the relative importance of conserving matériel compared with conserving life, the respective roles of position and maneuver, the concept of "firepower" as opposed to that of occupation of territory, and so on. Military doctrine, by developing a mental framework within which operational decisions can be made, is intended to make the task of modern commanders more manageable.

Military doctrine occupies a central place in the capability judgments of a state. Because it governs the makeup of the military machine, the principles that will affect its employment, and the point of view and professional orientation of its officer corps, it constitutes one of the filters through which raw military potential must pass before a sophisticated evaluation can be made of a state's real military capacity. American military doctrine has always emphasized firepower and maneuvering as the ingredients of victory, and has argued that an offensive posture is both less costly and more productive than a defensive one. Military doctrines can vary along several important parameters. For instance, for Americans, preservation of manpower has always ranked higher than that of matériel. The maintenance at all times of a force ready to fight is another standard American tenet, although one developed only since World War II. These principles contrast with the relatively low rank given by Chinese military thought to the conservation of life and the emphasis on small-group irregular tactics developed by Mao Tse-tung. Soviet doctrine emphasized massed firepower and placed less emphasis on maneuvering and mobility. All of these considerations (to which analogues could be found in military doctrines of all states) have a significant effect on the way the state's armed forces are constructed and used. They are important to both the foreign policy planner contemplating military action and the policymaker evaluating the potential of another state.

The Doctrinal Crisis: Is This a New Era?

The great crisis currently facing scholars of military doctrine involves an estimate of the impact of the new technology on the classic principles of warfare. Do these rules of strategy and tactics—evolved over the centuries and absorbing earlier technological advances from the bow and arrow to the tank, the "blockbuster" aerial bomb, and the technique of "vertical envelopment" by airborne forces—still apply in the era of thermonuclear warheads on intercontinental ballistic missiles? One school of thought argues that changes in warfare are entirely quantitative and not qualitative, and that the historic doctrines of warfare need only be adapted to new conditions. Another group contends that modern weaponry has changed the meaning of warfare, and entirely new concepts are required before men can exploit this as-yet-untried range of capability.

Traditionalists argue that the new weapons are no more than advanced versions of classic types. A thermonuclear bomb has the explosive potential of 50 million tons of TNT. Although a frightening figure, this comparison suggests that it would be possible to duplicate the blast of a hydrogen bomb by traditional means. Missiles are no more than improved delivery systems; the entire history of warfare involves gradual advance in delivery techniques, from the individual foot soldier carrying his spear, through rifleman, cavalryman, tanker, airplane pilot, and now the missile operator. Each advance, although not eliminating the human element, has involved increases in both the speed and reliability of the delivery of a weapon to its target. Thus, the argument goes, there is no conceptual difference between the doctrines of Caesar's legions and those of contemporary ICBM squadrons. Only the technical details of mobilizing and employing the individuals and matériel are new.

The opposite position, as discussed earlier, stems from the belief that destructive capabilities, such as those of hydrogen bombs and delivery systems using precision guidance and multiple independently targetable warheads, have made a travesty of the established doctrines of warfare. Not only have modern weapons endangered the survival of the political system that they are supposed to regulate, but they have also made war a cruel deception and a recipe for holocaust.

Advocates of new doctrines go in two different directions from this basic premise. One school contends that a new theory of total war must be developed, founded on principles different from historic practice and emphasizing the major characteristics of the new weapons: destructiveness and rapidity of delivery. The other group contends that war has been rendered obsolete, and that the principal military mission of the future will be to prevent recurrence of combat rather than to win a war.

Whatever direction this dispute might take in future, there seems little likelihood that prudent policymakers would take the risk intrinsic to modern war until they had resolved the doctrinal dilemma to their own satisfaction. So long as military specialists continue to deepen the gaps between the several schools of thought, the use of armed force on an organized basis by any major state remains highly problematic. The recent war in the Persian Gulf illustrates that, under the right conditions, armed conflict is still possible, but the uncertainties about motives, escalation, and termination that surrounded that conflict reflect some of the points we have made.

Doctrines of Total War

Deterrence. Deterrence—the capacity of modern weapons to dissuade another state from initiating warfare—is one of the pervasive doctrines of the new military era. This notion has always been part of military lore, but the peculiar qualities of the new techniques have made deterrence more significant than ever before.

Much thought has gone into the ramifications of the deterrent mission of modern military establishments. The development of massive nuclear arsenals by both major powers during the Cold War led to the acceptance of "nuclear parity," whereby each side recognized that any attempt to achieve nuclear superiority would result only in a reescalation of the arms race. Deterrence came to be based on "assured destruction," the premise that a state's retaliatory capacity should be such that, regardless of the damage inflicted by a first strike, the enemy would immediately receive an unacceptable amount of return damage to its cities, industrial capacity, and clusters of population. This approach, known as a "countervalue" theory, has been supplemented by the "counterforce" concept that bases deterrence on the development of capability sufficiently well aimed to destroy the enemy's military capacity while leaving cities and populations relatively intact. The neutron bomb, for instance, is designed to enable targeting of military concentrations for maximum deaths without the destructive blast force and fires associated with other nuclear weaponry. In practice, all states with adequate scientific and industrial means have attempted a policy that partakes of both capabilities. The ultimate deterrent, regardless of the counterforce-countervalue mix, remains the ability of a state to assure an unacceptable level of damage to another state's society.

The Nature of Response. Though part of deterrent policy, determining a state's appropriate response to a military-political provocation is in itself a doctrinal issue of considerable importance. As in deterrence, several different approaches have been proposed. We shall look at the way the controversy has developed in the United States, although all major states have addressed the issue.

An early school of thought favored "instantaneous response," more popularly known as "massive retaliation." Those advancing this argument contended that any direct Soviet-American armed conflict was inevitably a total war, and they urged that whatever strategic advantage lay in the first strike should be retained by the United States. The theory of response, therefore, was that the moment a Soviet provocation crossed the threshold of tolerability, the full weight of American nuclear capability was to be unleashed on the entire spectrum of targets in the former U.S.S.R. The advocates of this doctrine insisted that it not only insured the optimum basis for accepting total war, but also contributed to the efficacy of deterrence. No aggressor, certain that total war would result, would risk overly taxing an admittedly unclear measure of tolerance.

When the policy of massive retaliation was espoused in the mid-1950s, the United States possessed the ability to destroy the military forces of the former U.S.S.R. with little likelihood of serious retaliatory damage. However, the subsequent rapid growth of Soviet strategic nuclear power undermined the assumptions of massive retaliation. The balance of terror meant that the threat of massive retaliation was to some degree reciprocal. Therefore, the United States could not massively retaliate in any general or large-scale war without risking enormous damage at home from Soviet strategic forces.

A second major implication of the balance of terror was that strategic nuclear forces were much less credible in the deterrence of local aggression. Critics of massive retaliation argued that the threat was not effective in deterring local or limited war because it was not believable. As a result of such criticisms, a more sophisticated position known generally as "flexible response" was developed. Its basic rationale was that the United States should not commit itself to an all-out immediate response to a challenge, but should allow for a "pause for decision" before taking action, and then respond only at a level adequate to neutralize the immediate threat. Responsibility for escalating the conflict would then rest upon the enemy, and the United States would be free from the danger of initiating an unnecessary total war.

U.S. policy, long officially committed to instantaneous response, has shifted to a version of flexible response, with a wide range of force capabilities that provide multiple response options. Although this shift was hailed as a basic doctrinal overhaul, the United States still retained the right to initiate nuclear warfare in the event of an unbearable but nonnuclear provocation from the former Soviet Union. A fully implemented SDI program, as discussed earlier, would require yet another revision of the U.S. policy, as it must be presumed that one or more nations would soon possess the capability to destroy some or all of the other nations' intercontinental ballistic missiles while in flight.

Limited Nuclear Options. Since the United States is strategically more interested in deterrence than in initiating war, it has sought to maintain great retaliatory capability and yet avoid increasing tension and the probability of war. However, if deterrence fails, it must be capable of successfully conducting and limiting the war that has been forced upon it. The development of new technologies embodied in the B-1 and Stealth bombers reflects the continuing U.S. emphasis upon maintaining a flexible response capability.

In the mid-1970s, the United States promulgated a new doctrine of limited nuclear options. In order to limit the chance of uncontrolled escalation if war occurred, the United States introduced flexibility into its nuclear employment planning by incorporating the capability to react in a more selective way against enemy military targets. Such a capability, it was argued, would enable the United States to tailor its strategic response to the nature of the provocation rather than being forced to choose between a massive response against enemy cities or doing nothing. Since there is great uncertainty about how a nuclear war might start, responses should be available to deal with a wide range of possibilities.

Opponents of limited nuclear options claim that as nuclear war becomes more manageable, it also becomes more likely. A policy of "limiting" a nuclear response might mean that the horrors of nuclear weapons would become obscured. The ability to destroy only military targets, sparing population centers, seems to lower the cost of nuclear war, and the psychological barriers inhibiting policymakers from employing nuclear weapons might be weakened. Further, leaders might believe that a limited response could be controlled, implying a degree of precision that belies the traditional notions of nuclear retaliation.

Nevertheless, as the major powers accepted nuclear parity, they also came to view additional weapons systems and upgraded capabilities in terms of war fighting and war termination, should deterrence fail. Although it is hardly a pleasant prospect, the fact remains that analysis of such an event requires deliberate and thoughtful treatment prior to its occurrence if the pressures for escalation to general nuclear war are to be avoided.

Defense and Survival. Estimates of the casualties that would be produced by a nuclear attack on an urbanized state are uncertain—since no one knows what would actually happen—but all are terribly high. Further uncertainty arises when the effect of nuclear war on the environment is considered. Everyone agrees that the impact on combatant nations and their neighbors would be catastrophic, though considerable doubt exists as to the degree of damage in the global environment that would result. "Nuclear winter" was a much-debated concept in the 1980s and has gained acceptance by many, including the U.S. Department of Defense.

According to nuclear winter theorists, a heavily fought nuclear conflict would release tremendous quantities of smoke and dust into the atmosphere, thus preventing the sun's rays from reaching the Earth. The lack of sunlight would create subfreezing temperatures over most, if not all, of the Earth's surface. The effect is threefold: the possible extinction of humankind; the potential destruction of the party initiating the first strike; and a threshold for such disaster that cannot be accurately measured.

Concern over the prohibitive cost in human life has resulted in numerous studies of civil defense prospects for national survival after a major blow, and these discussions cluster around two major points. One concerns the defensive measures civilian populations might take, including evacuation, shelter, permanent underground installations, and fallout and radiation protection. This entire subject suffers from a number of conceptual and practical difficulties: If the nuclear winter theorists are correct, the issue of civil defense is indeed quite hollow. Since there is no reliable experience on which to build, the extent to which the theorists and responsible officials are themselves persuaded of the utility of their measures is debatable, and public fatalism and widespread apathy reflect a profound belief that initiation of nuclear war is simply the end of everything. No major state has more than scratched the surface in the field of passive defense, although the former Soviet Union had a much more substantive program than did the United States. Soviet civil defense measures appeared to be predicated on the assumption that planning could substantially ameliorate the destruction of a nuclear exchange, but government response to such events as the Chernobyl nuclear plant disaster have tended to undermine the credibility of official Soviet approaches to disaster planning.

Theorists of recuperation also have little evidence to support their dogmas. Their usual criterion is the rapidity with which the attacked state might be expected to restore its productive plant to preattack levels, and estimates vary according to the optimism of analysts and their evaluations of their opponent's strategy. Only a few theorists have addressed the question of human response to a destructive attack and inquired into the extent to which battered survivors would perform public reconstruction after their private lives had been shattered. It is generally agreed that a nuclear onslaught would destroy political democracy and individual freedom, and this conclusion raises the question, "How would a population accustomed to an open society respond to the imposition of an authoritarian regime in the midst of smoking ruins and wholesale death?"

In summary, we would suggest that the size and destructive capability of modern nuclear arsenals have, at the conceptual level, muted discussion of defense, survival, and reconstruction. Until a credible defense system seems possible, initiation of total war will remain a risk of unpredictable dimension.

Doctrines of Limited War

We have scrutinized the doctrines advanced and developed by theorists of total war. However, since war continues at the nonnuclear level, it is obvious that the balance of terror and reciprocal deterrence have not eliminated warfare that is less than total. Limited war doctrines acknowledge the deterrent power of nuclear weapons but challenge their universal effectiveness. As discussed earlier, nuclear weapons may deter a nuclear attack, but they are not credible deterrents against relatively minor provocations. Such challenges can best be met by conventional responses, with the ensuing conflicts fought to a political decision without escalating to apocalyptic proportions.

What does the concept of "limited war" mean in a nuclear age? To say that all wars short of general nuclear war are limited may be accurate, but it is analytically unsatisfactory. What distinguishes limited war from total war is deliberate restraint, and this deliberate restraint can be thought of in terms of limitations—limitations on objectives and limitations on means.

When the power available to one or more contenders is physically limitless, there must be a degree of self-restraint imposed on political objectives. An attempt to obtain total victory might force the conflict across a threshold beyond which the costs to both contenders vastly exceed the potential gains to either. In limited war, therefore, the most extreme outcomes—total victory or total defeat—become for all practical purposes irrelevant. Contenders must be willing to tolerate an outcome neither had foreseen, in which the objectives of both are achieved imperfectly or not at all.

Conventional War. The most common formulation of the limited war position is cast in terms of "conventional war"—war fought with high-explosive rather than nuclear weapons. The division between conventional and nuclear war is blurred by "tactical" nuclear warheads, which are deployed on or near the battlefield in the form of artillery shells, bombs, and even by rucksack, and which often have yields in the high-explosive range.

Chemical and biological warfare adds its own element of terror. Recent conflicts in Afghanistan, Iran/Iraq, and Southeast Asia have all seen the use of chemical or biological weapons in conflicts of extended duration. The danger is that as these weapons are used more often, inhibitions to their use will decline. Chemical warfare was fully integrated into the former Soviet Land Forces battle order, and the United States, citing the obsolescence of its (allegedly) deterrent stockpile, began modernizing its chemical weapons in the late 1980s. However, at the same time the United States began promoting adherence to the Chemical Weapons Convention (CWC) signed on May 3, 1993, by 130 countries. This convention bans production, acquisition, testing, stockpiling, retention, and transfers of chemical weapons. The United States is a signatory of CWC and has already begun dismantling its chemical weapons. Nearly 150 countries are now signatories of CWC.

Debate persists over the advisability of employing any nuclear weapons, even in a limited role. Nevertheless, both the United States and the former Soviet Union maintained a nuclear capability for their frontline forces. While the permission for use would have come from higher up the chain of command, the desperate tactical situation of a local commander, coupled with a breakdown in communications, could certainly have led to early utilization of nuclear assets. Such battlefield isolation is expected to be the rule rather than the exception on the modern battlefield.

Most analysts agree that when the nuclear "firebreak" is crossed, the complex relationship among the stationing of the tactical systems, their ranges, their basic nature (aircraft, artillery, missile), and the strategies under which they are employed may lead to a rapid self-propelling jump to total war. Contrary arguments are possible, but the great uncertainties associated with the introduction of tactical nuclear weapons to the battlefield generally exclude them from the range of attractive military options in "limited war," and they have been relegated to a deterrent role (as in Europe) or to the status of additional help if deterrence fails.

The record of the Cold War period shows that the West could meet its opponents on the battlefield without the war's becoming total, as shown by the experiences of Korea, Vietnam, and other crises. However, since limited war means limiting political objectives, a war between nuclear powers can be kept at a subnuclear level only if each side recognizes the imperative requirements for self-restraint and limits its objectives accordingly. The lesson was learned in Korea and relearned (with variations) in Vietnam.

Revolutionary War. There have been frequent revolutionary wars during the latter part of the twentieth century. The causes of revolutionary war are varied but usually stem from economic, social, racial, religious, or colonial dissatisfactions. Since nuclear deterrence has little impact on the initiation and prosecution of revolutionary war, such wars may become the most prevalent setting for the use of military force as we enter the twenty-first century.

The U.S. involvement in Vietnam focused attention on the nature of revolutionary conflict and the role of military force in a counterrevolutionary environment. As a form of strategy, counterinsurgency is applicable only in those special situations where the basic ingredients are present: a population alienated from its government and gripped by widespread disaffection, and a government that lacks energy and efficiency in dealing with both the guerrilla threat and the social, economic, and political conditions that spawned the revolution in the first place. It is of limited relevance to those states, including most leaders of the Western bloc, whose interest lies less in overturning governments and promoting revolution than in stabilizing and harmonizing relationships. Counterrevolutionary activity—strategically a doctrine of defense rather than attack—has an unquestionable military dimension, but just as the revolution has its roots in social unrest, so campaigns against guerrillas would more profitably be based on social reform and would employ military operations only as a secondary tool.

The failure of U.S. policy in Vietnam was based, in part, on the misconception that the war could be prosecuted using a strategy of limited war wherein the application of military force would bring the Vietcong and North Vietnamese to negotiate a tolerable outcome. American objectives, limited from the start, became increasingly more limited under domestic and international pressure, whereas the objectives of the revolutionaries were total—reunification of all Vietnam under the leadership of the North. However, it remains doubtful that even unlimited application of military force by the United States would have achieved the long-range goals pursued. Further, policymakers were convinced that U.S. strength and power would prevail as it had in World War II, the most formative experience of their lives. This mistaken premise inhibited the proper assessment of information because the negative assessments of American progress made by informed advisers in the field were passed over in favor of the positive evaluations produced by less-informed observers sent to Southeast Asia on short "fact-finding tours."

THE ARMS RACE AND ARMS CONTROL

With the logic of military action so open to question under contemporary conditions, it is not surprising that states have been pursuing the issue of securing some release from the grim pressure of potential destruction. Two interacting political trends have accompanied the conceptual discussion of military matters since the dawn of the nuclear era. The major military powers embarked on a massive arms race conducted primarily in the categories of new weapons and delivery systems. At the same time, significant efforts have been made to discover workable formulas for arms reduction, arms control, and ultimately, disarmament. These enterprises represent attempts by governments to develop a larger margin of relative security in a world grown more dangerous.

The Arms Race

The arms race between the Soviet bloc and the Western bloc during the Cold War era was as much a technical as a military contest, and though it is now decelerating, many of its dynamics are still in operation despite changes in the former Soviet Union and Eastern Europe. At its height every state involved sought advances in quality as well as quantity of weapons. The major categories of effort have included the increase in explosive "yield" of large nuclear bombs, the miniaturization of nuclear warheads for tactical purposes, the improvement of delivery systems—primarily in longer-range and more accurate missiles—and the development of multiple independently targetable reentry vehicles (MIRVs).

The rationale of that, or any other, arms race is devastatingly simple. Although military theorists questioned whether either side could ever gain a meaningful advantage, neither dared to relax its effort lest the other succeed in achieving a technological and military breakthrough. Each new move brought its inevitable countermove, which in turn triggered another step, and so on. In addition, every new move that made weapons more effective and war more horrible also augmented the deterrent effect of military power. As we have argued, a case has frequently been made for the arms race as a force for peace, in that it progressively narrowed the range of military action enjoyed by states.

Yet others have argued that there was also a point of vanishing returns. When each side developed a truly finite deterrent (possessing the capacity to destroy the other completely), any further refinement could be seen as merely "conspicuous consumption." The stakes became no more than prestige, with faint possibility of achieving any meaningful psychological advantage over the other contestant. However, as in the antiballistic missile (ABM) debate, it occasionally appeared plausible that a technological advance by one side could upset the precarious balance. Specifically it seemed that one major power, the former Soviet Union, could so degrade the assured destruction capability of the other that mutual deterrence would be eroded to the point of dangerous instability. Part of the debate revolved around which measures to take—offensive or defensive—if the Soviet ABM was indeed effective. It was apparently technologically feasible to overwhelm the ABM offensively (through pure saturation and sophisticated tactics), possibly restoring the deterrent balance, but at the great additional cost always attending massive increases in total weapons systems. This grim prospect of a costly upward arms spiral with no prospective increase in security convinced the major powers that they should explore new ways to limit the arms race.

Strategic Arms Limitation

In May 1972, after some thirty months of negotiation, the first significant agreement on levels of nuclear armament was finalized by the United States and the former Soviet Union in the form of a Strategic Arms Limitation Agreement containing an ABM Treaty and an Interim Agreement on offensive weapons.

The ABM Treaty, the tenure of which is indefinite, limited each signatory to the development of 200 of its ABMs in two equal fields. The treaty also established a number of prohibitions against qualitative improvements in ABM capabilities by banning space- and sea-based systems. In a 1974 amendment to the ABM Treaty, the United States and the former Soviet Union agreed to limit ABM deployment to 100 missiles in one site. In 1976 the United States closed its operative site, while the former Soviet Union continued to maintain a limited ABM capability around Moscow.

The Interim Agreement on the Limitation of Strategic Arms was an attempt to freeze certain aspects of the offensive weapons competition between the United States and the former U.S.S.R. for a five-year period. The Interim Agreement dealt with intercontinental ballistic missiles (ICBMs) and submarine-launched ballistic missiles (SLBMs). It did not deal with manned bombers, tactical nuclear weapons, or intermediate-range missiles. A protocol to the Interim Agreement translated certain provisions of the document into concrete figures, setting numerical limits on numbers of ICBMs and SLBMs. Although the Interim Agreement expired in October 1977, both sides pledged to abide by its provisions pending the outcome of negotiations for a second Strategic Arms Limitation Talks (SALT II) accord. An agreement "in principle" was signed at Vladivostok in 1974, and the two sides continued trying to reach agreement to limit the numbers of all offensive strategic nuclear weapons and delivery vehicles.

Negotiations to reduce arms were halted after the Soviet invasion of Afghanistan in 1979, and the U.S. Congress refused to ratify the completed SALT II agreement, although both nations continued to abide by its provisions. Serious negotiation did not get under way again until the mid-1980s with the Strategic Arms Reduction Talks (START) and the Intermediate Nuclear Forces (INF) accord reached in 1987.

The Future of Arms Control

A dismal page in the history of world politics between 1945 and 1963 was the utter failure of any attempts to reach an agreement on arms reduction or arms control. All the abortive projects, different only in detail, shared the same fate. Plans were advanced for elimination of nuclear weapons, reduction of conventional armaments, cessation of nuclear testing, and various inspection schemes to reduce the probability of cheating or surprise attack. All came to inglorious ends, and the arms race appeared to have been accepted by the major powers as unavoidable and necessary for the security of their respective nations. Yet both East and West had embraced the principle that general and complete disarmament, except for international security forces, was the goal for which all must strive. Progress was halted, not on matters of principle, but on the nature and sequence of steps to be taken to achieve the eventual end. Each side had an initial sine qua non on which it insisted in full knowledge that the other would reject it: The former U.S.S.R. demanded nuclear parity and abolition of nuclear weapons by treaty before it would consider any implementing steps, while the United States demanded full acceptance of a "control and inspection" system as a prerequisite to any consideration of the substance of disarmament. No negotiations were able to pass over this initial hurdle, and all broke off in mutual recriminations. The Soviets claimed that U.S. concern with inspection was a cloak for espionage, while the United States found the Soviet attempt to forbid use of nuclear weapons in war a sinister plot to undermine American security. With the advent of Soviet nuclear weapons parity and the celebrated political "détente," both sides were able to overlook prior objections and initiate some encouraging steps toward arms control accommodation. These steps include the Nuclear Test Ban Treaty (1963), a treaty barring the interjection of nuclear weapons into outer space, signed in 1966; the Nuclear Nonproliferation Treaty of 1968; the Sea Bed Treaty of 1972, which prohibits weapons on the ocean floor; the Threshold Test Ban Treaty (1974), limiting the size of nuclear explosions to 150 kilotons; and the SALT I Agreement, discussed earlier.

Arms control negotiations conducted in 1978 included the efforts for a follow-up on the Strategic Arms Limitation Agreement, Mutual and Balanced Force Reduction talks designed to reduce force levels in Central Europe, attempts to limit the level of military presence in the Indian Ocean, and preliminary consultations on a comprehensive test ban agreement to eliminate all nuclear explosions, for both military and peaceful purposes.

The future of arms control holds great promise and numerous challenges. A thaw in the late 1980s in relations between the United States and former Soviet Union allowed initiatives to be undertaken that were surprising in scope and depth. An agreement was signed, on intermediate-range nuclear force (INF) in 1987. INF covered intermediate- and short-range ballistic missile and ground-launched cruise missiles. In 1991, the START Treaty limited the United States and the former Soviet Union to 6,000 accountable warheads on 1,600 strategic offensive delivery vehicles. The START II Treaty, which the United States and Russia signed on January 3, 1993, permits each nation to deploy, at most, 3,500 ballistic missile warheads and heavy bomber weapons on their strategic offensive nuclear forces. This represents a reduction by more than two thirds when compared with the forces the United States and the former Soviet Union had deployed in 1990, before they signed the original 1991 START Treaty.

The lengthening list of arms control agreements negotiations, however heartening, does not mean that the threat of nuclear war has been eliminated. Technological advances in weapons systems have multiplied the destructive power of each superpower's nuclear arsenal even as agreements designed to limit them have been instituted. States do not sign arms control agreements for altruistic or humanitarian purposes; they must serve the national interest. However, such agreements can reduce the probability of war by reducing tensions or limiting the levels of armaments. They will serve as a valuable instrument in developing an environment in which the threat of nuclear destruction is not the preeminent fact of international life and in moving toward the eventual demise of the "balance of terror."

The Role of Political Decision

Disarmament, like the arms race, is much more a political than a military and technical question. In the absence of broad, meaningful participation by the majority of the citizens of all countries—but most importantly the great powers—in the formation of security policy, achieving disarmament depends to a large extent upon the actions of small decision-making élites. Their motivations encompass economic, ideological, and strategic factors. Billions of dollars are invested in perpetuating arms production, and enormous profits are derived from arms research and arms purchases. Large profits enable self-interested parties to command political influence disproportionate to their numbers. For instance, U.S. weapons contractors insured that each state or congressional district participated in each major contract, and thus stood to lose jobs should it be canceled. In the absence of national economic conversion planning to anticipate and ameliorate such potential disruptions, the entire economy of the nation seemed to be held hostage to the continuing arms race.

In the recent past, the political preconceptions each side brought to the analysis of issues of arms control compounded the difficulty in reaching agreement about disarmament. Ideological "we're right/they're wrong" attitudes and strategic thinking, careful or not so careful, as well as economic considerations and interests, contributed to these preconceptions. So long as both camps felt that their security was better served by a continuing arms race, disarmament remained an ephemeral goal. So long as both preferred the great but familiar risks of a possible conflict to the unknown dangers of living under military wraps in an untried and possibly entrapping control system, there was not enough appeal in the new to justify abandonment of the old. So long as the shadow of the Cold War persisted and was used as a framework for policy, worn out though it eventually became, arms reduction was of limited political value to all but the most visionary and brave political leaders.

In the new context of international politics, however, a "Cold War" arsenal of arms is increasingly perceived as too expensive and of limited utility. Security is now understood in terms of balances—goals that do not require the same numbers of nuclear warheads and intercontinental delivery systems. Thus arms control and disarmament have become important tools of foreign policy. These developments are reflected, for instance, in the efforts of Ukraine, a Soviet-successor state that "inherited" strategic weapons, to trade the elimination of these weapons for Western security guarantees and economic aid.

RECOMMENDED READINGS

ARON, RAYMOND. *On War.* New York: Norton, 1968.

BONDURANT, JOAN. *The Conquest of Violence: The Gandhian Philosophy of Conflict.* Rev. ed. Berkeley: University of California Press, 1965.

CLAUSEWITZ, KARL VON. *On War.* Princeton, NJ: Princeton University Press, 1976.

GEORGE, ALEXANDER L., ed. *Avoiding War: Problems of Crisis Management.* Boulder, CO: Westview Press, 1991.

HAMPSON, FEN OSLER. *The Allies and Arms Control.* Baltimore: Johns Hopkins University Press, 1992.

KLARE, MICHAEL T. *American Arms Supermarket.* Austin: University of Texas Press, 1984.

LESHAN, LAWRENCE L. *The Psychology of War: Comprehending Its Mystique and Its Madness.* Chicago: Noble Press, 1992.

NORTH, ROBERT C. *War, Peace, Survival: Global Politics and Conceptual Synthesis.* Boulder, CO: Westview Press, 1990.

RAMBERG, BENNET. *Arms Control Without Negotiation: From the Cold War to the New World Order.* Boulder, CO: Lynne Rienner, 1993.

RAPAPORT, ANATOL. *The Origins of Violence.* New York: Paragon House, 1989.

REARDON, BETTY. *Sexism and the War System.* New York: Teachers College Press, 1985.

ROTBERG, ROBERT I., and THEODORE K. RABB, eds. *The Origins and Prevention of Major Wars.* New York: Cambridge University Press, 1989.

STOESSINGER, JOHN G. *Why Nations Go to War.* New York: St. Martin's Press, 1974.

TAR, DAVID W. *Nuclear Deterrence and International Security: Alternative Nuclear Regimes.* New York: Longman, 1992.

WALTZ, KENNETH N. *Man, the State, and War: A Theoretical Analysis.* New York: Columbia University Press, 1959.

WITTNER, LAWRENCE S. *The Struggle Against the Bomb.* Stanford, CA: Stanford University Press, 1993.

WRIGHT, QUINCY. *A Study of War.* 2nd ed. Chicago: University of Chicago Press, 1965.

ZIEGLER, DAVID W. *War, Peace and International Politics.* 6th ed. New York: HarperCollins, 1993.

Chapter 10

THE ROLE OF BELIEF SYSTEMS: IDEOLOGY, NATIONALISM, AND RELIGIOUS FUNDAMENTALISM

One of the features of contemporary world politics that distinguishes it from the "classic" pattern of an earlier era is the manipulation of mass beliefs and popular ideas by decision makers. The impact of mass movements of vast size and compelling force has diluted the once-exclusive control of foreign policy exercised by highly skilled élites. Mass as well as individual ways of thinking have been targeted for manipulation by both domestic and foreign agencies.

THE NATURE OF IDEOLOGY

The term *ideology* was initially used when French revolutionaries wanted France to be governed by the principles of the French Revolution. Today, an ideology may be defined as a self-contained and self-justifying belief system that incorporates an overall worldview and provides a basis for explaining reality in general and, specifically, social experience. Beginning with certain postulates about the nature and role of the individual, an ideology develops from these a theory of human history, a moral code, a sense of mission, and a program for action. All ideologies purport to embody absolute truth, reinforced with certain supernatural (or superhuman) justification. Adherence to the system is thus both a rational and a moral act, and disagreement is not only an error but something like a sin.

Ideologies are not new in world politics. Every system of government and every national group has at some time found it expedient to ground its international conduct on what it conceived as eternal truth. But the mass movement, defined here as an ideology with implications of social action that gathers sufficient adherents to become a real force, is a more contemporary political phenomenon. Ideological formulations of issues have colored the bulk of the modern world's confrontations within and between states.

An ideological approach to world political problems displays certain marked characteristics. Ideology leads inescapably to the formulation of problems in moral terms. An international dispute thus becomes a clash between good and evil with the stakes never less than absolute vindication or total defeat. Ideological controversy (which is inevitable in any contact between states embodying total belief systems) is not susceptible to compromise or accommodation: No ideology permits bargaining with evil. Furthermore, ideologically-oriented policy can never "succeed" in the sense that strategic calculations can be crowned with success. States cannot kill ideas, only people; wiping out a population in no way destroys their unpopular beliefs.

Ideology and Contemporary World Politics

In a manner unknown to history since the great shocks of the Renaissance, the Reformation, and the Industrial Revolution washed away the underpinnings of the unified society of the Middle Ages, individuals have turned to all-encompassing belief systems to explain reality. In contrast to the rational person who was the ideal of the eighteenth century and the optimistic person who characterized the nineteenth, the present century has had at its center the "true believer." Individuals adrift in a universe that grows more difficult to comprehend and cope with every day have frequently found relief and comfort in systematic, comprehensive systems of belief.

This tendency, running through the entire fabric of our social life, is sharply reinforced in matters concerning world politics. The world has grown uncomfortably smaller, and national groups everywhere have been wrenched from a cultural isolation that had endured in some cases for centuries. However, the great increase in the number of global problems demanding solution has been accompanied at times by a decrease in the apparent probability of their solution. Faced with an agonizing dilemma of impossible choices, entire societies have fled from the reality of coexistence (in its literal sense) to the refuge of an ideological utopia. As a result, tension, danger, and potential explosiveness in international politics have at times risen to levels that have no parallel in history.

Ideology seems to thrive in an environment of social stress, particularly the malaise generated by limited resources and choices for action; whereas pragmatism, in a sense the opposite of ideology, is more often characteristic of societies enjoying greater material abundance. Simply put, when life is difficult, people seek an explanation for their hardship, and, when life is easy, they are content to leave well enough alone. This generalization accounts, to some extent, for the popularity of a variety of radical ideologies in the poorer states of the Global South. To the extent that richer societies have formulated and embraced belief systems, these systems have justified and legitimized their control of power and wealth. For example, Max Weber, the German sociologist, studied the simultaneous rise of Protestantism and capitalism in the Western world and found that the two systems of thought and action mutually reinforced each other.

Because ideologies frequently represent divergent material positions, they have often clashed. This tendency to conflict is further reinforced by the individual's self-righteous protection of his/her ideology, a response that arises from the key symbolic and psychological role ideology can come to play in personal and collective life. Any threat to the ideology may be taken as a direct attack on personal identity and lifestyle. Such identification can be so complete that the death of an ideology is perceived, and felt, by some as the death of self.

Often beginning modestly, as they grow in influence most ideologies have come to claim for themselves universal truth. Also, many have peaked quickly and become outmoded rapidly, going through stages of messianism, corruption, misuse, and eventually—as circumstances change—meaninglessness. In fact, as exemplified by the contemporary evolution toward democracy and capitalism in formerly communist Eastern European states, ideologies may foster the emergence of their own antithesis.

Indeed, the role of ideology in both rich and poor societies is currently undergoing change. Although it is still too soon to make any detailed predictions, we would suggest that the ideological conflicts that may arise in the coming decades are likely to be shaped by the commodities and conditions that will be prized and sought after—that is, such things as food, energy, technology, liberty, and quality of lifestyle. There are, for instance, already clearly discernible ideological tensions between those who want to protect and preserve our natural environment and those who wish to exploit resources in the name of growth: two groups divided by very different basic values and conceptions of social welfare. Finally, one should bear in mind that though some ideologies may die, from their ashes new ones may be born, and others may adapt, mutate, or otherwise change to meet the demands of a changing international system.

Ideology and Foreign Policy

The role of ideology in world politics—how ideology affects foreign policy and the resulting implications for international relations—has become an increasingly important subject. This issue has been magnified by the challenge of recent ideological formulations of world politics.

Ideology has helped focus foreign policy by telling us who our enemies are and why they are our enemies. From this beginning, we then use familiar formulations such as "The friend of my enemy is my enemy" and "The enemy of my enemy is my friend (perhaps)." Though at times confusing in application, in theory a prevalent ideology is supposed to identify states, nations, and peoples as friend or foe.

Though enemy formulations may seem simplistic when talked about in such abstract terms, one should not underestimate their power. Such seminal ideas of friend and foe are incorporated at a very early stage in the process of policy development—a stage when the most basic goals and interests are defined. An example may be as straightforward as a great power deciding it is in its interest for key Global South nations to have regimes more friendly to itself than to its main rival.

Enemy identifications derived from a dominant ideology may come to be accepted on faith, and such acceptance would hinder a rational ongoing assessment of national interest. Unquestioning faith, in itself, helps to explain why so much careful policy planning backfires. Ideology can blind policymakers to both certain aspects of a situation and to the real interest at stake.

What has been described so far is perhaps the worst-case scenario for the effect of ideology upon foreign policy, though it unquestionably prevailed from time to time during the Cold War. Its day seems to be waning as we distance ourselves in time from the midcentury events that gave rise to that conflict. Ideology may not affect policy at such a fundamental level on all issues. There are certain levels of action and decision on which either ideology or realism is predominant, and between these two extremes some sort of balance may be achieved. We can say that, although ideologically blinded policymakers may think they are acting rationally, ideology has the potential to make seemingly realistic appraisals grossly inaccurate, for it colors the beginning assumptions from which event interpretations and policy decisions are developed.

How may we assess the extent to which ideology conditions foreign policy decisions? First, we would suggest that in making this determination one should put more faith in what a state does than in what its spokespersons say. That is, one can better infer a state's intent from a series of actions related to an issue or situation than from a series of statements, because verbal consistency does not necessarily imply consistency in action.

The conflict is therefore between the systematic worldview imposed by an ideological approach to action and the uneven, incomplete, and paradoxical fashion in which the real world impinges upon a state. Ideology and national interest both have their roots in a system of values, but they differ in how they dictate action. Ideological formulations make generous use of concepts of inevitability or impossibility and lead to one-dimensional foreign policy thinking. A pragmatic national interest is fixed only in its (possibly utopian) view of the future, and may be quite flexible in its intermediate goals and objectives and in the tactics adopted for their achievement.

When ideology becomes the basis for formulating national interest and long-range goals, a successful foreign policy may be possible if these aspirations are deeply rooted in the social dynamic of a people and if the government is adept at tactics. But if ideology intrudes excessively into situational analysis and state action is made dependent on imperatives of belief, statecraft in the classic sense is largely impossible.

IDEOLOGY, MYTH, AND REALITY

In many societies, myths help individuals cope with the realities in social life and make those realities comprehensible. By myths we mean symbolic explanations that endow individual and collective actions with broader, often transcendent meaning. The cosmologies of most traditional societies, for instance, consist of sets of mythic narratives that explain how archetypal figures, natural and supernatural, brought the experienced universe into being.

We would suggest that, though it is not often discussed in such terms, political society is invariably validated by myth. Even such theorists as Hobbes and Locke, who appeal to reason for a basis of political society, posit such notions as "rational man" and "natural right," the existence of which are taken for granted, or on faith. Such myths are "reality" organizers; they provide common cultural identity and a sense of history and roots, and in so doing are indispensable. To act, individually or collectively, we must believe in something.

Successful political action demands a convincing ideology, but the issue is not whether ideology is only predicated upon myth, nor whether myth and reality are identical. Society and consciousness are always changing, and ideas and images can only be real in a given historical context. The myth of Pegasus had an operational reality in the classical Golden Age, but not in a modern positivist universe. Beauty is what is considered beautiful at a particular time; heroes have done what is heroic in the context of a particular culture.

However, in a changing world the subjective ground of myths is in flux, and the myths themselves may become outmoded and eventually be discarded. As myths become obsolete, so do the structures they support. We are experiencing this process today as formerly powerful symbols are rejected and more and more peoples find themselves searching for new explanations of their social experience and new directions for collective action.

We would suggest that contemporary international political life requires a powerful, new, accessible myth to give individual and social life meaning in the "global village." Furthermore, if the rise and fall of past civilizations are at all instructive, such a myth to be effective must rekindle a sense of transcendence, a belief in the ultimate meaning of human experience in an awe-inspiring and mysterious universe. Yet the destructive dynamics of enemization might be revived by any new myth, and the more deeply it is felt, the more real is such a danger. Herein lies the challenge and difficulty for effective policy making, because politics without some element of myth is empty and incapable of inspiring collective effort, while the wrong myth can unleash untold destruction in our age of high technology.

IDEOLOGY IN WORLD POLITICS: THE COLD WAR

The post–World War II era marked a challenge to the traditional criteria and concepts of the classic international system. New ideas appeared to compete with the time-honored principles of statecraft. Their advocates sought, with varying success, to apply them in a nontraditional world. We may view these as ideologies, each seeking an appropriately changed situation in which to be applied.

By 1950, three such ideologies had found more or less clear expression, and their subsequent interplay gave the postwar world its characteristic form. Since all ideologies other than simple nihilism incorporate a utopian vision of perfect order, these doctrines may be initially compared in terms of the ideal each considered itself to be serving.

The first was the worldview of communism. Its utopian vision was of a classless and therefore stateless society where individuals would live in relatively unfettered community. It emphasized protection of existing communist beachheads in the world and, at a somewhat lower priority level, extension of communist influence by persuasion, subversion, and war. Purporting to be "scientific," its perfect world order was believed to be attainable, feasible, and inevitable.

The second great utopia was projected by the United States. American doctrine envisaged a world organized under law into a peaceful and harmonious society of states, where individual and group obligation to humankind placed limits on the freedom of states—a translation into world political terms of the familiar domestic political outlook of Americans. One important effect of such developments was to be the enrichment of Americans in the marketplace of the world, and the maintenance of the standard of living to which Americans had become accustomed, whatever the consequences (within some limits) for the rest of the world. Committed ideologically to free will and personal responsibility for action, the United States could not predict the inevitable realization of its dream, only its possibility.

The final ideology was the nonalignment of the anticolonial world, eventually given many specific forms but first verbalized clearly by independent India. Its utopia was a world in which distinctions among states were downplayed in favor of global cooperative efforts to alleviate the material misery of the human race. In practice, this belief system meant estrangement from the East-West agenda of world affairs and emphasis on issues of development, race, and cultural diversity in the name of a higher morality.

From each of these utopian postures was derived a set of policy goals to be pursued by a believing state compelled to exist in a nonideal world. To communists these goals included prevention of any hostile coalition strong enough to menace existing communist systems and preservation of sufficient instability and tension in the noncommunist world to permit continued expansion of communist power. For Americans the requirements included adequate stability in the world to give existing mechanisms of international organization a chance to survive and grow, while at the same time preserving the uniquely favorable position enjoyed by the United States. Nonalignment requirements were somewhat more numerous, beginning with the simple idea of early liquidation of colonialism and extending to establishment of inhibitions and limitations on all major states by international mechanisms. The nonaligned wished "a plague on both your houses" to the superpowers, but generalized the curse to include all aspirants to high status and a broad sphere of power in the global system. Such an attitude did not impede them from, at times, playing the superpowers against each other in an effort to extract the maximum amount of foreign aid.

Out of the clash of these requirements came the subject matter of world politics from 1945 to the end of the 1980s. The Cold War itself, especially in its acute phase, brought the minimum demands of the United States and the former Soviet Union into close and often irreconcilable juxtaposition.

The Former Soviet Approach to the World: A Form of Communism

The former Soviet Union in the aftermath of the August 1991 coup has disintegrated into the Commonwealth of Independent States (CIS). One consequence of this momentous event appears to be the end of communism as a guiding ideology for the peoples (once) grouped in this vast federation. Such cloture provides a unique vantage point from which to assess the influence of the former Soviet version of this ideology on the international system.

The former Soviet Union, thanks to its official ideology and one-sided propaganda attack on domestic consensus, had for seventy-four years, 1917–1991, a clear and comprehensive orientation to both domestic politics and international relations. Marxism and its later derivations professed to unlock the riddle of history and to enable true believers to understand the basic nature of world politics.

During this period, the former Soviet Union viewed itself as a revolutionary power committed to the destruction of existing institutions and patterns and their replacement by an entirely new order. Such an approach necessitated the assumption that all existing international arrangements were inherently temporary (except those already under Soviet control) and subject to change by Soviet initiatives. Any understanding or agreement with noncommunist powers was by definition tentative and designed only to serve a longer-range strategic purpose. Conflict was to be protracted indefinitely until victory crowned the entire effort and utopia became a fact. Such an outlook was, according to our previous definition, revisionist in the extreme.

However, a distinct evolution can be traced in the Soviet attitude. Beginning from a position of a great psychic and physical insecurity, Kremlin leadership felt obliged to strike a continuously militant pose and to fight with words battles they were incapable of prosecuting in action. As the processes of history subtly modified the nature and expanded the dimensions of the world role played by Moscow, and as the Kremlin itself gained in self-confidence and prestige, the necessity for extreme positions and language gradually diminished. Moscow's interest in preaching the message of revolution diminished in direct proportion to its increasing stake in preserving the existing order. Far from persisting as a revolutionary and radical force in world affairs, Soviet policy became more like the nineteenth-century ideal of a great power functioning within the European concert; that is, the former Soviet Union gradually came to resemble a status quo power in more and more aspects of its foreign policy.

More recently, prior to the collapse of the Soviet system, one witnessed a tremendous ferment and change in the approach of the former Soviet Union to the world. One way of viewing Soviet foreign policy from 1985, the beginning of Mikhail Gorbachev's *glasnost* and *perestroika,* until its collapse in 1991, is that the former Soviet Union was the first superpower to perceive and attempt to take advantage of a fundamental shift in security needs that makes economic considerations more important, past a minimal level of security, than military ones. Though the former Soviet Union may have been singularly poorly equipped to cope with these new conditions, President Gorbachev was at least perceptive enough to realize that the domestic and international priorities of Joseph Stalin and Leonid Brezhnev would not see the Soviet people into the twenty-first century.

The U.S. Approach to the World: A Form of Democracy

The U.S. approach to the world is the result of a peculiar mixture of vigorous tradition and accidental historical circumstance. There are three important elements that contribute to the contemporary orientation of the United States to international politics: (1) the traditional American outlook on international relations; (2) the new sense of national importance and mission that came with victory in World War II and the role of leadership that the country was forced to play in its aftermath; and (3) an increasingly realistic approach to the international political environment, derived from accumulated experience. Each makes its own contribution to the conceptual framework of American foreign policy.

American culture portrays world politics as taking place within a universal system and order governed by and amenable to both logic and morality. Individuals who operate the controls of government are rational and moral creatures; the purpose of world politics is advancement of the common interests of humankind, to be achieved through cooperative action by all states and the solution of "problems" as they arise. Peace marked by amicable resolution of differences and a steady stream of formal (i.e., legal) agreements on particular issues is the normal condition of the world. War is abnormal, the result of the unpredictable appearance of individuals or groups who insist upon immoral and illegal behavior. As an abnormal system, war is outside world politics proper. The task of the state caught in a war is to end it as soon as possible, punish those responsible, and "get back to business" with minimum loss of time.

Although never put so badly as we have summarized it here, this ideal has animated American action for a century and a half. This was the image of utopia—strengthened by institutions for both affirmative cooperative behavior and the punishment of evildoers—for which the Wilsonians fought so hard after World War I. It still affects the conceptual and the operational atmosphere in which American policy is decided, and it remains in some form as a recognizable key ingredient in the American self-image. Any more elaborate or sophisticated strategic interpretations must build upon these principles if their advocates wish them to gain public acceptance and support.

The second element in the American worldview is the new sense of historical importance with which the postwar generation has been forced to come to terms. Through World War II, Americans were permitted by history and their own code to conceive of themselves as virtually nonparticipating observers of the world political process, dealing with an intrinsically corrupt system at arm's length and trapped into direct involvement only on widely separated occasions. The country's normal world mission was to act as a moral example. When events conspired to draw the United States into the thick of battle, the national purpose was to set things right, to provide others with a more reliable guide to future action by institutional change, and then to retire gracefully to a remote observation of the eccentricities of world politics. Yet, the policy and security apparatus of the nation was often not prepared to follow in its actions and methods those moral precepts that the majority of American citizens believed ought to be central to their nation's foreign policy.

Much of this philosophy was swept away by World War II, the birth of the nuclear age, and the beginning of the Cold War. Once the most reluctant of dragons, the United States moved within a relatively few months between mid-1947 and early 1949 into complete acceptance of a starring role. The phrase "responsibilities of world leadership" fell more often from American lips, and with each hearing became more palatable. Today Americans enjoy their key position as one of the arbiters of humankind's fate, even though they may occasionally betray a nostalgic yearning for the days of happy isolation. The thought that some portion of the Earth for which the United States has assumed primary responsibility—such as Western Europe—might wish to throw off U.S. sponsorship and strike out on its own causes serious tremors in American political and strategic circles.

Finally, the gradually increasing realism of American thinking about world affairs should be mentioned. What we have called the American outlook on international relations was, at least until World War II, accepted less as a utopian dream than as a serious description of world politics, an illusion that had survived almost undisturbed all the shocks of the twentieth century until 1939. The searing experience of World War II, however, began the eye-opening process that was further reinforced by the ensuing Cold War.

Let us indicate briefly the major elements in the new realism. First, the United States is less inclined at the end of the twentieth century than it was in the 1950s to seek absolute solutions to problems, or even to formulate issues in simple black-and-white terms. Second, Americans now appreciate the irrelevance (or at least the frequent inapplicability) of private morality, ideologically conceived, to the behavior of states. Third, there is reduced acceptance in U.S. policy of the constant alternation of crisis and relaxation and a correspondingly greater search for a significant dimension of positive and affirmative action. Finally, U.S. policymakers speak less about the general good of humankind and more explicitly about the promotion of a specifically American interest.

These disparate elements combine to produce a reasonably clear and workable worldview for the use of U.S. strategists. The United States now conceives of the international system as unstable but capable of being stabilized, as disorderly but capable of order, and as potentially warlike but capable of being structured on a continuing basis of peace. The image of the world adopted by the United States thus contains its own built-in action imperatives: The United States is obliged to seek solutions to global problems that impinge on the pursuit of U.S. interests.

The policy of the United States basically promotes the creation of a peaceful, orderly, and stable world—a translation into operational terms of the prevailing national myth. Although popular treatments of the subject emphasize that achievement of U.S. ends would benefit the entire human race, in reality the motivations underlying such a formula are the most practical American strategists can discover. A world such as this would be one in which U.S. security risks were reduced almost to the vanishing point, U.S. economic and status-prestige concerns received full satisfaction, and the final vindication of American doctrines about the individual and society would be complete.

For Americans, the most salient consequence of the end of the Cold War and Russia's—and communism's—decline has been that it leaves the United States without a compass to guide its foreign policy or, as critics might put it, "a foil to justify American continued meddling in other people's affairs." It has also left concerned American citizens, as well as politicians, without an established framework to judge the wisdom (or lack of wisdom) of U.S. actions in world politics.

The Global South Approach to the World

Global South approaches are diverse in form, and they have certainly not offered a uniform blueprint for world reform or revolution. Most frequently they have been nationalistic, antihierarchic, and socialist in orientation. Global South nationalism (discussed in more detail in the next section), ranging in content from tribal factionalism to pan-Africanism to pan-Arabism to Islamic fundamentalism, has been used as a means of recapturing past glories or coping with the immediate and future problems of building modern societies. It has often sought to demonstrate that emerging countries of the Global South could and would take their rightful places in the world, despite the old Western claim that they are incapable of doing so, and would overcome their perceived inferiority in the white-dominated Western world. This imposed inferiority has left a deep emotional scar, causing Global South leaders repeatedly to assert their nationalism in order to prove their viability and dignity.

In their colonial past, many of the new states were denied racial equality and national political freedom. Rebellion against this enforced inferiority and the drive for acceptance and racial equality developed into revolutionary urging.

Nonwhite, non-Western, and non-Establishment characteristics were proclaimed to be the framework of a unique personality of which its possessors should be proud. What began as an attempt to give the Global South a sense of personal worth and self-respect rapidly changed into a reaction to white and Western domination that could easily be distorted into Global South (counter)racism.

Proceeding from the premise that equated Establishment-West-white supremacy and capitalism, many Global South leaders have seen these interests continuing in a postindependence attempt to exert de facto political control by economic means. They saw the independence and progress of their new states threatened by covert foreign economic domination, which was denounced as the direct cause of the immediate failures of the postindependence period.

The Global South's universal predicament is mass poverty. A lack of appropriate skills and managerial talents, inordinate income differentials, and the desire to overcome a colonial self-image are the intertwined problems of these societies, exacerbated by oppressive foreign debt burdens and excessive military establishments. Many of their leaders believed that socialism was the only answer to the need for a moral and just social order. Human dignity, social justice, and equality of opportunity are promoted as the highest social values.

The Global South views the global system differently than does both Western democracy and communism. Throughout their modern history, many of the new states have been victims of great-power rivalries. The disparate strands of their foreign policies were derived from several basic assumptions: Neocolonialism or neo-imperialism posed the principal threat to their existence; American-Soviet confrontation was merely a struggle for power and domination of smaller states; and the bipolar international system did not accommodate their interests and objectives.

From these basic attitudes, the countries of the Global South have come to place great stress on international and regional organizations. They feel that the UN and other organizations should exert a strong influence in settling international disputes, even among great powers. International organizations became vehicles for increasing the political power and influence of traditionally insignificant states, which were attempting literally to force the great powers to pay them heed.

As stated earlier, the countries of the Global South adopted a strategy of nonalignment in an attempt to transcend the dominant ideological split. As translated from precept to practice, nonalignment was designed to serve specific functions—to reconcile national sovereignty and the requirements of security; to harmonize political independence and economic dependence; to maintain and enhance national solidarity; to maximize foreign policy alternatives and power in world politics. Nonalignment played another role for these states, one that is derived from domestic political considerations. It acted as a rallying point to mobilize widespread support behind governmental actions vis-à-vis the external world. States were caught in the middle of domestic factional struggles among various groups. Some were frequently closely identified with the values of the Western tradition; others were ultranationalists whose response to the outside world sometimes bordered on racism; and still others were quasi-Marxists, neocolonialists, or socialists inclined toward emulation of the former Soviet or Chinese statist models.

To preserve an already tenuous and strained national unity, create a national consciousness, and develop economically, leaders of the Global South tried to pursue policies that would satisfy everyone. Nonalignment, in particular, seemed to offer the possibility of avoiding the disasters of civil war or domination by the superpowers during the Cold War. An assertive foreign policy and a demonstration of willingness to support, cooperate with, and receive aid from both blocs satisfied the domestic factions in the interest of unity.

The rapprochements that occurred between the two major blocs rendered the nonalignment movement ineffective as a viable strategy for the Global South. Furthermore, the demise of socialism and communism in the former Soviet Union and Eastern Europe and their attempt to move toward a free-market capitalism have tended to discredit socialism as an alternative model and deprived nonalignment of its raison d'être. If there are no longer two distinct blocs, there is no middle—and no place from which to play each side off against the other. These developments, coupled with the chronic problems of underdevelopment, combine to make the contemporary landscape of the Global South more vulnerable than ever to outside influence.

NATIONALISM: OLD AND NEW

Though usually not referred to as such, nationalism is one of the oldest ideologies. Nationalism can be defined as the common sentiment of solidarity that transforms a people into a nation and expresses itself in an attitude that assigns the collective activity of the state a high (frequently the highest) place in the hierarchy of social value. Nationalism is one of the most influential elements in world politics today, as it has been since the French Revolution. It grows from a variety of sources, but some of the more obvious factors that impel individuals to join with others in a national group include a common language, religion, historical background, cultural tradition, and race. Several of these may interact in subtle ways to reinforce a group's cohesive tendencies. The nationalist ethos is best expressed in the broadly based and deeply felt social identity from which the state derives its purpose in world politics. It is also reflected in a complex variety of symbols: external enemies, myths, heroes, history, and folklore.

Traditional European Nationalism

Rudimentary forms of nationalism can be traced to the states of antiquity. Ancient peoples commonly considered themselves divinely chosen and guided, and they believed that their gods were the sworn foes of other states. Regarding themselves as greatly superior in all aspects to the rest of humankind, other cultures were appreciated only to the extent that they reflected similar values.

Development of the European states system and the expansion of Western civilization gradually brought into sharp focus the effects of nationalism on world politics. The Hundred Years' War (1337–1451) between France and England is considered by many to mark the beginning of modern nationalism. The initial foundations for the union of Normans and Saxons into the English were laid in England during the twelfth and thirteenth centuries, to be fully achieved by the middle of the fourteenth. In France, an elementary form of French national consciousness first appeared during the Hundred Years' War. The French, however, lacked the more elaborate political institutions of the English, and consequently the development of full national identity was slower in France than in Britain. By the seventeenth century, however, both England and France had become nation-states in almost a contemporary sense, to be followed shortly by Sweden, Holland, Spain, and Denmark.

The unifying influence of nationalism, which initially brought order and stability within these few countries, has gone on to foster the development of a highly diverse community of sovereign states. During the early stages of this growth, nationalism promised peace, order, and justice predicated on the fulfillment of national aspirations. The paradox of nationalist feelings, however, was highlighted after the middle of the eighteenth century, in that since that time it has functioned more as a force of disintegration and fragmentation than of unity.

The development of world politics since the middle of the eighteenth century furnishes much evidence of how difficult it is to promote nationalism without aggravating the conditions of world order. A people's aspiration to create a nation-state has almost always conflicted with territorial claims of other states. Nationalists, generally not satisfied with internal achievements, have often sought glory through expansion and empire, whether territorial, economic, or cultural. Furthermore, intense nationalistic identification tends to undermine flexibility in policy and the capacity to compromise in interstate disputes.

The series of major wars that have been waged since 1815—especially World Wars I and II—embodied overt attempts to apply the principles of nationalism. Almost every one was fought by one or more belligerents in the name of national self-determination, and the results of these wars were reflected in peace settlements allegedly predicated upon the same principles. Yet a victory of nationalism, instead of bringing peace and order to world politics, only led to an exchange of the roles of oppressor and oppressed. Far from creating a more stable system, nationalism contributed to the fragmentation of world order and increased already-existing tensions.

More recently, with the end of the Cold War, nationalism has created a polycentric mosaic in place of the two supranational ideological blocs that emerged after World War II. However, it shows no potential for developing into a political concept broad enough to unite political institutions, ideologies, and economic systems in the same way that science and technology have compressed the world, and it is, therefore, highly problematic for the global future.

Nationalism in the Global South

The impact of European nationalism on the Global South has been explosive, partially because the environment was peculiarly prepared to respond to the stimulus of these ideas. As discussed earlier, since the middle of the nineteenth century, Asian, African, and Caribbean peoples coming into contact with the expanding West had been searching for some orienting concept upon which to base an adequate response. With their old societal and personal values eroded by the technological transformation everywhere in the less-developed world, these peoples found in nationalism a method of giving new meaning to their lives.

The non-Western world found it essential to try to reconcile tradition with the demands of modern thought and life. Success in this effort has been minimal because of the peculiar dimensions of the problem. Non-Western leaders, seeking a sufficient mass revival to produce a political and cultural renaissance, fear revolutionary change. Caught between the necessity of doing something and the reluctance to do too much, leaders in the non-Western world discovered that old codes no longer met pressing social and political needs, but newer Western ideas were in many respects unpalatable. This paralyzing contradiction seriously hindered the promotion of positive social change in the Global South.

A nation-state in the Western sense is difficult to construct within the boundaries of countries in the Global South. These states do not reflect spontaneous political growth, but rather the aftereffects of the division of the world by European colonial powers. In many instances, no concept of nationality exists, and communal and tribal loyalties still form the central core of the society. Government is minimal in organization and in effect, and the visible symbols of national identity are few and unimportant.

Thus nationalism in Asia and Africa has often been incoherent in its expression. Past glory is evoked at the same time that the people are exhorted to abandon their old ways and join the mainstream of modern life. The non-Western world wants simultaneously to escape from the "vulgarities" of Western life and to emulate the comforts found there. Nationalism in the new states seems at times to be more a reflection of culture shock than it is a cogent belief system and a basis for governmental action.

Despite these shortcomings, non-Western nationalism evokes a sense of self-respect that was unknown during the colonial period. It can stimulate social solidarity and has helped to create communities to which diverse peoples have come to claim common loyalty. Finally, it has created the national unity of purpose and readiness to sacrifice required for development and survival in a hostile environment.

The élites of the nationalist movements, usually products of modernization or militarization, have been the mediators between the old and the new. They have been required to set the ends and employ the means of modernization, yet the values and techniques that they have adopted have often been inappropriate to the conditions of their societies. More often, the élites subverted the existing order and society, seeking change primarily to satisfy their own needs. Thus their desire for change is in part a narrow personal wish, but it is also rooted in their desire to bring to their people the "better life." Cruelly, the amount of change needed to arrive at political and cultural awakening inevitably disrupts orderly transition. The endeavor to create a national state through common effort frequently runs into opposition from traditional groups that only strengthens factionalism and division. Such obstruction of nationalist ideals has often been met by the creation of one-party states that have suppressed opposition and dealt ruthlessly with dissidents and separatists, thereby undermining the legitimacy of the symbols of nationalism.

RELIGIOUS FUNDAMENTALISM

Fundamentalism is a kind of pathology of culture that arises by taking some of the basic tenets of tradition and, under the pressure of economic or social insecurity, desiring to secure one's self by sealing off others or seeking revenge on them. In all conflict situations, people under stress react by reducing their own beliefs to a small workable subset in order to fight others or protect themselves. But this reaction closes off the ability to hear and communicate.

Religious fundamentalism is a defensive social and political movement—a reaction to fast-paced modernization in a changing world. It is basically a struggle for self assertion and identity, together with a latent dissatisfaction with what the consumerist, materialist society offers around the world. Accordingly, this struggle has become an attempt by fundamentalists—Hindus, Muslims, Jews, Christians, and others—to preserve their religious culture and through it the sociopolitical viability by which they can define themselves.

Consequently, the world is experiencing a period of paradoxical struggle between old and new cultures, between traditionalism and modernism, in which the modernist attitude of cultural superiority reinforces an alien Western, secular system of values and therefore accelerates the displacement of already-weakened traditional cultural norms. New symbols of legitimacy and status—nation-statism and wealth—are introduced, while many traditionalists lose faith in their own cultural heritage.

Islamic Fundamentalism: A Case Study

Islamic fundamentalism is not an enemy of the West. It is not really a religious movement, nor is it, as some fear, expansive. Islamic fundamentalists seek to restore an old civilization, not create a new empire. Among the world's historical powers, only the Muslims, as people, have not reversed the decline in their global status. The Japanese, the Chinese, and the Europeans have all regained their world influence.

The Islamic people are trying to preserve their culture, and fundamentalism is a way of defining who they are. In this respect, the fuel that feeds the Islamic revival is similar to the impetus behind Hindu, Jewish, or Christian fundamentalism. In fact, the tension between nationalism and religion in the Islamic world bears a similarity to a split in Israel. Everywhere there is a latent dissatisfaction with what the materialist, consumer-oriented society offers. Such categories as Islamic fundamentalism, therefore, are not so much descriptions of political discontent as they are manifestations of an underlying social and cultural malaise.

The contemporary Islamic revival is based on a long history of responses to the challenges encountered by Islam. Traditionally, Islam has provided two channels of response to challenges: *Tajdid* (renewal) and *Islah* (reform). During the late eleventh and early twelfth centuries, Muhammad al-Ghazzali reconciled mysticism with mainline Islam. Two centuries later, Ahmad Ibn Taymiyyah dealt with the challenge of idolatry and social upheaval brought on by the Mongolian invasion. During the sixteenth century, Mogul emperor Akbar allowed infiltration of Hindu ideas, but the Islamic reformer Ahmad Sirhindi opposed this and sought to purge Hinduism from Islam. And in the nineteenth and twentieth centuries, Western infiltration of the Islamic world has become complete. A response, not quite clearly defined, falling short of renewal and reform, is in the making.

Beginning in the late nineteenth century, Islamic reformers such as Muhammad Abduh and Jamal al-Din al-Afghani, impressed by European scientific and social advances, began an agonizing appraisal of the declining conditions in the Islamic world. A new school of thought, *Salafiyah* (pure ancestry), developed. Its aim was the reconciliation of Islamic precepts and Western social organization. In the early twentieth century, Egyptian reformer Hasan al-Banna moved the Islamic revival from the realm of individual reforms to a popular movement by introducing the concept of mass organization. Sayyid Qutub, successor of al-Banna, built upon the latter's contribution by using the tool of ideology in an amalgam of fascist and Marxist organizational principles. The Islamic revival was transformed into a political movement exemplified in the emergence of the Green Shirts and the Muslim Brotherhood in Egypt and the array of Islamic groups that continue to develop in today's Islamic world, including the Islamic Salvation Front in Algeria, Muhammad's Army in Jordan, al Nahdah in Tunisia, Hamas in the Occupied Territories, and Hizballah and Jihad in Lebanon.

The Islamic revival is a powerful movement that touches upon every aspect of life for Muslims. Yet, there is great diversity within and among the various Islamic groups, reflecting local, national, cultural, and economic realities.

Unfortunately, there is a growing tendency in the West to lump all Islamic groups together, thus complicating Western abilities to understand the full range of Islamic forces at work. When Americans attack fundamentalism or Islamic-oriented governments, they are assaulting, among others, friends of the United States like Saudi Arabia and Pakistan. Iraq and Syria, two countries usually perceived as among America's adversaries, are the most secular of the Arab states. Like the media, U.S. policymakers have often proved themselves to be surprisingly myopic, tending to view the Islamic world and various groups solely through the prism of extremism and terrorism. Though this reaction may be understandable in the light of events in Iran and Lebanon, it fails to do justice to the complex reality of Islamic revivalism and undermines U.S. interests in the Middle East and the Islamic world.

Common to the members of the Islamic revival is the affirmation of an Islamic ideological alternative to secular nationalism, Western capitalism, and socialism. The failures of Pan-Turanianism (unity of the Turks), Pan-Arabism (Arab unity), Arab nationalism and socialism, and Iranian nationalism have left an ideological vacuum. Far from a monolithic reality, the Islamic revival, as a movement, is as diverse as the countries in which it is occurring. It spans the political and ideological spectrum, influenced as much by the local sociopolitical conditions as by religious faith. For example, women serve in the security system of Muammar Qadhafi's populist Libya, yet women cannot drive vehicles in Saudi Arabia. Women enjoy voting rights in Pakistan and Iran but are disfranchised in Sudan. Most recently, Islamic electoral successes in Algeria, Jordan, Sudan, Yemen, Lebanon, and Tunisia blend Islamic precepts with Western political discourse.

Despite vast disparities in their methods, however, Islamic groups hold in common a set of ideological beliefs. They view Islam as a total way of life, for personal conduct as well as for the conduct of state and society. Westernization is regarded as the primary cause of the political, economic, and social ills of Muslim societies. Finally, followers of the Islamic revival movement believe that the introduction of the *Shariah* (Islamic Law) will produce a moral, just, and self-reliant society.

Islamic groups such as Hamas, Jihad, Hizballah, and an array of small radical organizations go beyond these principles, seeing Islam and the West as being involved in a historic power struggle of considerable duration, beginning with the Crusades and continued under European colonialism, Zionism, and American imperialism. The West, especially the United States, is blamed for its support of unjust regimes in Morocco, Egypt, Kuwait, and Saudi Arabia; for its unconditional support for Israel; and, more recently, for backing the military usurpation of civilian government in Algeria. These radical groups, therefore, consider violent struggle against unjust Islamic rulers and the governments that support them to be a justifiable strategy of liberation.

Islamic ideology and movements—Islamism—have become an integral part of Islamic society and will inform Islamic domestic and international politics. These Islamists are found among the Western-educated as well as the untraveled, among literates and illiterates alike, transcending all classes, professions, and gender and age groups.

The power of the Islamic revival is manifested in many ways. As stated earlier, candidates running as Islamists have won elections in many Islamic countries. This revival has produced a new class of modern and educated Islamist élites who are no less visible than their secular counterparts and in every way as competent.

The Islamic revival has developed into a broadly based social movement, functioning today in virtually every Islamic state and in communities around the world. The goal of this revival is to transform society through the transformation of individuals. Organizations known as *Da'wah* (Islamic Call) exist at all levels of education, in all forms of communication, in banks and investment houses, in every type of social service, and in the police and military. Student associations are present in every Islamic country and elsewhere. Indeed, Islamic revival has produced a new generation of Islamists in every profession at every level in the Islamic world.

True, a minority of Islamic groups will continue to use violence. They will disrupt rather than overthrow governments and will substantially alter their societies. Algeria, Egypt, Lebanon, Morocco, Tunisia, and the Gulf Arab states remain prime candidates for future problems with these violent organizations. Yet the moderate majority of Islamist groups, including Islamists in the former Soviet republics and in the Balkans, will continue to pursue a policy of gradualism, seeking to bring about change from below.

The Islamic revival will not die but will not become mainstream, either. The multiplicity of Islamic militant groups fosters dissension among them and works against hegemony by any single organization.

RECOMMENDED READINGS

APTER, DAVID E., ed. *Ideology and Discontent.* London: Free Press, 1964.

BELL, DANIEL. *The End of Ideology: On the Exhaustion of Political Ideas in the Fifties.* Rev. ed. New York: Free Press, 1965.

CHOUEIRI, YOUSSEF M. *Islamic Fundamentalism.* Boston: Twayne, 1990.

ESPOSITO, JOHN L. *Islamic Threat: Myth or Reality?* New York: Oxford University Press, 1992.

FANON, FRANTZ. *The Wretched of the Earth.* New York: Grove Press, 1965.

FULLER, GRAHAM E. *Islamic Fundamentalism in the Northern Tier Countries: An Integrated View.* Santa Monica, CA: Rand Corporation, 1991.

HAYES, CARLTON. *The Historical Evolution of Modern Nationalism.* New York: Macmillan, 1963.

HOBSON, JOHN. *Imperialism: A Study.* Ann Arbor: University of Michigan Press, 1965.

HOOK, SIDNEY. *Marx and the Marxists.* Princeton, NJ: Van Nostrand, 1955.

MOUSSALLI, AHMAD S. *Radical Islamic Fundamentalism: The Ideological and Political Discourse of Sayyid Quatb.* Beirut: American University of Beirut, 1992.

PISCATORI, JAMES. *Islamic Fundamentalism and the Gulf Crisis.* Chicago: Fundamentalism Project, American Academy of Arts and Sciences, 1991.

POSTER, MARK. *Politics, Theory, and Contemporary Culture.* New York: Columbia University Press, 1993.

SAID, ABDUL AZIZ, and DANIEL COLLIER. *Revolutionism.* Boston: Allyn and Bacon, 1971.

SICK, GARY. *Islamic Fundamentalism.* New York: Conference Board, 1993.

SISK, TIMOTHY. *Islam and Democracy: Religion, Politics, and Power in the Middle East.* Washington, DC: United States Institute of Peace, 1992.

WALKER, R. B. J., ed. *Culture and Ideology and World Order.* Boulder, CO: Westview Press, 1984.

WATSON, MICHAEL. *Contemporary Minority Nationalism.* London: Routledge, 1990.

Chapter 11

HUMANKIND, TECHNOLOGY, AND THE ECOSYSTEM

We live in an age of unprecedented technological progress. The contemporary assault of human intelligence upon the secrets of the natural world has yielded spectacular discoveries, and the twentieth century has seen more changes in the conditions of human existence than have occurred in all previous recorded history. Inevitably, the technological revolution of this century has had a profound effect on the politics of states. We have already noted the impact of advanced technology on the theory and practice of warfare, as well as the reevaluation of long-standing postulates. These developments have been paralleled in most other dimensions of world politics. In fact, the very organizing assumptions of state life have been called into question by a newly engendered technical interdependence. This new parameter, created by our increasing capacities to communicate among ourselves and to intervene in our natural environment, continues to raise new questions and issues for the global political agenda.

In this chapter we shall examine six of the many technology-related issue areas that are contributing to change in the substance and style of international relations. We shall note their similarities in modifying and perhaps transforming world politics, and we feel that our conclusions are generally applicable to most other technological issues.

The six we have selected for brief analysis and evaluation are (1) energy; (2) the conquest of space; (3) the question of population, hunger, and poverty; (4) mass communications; (5) the new patterns of economic production, consumption, and distribution; and (6) the "information revolution."

ENERGY

During the last quarter of the twentieth century, energy has become a primary issue in the global system. A drastic increase in the price of petroleum imposed by the Organization of Petroleum Exporting Countries (OPEC), combined with the Arab oil embargo of 1973, served to disrupt the pattern of global economic growth, both in the center and in the periphery. Despite the subsequent oil "glut" in the 1980s, governments, some more slowly than others, have reappraised their energy policies, taken some measures to alter patterns of consumption, and begun to search for alternative sources of energy.

Fossil Fuels

Fossil fuels have been the prime source of energy for the past century: Crude oil, natural gas, and coal have been employed to serve the majority of our needs. The supplies of fossil fuels, being the residue of extraordinarily long geological processes, are necessarily limited. Furthermore, when one considers that the global process of modernization has created an ever-increasing demand for energy—to run cars, factories, appliances, heating and cooling systems, and so on—it is obvious that fossil fuels will have high salience in the interaction of states.

It is useful in this connection to distinguish a *shortage* from a *scarcity* of energy. A scarcity is a situation in which the goods in question are available in the marketplace to anyone willing to pay the higher price that their scarcity entails. Although it is doubtful that an actual shortage of fossil energy resources will be encountered in this century, the need to establish alternative energy sources is nonetheless pressing—sources of energy from which all of humankind can benefit, not merely those who are able to pay the high and erratic prices of energy from scarce, nonrenewable sources.

Nuclear Energy

Nuclear energy is the most widely used nonfossil energy source because it has certain obvious advantages. First, because so much energy can be released from such a small quantity of fissionable matter, and because the supply of elements from which the necessary isotopes can be made seems to be large, this technology appeared to solve the problem of long-term energy availability.

For just this reason, the development of civilian uses of atomic energy was immediately relevant to the pattern of world relationships; that is, it appeared to make possible a "second industrial revolution." States that became industrial giants in the days of coal-iron technology had accidentally been endowed with deposits of these raw materials, of which coal was the more important. Great economic power and world political leadership were built on this base, and states without adequate sources were condemned to second or even lower rank. The rise to importance of OPEC provides a contemporary example of this same phenomenon.

Nuclear energy, however, could equalize the conditions of competition by making energy availability no longer dependent on serendipitous natural endowments. Nevertheless, the opportunity for nonindustrial states to skip the coal-oil stage entirely and to move directly into this more advanced technology was compromised by its high capital cost. In fact, industrialized states had an advantage right from the start in their relatively large supply of scientists, technicians, and production specialists, but this advantage was not permanent. Thus there still remained the expectation that the exploitation of nuclear energy could result in a substantial reordering of the relative production ranking held by states and might also culminate in a narrower spread between the top and the bottom. But, for several reasons, as we shall see, these changes have not happened.

Nuclear Energy and World Politics. The military uses of nuclear energy have been a factor of division and have intensified competition and tension in the relations of states. Though each state possessing nuclear power has sought to confine its advances to itself and to monopolize all its rewards, proliferation has occurred through sale and reprocessing. The peaceful use of nuclear energy, however, has stimulated new dimensions of international cooperation for a number of reasons.

First, if states approach the development of this technology separately and individually, they are condemned to the expense of repeating each stage in the process, whereas cooperation has enabled many to build on the totality of everyone's findings.

Second, for the most effective use, nuclear energy arrangements should be on a larger scale than most smaller states can develop. Cooperation in establishing supranational research and development programs could, therefore, result in dividends beyond the capacity of individual states to muster.

A third factor is the "self-image" of the scientific community. Committed by professional values to freedom of knowledge and the exchange of ideas and findings in a common pursuit of truth, nuclear-related scientists have over the years strongly urged governments toward cooperative ventures in this area.

The two most conspicuous examples of international cooperation in the exploitation of nuclear energy for peaceful purposes have been the International Atomic Energy Agency (IAEA), established in response to U.S. initiatives under the auspices of the UN, and the European Atomic Community (EURATOM), set up by the six original states of the European Community. These two agencies have contributed to a relatively successful and fairly stable, if somewhat loose, international nuclear energy regime that provides for joint and cooperative exploitation of the peaceful possibilities of nuclear energy.

In recent years, however, the nuclear "genie" has come to be perceived as a demon by an increasing number of citizens of the advanced industrial societies. This new attitude has been engendered by a series of both major and minor accidents, caused by technical breakdowns in nuclear plants, coupled with a more widespread and profound appreciation of the problems of waste disposal and other forms of environmental degradation associated with current nuclear technology. Some have wondered if economic growth is really worth these kinds of hazards. The issue has become very complicated because many industrial states had already made enormous investments in nuclear power only to later discover its darker side. The major accident at the Chernobyl nuclear plant in Ukraine appears to have been a landmark, because many policy changes followed in its wake. For instance, Sweden, the country most seriously affected by fallout from the accident (after the former Soviet Union itself, of course), made the historic decision to phase out nuclear power altogether! Other countries have been forced by concerned citizens to take many extensive (and expensive) measures to insure reactor safety and to reevaluate the long-term role of nuclear energy in satisfying their demand for power. This event also revived the previously lukewarm official interest in developing new, renewable, and less threatening forms of energy.

Solar Energy

Recently, we have come to appreciate that there really is no scarcity of energy as such. Vast quantities of renewable, nonpolluting, and cost-free energy fall every day upon all parts of the earth in the form of solar radiation. Even the fossil fuels, whose quantities are limited, consist of solar energy that was trapped and stored millennia ago by green plants. Both wind and water, two other sources of energy, derive their power from the sun's irregular heating of the Earth's crust and the evaporation of its bodies of water.

Research into the direct collection, storage, and use of this plentiful energy source is proceeding at an accelerated pace. It is now economically feasible to utilize solar energy to heat water, and there are signs that new processes may soon make it as economical as nuclear plants for generating electricity—with no significant environmental costs. Such considerations may mean that a third, even more dramatic, industrial revolution could result from the widespread exploitation of solar power. Also, it should be noted that most of the countries of the Global South are plentifully endowed with sunshine, and, since they cannot afford to pay for all the fossil fuel they need for development, this new technology holds a special promise for them.

Appropriate Technology

A third industrial revolution would depend upon a variety of technologies, not simply those related to solar energy. The term *appropriate technology* denotes combinations of technological methods, both traditional and innovative, that are scaled in size, cost, and degree of complexity to the situations to which they are applied. Thus it is a strategy for the selection and implementation of technological methods that are effectively calibrated to situational needs, resources, and priorities. For instance, in many rural areas in the United States it may be more effective to install a variety of dispersed energy-production devices such as windmills or solar heaters than to build new centralized power plants, no matter what their energy source.

More particularly, there is a sentiment in much of the developing world that technology transfer has failed, and that local problems must be somehow approached through methods and means endogenously defined and engineered. Also, as we have mentioned earlier, even if they wished to do so, few Global South countries can pay the price of the increasingly expensive imports of equipment and energy necessary to fully imitate Western-style development. Instead, there has been a move toward trying to add on by increments to the technological capacity of an indigenous society, rather than replace it with the Western way of doing things, and thereby to involve the local people in the creative process of defining their own social and economic development. The results of such efforts have been generally positive, despite the fact that many Global South leaders have seen appropriate technology as just another ruse to get them to accept "second best."

THE EXPLORATION OF OUTER SPACE

The nuclear age dates from 1945, but the space age has been a reality only since 1957 when the former Soviet Union launched the first artificial space satellites, followed in 1958 by the United States. Since that time, efforts to gather more scientific information about the reaches of space and to launch vehicles and persons deeper into the universe have steadily continued with more and more countries becoming involved. Moving from small Earth-orbit satellites, through manned landings on the moon and unmanned landings on Mars, to plans for international manned missions to Mars in just over thirty years is remarkable. Such a quantum leap in human civilization has undoubtedly had a major impact on international politics, and we shall see that the influence has been both profound and varied.

Humankind's venturing out into space has begun to change our understanding of ourselves. Despite the projection of national rivalries into this domain—the so-called space race—space exploration has in fact done much to foster collective action among states and to help them see the limits of such concepts as national sovereignty. At the moment, according to international law, none of the celestial bodies (i.e., the rest of the universe) are subject to national annexation. Also, there are international conventions to insure that astronauts in difficulty should receive aid from whomever can give it, regardless of national identity. The fact that humans have seen the Earth from the vantage point of space seems to have been a watershed in human history, after which the lack of unity among humanity and harmony with the Earth seems anachronistic. From the vantage point of two hundred years in the future, if civilization succeeds in reaching that point, the beginnings of space exploration may be seen as the precursor of truly transformational change.

The Military Uses of Space

Space capabilities have added an entirely new dimension to questions of national security. In military terms, the development of intercontinental ballistic missiles—projectiles that enter outer space while in flight to their targets—profoundly changed the notion of international warfare and national defense. From this situation came the new concept of deterrence, which, as we discussed earlier, introduced interdependence into the security question.

Second, satellites can now provide almost inconceivably detailed information about other countries, making it nearly impossible to carry on military actions of any scope without being detected. This capability further restricts the utility of force in world politics because the element of surprise is greatly reduced.

Last, we should mention the contemporary debate about the possibility of putting in place an effective "shield" against missile attack, consisting of satellites capable of destroying missiles in flight. Whatever the merits of this idea, it would have been inconceivable except in the realm of science fiction only a few decades ago, but in the wake of tremendous progress in space science and engineering, it has attracted serious interest and investment. Furthermore, at the time of writing, there is serious discussion about making the system international, rather than national in scope, as the United States and Russia consider the possibility of pooling their efforts in this area.

Cooperation in Space

A countertrend to the development of missiles and spy satellites also began to manifest itself as early as 1961 and 1962—a strong urge toward the cooperative exploration of space without political overtones. Proposals for cooperation had been frequent even during earlier stages, but the pressure for political and possibly military advantage had prevented their implementation. Proposals to declare space "out of bounds" to the East-West confrontation and to share both the costs and the findings of further explorations were accepted in principle, but considerations of timing, prestige, or national security blunted these preliminary efforts.

However, when Premier Nikita Khrushchev of the former Soviet Union congratulated the United States on its first manned orbital flight in 1962, he raised the possibility of the two countries' developing ways of extensive cooperation in the future penetration of space. The U.S. response was affirmative, and the negotiations for the formulation of areas and techniques of joint interaction were immediately initiated in a climate of relative goodwill and free exchange.

The apparently sincere acceptance of cooperation in space by the two states that had been competing so grimly was both important in itself and profoundly suggestive. Furthermore, the test ban treaty of July 1963, which, among other things, banned nuclear testing in outer space, and President John F. Kennedy's revolutionary proposal before the UN for joint Soviet-American exploration of the moon were both indications of the different posture being assumed by the United States. Later, in May 1972, the United States and the former Soviet Union signed an agreement to cooperate in the exploration and use of space for peaceful purposes.

This cooperation attained its high point with a docking of U.S. and Soviet space vehicles in orbit about the Earth in 1975 (the Apollo-Soyuz flight), and then deteriorated in the climate of renewed hostility that prevailed in the early 1980s. However, there has been a general realization among states that are engaged in space research (now including the members of the European Union) that no single state can afford the expense of such ambitious projects as the manned exploration of other planets. Thus international cooperation has become a practical necessity.

The UN has been a major forum for discussion and resolution of conflicts in regard to space. In 1963 the General Assembly adopted the nine-point Declaration of Legal Principles Governing the Activities of States in the Exploration and Use of Outer Space. This declaration recognized the "common interest of man" in space activities: The exploration and use of space and celestial bodies should be for the benefit of humanity; that is, as we mentioned, they are not subject to national appropriation or claims of sovereignty. All are free for use by all on the basis of equality. States retain ownership of their vehicles and control over their personnel, but astronauts are considered "envoys of mankind," to receive all possible aid in event of emergency. This declaration was expanded upon by the Outer Space Treaty (Treaty on Principles Governing the Activities of States in the Exploration and Use of Outer Space, Including the Moon and Other Celestial Bodies). The latter treaty was signed in January 1967 and is now in force in most of the states of the world.

The average person is perhaps most affected by the great boost space technology has given to global communications. In 1962 the United States created the Communications Satellite Corporation (COMSAT), a corporation with stock held by the public and by American communications companies, with several of the directors appointed by the president. COMSAT, in turn, was the American representative and the manager of the International Telecommunications Satellite Consortium (INTELSAT), which functions under special and interim agreements to supply some 90 percent of all present international telecommunications traffic through communications satellites. The former Soviet bloc had a similar system based on the Soviet Molniya (lightning) system. Recently, several more such satellites have been put into orbit, both broadening the scope and improving the quality of global communication.

In summary, we can say that space holds unlimited promise for the human race, but the realization of these possibilities demands social as well as technological evolution on our part. There are already signs of such developments, as humankind seems poised to forge ahead with unprecedented international cooperation in this field.

POPULATION, HUNGER, AND POVERTY

Science and technology, joining forces in the fields of public health and preventive medicine, have brought to the world one of its largest contemporary problems: the population question. The number of human beings on Earth today is by far the largest in history. One significant study points out that one third of all the people born in the entire history of the human race are alive today.

Only in the recent past have political leaders become alarmed by the steady acceleration of birth rates in many parts of the world. Now that population has acquired a political dimension, it has become a matter of great concern to many governments. Though difficult to master, there are signs that concerted collective effort can make some impact on this issue.

Population, however, is one strand of an intricate web of related problems of development. While the genesis of the population problem in a general sense can be traced to advances in health and well-being, its resolution has only been successful when population is seen as one aspect of a general problem—lack of adequate nutrition, health care, and self-sufficiency among a large portion of a country's people—in other words, hunger and poverty.

It should be noted at the outset that the story of poverty in the twentieth century in the Global South is not completely gloomy. According to a standard of measurement agreed upon by United Nations and nongovernmental agencies that work with these issues (50 or fewer deaths in the first year per 1,000 live births), more than fifty nations have ended hunger as a basic issue in their societies since 1960. None of them has accomplished this feat without at the same time resolving the crisis of rampant population growth. While many of these countries, such as Sri Lanka, still have serious problems, which could lead to a return of massive hunger and excessive population growth, most have consolidated these gains rather impressively.

Causes of the Population Problem

The population of traditionally agrarian societies always stabilized at the maximum supportable by local supplies and prerequisites of living. It was kept in check by "Malthusian restraints": war, epidemic, famine, and disease. For instance, a predominantly youthful population (because of short life span) and very high birth and death rates were generally regarded as characteristics of most peripheral, Global South societies.

However, since the beginning of the twentieth century (and in some cases earlier), these societies have begun to benefit from public health measures, improved sanitation, and modern medicine. The results have been spectacular: Death rates have dropped at a dramatic rate, primarily in infant mortality and in epidemic diseases, while birth rates in most cases have either remained constant or increased further. As more infants survived to become parents, population figures soared, with the result that population pressures began to force the hand of many governments.

Political, Social, and Economic Effects

The consequences for the states directly affected by the population problem have been simple and devastating. Since no government can accept starvation as a way of bringing food supplies and public demand into harmony, all must acknowledge their responsibility to provide for the hungry. But this acknowledgment does not reduce the scope of the problem—birth rates remain high, and for many years the crisis has intensified. It was frequently difficult to put the necessary long-term measures into effect because the short-term crisis demanded so much energy and attention.

Within many newly independent countries, the constant specter of starvation has haunted everyone. Although for centuries this situation was accepted as a part of life, in the contemporary era processes of social change have been at work in once-quiescent societies. Political discourse in such societies grew more extreme as distress provided the catalyst for the political awakening of the masses. Governments were increasingly less able to withstand these pressures and more inclined to take desperate measures to safeguard their authority.

At this point, the problem became pertinent to world politics. Governments under such pressures at home are neither forces for stability in world politics nor free to make long-term international commitments. A state with accelerated population growth was incipiently revolutionary, even though population pressure could not be relieved just by a change in regime orientation. Also, desperate regimes seeking to divert the antipathy of an increasingly stressed society from themselves may suggest that certain foreign powers are responsible for the country's difficulties.

It is thus reasonable to assert that the reproductive habits of individuals in the tropics have been and are of direct relevance to the modern industrialized states. Population pressure has contributed its share to the militancy of the Global South demands for reform in the world economic system, and it should be taken into account by the developed market economies when they confront these issues. However, we would not want to argue that the principal motivation for a response from the industrial North to the problems of hunger in the Global South should be enlightened self-interest, in a negative sense of threat avoidance. In fact, it may be possible for the center to largely protect itself from any direct consequences of the Global South food shortages. Rather, we would suggest that help should be motivated by empathy and a feeling of common humanity. It is interesting in this regard to note that the results of privately organized and administered national campaigns for famine relief for Africa in the mid-1980s exceeded in many cases the official contributions of certain developed states. In a more positive sense, enlightened self-interest can also play a role. The successful development of the Global South will benefit all humanity, including the more-developed economies in search of greater markets for their production. In this regard, one could argue that humanity is currently operating at a tremendous handicap as it tries to solve its many problems because the full contribution of one fourth to one half of our number is wasted.

Avenues of Solution

As we have already mentioned, great successes have been achieved in fighting the interrelated scourges of poverty, hunger, and overpopulation. A combined internal and international approach offers further promise for the future.

Internally, initiatives that focus on giving hungry people opportunity—making it possible for them to either grow enough food to feed their families or earn enough money to buy sufficient food—have been very effective when combined with the provision of basic health care, family planning education and assistance, and literacy programs. Programs that focus on improving the resources and abilities of women have been particularly effective, as have small "microenterprise" loan programs, which provide credit for the poor to start or improve small farms and businesses.

Globally, the population problem can best be attacked by development programs, funded and guided by international organizations. There is a clear tendency for the rate of population growth to slow as a society industrializes and the standard of living rises. People do not feel that so many children are necessary, and they appreciate the need to educate those they have. It is important that flexibility be maintained to implement different solutions to similar problems in different areas. For some regions, the growth of cash crops for export must be diminished so that people do not die of starvation next to fertile fields that could provide their sustenance. For others, small-scale nonagricultural development assistance can provide people with the necessary income.

India and China both have made spectacular progress in this area, though not all would approve of the entire range of their methods. China, with one fifth of the world's population, has basically ended the problem of hunger by allowing market forces to replace the commune system, thereby providing the initiative responsible for a greater productivity. China has adopted various economic measures to offset the adverse influence of price hikes on the standard of living, and has began to provide decent living by increasing the purchase price of food grain, cotton, and other farm and sideline products. India, while still suffering from chronic undernutrition in almost half of its population, has established both the grain self-sufficiency and the grain storage and transportation infrastructure necessary to insure that a serious famine will never again erupt there.

Last, we should mention the spread of the AIDS virus, which could conceivably radically alter the population problems of the Global South. Though an accurate monitoring of the diffusion of AIDS in societies with limited public health facilities is impossible, the World Health Organization (WHO) has already seen fit to warn African leaders that they should plan to have significantly reduced workforces in the coming decades because of the ravages of the virus on their productive population. There appears to be little reason to think that other, poorer regions will be able to avoid a similar fate.

Population and Global Politics

Some ecologists and biologists argue that the pressure of population is the most influential single factor in shaping the future of the human species. In political terms they contend that ideological and nationalistic drives pale in comparison with the frantic search for subsistence by two thirds of the world population. Unless this challenge is met head-on, they contend, a new wave of barbarism will threaten to sweep the planet.

Regardless of how seriously these warnings may be taken, we cannot escape the conclusion that the global system must adjust to this stark phenomenon. Whether it leads to war and destruction or to a new cooperative climate for solving common problems, the inadequate conditions of a significant fraction of humanity are a political problem of the first order, about which we will hear more in the years ahead.

MASS COMMUNICATION

Mass communication devices and techniques are another entry in the list of technological advances that have revolutionized life in the twentieth century. It is now possible for one person to communicate simultaneously with an audience numbered in the billions. The development of commercial satellite telecommunications that began in 1965—the Early Bird system and subsequent development with possibilities of direct-broadcast satellites—seems to indicate that an even greater role can be played by the communication media in the future. This capability to affect the emotions and increase the knowledge of vast numbers of people within a short time span has had a profound effect on patterns of social life everywhere. Information, entertainment, intellectual stimulation, and political leadership are all part of the content of the mass media. For instance, the "Live Aid" broadcast in July 1985, a musical concert that raised money and consciousness for ending hunger globally, reportedly watched by two billion people, combined several of these elements. Anything so powerful in its impact directly affects world politics as well.

Mass Media in World Politics

The primary relevance of mass media to world politics has already been noted in our discussion of propaganda. New techniques of conveying messages to an audience have led to great advances in propaganda effectiveness. We identified four different audiences for national propaganda efforts: the state's own people, the people of its allies, the people of neutral or uninvolved states, and the people of its opponents. In reaching each of these audiences, the propagandist makes extensive use of the mass media.

At home, electronic media (such as radio and television) are used widely, with applications varying according to the richness of the technical installations and the sophistication of the home audience. Printed and visual media—books, magazines, motion pictures, posters—also play a large role. The problem of access is much more complex when a foreign audience is being approached. The audience is in no sense "captive" and must be reached more circumspectly. Radio, as yet the only real global medium, is especially valuable because home radio receivers are common everywhere and the technique of beaming shortwave broadcasts is so well developed.

Television, though it has a much more profound impact and has become very sophisticated in the developed countries, is not yet widespread in the Global South. There are still a large number of people who have never seen a television set and millions in whose lives the medium plays almost no role. Among élites in many Global South nations, however, television is a major factor. The lack of indigenous television production and broadcasting facilities in these countries means that what is viewed on television is mainly produced in the developed nations. This fact has exacerbated problems of alienation—both of élites from their own cultures through "Westernization," and internally between élites and the masses.

Today, critical problems of communication policy confront all states with far-reaching decisions. Not only will these decisions affect domestic policies for some time to come, but they may also restructure the coming international communications regime.

Destructive and Constructive Applications

The methods of mass communication, like almost any technical skill, are neutral and without policy significance. However, they may be put to destructive and dangerous uses, or they may serve constructive ends—the decision is left to responsible policymakers. Examples of both categories abound in the contemporary world.

Destructively (at least potentially), mass media are appropriate for intensifying nationalist hatreds and tensions. The media can help work the people of one state into a condition of intensive hostility toward another people, and great pressure may be generated. Adamant public positions on crisis issues can be developed, while equally powerful drives for adoption of new policies can be unleashed. Perhaps more significant than any of these is the role of mass media in filtering and interpreting the flow of information received by the audience. Whether acting on its own or as a tool of the government, the mass communication machine in any state is the means whereby individual citizens acquire both factual data and authoritative interpretations of the problems their government faces. The state of mass opinion in a modern society at any particular moment is to a large extent the work of the mass communicators in that society.

The political significance of mass communication techniques derives from the opportunity they offer governments to monopolize communications in a society. This degree of centralized information generation and diffusion was not possible in the past. In traditional societies there were storytellers in every town; now the state (or the media establishment) is the only legal storyteller.

Constructively, mass communication media are potentially important to the creation of a global consensus. In today's rapidly moving world, opinion can focus on a particular issue in time to affect its outcome only if the mass media convey the information widely and quickly enough. Technical execution of the task is relatively simple, in view of the advanced state of the art. A cohesive world community is conceivable only if individuals are tied to a single and responsive communications network, and there are signs of evolution in this direction.

PRODUCTION, CONSUMPTION, AND DISTRIBUTION

Another technological problem is constituted by great changes in world production, consumption, and distribution of economic goods. Each of these three areas has been affected directly by the technological revolution we have analyzed throughout this chapter. So vast are the economic implications of modern technology that we can do no more than suggest a few of the leading considerations.

New Production Techniques

Almost every aspect of industrial technology has affected production in a remarkable way. Best known of the new techniques is *automation*—the application of electronic controls and simplified patterns to the production of high-quality goods by only a fraction of the labor force formerly needed. Even nonautomated industry has been so revolutionized by new techniques that almost any factory built before 1945 is obsolete today. This point was dramatically demonstrated by the industrial success of the war-devastated states of Europe after 1945. Forced to rebuild industrial plants from the ground up, they were able to incorporate new arrangements and techniques, with a consequent impressive gain in productivity.

The principal result of new production techniques has been a great increase in the capacity of the world economy to produce goods of all sorts. More goods are available for consumption than ever before, and the trend is toward a continuation of the upward spiral of productivity. This phenomenon is independent of any considerations of profit margins, markets, or employment. It is simply a macroeconomic conclusion that the world, viewed as a unit of production, is increasing its gross product at a significant rate. The social and political consequences are functions of decisions made in other contexts and cannot be inferred from the mere fact of an upward trend in production.

Rising Consumer Expectations

Paralleling the revolution in production technique is an analogous upward curve in the rise of consumerism in the industrial states and more recently in the Global South. Regardless of the standard of living enjoyed by an individual, the urge for consumerism is constant. Although the United States, with its consumption economy of "affluence," has long set the trend for higher standards of living, Western

Europe, the Commonwealth of Independent States, and the semi-industrialized societies in the Middle East, Latin America, North Africa, and South Asia have followed suit.

Worldwide interest in consumption of economic goods has placed many governments in a dilemma. Many, particularly in presocialist and developing countries, were committed to collectively phrased nationalist goals whose attainment called for a significant portion of national production to be committed to the "public sector" of the economy, but a heavy burden of armament and the capital formation prerequisite to industrial development required that individual consumption be limited. However, the increasingly vocal demand of the mass public for more of the "better things of life" inhibited the vigor with which the government could continually demand sacrifice and dedication to necessary public programs. This dilemma was one major contributing cause of the swing toward capitalism in those societies.

The Problem of Distribution

The states system divides the world into a collection of national economies that are supposed to be self-sustaining. Some of these are productive of surpluses, while others can do no more than budget deprivation. At the subsistence level, for example, today's food production potential is adequate to feed the entire population of the world. In other words, hunger exists because of failures of distribution. (This is not to suggest that improved international food distribution represents a complete solution to the hunger problem.)

How, within the present structure of the world economy, can distribution be rationalized so that increased productivity can be reflected in increased consumption and a richer and better life for everyone? This is an extremely difficult question that admits of no simple answer. In some respects, the current situation is a *product* of the states system, and it may not be reasonable to expect a real solution within the current structure of global affairs. Alleviation of the more severe aspects of the problem may be possible though, insofar as the center states realize that some *reform* of patterns of global distribution is necessary simply to insure that they retain their favorable position within the structure. Distribution reforms will need to be accompanied, especially on the subsistence level, with increased local self-sufficiency. The relief for peoples left destitute by their dependence on a fluctuating global economy lies both in increasing their control over that economy and in decreasing their dependency upon it.

Political Significance

The political ramifications of these general observations are self-evident. The basic economic issues of production and consumption have been sharpened by the technological breakthroughs of the contemporary era. Politically, the world has most often emphasized division and separateness; economically, the maximum social advantage is attainable only in a system emphasizing unity and joint action. The economic problems of the contemporary world are insoluble on a state level, except for a few fortunate states of great expanse and rich resource endowment. Perpetuation of a predominantly nationalist approach to global economic issues can do no more than buy time, and it may possibly worsen the situation in the long run. Here, as in other areas, no automatic or guaranteed response to the challenge of technology exists, because the problems encountered are unprecedented in global political experience.

The world community has, however, responded en masse to the devastating impact of technological advances on the global environment. The United Nations Conference on Environment and Development, the "Earth Summit," held June 3–14, 1992, in Rio de Janiero, addressed key issues and strategies aimed at halting environmental destruction caused by exponentially increasing production and consumption. The Rio Summit was indeed unique, as 118 heads of state and leaders of the major nongovernmental organizations attended. The tangible outcome of the summit was the creation of four important regimes:

Rio Declaration of Principles

In signing the Declaration of Principles, states agreed to refrain from practices that damage the environment of other states. Canadian concern about acid rain caused by U.S. industry is a prime example of the issues this agreement addresses.

Climate Convention

The Climate Convention seeks to limit the allowable emissions of various gases that affect the Earth's climate.

Biodiversity Treaty

The thrust of the Biodiversity Treaty is to insure compensation to the source state for natural resources used by another state for profit. This treaty addresses the concerns of Global South states, whose natural resources have often been coopted by industrialized nations for the production of finished goods.

Agenda 21

Agenda 21 acts as a blueprint for environment policy well into the twenty-first century. It calls for environmental cooperation and mutual respect among signatory states.

THE INFORMATION REVOLUTION

Advances in computer technology, from the so-called supercomputers to the development of ever-more-powerful personal computers, along with the accompanying capacity to transfer enormous quantities of electronically coded information over great distances in the twinkling of an eye and the much-discussed "information superhighway," are revolutionizing world civilization. This field also has many ramifications for international politics, but owing to the speed of innovation in data-processing technology, anything we state here must be considered tentative.

There is little doubt that a state's level of "computer literacy" has become an important element of national capability in the late twentieth century. For example, government leaders of "closed" societies came to realize that they could not both promote the spread of information technology in their societies and retain control over information. That is, for some decades it was possible for such governments to dominate these means for their own purposes, but in the era of personal computers and modems, international competitiveness required that the masses be allowed to share in the flow of information, and this need created pressures toward more "openness" in all areas of social life.

In the area of intelligence, computers play an enormous role because one of their most important capacities is to store and process huge amounts of information and, when asked, to look for patterns in the data. These functions, when combined with the observational capacity of satellites, make it much more difficult for any of the major actors to carry out clandestine actions on any significant scale. This factor would seem to contribute to stability and a reduction in the practical uses of military force in foreign policy (at the major power level). Computers have also been incorporated into all of the major powers' weapons systems, and therefore accuracy has improved to an almost unimaginable degree. It is now possible to hit very small targets over tremendous distances, a fact that has greatly augmented the destructiveness of even conventional weapons.

Computer technology further contributes to transnational global interdependence through the growth of networks of users, sometimes widely dispersed over the face of the globe, who communicate over telephone lines and exchange programs and data. Though such exchanges are to some degree controllable, they represent a wholly extrastatal form of international contact between private individuals.

To date, the distribution of computer capabilities reflects the general stratification of the international system, and many Global South nations see as much threat as promise in the new technology. They appreciate that information is power, and because they are not yet able to wield these tools effectively, they are sometimes subject to manipulation by the more powerful. Consequently, they have tried to shield themselves from transnational data flows to some extent, and to find other means to gain time to integrate the new technoculture into their plans for national development. This process represents a tremendous challenge, even just on a practical level, because contemporary computer technology is still rather delicate and requires special infrastructural support in warm, humid tropical climates where power supplies may be irregular.

All in all, we would say that the computer has accelerated the pace of international relations, as it has many other dimensions of life. Furthermore, there are signs that it is changing our civilization in ways so fundamental as to inevitably modify the way states relate to one another.

RECOMMENDED READINGS

BRONOWSKI, JACOB. *The Ascent of Man.* Boston: Little, Brown, 1976.

BROWN, LESTER, et al. *State of the World, 1994.* New York: Norton, 1994.

DANIELS, NOMSA D. *Protecting the African Environment: Reconciling North-South Perspectives.* New York: Council on Foreign Relations, 1992.

GEORGE, SUSAN. *Feeding the Few: Corporate Control of Food.* Washington, DC: United Nations, 1992.

KIRDAR, UNER. *Change: Threat or Opportunity for Human Progress?* New York: United Nations, 1992.

KORTEN, DAVID. *Getting to the Twenty-First Century: Voluntary Actions and the Global Agenda.* Hartford, CT: Kumarian Press, 1990.

KRASNER, STEPHEN. *International Regimes.* Ithaca, NY: Cornell University Press, 1983.

LAPPÉ, FRANCES M., and JOSEPH COLLINS. *World Hunger: Twelve Myths.* New York: Grove Press, 1986.

LINDBLUM, CHARLES. *Politics and Markets: The World's Political Economic Systems.* New York: Basic Books, 1977.

MOWLANA, HAMID. *The Passing of Modernity: Communication and the Transformation of Society.* White Plains, NY: Longman, 1990.

ROSZAK, THEODORE. *Voice of the Earth.* New York: Simon & Schuster, 1992.

SCHILLER, H. I. *Mass Communication and Cultural Domination.* White Plains, NY: International Arts and Science Press, 1976.

SKOLNIKOFF, EUGENE B. *The Elusive Transformation: Science, Technology, and the Evolution of International Politics.* Princeton, NJ: Princeton University Press, 1993.

STERN, PAUL C., ORAN R. YOUNG, and DANIEL DRUCKMAN. *Global Environmental Change: Understanding the Human Dimensions.* Washington, DC: National Academy Press, 1992.

WHITE, RODNEY. *North, South, and the Environmental Crisis.* Toronto: University of Toronto Press, 1993.

YOUNG, ORAN R. *International Cooperation: Building Regimes for Natural Resources and the Environment.* Ithaca, NY: Cornell University Press, 1989.

Chapter 12

INTEGRATION, INTERDEPENDENCE, NORTH-SOUTH RELATIONS, AND DEVELOPMENT

For three hundred years the nation-state has been considered not only the basic unit for the conduct of political relations among peoples, but also the basic unit of economic organization. However, once the industrial revolution had launched the great transformation in the method of production and the associated reorientation in human life that continues today, the limits of the state as a structure for rational economic life became gradually more and more apparent.

Despite the theoretical compatibility between political sovereignty and economic autarky, no contemporary state is economically self-sufficient. All are in some measure dependent on outside sources for some share of their economic goods, or they require external markets to sell their products. Resources are not distributed among states in any recognizable proportion to demand; raw materials inadequately supplied in one state may be in surplus in a neighboring state. In fact, many commodities are obtainable advantageously or even exclusively only from certain favored states. Since all people today have economic goals, these differences in physical, political, and economic circumstances lead to different and often conflicting economic policies by governments. And yet, the economic well-being of all individual members of the system depends on the discovery and implementation of means to coordinate these conflicting policies. Here lies, we would suggest, the central paradox of contemporary international economic relations.

INTERDEPENDENCE, INTEGRATION, AND CONVERGENCE

There is a tendency to confuse the two concepts of integration and interdependence. *Integration* is the process by which two or more actors in the global system become one. When applied to states, the term refers to the building of supranational communities in which there are shared social, economic, political, and communication systems. Emphasis here is on the term *process* because very few, if any, such experiments have yet been completed, and it is not yet clear to what degree they will eventually become integrated.

Interdependence can be defined in a number of ways, but it is most commonly used to refer to a state of affairs of mutual dependency; that is, the negative effects of a disruption of two or more states' relations would be fairly equally distributed among them. This condition, where it exists, has usually arisen fortuitously. There has also grown up a set of cooperative arrangements, of greater or lesser formalization and institutionalization, to enable states to cope with issues in international relations that affect them jointly. These arrangements have come to be called international regimes.

Integration

Integration is usually analyzed within the contexts of functionalist and communication theory. Functionalism, developed by David Mitrany and Ernst Haas, asserts that the nation-state cannot respond adequately to the technical, economic, and social challenges of modern society.[1] Mitrany proposed a restructuring of the global system into a horizontal organization consisting of international administrative units instead of a vertical organization based on nation-states. Mitrany believed that such a structure would provide more value satisfaction for all people and help to reduce or even eliminate international conflict. Sovereignty would lose its meaning, cooperation would increase, and technology would overshadow diplomacy.

For Ernst Haas, functional integration is possible only in pluralistic societies where power is not monopolized by a single group but is shared equally by all groups. Political disagreements should not alter the consensus on basic values. Rather, successful economic integration, by demonstrating the benefits to be gained through cooperation, opens the way for a gradual political integration through centralization of the decision-making process. The result is the creation of a new statelike political community.

Karl Deutsch made an important distinction between two types of political communities: the pluralist community where groups maintain their autonomy

[1]See David Mitrany, *A Working Peace System* (Chicago: Quadrangle Books, 1966), and Ernst B. Haas, *Beyond the Nation-State: Functionalist and International Organization* (Stanford, CA: Stanford University Press, 1964).

and the complex community where groups enjoy no autonomy.[2] In the complex community, groups are swallowed up in a central unit. This type of integration requires common values, perceptions, and traditions. In the pluralist community, values, perceptions, and traditions are compatible but not identical. Relevant élite groups in each state, though acknowledging and acting on common interests in some areas, retain their unique points of view. According to Deutsch, pluralist integration is easier to achieve, and therefore historically more frequent, than complex integration.

Interdependence

Interdependence carries with it the potential for both conflict and cooperation. On one hand, increased mutual vulnerability may induce moderation and cosmopolitanism. Also, it has become nearly impossible to contain the spillover of new science and technology across national boundaries. More seriously, in a system that continues to lack effective central guidance, interdependence poses grave threats to global stability. An incident in a region exporting raw materials could have dramatic consequences in another region. The 1973 oil crisis was a dramatic example.

We should point out that at present the so-called "web" of interdependence is very unevenly spread in the world. The major industrialized market economies, as represented in the Organization for Economic Cooperation and Development (OECD), experience the most extensive form of economic interdependence, which compels them to hold regular economic summits to coordinate their monetary and trade policies.

However, a strategic balance also represents a kind of interdependence in the realm of security. This is most clearly embodied in the concept of *stable deterrence,* which implies that *any* disruption of the balance, even in one's own favor, is a danger to peace. The processes of arms control and disarmament can also be seen in this light, because no one can take any meaningful initiative without assurance that the other side will reciprocate. The contemporary process of arms reduction, which began between the United States and the former Soviet Union some years ago, has evolved in this direction.

Finally, we should mention the environment, though we treat it in more detail later. There is perhaps no single issue area in world affairs that better highlights the gap between the functional capacities of the traditional states system and the policy demands being put on it in the modern world. All human beings share a dependence on the biosphere for survival, and an intelligent approach to regulation of humankind's intervention into the biosphere requires *at least* extensive policy coordination among states. To take one example among many, the current lamentable condition of the Mediterranean and the North Seas, together with the difficulties that the governments most directly concerned have in com-

[2]See Karl Deutsch, *Political Community at the International Level: Problems of Definition and Measurements* (New York: Doubleday, 1952).

ing together to assess costs and initiate cleanups, clearly portrays our contemporary dilemma.

Technological advances have fostered increased interdependence in the present global system, but institutions have not kept pace. As we mentioned earlier, regimes are the principal means of coming to terms with the need for international cooperation under conditions of anarchy, but they are interstate structures and are thus subordinate to national sovereignty and interest. There is a tendency for a successful regime to persist for some time when benefits unattainable through unilateral action are realized by all the parties involved. However, there is still reason to doubt whether such arrangements will prove sufficient to cope with the increasing number of global issues that are a product of and are influenced by the contemporary condition of interdependence.

Convergence Theory

In recent years the attention of the world has been seized by the vast changes in Eastern Europe and the former Soviet Union, the end of the Cold War, and the repercussions these developments have had on the entire constellation of international relations. What perhaps is not so well appreciated is that there is an emerging consensus about the value of pluralist democracy and free-market capitalism as a pattern for social organization. This evolution lends new credibility to the ideas of those who for decades have been predicting such events, and we feel a brief survey of their prescient analyses is helpful in understanding the present and in thinking meaningfully about the future of these trends.

The concept of peace through convergence between diverse actors, which is clearly related to the general phenomenon of interdependence, is quite recent. Of course, we can find "great ancestors" of the idea—Alexis de Tocqueville foresaw a common trend toward democracy as a result of industrialization beyond the rivalry of the United States and Russia. Max Weber observed that social systems are "mixed orders" in constant evolution and perpetual change. Thorstein Veblen predicted the growing power, in every industrial society, of a new class of decision makers: the managers. But the contemporary notion of interdependence appeared first during the 1950s in the works of economists, sociologists, and political scientists of diverse outlooks, who argued that there was a new mixed, or synthetic, system emerging from interaction between economic development techniques and patterns of social organization.

In the West, this phenomenon was initially seen in the growth of every economic sector—the growth of the public sector, the growing budget of government, antitrust measures, comprehensive planning and cost/benefit analysis, and measures against inflation that affect prices, salaries, and state aid. In Marxist societies, it was reflected in specialization in production, new technocracy with managerial skills, income according to productivity, use of monetary indexes and capital interest, individual consumption and more meaningful free choices, acknowledgment of international trade, and a certain decentralization and autonomy in the economic decision-making process.

According to Walt Rostow, by midcentury there was only a one-stage difference between the development of Western capitalism and socialist societies, and it was a difference in degree and not in kind. The former Soviet Union was technically and psychologically ready to enter the mass consumption society.[3] The remaining obstacle was the government's decision to spend an increasing part of its budget in defense appropriation and heavy industry—a policy characteristically viewed in the West as promoting the goal of world supremacy and dominance. This era has proved, however, just as Rostow predicted, to be only transitional, and the evolution toward mass consumption could not be stopped indefinitely.

The dynamics of convergence were further explicated by John Kenneth Galbraith.[4] Briefly summarized, he argued that the technological revolution was transforming both capitalist and socialist systems, which were similar in their technostructures, into new industrial state syntheses. The technostructure, a product of business managers and state appointees, was seen to reduce conflict between political and economic power. Basically, both systems found themselves putting more emphasis on production, capital, and technology, and in this they tended to converge.

The late Soviet physicist and dissident Andrei Sakharov emphasized that social development in the United States and the former Soviet Union had created more complex structures and forms of management with a new class of managers whose social character in both countries was very much the same.[5] Sakharov's remarkable vision of the future includes four stages of development: (1) political democratization in Marxist societies and the victory of peaceful coexistence in the capitalist countries; (2) transformation of ownership structure in capitalist societies and collaboration with socialist countries under the prudent leadership of the liberal bourgeoisie; (3) collaboration of socialist and capitalist countries to assist the Global South; and (4) scientific and technological revolution within the socialist and capitalist systems that will lead toward the creation of a world government and the disappearance of contradictions between the two systems.

This vision of convergence is quite optimistic, anticipating the end of ideology, the meeting of the socialist and capitalist systems, and the appearance of a new person and, in fact, a new world. We can read some confirmation of his initial predictions in current events, and the possibility of others in signs of discontent in the capitalist societies. However, the somewhat darker predictions of other writers, such as Herbert Marcuse, also have plausibility.[6] Marcuse argued that both socialists and capitalists, through technological progress, were moving toward a dehumanization of social relations, and that future generations would be

[3]See Walt W. Rostow, *The Stages of Economic Growth.* 2nd ed. (Cambridge: Cambridge University Press, 1971).

[4]See his book *The New Industrial State.* 2nd rev. ed. (Boston: Houghton Mifflin, 1972).

[5]See Andrei Sakharov, *Sakharov Speaks* (New York: Alfred A. Knopf, 1974) and Harrison Salisbury, *Progress, Coexistence and Intellectual Freedom* (New York: Norton, 1968).

[6]See his book *One Dimensional Man* (Boston: Beacon Press, 1964).

dominated by an antihuman technology controlled by cliques of manipulative technocrats.

One trend, which had been omitted from most visions of convergence until it became popular in the 1980s, was the reduction of the economic role of government in capitalist societies. The conservative swing in the West aimed at providing more room for the entrepreneur by reducing the role of government in various sectors, and it is precisely this model of capitalist development that represents the new order for states that have rejected socialism. However, it could well be that just as this model is establishing itself as the global "orthodoxy," its credibility in the developed countries is being called into question in light of mounting social problems, which many electors perceive as requiring renewed government intervention in the society and economy. We would suggest that the basis of true convergence may ultimately involve some movement of capitalist societies back in the direction of enlightened social welfarism.

Second, even assuming a fairly steady and recognizable economic and political convergence, there is no guarantee that either will be of long duration. We have argued that politics is largely a cultural activity, and democracy and capitalism must ultimately be reconciled with the cultures in which they exist if they are to flourish. Cultures are not immutable, but they have proved resistant to change, and the implementation of new social programs must be carried out with pragmatism and flexibility. Observation of contemporary developments in Russia and other former Soviet republics reveals to what extent traditional forms of xenophobia, such as anti-Semitism and pan-Slavism, are reemerging under the stress of the program of economic and political reform.

Finally, there is again no guarantee that the process of global convergence, though certainly an improvement in the short run, will ultimately produce stable peace and long-term benefits. There are still many old issues to work out (e.g., the proliferation of nuclear weapons), and many new ones are emerging (such as the control of drug trafficking), which suggest that convergence, like interdependence in general, seems to hold as much threat as promise, and we can only hope that as the process accelerates, a sense of supranational solidarity will develop with it.

NORTH-SOUTH RELATIONS AND THE NEW INTERNATIONAL ECONOMIC ORDER

The global system comprises the "developed" countries (the North)—the affluent countries in North America, Western Europe, and Japan, which account for about 15 percent of the world population but more than 60 percent of world income—and the "less-developed" or "developing" countries (the Global South)—scores of poor countries in Asia, Africa, and Latin America that comprise most of humankind but possess little of the earth's bounty. Both the North and the South conduct economic relations within a framework that is not currently redistributing wealth and is disadvantageous to the South, which remains characterized by underdevelopment and its ensuing social consequences. The North and South advocate development, yet each views the methods to achieve it from a different perspective.

A New International Economic Order?

The North's development strategy consists of improving the sectors of the less-developed countries' economies that produce the raw materials needed for the North's industries and consumption. The developed states generally discourage heavy industry in the less-developed countries that have the potential of competing with the production of manufactures in the North. The developed states protect themselves from competition through the application of quotas, tariffs, and what are called nontariff barriers to trade (product specifications, health regulations, etc.).

The South, largely because of either direct colonial subjugation or at least dominance by the West, has produced primary goods (i.e., raw materials and agricultural products) for export. This production has been the principal, and in some cases the only, means at its disposal to gain the foreign exchange necessary to purchase capital goods necessary for industrialization. Unfortunately, since World War II, prices paid for their main exports have been steadily declining, thus making the South's position ever more difficult. Also, what industry there is in the South suffers from the discriminatory practices already mentioned when it tries to export to the North. When countries in the South have borrowed, their limited earnings from trade have fallen increasingly short of being sufficient to service their loans. Thus, no matter what angle one looks at it from, the current economic structure does not seem to meet southern needs.

While the North and South are dependent upon one another, each group's dependence varies in terms of raw materials, capital, technology, industrial capacity, political and military power, and cultural vitality. The North is highly industrialized and possesses much capital and military power, but it is dependent upon raw materials. Although the South is economically, militarily, politically, and culturally weaker, it can exert some leverage through its possession of raw materials.

Though there is some degree of mutual dependence between the North and the South, it is highly asymmetric and does not substantially offset the disadvantages experienced by the South in the present international economic order. In fact, the position of the less-developed countries is often described as *vulnerable,* because they are significantly affected by even minor disturbances in the global economy and have very limited means to cushion themselves against or recover from such shocks. The effect of the rapid and steep increase in oil prices upon the non-OPEC Global South is a dramatic case in point.

The North-South dialogue has consisted of a series of discussions and debates that have been going on since the postwar economic system was first discussed in the 1940s and that came to a head during the first special session of the United Nations General Assembly on the New International Economic Order in 1973. In the following numbered paragraphs, we present both the South's original proposals for change in global economic relations and the developed countries' reactions to those proposals.

1. *Orientation of the international monetary system, and especially its central institution, the International Monetary Fund (IMF) toward the interests of the developing world:* The IMF was established in 1944, as part of the so-called Bretton Woods system, which laid the foundations for the global economic system of subsequent decades. This institution was designed to help countries with short-term balance-of-payments problems. After contributing to a common fund, member countries could borrow back when they were temporarily short of foreign exchange. Though perhaps a reasonable program in 1944, the IMF is now considered by many to be inadequate to deal with the chronic (rather than short-term) foreign exchange problems of the developing countries, the majority of which were not even independent in 1944 and whose interest were not considered when the post-war system was conceived. In 1993 the IMF and World Bank switched the economic measures that it used to rate the relative strength of each member country's economy from gross domestic product (GDP) to a new scheme of purchasing-power parity (PPP). Because GDP ranks domestic production in U.S.-dollar terms, it is subject to currency fluctuations. Conversely, PPP gives a more accurate picture of economic strength by comparing prices of various goods and services common to all member states.

2. *The creation of more production cartels along the lines of the Organization of Petroleum Exporting Countries (OPEC):* The 1973 oil embargo and subsequent pricing policy of OPEC seemed to be a replicable model of southern power in the global political economy. It was felt that many other cartels and commodity producers' organizations could be formed or strengthened in order to compel the North to make concessions to southern demands, and more generally to redirect more wealth from the North to the South as OPEC had done. Areas thought to be ripe for such an evolution were cocoa, coffee, copper, and tin, among others.

3. *The formulation of more favorable commodity agreements to regulate prices and quantities:* As mentioned previously, commodity prices have tended to go down since World War II, and these falling prices have had a devastating effect on the earnings of southern economies, which are integrated into the global economy as producers of these commodities and which have limited capacity to diversify their exports. Since successful development planning requires some stable expectation of foreign exchange revenues, it was suggested that an international fund be established to back up stable commodity prices. Thus, when the world price fell below a certain minimal level, the difference would be made up from the fund, and when it rose above this level, the difference would go into the fund for future use in bad years. Such a scheme has operated on a limited scale between the African, Caribbean, and Pacific (ACP) group of countries and the European Community, and is known as STABEX.

4. *Linkage of export prices in the developing countries to the prices they have to pay for imports (known generally as indexation):* The demand for linkage arises from the fact that, as commodity prices have fallen, the southern countries have found

themselves obliged to export more and more to obtain the capital goods necessary for development; that is, it has become necessary to sell more tons of "bananas" abroad to buy the same "tractor." The problem has been aggravated by inflation in the northern countries, which has further contributed to what economists call the deteriorating terms of trade of the South. Indexation, together with commodity price stabilization, would help development planners in the South to rationalize the relationship between imports and exports to a certain degree, and they would be able to count on at least a relatively stable level of foreign reserves over time.

5. *Extension of preferential treatment in trade:* The postwar economic order was based on free trade, and the most basic element of a free-trade regime is the "most-favored nation" principle. This principle insures that no group of countries may establish special trading arrangements among themselves that would exclude others. So, under GATT, if a country grants access to its markets or reduces tariffs for some goods for one country, it must do so for all other members of GATT. The South, however, felt that their economies were entitled to special treatment because they both needed access to northern markets and felt they must protect many of their weak new industries from foreign competition. In effect they wanted special, or preferential, treatment under GATT.

6. *Recognition of developing countries' permanent sovereignty over their natural resources (sometimes referred to as "economic sovereignty"):* Many southern countries discovered that political sovereignty did not automatically bring them control over their economies. Newly independent countries and others that were heavily influenced by foreign investment and manipulation wanted to redress this situation by exerting full juridical control over the conditions of operation of multinational corporations and the conditions for any financial compensation paid in the wake of nationalization of foreign-owned firms. The latter point has been the source of much controversy because traditional international law, reflecting the interests of the former imperial powers, posits the existence of an international standard of compensation. Essentially, the South wanted economic sovereignty recognized as a logical and necessary corollary of political sovereignty.

7. *Transfer of advanced technology to the developing countries on preferential terms.* The southern states simply lost patience with northern proclamations of interest in promoting southern development when in fact the amount of technology actually transferred to the South, measured in terms of either northern capacity to provide or southern capacity to absorb, was very limited. The southern states increasingly adopted a point of view that saw northern development as having occurred at the expense of the South, and felt that the North should provide them with the technology of development as compensation. This policy would also be of long-term benefit to the North because as the South became more developed it would become more of a market for northern high-tech exports.

To this list we would add the more contemporary issue of *debt rescheduling,* which has arisen because of the pressures unfavorable terms of trade have put on the developing countries' ability to pay off their international loans. Furthermore, countries that do not produce oil are required to use much of their limited export earnings to pay for petroleum imports. Yet another contributing cause to the debt problem is the fact that loans were taken out with variable-rate interest, with the result that, as inflation increased in the donor countries, so did the debt of the borrowers. The net effect of these factors, not all of which can be considered the "fault" of the South, is to greatly reduce the actual foreign exchange available to poorer countries to acquire the capital goods and infrastructure necessary for development. Hence, the demand for less stringent ways to pay off debts, and, in the case of the poorest of the poor, the canceling of some debts, has become more strident.

The North regards these demands as far reaching and fundamentally threatening. The developed countries feel that the proposals of the South would dismantle the market-based global economic system, in which the industrialized countries have generally prospered. Furthermore, rebuttals from the North suggest that these demands would also create a severe imbalance in the developed countries because they would tend to favor the economies that were less integrated in the world economy because of their considerable reserves of raw materials. In other words, they would be harder on Europe than they would on the United States.

On the "threatening" proposal of cartels along the lines of OPEC, it can be argued that cartels have a limited exporting power because the developed countries can in most instances use other raw materials (or synthetics) as substitutes. The development of production techniques would thereby reduce the consumption of raw materials, and those still imported could probably be attained from countries that did not belong to the cartels. As time passes, it becomes increasingly clear that the influence of OPEC in the 1970s was a unique phenomenon, which, though theoretically reproducible, is very difficult for other producer groups to achieve.

The third proposal, on indexation, also meets the opposition of the North—again because of the imbalance it would create. Developed countries with low inflation rates would suffer from the indexation of raw material prices, while countries with high rates of inflation would profit. However, the objections to this demand go further. Indexation would serve to offset the "market forces" that determine the structure of the world economy, and capitalist thought has been based for centuries on the notion of "free" markets as the best way to distribute wealth. That the current international market system works in such a way as to favor the North is beyond question. Indexation would substitute a welfare ethic at the global level for the current highly unequal competition.

The new international economic order as envisaged by the South also meets skepticism in the North regarding its effectiveness in bringing about development. This critique is based on the fact that more than half of the raw materials exported in the world come from the industrialized countries of the North. Accordingly, the argument follows, any measure to support prices in the South would benefit the main exporters of raw materials, which ironically have long since reached the stage of takeoff.

The South's demand for the extension of preferential treatment in trade also faces opposition in the North. The North feels that generalized trade preferences (i.e., special access to certain northern markets not enjoyed by other states) should be granted slowly and incrementally to avoid social and economic problems in the developed countries. That is, they do not wish to be flooded with cheaper imports that would harm their domestic industries. In regard to the proposal of the South to promote industrialization, the North favors industrialization on a sectoral basis, and on a basis not competitive with the industries of the developed countries.

As with industrialization, the transfer of advanced technology also provokes the North's protectionist tendencies. Most of the advanced technology in the South is within the jurisdiction of multinational corporations that monopolize technology in order to promote their economic interests. The MNCs seek to retain control of patents and discourage or exclude competitors. The South obviously desires to gain access to this valuable technology, but has so far proven unable to do so.

In conclusion, the developed states see the proposals of the less-developed countries as contributing to imbalances within the global system that would be favorable only to the less-developed countries. The developed countries would like to avoid any modification of the patterns of economic exchange that threaten their favorable positions. However, there has been increasing evidence in recent years that the developed countries must do something to alleviate the crisis in the South because they themselves are being negatively affected by it. For instance, they require markets for their capital goods, but a country that is earning very little foreign exchange and paying out a large portion of what it does earn for debt servicing cannot import very much. Thus at least a few of the reforms put forth may be realized—not through altruism but as an expression of northern self-interest. One can also be sure, however, that these adjustments will present as little threat as possible to the North's favorable position in the system.

The more profound question is whether the current international system can really accommodate the aspirations of the Global South. To be sure, their demands have been expressed almost entirely in economic terms (now that the process of decolonization is nearly completed), and they are among the most jealous guardians of their national sovereignty because it was so recently and painfully gained. However, the international economic system and the states system are products of the same process of historical evolution, and to significantly modify one may not be possible without changing the other. We would suggest that in an increasingly interdependent environment, issue areas refuse to remain distinct, and reform, to be effective, must be more comprehensive than heretofore proposed. Otherwise, the basic structural deficiencies remain and could produce even more serious problems.

DEVELOPMENT AND APPROACHES TO DEVELOPMENT

As we have indicated, the less-developed countries face formidable obstacles in their efforts to modernize. In every dimension of collective life—social, political, economic—change is endemic. Many of these lands have undertaken the colossal task of superimposing a modern nation-state onto a traditional culture that finds it almost wholly alien. The equivalent process took centuries in Europe and was quite gradual. In the contemporary developing world, history has, in this sense, been greatly accelerated. Goals for social change are expressed in terms of generations, or even decades. Thus the problem of development has assumed enormous significance in recent years.

Approaches to Development

Both Western and communist conceptions of the development process have been ambushed by events in the Global South in recent years. A conceptual crisis accelerated by the declining intensity and end of the Cold War and the erosion of shared values in industrialized society has even created doubts about the validity of shared visions of the future and the inevitability of progress endorsed by both Marxists and conventional theorists.

Theories of development, especially the notion of a "revolution of rising expectations," have presented serious policy dilemmas for the major industrialized countries, especially the United States. On the one hand, failure to promote development (understood as *both* economic growth and more equitable distribution of wealth) effectively in a world where communication has raised levels of expectations would seem almost to guarantee social upheaval. On the other hand, rapid development tends to upset traditional social structures in such a way as also to accelerate unrest. This situation seems to have no simple solution.

The ebullient optimism that kicked off the 1960s as the "decade of development" has degenerated into theoretical and policy frustration. Some development did, of course, take place. But the optimistic thesis of gradual peaceful change and the rise of social democracy, espoused by Western liberals, has not yet been justified, though recent events are to some extent encouraging. Even more dramatic has been the near-universal collapse of Marxist-oriented approaches to development. In fact, the end of the Cold War has reduced the commitment of the industrial nations to sponsoring development. It has proved expensive, complicated, and ambivalent as a policy goal. More recently, the growing world ecological crisis has raised doubts about the adaptive value of industrialism in its present form, even for advanced states.

A given state is still generally considered to be underdeveloped if it fails to fit a model structured by Western notions of politics and community. If it lacks democratic, competitive political parties and a high standard of living, it is, almost by definition, underdeveloped. Most policymakers still assume that a people emerging from colonialism and poverty will eventually express its independence in a systematic effort to construct a modern state.

This outlook was first articulated in the few early postwar analyses of the newly independent states of Asia and Africa. These were largely historical, administrative, and anthropological studies. Historians were generally preoccupied with the origin and evolution of particular states. Political scientists engaged in comparative analyses of newly formed constitutional, electoral, and legislative processes, employing the conceptual scheme of the Western political tradition. Anthropologists, alone among social scientists, as a result of their appreciation of human cultural diversity, opposed the imposition of alien rule on weaker societies.

Because the early transitional period in the new states of the Global South was characterized by stubbornly persisting political instability and social discontinuity, early enthusiasm for independence and the happy anticipation of these states evolving along modern democratic lines began to fade. The prevalence of turmoil, instead of the expected development of stable institutions and economic growth, led to a reexamination of prior assumptions. Using such indexes as per capita income, literacy rates, and levels of industrialization, economists and sociologists associated political instability with economic backwardness. Some emphasized the need for economic and military assistance to countries threatened by communist aggression and infiltration, thus limiting their analysis to the context of the Cold War. Thus, as the U.S.–U.S.S.R. rivalry intensified, the practice of international development and alternative approaches to the problems of modernization (communist versus democratic) acquired considerable status as important foreign policy issues.

Western social scientists were reluctant to see the issues of modernization as comprising a meaningful whole. They tended to conceive the problem in terms of unprecedented speed and intensity of social change, and found it difficult to make their assumptions explicit or to relate theory to specific issues. Still, the resulting concern with modernization problems, as issues in themselves, had the salutary effect of forcing the social sciences to devise new categories and techniques of analysis of the phenomena of rapid social and political change.

The effort to gain a deeper understanding of political development, as contrasted with the exclusively technical problems of economic development, is regarded as one of the most significant advances in social research of the Global South. Resting on the assumption that an important relationship exists between social, economic, and political development, this approach was seen to offer the policymaker a fresh and more realistic method for assessing the long-range problems of development.

Because of the often extreme difficulties encountered by the Global South in building modern, politically viable states out of traditional societies, political development was recognized as the key to the overall process of modernization. It came to be generally assumed that political development was a precondition of fully successful economic development. Accordingly, social scientists attempted to analyze the problem systematically by using more general concepts such as *legitimacy, stability, adaptation, articulation, aggregation,* and *integration* in place of concepts like *constitutions, elections, interest groups,* and *legislatures.*

This approach was able, at least to some extent, to identify and analyze the political and cultural systems and subsystems in states with diverse levels of political sophistication. It advocated an empirical analysis of political functions and the processes of change and modernization without regard to culture or geographical peculiarities. Because of its greater precision, the behavioral approach provided a more universal set of analytic concepts for the study of comparative politics. But, at the same time, it minimized the importance of values and goals by placing primary emphasis on processes. In short, the subjective, human dimension of modernization was largely left out.

One implication of this approach was that no particular model could be claimed to represent a necessary or ideal precondition for economic and social development. Even in the twentieth century, industrialized states have experimented with or accepted divergent governmental institutions. These have ranged from monarchies to multiparty democracies, from oligarchic capitalism to democratic centralism. It was also occasionally argued that the new states might require innovative forms of governmental institutions related to their own societal values and traditions.

However, analysis of development often assumed that contemporary social and economic conditions in the Global South give rise to, or require, a specific mode of political development, and this premise reflected certain, perhaps unconscious, value judgments of the Western analyst. The most popular approaches are based on assumptions that democracy is a symptom of modernity, that it is the ideal form of political development, and that it is a prerequisite of development. We would suggest, however, that democracy has produced so many hybrids and derivations and is applied to such a multitude of aphorisms that it has lost its meaning—unless precisely defined within the organic framework of a given state.

Beyond Economics, Toward Adaptation

Historically there have been many human value systems. Therefore, no transcultural standard exists (yet) with which to judge the relative merits of one system against another. We would argue that it makes little sense to divide humanity into "traditional" and "modern" cultures. All cultures are constantly evolving, and none stand still. Furthermore, historical precedents of encounters between developed and less-developed societies illustrate that the less-developed society does not become a carbon copy of the more advanced one, but rather a hybrid society. Since the imported values and technology do not affect all segments of the less-developed society equally, certain groups—the army and the intelligentsia most often—are more adaptive. The techniques of cultural innovation designed to oppress or indoctrinate—arms and ideas—are most readily acquired by the élites of the less-developed society.

From the Western-culture-centric point of view, the struggle of former colonies to emulate the technology, lifestyles, economic practices, and other characteristic behavior of the West is referred to as "development" or "modernization." However, how valid can such a judgment be if many aspects of Western culture are perceived as increasingly nonadaptive even to Westerners? It is quite possible that the societies that put up the greatest resistance to the technocratic mentality may be vindicated by history as having refused to go down a blind alley. We may believe, or wish to believe, that the present transformation from agriculture to "technoculture" (for want of a better word) now sweeping the planet will eventually produce modes of behavior consistent with the ecology of the Earth, but such an outcome is neither inevitable nor self-evident.

The usual focus of the study of development—on the nation-state as the unit of analysis—seems to be too narrow, and the common assumptions that modernization can be achieved on an incremental, nondisruptive, and above all peaceful basis appear to be the height of wishful thinking. In many parts of the South, the average regime has had a life cycle of only a few years or even a few months. The other major complex of issues—covering which ideology or strategy of development will be adapted—seems to suffer from the same myopia. Recent findings in the field suggest that *any* regime that invests heavily in mass education and industrial development begins to look more like an industrialized state. Russia began modernization (by emulating European states) with Peter the Great. By 1912, five years before its revolution, Russia was already the fourth-ranking industrial power. Japan consciously chose to emulate Great Britain in its drive for technoculture. Is it really very likely to have made any difference over the next five hundred years if Japan had instead chosen France or Germany?

The economic standard commonly used as the primary criterion of development is being increasingly questioned by both emerging societies and the West. Though currently seeking more Western technology, China has resisted fully emulating the Western pattern of growth because the Chinese have viewed the Western concept of development as a residual form of imperialism and as a cover for a continuing exploitative arrangement between imperial powers and their former colonies. Western ecologists, on the other hand, have pointed out with increasing emphasis that the drives for ever-increasing per capita gross national product (GNP) and energy consumption in industrial and industrializing societies—both usually seen as indicators of development—rather than overpopulation, are major contributing causes to the worldwide environmental crisis. Some long-range planners have even begun to talk about advanced societies where declining population, dropping energy consumption, and negative aggregate GNP growth would be viewed as "progressive."

Our view is that *development,* with its connotation of "bigger is better," is a misnomer. A more appropriate term might be *adaptation.* An adaptive society might well pursue stability as its ideal rather than uncontrolled growth. This is a more comprehensive, more pragmatic, and more open-ended approach to the subject. Human societies are faced with different challenges at different times, and it is the ability to assess current problems accurately and initiate appropriate responses that leads to success and prosperity on all levels. Furthermore, we suggest that development should be considered in normative and moral terms and not just as an economic or technical problem.

Sustainable Development: Problems and Prospects

Sustainable development refers to a process through which human beings choose and shape their futures within the context of their environments to achieve a humane and creative society. It is concerned with the dignity of the individual, a secure level of self-esteem, and the establishment of institutions appropriate for these ends. Development involves modernization and humanization.

Development is a process whose goals are to realize the human potential for total societies and for the total human being and whose success hinges upon the satisfaction of those goals. Worthwhile goals common to humanity can be found in the various documents on human rights, including the United Nations' Declaration of Human Rights, International Covenant on Economic, Social, and Cultural Rights, and International Covenant on Civil and Political Rights; Pope John XXIII's *Pacem in Terris;* and Global South declarations. Obviously, these documents reflect the weaknesses and strengths of the United Nations and the historical context and cultural realities of the time, and we expect efforts to define the goals of human existence to continue.

Therefore, a *developed* or adaptive country is one where the obstacles to human freedom, community, and creativity have been as nearly eliminated as possible, where the social, economic, political, and cultural institutions support and stimulate freedom, community, and creativity for all persons, where there is a nearly approximated norm of equal dignity and respect for all persons and groups, and where there are no *extremes* of wealth and poverty among the population. Individual human and societal growth are interconnected and the process is open-minded.

Development goals, in our scheme, are the furthest projection of human objectives consisting of hopes and ideals, the components of the ideal society—that is, the best possible society that can be imagined. Development objectives are the concretely defined goals, considered reasonable and realizable within the limits of available technology and resources, that are established as aspirations within the context of an existing situation. Development targets are short-range objectives, usually those that are selected as the target level of a particular program (e.g., to raise the literacy rate from 30 to 70 percent—70 percent would be the immediate development target). It follows that targets and objectives should be consistent with and build toward the realization of consciously chosen and explicit development goals.

Modernization is the process of adapting technology for the uses of the society and attempting to make that society more rational, efficient, and predictable, especially through the use of comprehensive planning, rational administration, and scientific evaluation. Modernization also carries the connotation of a more productive society, at least in economic terms. Like development, modernization is always at least a partially conscious effort on the part of some, who therefore have a vision or model of what a "modern" society should look like.

Humanization is the process of enlarging and making more equal the dignity, freedom, opportunity for creativity and community, and welfare of individuals in society, as well as the restructuring of the institutions and culture of that society to support these goals. To summarize: Modernization plus humanization equals development.

The goals of development can be divided into two broad categories: the human quality of life and the infrastructure of the developmental process. The human quality and level of life include the following:

1. *Physical and Mental Health:* The state of life and consciousness that supports and stimulates the greatest self-knowledge, community knowledge, and realization through the maximization of physical and mental energy and creativity and through the maximum diminution of physical and mental malfunctions, diseases, and suffering.

2. *Security, Dignity, and Freedom:* The state of life of the individual and the group that supports and encourages the greatest self- and community realization through the maximum possible reduction of external threats to the integrity of the individual and the group.

3. *Education and Training:* The quantity and quality of facilities and resources available to individuals and communities to provide the skills necessary for the preservation, enhancement, and continuous re-creation of culture and the development of the talents and skills of the individual and the group to the maximum degree possible.

4. *Culture and Leisure:* The quantity and quality of time and cultural opportunities afforded, as well as facilities and resources, for groups and individuals, for cultural development and enrichment, for cultural creation, and for group and individual fulfillment.

The infrastructure of the development process includes the following things:

1. *The System of Ecosystem Maintenance:* Encompassing the conservation of natural resources, avoidance of pollution and waste, and health and safety support.

2. *Social, Cultural, Educational, and Communications Support Systems:* To enhance the goals of a developed society to expand the sense of community and human solidarity, and to stimulate cultural creativity and responsibility.

3. *The Political System:* The level and quality of participation in setting social, economic, and political guidelines for the society and the group, the level and quality of responsiveness, review, and accountability of political officials to their society, the efficiency of administration of public programs, and the level and quality of research and planning in the allocation of social resources and values.

4. *The Economic System:* The quality and adequacy of research planning in the use of human and natural resources for purposes of the production of goods and services, efficiency and adequacy of the quantity and quality in the production of goods and services, including working conditions, the distribution system, the supportive infrastructure (sanitation, transportation, and communications), and the level and quality of accountability of the economic system to the society for its research, planning, efficiency, administration, and allocation of resources.

Sustainable development is a self-conscious, participatory, and self-managed enterprise, seeking the full humanization of the person, or all persons, of the community and of the world system. It focuses on the diminution of impediments to human self-realization (poverty, disease, war); the provision of the skills necessary for self- —and community—expression and realization (communication and organizational skills); and the support and stimulation of human realization by positive action, through cultural creation.

The goals of development are to realize the human potential for total societies and for the total human being. Development is a process in which one of the principal "products" is the very process itself—the open-ended process—of the constant creation and re-creation of a global humanist culture. There are no "more-developed" and "less-developed" human beings or states—only "individuals and societies in development." Development becomes the permanent quest of every person, of all societies.

RECOMMENDED READINGS

ADAMS, NASSAU. *Worlds Apart: The North-South Divide and the International System.* London: Zed Books, 1993.

ALMOND, GABRIEL A., and G. BINGHAM POWELL. *Comparative Politics: A Development Approach.* Boston: Little, Brown, 1966.

BALDASSARRI, MARIO, LUIGI PAGNETTO, and EDMUND S. PHELS. *International Economic Interdependence, Patterns of Trade Balances, and Economic Policy Coordination.* New York: St. Martin's Press, 1992.

BRANDT, WILLY. *Common Crisis: North-South: Cooperation for World Recovery.* Cambridge, MA: MIT Press, 1983.

CHERU, FANTU. *The Silent Revolution in Africa: Debt, Development and Democracy.* London: Zed Books, 1989

EHRLICH, PAUL R. *The Population Explosion.* New York: Simon & Schuster, 1990.

GOULET, DENIS. *The New Moral Order: Studies in Development Ethics, and Liberation Theology.* Maryknoll, NY: Orbis Books, 1974.

HAAG, G., et al. *Economic Evolution and Demographic Change: Formal Models in Social Sciences.* New York: Springer-Verlag, 1992.

HEILBRONER, ROBERT. *An Inquiry into the Human Prospect: Looked at Again for the 1990s.* New York: Norton, 1991.

MEADOWS, DONELLA H., et al. *Beyond the Limits: Confronting Global Collapse, Envisioning a Sustainable Future.* Post Mills, VT: Chelsea Green, 1992.

SAID, ABDUL AZIZ, ed. *Protagonists of Change: Subcultures in Development and Revolution.* Englewood Cliffs, NJ: Prentice Hall, 1971.

SCHUMACHER, E. F. *Small Is Beautiful: Economics as if People Mattered.* New York: Harper & Row, 1973.

STAUDT, KATHLEEN A. *Managing Development: State, Society, and International Contexts.* Newbury Park, CA: Sage, 1991.

STEWART, FRANCES. *North-South and South-South: Essays on International Economics.* New York: St. Martin's Press, 1992.

THEOBALD, ROBIN. *Corruption, Development, and Underdevelopment.* Durham, NC: Duke University Press, 1990.

THOMAS, CAROLINE. *Conflict and Consensus in South/North Security.* Cambridge, UK: Cambridge University Press, 1989.

YOUNG, ORAN R. *International Cooperation: Building Regimes for Natural Resources and the Environment.* Ithaca, NY: Cornell University Press, 1989.

Chapter 13

THE WORLD ECONOMY AND THE MULTINATIONAL CORPORATION

We have mentioned that the altered and reduced role of military might in international relations has, among other things, increased the salience of economic issues. Global economic trends and processes have always generated parameters that heavily influence the foreign policy choices of states, and this statement is even more true of today's highly interdependent international system. Consequently, the multinational corporation (MNC) as the main instrument of global economic production and distribution has attracted increasing attention from scholars of world politics. In this chapter we will first introduce the concepts and elements of global economics that impinge most directly on international politics, and then go on to consider in some detail the role of the MNC.

THE WORLD ECONOMY: A PRIMER

International economics is a developed and complex field of study, and here we seek only to provide the ideas and vocabulary necessary to make an entry into the subject. We would, however, maintain that our approach to politics, as the maximization of social values, can be extended to economics, even though many mainstream works in the field give another impression. Contrary to the public image of the economy as an objective, nearly mechanistic, system that functions according to "laws," we see economic outcomes as the product of choices among social priorities.[1] It is because social priorities vary both within and among states that there are a variety of approaches to international economic policy.

[1]This point was central to our discussion of development in the previous chapter.

If there is a central concept in international economics, it must be "wealth," or, more specifically, the "wealth of nations," and here we are most concerned with the impact of differential levels of wealth among states on international political outcomes—put more simply, the relationship between power and wealth in international relations. Many of the issues in this area arise from the fact that, in the wake of the Industrial Revolution and European colonial expansion, the first truly planetary economic system came into being early in the twentieth century, but, as we have emphasized repeatedly, the world political system remains fragmented and anarchic. This anarchy continues to pose acute problems of policy coordination for all the world's states as they seek to survive and prosper.

Perspectives

In the introduction to this book we contrasted different views of the relationship between politics and economics, and writers on international economics usually adopt one of three basic points of view on this question, which can be characterized as *mercantilist, liberal,* or *Marxist.*

Mercantilism has often been portrayed as the economic "twin" of realism and neorealism. Mercantilists assess international economic issues from the point of view of a state with a national economy, trying to increase its wealth in order to maximize its potential and actual power relative to other states. This outlook is statist, competitive, and security conscious: Power is the end, and wealth a means. In this regard, mercantilist governments would promote industries important to strategic concerns and would assist national firms to take the lead in developing new technologies and capturing new markets before major competitors. They would not favor economic policies that, though bringing high profits, might increase the state's political or strategic vulnerability. For instance, mercantilists have at times advocated strict control over sales of high-technology equipment to states that are perceived as competitors in any area of world politics. In short, economic efficiency, in this case the maximization of exports, would be sacrificed, if necessary, for statist political ends.

For liberals, economic efficiency takes top priority, and this is understood to require global markets for goods and services that function in as free (i.e., unrestricted) a manner as possible. Free markets are viewed as the best means to create and distribute wealth, both within and among states. To maximize efficiency, and therefore wealth, in the global economy, liberals advocate the principle of *comparative advantage*—the principle that a given national economy should concentrate on producing and exporting things in regard to which it has a comparative advantage relative to other countries. Commodities it cannot produce as efficiently, it should import. Economic efficiency is maximized because all would produce what they produce best. Since the world economy has never been wholly "open" in the way liberals advocate, a characteristic goal of liberal policy is to reduce the amount of government intervention in specific economies and to create global economic regimes that promote free markets.

We have already touched on several elements of the Marxist perspective.

Seen from this viewpoint, the world economy as a whole is capitalist, as are almost all the national economies within it. In a capitalist economy the capitalist class—that is, those who *own* the means of production in society—receives the largest share of economic benefits; the workers—those who actually *produce* goods—receive proportionately less. In the past, Marx, Lenin, and others felt that the tendency of capitalist systems to overproduce would eventually so impoverish workers that they would unite to revolt against their "oppressors" and would take the means of production into their own hands and create a socialist society. However, in recent decades much of the world's capital has become transnationalized: multinational firms operate in many countries and are not closely tied to the fortunes of a single national economy or state (this topic will be discussed in detail later). Thus the "balance of power" among capitalists, workers, and the state has shifted dramatically in favor of the first.

For Marxists, this world capitalist economy is structured, as described in Chapter 12, in terms of a center of highly developed industrial states with strong political institutions and integrated societies, and a dependent, vulnerable periphery of underdeveloped, largely agricultural, raw-material-producing states with weak political institutions and divided societies. Marxists emphasize that this structure is inherent to a capitalist system of production, that the class tensions within countries and between the center and periphery countries will continue and increase as long as the structure persists, and that the inevitable result is the simultaneous enrichment of a very small global élite and the impoverishment and alienation of the majority of the world's people.

Considered together, these three perspectives reflect the problems of policy coordination that we have already referred to. Though interaction and cooperation among states are necessary to foster widespread prosperity, this kind of economic "openness" is in many ways incompatible with "national security" as traditionally conceived. Also, as we argued in our discussion of North-South issues, the continued impoverishment of the Global South serves no one's interests in the long run.

The Three *C*'s: Commerce, Currency, and Capital

There are basically three aspects to a state's foreign economic policy: (1) the conditions for trade with other countries; (2) the rules and procedures for fixing the value of its currency relative to others; and (3) the flow of capital into and out of the national economy. It is in the formulation and implementation of policies in these three areas that the "politics" of political economy is found.

All states trade with others, to a greater or lesser extent, and in the last hundred years the intensity and scope of world trade have increased tremendously. Trade, however, poses a fundamental foreign policy dilemma: Should the state apply the principle of comparative advantage and buy cheaper foreign goods even if these goods are produced domestically? If the domestic producers are important politically to the ruling regime or if they provide many jobs, undiluted economic rationality may not always prevail. Trade policy, therefore, is often a compromise that reflects some elements of liberalism and some of the power/security concerns of mercantilists, and that also seeks to be politically popular.

In the context of the world economy, the state can be thought of as a gatekeeper that sets the conditions for entry and exit of goods. If a state wishes to protect domestic producers from foreign competition, it can use any mix of tariffs, quotas, and nontariff trade barriers to limit the flow of foreign goods into the national economy. A state cannot, however, determine trade policy solely on this basis. If state A sets limits on the importation of goods from state B, state B may do the same. When this trend becomes widespread in the international system and the world economy becomes generally "closed," all states suffer because their export industries lose markets. These losses, in turn, can lead to a widespread economic slowdown with accompanying unemployment and social tension—an obviously unpopular situation that any government would seek to avoid.

This reciprocal dimension to trade is what led to the creation of an international trade regime, given formal expression in the General Agreement on Tariffs and Trade (GATT), which has been the main policy forum for discussion of trade issues. We discussed the origins and thinking behind GATT in Chapter 12, and since its creation after World War II several rounds of trade talks have generally brought tariffs down. The last one, the Uruguay round, was completed in 1993. The global trade treaty signed at the Marrakech Conference in 1994 provided for the creation of the World Trade Organization (WTO) to replace GATT. The new organization will serve to monitor trade and resolve disputes before they can damage the world economy. It should be emphasized that under GATT and the most-favored-nation principle, "openness" is the norm in the world economy, and exceptions to this norm are supposed to be negotiated through GATT.

The fluctuations of the world political economy have, however, prevented tariff reduction from continuing uninterruptedly, and many states have reverted to some elements of protectionism in recent years. However, GATT still serves to regulate these developments and to moderate their intensity. Global South states, though granted some special concessions to protect the "infant industries" of their developing economies, still tend to view GATT as a "rich man's club," and they have created their own forum to discuss trade issues, the United Nations Conference on Trade and Development (UNCTAD).

Another closely related problem of foreign economic policy is the value of the national currency relative to that of other states: This is called the currency's *foreign exchange value.* A state can, in theory, fix this value at whatever level it likes, but reciprocity once again comes into play. If state A reduces the value of its currency relative to that of state B, then A's goods (obviously priced in A's currency) will become cheaper to those paying with B's currency. Conversely, B's goods would become more expensive to consumers in A. This measure would then have the effect of simultaneously increasing A's exports to B and decreasing B's exports to A. However, B could take similar measures, and such "beggar thy neighbor" policies are just as destructive as trade protectionism to the world economy.

Therefore, efforts have been made from time to time, both on the global and regional levels, to regulate the foreign exchange values of currencies so that governments, businesses, and private consumers can benefit from the resulting stability. At the time of writing, there exists such a system within the European Union, known as the European Monetary System, but it is under severe strain, with certain members of the union having opted out of the EMS for indefinite periods. The last such system at the global level was based on currencies valued in terms of gold, which was itself priced at thirty-five U.S. dollars an ounce. In effect, the main currencies in the world were traded at their American dollar values, and American dollars were, in theory, redeemable in gold at the fixed rate.

This system operated from the late 1940s till the early 1970s, when it was understood by all concerned that there were too many U.S. dollars in circulation to ever be redeemed in gold. President Richard Nixon then took the dollar off the gold standard. From that time on, the value of the dollar vis-à-vis other major currencies has been determined by market forces—that is, by the demand for dollars in the world's currency markets at a particular time. Thus the price is not fixed, but rather "floats"—that is, fluctuates according to developments in the U.S. and world economies that influence demand for the currency.

Only a few major currencies are used for international economic exchanges, and these are determined by how stable their values are perceived to be. For instance, if country A's currency is subject to rapid and wide fluctuations in value, no one would want to hold much of it for very long. Therefore, if A wants to buy a commodity like oil from abroad, it has to first buy the dollars necessary for the purchase, which are then transferred for the sale of oil. Besides the dollar, other prominent international currencies include the German mark, the Japanese yen, the British pound, and the Swiss and French francs.

Thus, states whose currencies are not used for international transactions must always be concerned about their *balance of payments*—that is, whether the foreign exchange they earn (largely through exports) and the foreign exchange they spend are more or less equal. Many of the Global South states have had serious problems in this regard because the value of their currencies has fallen, thus cheapening their exports, at the same time that their need for foreign exchange to import technology and to repay loans has increased.

The principal global institution for dealing with these *monetary* issues is the International Monetary Fund (IMF), which we introduced in our discussion of the New International Economic Order in Chapter 12. It should be added here that in recent decades there have been more and more conditions associated with certain kinds of loans from the IMF. Basically Global South and Eastern European countries that have sought IMF help with their massive foreign debts have been required to reshape their domestic economies according to liberal free-market principles.

The third dimension of foreign economic policy concerns the international movement of capital. All economies rely to some extent on foreign capital, but some are more dependent than others, and a high level of dependence can influence a state's foreign policy in a number of areas. For instance, during the 1980s, in order to finance its huge arms buildup, the United States came to rely on Japanese (and other) banks to purchase the government bonds issued to raise the necessary funds. Many people were concerned that being America's creditor on such a large scale gave the Japanese a potential "lever" on U.S. foreign policy. In purely strategic terms, being dependent on outside capital is a sign of vulnerability.

There are two sources of foreign capital: foreign investment and foreign aid. The former can be either *direct,* which entails ownership of enterprises in other countries, or *portfolio,* which involves acquiring stocks and bonds in foreign companies without necessarily seeking a controlling interest. Foreign aid, as we have discussed elsewhere, is intergovernmental, either on a bilateral or multilateral basis, and involves grants, loans, and technical assistance.

Before we discuss the pros and cons of the multinational corporation as the main contemporary vehicle of foreign direct investment, it should be noted that the volume of capital movements in the world today, thanks to well-developed financial markets and electronic technology, is many times that of trade. These technical means have combined with a capitalistic, speculative mentality, to produce a very volatile environment for states' economic policymaking. A single wrong decision by a state about domestic interest rates, for instance, may lead to a "flight" of capital from domestic to foreign banks where greater profits are to be realized—a potentially serious blow to any economy. More and more government attention must be devoted to monitoring and, to the extent possible, steering these developments.

MULTINATIONAL CORPORATIONS (MNCs)

Though much has been learned about the MNC, its impact on the international *political* environment is still not clear. It is difficult to assess its relationship with other actors in the system and to evaluate its contribution to global development. Even the applicable tools of inquiry are somewhat alien to the political scientist, because they include such things as balance sheets, reports of board meetings, and stock market quotations rather than government white papers, event data, or the memoirs of decision makers. Though we are not accustomed to thinking of the foreign policy of IBM or General Motors, decision making by such companies has as much impact on global conflict and cooperation as that of a great many states.

In this section we will trace the origins and contemporary role of the MNC in the international political economy. We will also try to convey the very widely differing views on the contribution of MNCs to global welfare. The basic question is whether the activities of MNCs are among the fundamental causes of certain significant trends in the international system or merely part of the effects.

Historical Evolution of Multinational Corporations

Multinational enterprises are not a recent phenomenon. In 1902, F. A. MacKenzie's *The American Invaders* appeared in London, analyzing the impact of U.S. direct investment abroad stimulated by many American companies, among them

Otis Elevator, Singer Company, and General Electric. Even earlier, long before the coming of the Industrial Revolution, international financial institutions flourished in the fourteenth- and fifteenth-century cities of Venice, Barcelona, and Genoa. In 1689 the Bank of Amsterdam was established to finance the explorations of the Dutch East India Company, and the French Compagnie d'Occident was created in 1717 to foster trade with the Louisiana territories. By the nineteenth century the center of banking activity in Europe had moved to Germany, which had established affiliates in South America, the Far East, and Eastern Europe.

Multinational banking saw its golden age in nineteenth-century England, where much of the economic development of the United States (particularly railroads) was supported with capital originating in London. It was the failure of the British banking house of Baring Brothers that precipitated the first world financial crisis, a consequence of which was the massive depression in the United States in the 1890s.

Another early form of multinational business was the seventeenth-century trading company, which obtained grants from the crowns of Europe to monopolize colonial trade. Such companies were chartered by the competent mercantile powers—England, Holland, Sweden, Denmark, and Spain—and were manipulated as appendages of the political and economic policies of the country that chartered them.

However, it has only been since the end of World War II that the MNC has emerged as a pervasive force in world politics. Direct investment by multinational firms in states, as distinguished from portfolio investment, has been a conspicuous feature of national development, the results of which have been mixed. In the industrialized market economies the MNC has had a generally positive effect. In Australia, for instance, direct investment has been the most important source of capital formation for economic growth. In the 1960s, American, British, and Japanese corporations assumed a major role in furnishing technology and capital to exploit the significant mineral discoveries made there during these years. The role of direct investment in modernizing industries and stimulating domestic markets has also been perceived as beneficial in such diverse countries as Norway (hydroelectric power), South Africa (mining and gold), and Canada (oil, natural gas, and minerals), as well as Argentina and the United States.

However, direct investment in the less-developed countries has been associated with the persistent economic domination of the North over the South—a situation generally referred to in all its various historical forms as "imperialism." There is little doubt that the pecuniary interest of foreign firms played a major, though not necessarily determining, role in the process of European colonial expansion, as well as in the more contemporary relations of "neocolonialism." Neocolonialism refers to a condition in which, despite political independence, a new state is still vulnerable and sensitive to external manipulation because of continuing foreign control of its economy.

Although historically there is sufficient basis to draw such conclusions, often a passionate distaste for imperialism has clouded the separate issue of whether the "peripheral" state has derived *any* benefits from its relationship with the "metropole." The classic instance in this debate is India, where despite the undeniably inhibiting influences of the British presence, it still seems unlikely that the country could have undergone modernization alone.

One cannot fully appreciate the impact of the MNC without considering some startling figures. For instance, since the end of World War II, direct U.S. investment abroad has leaped from $19 billion to more than $323 billion, while foreign private investment in the United States, between 1979 and 1990, grew from $80 billion to $403 billion. The annual growth rate in investment has been approximately 10 percent. At present the United States has a GNP of approximately $5 trillion per year, and 25 percent of the world's total GNP is generated from branches and subsidiaries of U.S. corporations. Another 20 percent of the gross world product originates from European and Japanese MNCs.

Multinational corporations are in an excellent position to facilitate capital transfers between states, stimulate capital formation, and serve as a conduit for the transfer of technology. However, as self-interested profit-making firms, their goals and priorities in these areas do not always agree with those of their host countries. The question then becomes, "How do nation-states preserve their political, economic, and cultural identities and prevent the theft or abuse of their natural resources and environment, while still sharing in the benefits of rapid industrial growth of which the MNCs are the primary vehicle?"

The majority of the world's MNCs are based in the United States; of the 500 largest corporations in the world, 306 are American and 74 are from the countries of the European Economic Community. Moreover, 187 U.S. multinationals account for a third of the sales and half of the assets of U.S. enterprises. But not all the largest multinationals are American. For example, Philips, headquartered in the Netherlands, operates in some 68 countries. Japanese-based MNCs have expanded so rapidly that today Japan is the second-largest center of multinationals in the world, overtaking Britain.

What do these statistics suggest about the MNC as an actor in the contemporary world environment? Is it politically significant that the aggregate sales of General Motors are larger than many states' GNPs? Should we inquire how many armed divisions are controlled by General Motors, or does this inquiry merely beg the question? Is General Motors a largely independent actor in the global system, or are most MNCs only appendages of their home states' foreign policies?

The answers to these questions lie somewhere in the nexus of power and wealth explored earlier. For instance, MNCs control such vast quantities of money that they alone can precipitate the sort of monetary crises mentioned before by moving a small proportion of their funds from one country to another. The short-term liquid assets of private institutions are estimated to be 1200 billion U.S. dollars on the international financial scene, and the "lion's share" of this money is controlled by U.S.-based multinational corporations and banks.[2] Because of the enormity of the multinationals' assets, only a fraction needs to be moved for a

[2]*World Investment Report 1992: Corporations as Engines of Growth.* United Nations, Transnational Corporations and Management Division. Center on Transnational Corporations. New York: United Nations, 1992.

serious crisis to develop. In fact, it is certain that these largely American MNCs precipitated the devaluation of the American dollar in the monetary crisis of March 1973, as speculators unloaded dollars and purchased West German marks and Japanese yen.

Such effects are even more significant in developing countries, where the impact of a large MNC in such areas as tax revenues, inflation, and employment, as well as monetary issues, can contribute directly and dramatically to the level of support for the regime in power. As we will see in more detail in a later subsection, the governments of less-developed countries have often found themselves, initially at least, poorly prepared to bargain with such powerful and resourceful adversaries.

The actions of the firms involved, however, are not usually intended specifically to do political damage. Rather, MNCs pursue their own interest as economic actors, and this fact renders their role in international relations ambiguous. Insofar as the global economy is "open" and governments only interfere to a limited and controlled degree in the activities of MNCs that are based within their borders, the political impact of these firms will usually be indirect. It is true that the corporate interest of U.S. MNCs and the national interest of the United States as a nation-state frequently coincide, for the simple reason that material prosperity is a goal of all states, and the success of U.S. MNCs contributes in large measure to the economic well-being of the country. However, at times, as described previously, their interests diverge.

Why then do some writers persist in seeing the U.S. multinational corporation as a "tool" of American imperialism when a U.S.-based MNC can apparently pursue policies quite independent of—and in contradiction to—those of the U.S. government? Perhaps because such observers have been more concerned with the aggregate effects of U.S. global prominence than with the particular political and economic dynamics that produced it.

It must be admitted that the U.S. government has intervened on many occasions to protect private U.S. investments, particularly in Latin America, and it has considered doing so in other instances. However, there is just as much evidence that at times the government has used the protection of investments as an excuse to pursue, through intervention, other more strictly political objectives.

In other words, today's MNC should not be confused with an enterprise such as the British East India Company, created specifically to help achieve a goal of foreign policy. The very existence of the U.S. Trading with the Enemy Act and the conditions for its application are evidence that the possibility of conflicting interest between the business community and the state is acknowledged. There is no doubt that the U.S. government has tried to devise ways to control American businesses operating abroad.

Goals of Multinational Corporations

The classic formulation of the motivations of states is that they seek to increase their capability to pursue their national interests, largely defined in terms of security and economic growth. The classic formulation of corporate motivations, as we have been arguing, is the profit-maximizing model. However, even this model does not furnish an objective norm for corporate behavior but rather establishes limits beyond which the corporation cannot go. These limits suggest that although the profit-maximizing model is by no means an infallible guide to predicting multinational enterprise behavior, it is closer to the mark than other analyses that compare it too closely with the state; that is, the multinational corporation is not *power maximizing*. Among the factors that inform the decisions of the MNC to expand are the need to control resources, the saturation of home markets and access to foreign markets, scarcity of production factors at home, and preferential tax treatment in other countries. However, one of the inevitable by-products of *profit* maximization is political influence.

American MNCs often seek access to foreign markets to move behind the walls of tariffs and voluntary restraints that would make the export of U.S. goods to these states unprofitable. By having direct access to foreign markets, the MNCs are better able to guarantee a supply of products without the threat of such actions as dock strikes. Less-developed countries often insist that factories or refineries be constructed locally as joint ventures. If penetration of the market cannot be accomplished in any other way, then direct investment is the only logical alternative. Where relatively unskilled labor can be combined with sophisticated technologies, good reason exists for business expansion abroad.

One powerful motive for a U.S. move abroad arises when a native corporation has surplus investment funds for which it sees only marginal opportunities in the United States. Japanese multinational concerns have also accelerated direct investment abroad in recent decades. Japan's direct investment was 16.044 billion U.S. dollars in 1984 and rose to 53.4 billion in 1988.[3] Among the reasons cited for the activity of Japanese multinationals are increased yen revaluation that has made Japanese exports prohibitively expensive, scarcity of land for such industries as aluminum and oil refining, the rise in Japan's labor wages, and the economic advantages of investing in countries with abundant natural resources.

Charles Kindleberger has observed that in a world of perfect competition "direct investment cannot exist." Nowhere is this observation made more evident than in the differential rates of taxing multinational enterprise income that exist in different states as inducements to multinational firms.[4]

Changes or fluctuations in a state's posture toward MNCs are factors to be weighed in predicting behavior. Often states provide outright subsidies to multinational enterprises, which can reach 40 percent of the investment, as in Great Britain. Finally, it should be emphasized that when multinational enterprises decide to invest in a specific state, it is not necessarily in anticipation of a high rate of profit but for the contribution that plant will make to the multinational corporation's worldwide operation. Thus it may be that producing an item in country X

[3]*Statistical Report of The United States,* 1990.

[4]Charles Kindleberger, *Economic Laws and Economic History* (New York: Cambridge University Press, 1989). This point was also made in an earlier publication, "Group Behavior and International Trade," *Journal of Political Economy* Vol. 59, No. 1, February 1951.

will contribute to profits made in country Y where the item is combined with other technological resources and where the item could be produced only at a prohibitive price. This process can lead to what is known as "transfer pricing," whereby the multinational enterprise adjusts its prices on intracompany sales to minimize losses and maximize profits. In this fashion, MNCs can seek to take their profits in states with a lower tax rate or circumvent the policies of states that seek to prevent repatriations of profits that might produce negative effects on their national balance of payments.

The Relationship Between Multinational Corporations and Nation-States

The ranking of countries and corporations according to the size of their annual products raises the issue of multinational corporations evolving into "powers" more formidable than many states. The economic dimensions of the multinational enterprise are indeed staggering, as the previous discussion of world production and direct investment has indicated. Determining whether MNCs can encroach on or obscure the importance of the state, however, depends on what preconceptions one brings to the analysis of their respective roles in the global political economy.

Though MNCs require some measure of global stability to operate, they are also able to benefit from the anarchy of the states system because, as we have seen, by operating transnationally, they can frustrate national-level efforts to control them. However, we would suggest that their expansion has not been at the expense of the nation-state per se. Rather, the nation-state as an institution has proved itself to be inadequate to deal with the increasing agenda of essentially *global* issues. The regulation of multinational business, about which we will say more, is only one such issue. Others would include such problems as the reduction of widespread poverty, the control of illegal drug use, the maintenance of environmental quality, and the establishment of more equitable and effective global trade and monetary regimes. Furthermore, signs of neoprotectionism indicate that the state in the industrialized countries is still capable of using the means at its disposal to influence patterns of production and consumption.

We would suggest that in each situation the relationship between the multinational enterprise and the state will be forged out of a relative advantage-disadvantage calculus. Generally speaking, the government of an enterprise's *home* state will be better able to deal with the MNC than the *host* states in which it operates. Each such relationship, however, evolves over time as both government and corporate decision makers learn more about each other and the environment in which they act.

Canada presents an interesting case in this regard. There has been long-term substantial direct investment of U.S. firms within the country, and though this has always been the source of some friction, it is only quite recently that serious concern has arisen about the detrimental effects of this situation for Canadian sovereignty. By contrast, in Southeast Asia, direct investment has become an object of national resentment on the part of host countries, renewing the old detestation of Japanese domination. Japan, which relied upon Indonesia for nickel, copper, timber, and low-pollution oil, has extended more low-interest, long-term loans to that country than to any other Asian state. Indonesia, on the other hand, has sought to balance Japanese investment with German, French, and British investments. Japan and Indonesia have split over Indonesian demands for Indonesian-based and -controlled export industries, and the Indonesian government has on occasion threatened reprisals if the Japanese do not invest in more infrastructural projects.

Thus, despite the considerable degree of emotional conflict between MNCs and host countries, there is scant evidence that the MNC has emerged as an arbiter of political affairs. Clearly, the most celebrated example of an attempt by a multinational corporation to interfere in the political affairs of a state is the Chile-ITT affair, which indicated that, although a multinational enterprise may have political thoughts, it possesses limited influence to put them into effect.

The investigations of the ITT affair by both the U.S. Senate and OPIC revealed the extent of ITT's unconscionable scheme to influence the outcome of the presidential elections in Chile so as to avoid the possible expropriation of its subsidiaries in that country. The ITT executives received a sympathetic hearing from high government officials in Washington, but nevertheless there is no direct evidence to link the corporation to the downfall of the Salvador Allende government in 1973.

The ITT affair should not obscure the fact that Latin American governments have moved quite freely to nationalize and expropriate U.S. multinational corporations. Peru expropriated the assets of International Petroleum and W. R. Grace Company. Bolivia expropriated the Gulf Oil Company, and in Chile the Ford Motor Company and Bethlehem Steel Corporation were forced to terminate their operations.

Multinational Corporations and the Global South

Although the MNC has rarely conceived of itself as a political actor, it is equally clear that its impact on the economic affairs of states has grown steadily, creating a special interest in its transactions with the Global South countries. Despite the fact that much of the thinking and analysis of the relationship between the multinational corporation and the Global South countries is characterized by mutual recrimination, their interaction is much more complex than might at first be appreciated. The basic question is whether the Global South countries have benefitted from the presence of the multinational enterprise. Corollary issues include these: Do the MNCs dominate the host countries? Who receives the lion's share of the profits? Has the MNC adversely affected the Global South countries' balance of payments?

The oil-exporting countries, particularly those in the Organization of Petroleum Exporting Countries (OPEC), constitute one of the more important cases in this regard, not least because the bulk of U.S. direct investment in the less-developed countries is in petroleum. It is only in recent years that host countries have managed to use the multinational enterprise for their own purposes, not in a zero-sum situation but rather as participants in the rewards of oligopoly. After almost a half century of outright exploitation by the oil cartel since 1928, the oil-producing countries began to control their oil. Members of OPEC managed to raise their share of the profits on crude oil production from 10–15 percent to 80–85 percent.

A major factor in the change in the bargaining position of these states has been the competition among the multinational corporations that have entered the market since 1950. The history of OPEC, though tumultuous, shows that the oil-producing states are capable of driving hard bargains with MNCs and resorting to nationalization of industries where the national interest is believed to be served. In 1972, Iraq and Syria nationalized the assets of the Iraq Petroleum Company in their territories. Turkey and Ecuador also moved to strengthen the position of local producers with foreign competitors. In summary, viewed both in terms of maintaining a rising share in profits and capital assets as well as enjoying an oligopolist position with respect to the rest of the world, the relationship of the oil-producing states to the multinational enterprises has been more like client-agent than master-slave.

However, the OPEC experience has not, to date, been reproduced in other areas. Few other products, whether agricultural or mineral, enjoy the same inelasticity of demand as petroleum. Also, expropriation has produced mixed results in some sectors. In Zambia and Zaire, government takeovers, or partial takeovers, had disastrous effects in the copper industry. The copper MNCs were much better equipped to cope with the vicissitudes of the world copper market—a fact appreciated too late by the governments as they watched their export revenues steadily dwindle.

Overall, the "exchange" between the center and the periphery through the medium of the MNC is unequal. Harry Magdoff has noted that between 1950 and 1965 the flow of direct investment from the United States to Latin America amounted to $3.5 billion, whereas income on capital transferred to the United States came to $11.3 billion, a surplus of $7.5 billion in favor of the United States.[5] In Europe, U.S. direct investment was $8.1 billion, with $5.5 billion in profits transferred back. Profit rates are in fact higher in Latin America and the Middle East because investments in the extractive industries such as petroleum are consistently higher than those in the service and manufacturing industries. George Lictheim, a European socialist, has argued that these statistics "merely underscore the familiar fact that 'uneven development' is a source of surplus profit for the advanced countries—it does not prove that no development takes place."[6]

One area of controversy concerns the overall effect of foreign investment on a host country's balance of payments situation. If the investment is in "import

[5]Harry Magdoff, *The Age of Imperialism* (New York: Monthly Review Press, 1969), p. 198.
[6]George Lichtheim, *Imperialism* (New York: Praeger, 1971), p. 152, note 14.

substitution" industries—that is, those intended to produce something the country was formerly importing—then it should improve the balance of payments. However, a large portion of the industries established in peripheral countries in fact import raw materials to function! Also, if what is produced can be exported, this factor would be another positive influence, but many local subsidiaries of MNCs do not export much, because they are primarily geared to local markets. Finally, MNCs take a large percentage of their profits out of the country, and they have access to foreign exchange to do this. In fact, most of the contemporary research on this question indicates that the overall effect of MNCs on the balance of payments of developing countries is negative.

A crucial factor in determining the future relations between MNCs and the less-developed countries is the question of technology transfer. The MNC has been touted as the great vehicle of economic modernization through the installation of modern production facilities in peripheral states, thereby assisting the people to become more technologically sophisticated. This claim is true to the extent that those employed are taught new skills. However, because the foreign-owned production facility is often an enclave almost wholly isolated from the rest of the host society, the skills imparted are of limited relevance outside the factory. Also, since these firms tend to use highly capital-intensive technology, only a very limited number of workers ever acquire any new skills, so to speak of a general "transfer" may be quite misleading.

Furthermore, an MNC will not necessarily "transfer" its most advanced technology unless there is a compelling reason to do so. If production is for an internal market and competition is limited or nonexistent, it would in fact be most profitable to offer a product that only meets minimum local standards. For instance, it is not uncommon for major car brands assembled in developing-country plants to have components (such as braking systems) that have been superseded by more modern, or even safer, variants in the home country. So in one sense, the so-called technology transfer may only serve to further entrench the realities of international stratification.

There is an even more pernicious dimension to this issue. Though regulations on industrial production designed to protect the natural environment are far from adequate in the industrialized market economies, they are practically nonexistent in many countries of the Global South. The development and implementation of environmentally benign production processes cuts into a firm's profits, initially at least. If they do not have to invest in such measures in a host country, they are not likely to do so, and as a result the society in question will receive an industrial infrastructure that could well produce harmful side effects for workers and the population at large. Such practices certainly call into question the long-range utility of the MNC's technology transfer function.

On a different note, some argue that the future challenges to national sovereignty will be in the cultural sphere of activity, not in the political or economic sphere. For instance, an MNC may clash with ethnic subcultures, as was the case in Canada where Premier Robert Bourassa of Quebec intervened in a language dispute between General Motors and the United Auto Workers at an assembly unit outside Montreal. General Motors had rejected demands that French be made the language of work for 2,400 assembly-line workers.

The degree to which an MNC is a vehicle of cultural imperialism is difficult to determine precisely, but it undeniably does exert this kind of influence. Fast-food chains and soft drink manufacturers are perhaps the most obvious, with such firms as Pizza Hut, McDonald's, Coca-Cola, and Pepsi-Cola having come, through their global distributive networks, to influence the culinary habits of a wide diversity of cultures. Some of these effects can be more than banal, as witnessed by the Swiss food-processing firm that, through its advertising, convinced many mothers from the Global South, who often had no access to clean water, to prepare instant formulas for their babies rather than breast-feeding them.

Regulating the Multinational Corporations

The rapid growth of MNCs in recent years has attracted public attention, and to some extent alarm, in the United States, Western Europe, and Japan, where the vast majority of corporations are based, and of course in the developing countries, where they have proved so influential. There is a loose consensus of opinion in official circles that something should be done to regulate their activities. Such a development would, in the longer run at least, also benefit the MNCs by establishing more clearly defined parameters for their activities that would assist them in planning.

One result of this growing concern was the creation during the mid-1970s of two UN-related bodies to investigate the possibilities of MNC regulation. They are the Commission on Transnational Corporations and the Center on Transnational Corporations. The main task of these bodies, besides research, has been to draft a code of conduct for multinational enterprise. The code is supposed to achieve certain purposes, primary among which is trying to get the MNCs to act in agreement with the development goals of their host countries—thereby augmenting their contribution to development and minimizing the extent to which they frustrate local targets and programs. Means to this end include provisions to increase the bargaining capabilities of the host countries vis-à-vis the corporations and efforts to reduce the likelihood that MNCs might resort to illegal or otherwise unacceptable business practices (i.e., corruption).

The code also seeks to promote a general intergovernmental agreement on rules relating to MNC operations that would serve as an international standard for domestic laws in this area. Furthermore, the code is designed to improve national legislation by specifying principles of jurisdiction, making it more difficult to evade national regulations, and assisting in the sharing of information and intergovernmental coordination.[7]

Unfortunately, the commission itself has been divided on key issues affecting the code. The center states did not want the code to be legally binding on corp-

[7]United Nations, Center on Transnational Corporations, *Transnational Corporations: Issues Involved in the Formulation of a Code of Conduct* (New York: United Nations, 1976).

orations, while the Global South and socialist states wanted it to be binding on corporations but voluntary for governments. Also, even if a comprehensive code were agreed upon, the problem of enforcement remains, and within the current anarchic states system the possibilities of enforcement are necessarily limited. In light of these difficulties, the prospects for international regulation procedures to significantly alter the role of the MNC in global development in the foreseeable future are limited.

Conclusion

In this chapter we have tried to make a few basic points about the multinational corporation as an actor in international relations. First, it acquires some political influence as a result of the impact it has on the economies of the states in which it operates. However, it is only in certain Global South countries where for many reasons the institution of the state is not well grounded that any real challenge to sovereignty could be said to exist.

Second, to date the MNC has been at best a highly imperfect agent of development in the Global South. The gap between MNC interests and goals and host country interests and goals has made for much frustration and disappointment, and in some cases even totally counterproductive results.

Third, effective international regulation of MNCs is still a long way off. Undoubtedly, the efforts made to formulate a code of conduct will have some impact on the behavior of corporations, even if only cosmetic. Still, it is probably safe to assume that MNCs will continue to take advantage of the anarchy of the states system as long as they are free to do so.

The global political economy, however, is not static. There are signs that after a few decades of negative experience host governments have learned more about dealing with MNCs, and MNCs have also learned more about the variety of environments in which they must operate. Thus there are new sorts of arrangements being made between state and corporation that represent a more equitable distribution of benefits, though they are certainly not yet equal exchanges.

For instance, a host government may allow an MNC to establish and run a plant for a fixed period, taking out a generous amount of profits, and in exchange the plant will revert either to the government or to local private ownership at the end of the agreement. Thus the MNC can operate without fear of expropriation, and the host country can hope to move gradually toward more locally controlled production. Such developments indicate that it is possible to favorably modify what has been most often an exploitative relationship. However, whether foreign corporations will ever come to define their interest in a way compatible with the aspirations of their host societies and begin to act accordingly is perhaps the most important question that remains to be answered as we look toward the future.

RECOMMENDED READINGS

ANDERSON, KYM. *The Greening of World Trade Issues.* Ann Arbor: University of Michigan Press, 1992.

BARNET, RICHARD J., and JOHN CAVANAUGH. *Global Dreams: Imperial Corporations and the New World Order.* New York: Simon & Schuster, 1994.

BARRAT, BROWN M. *Fair Trade: Reform and Realities in the International Trading System.* London: Zed Books, 1993.

DESTLER, I. M. *American Trade Politics.* 2nd ed. Washington, DC: Institute for International Economics, 1992.

DUNNING, JOHN H. *Multinationals, Technology, and Competitiveness.* London: Unnin Hyman, 1988.

EVANS, PETER B., et al. *Double-edged Diplomacy: International Bargaining and Domestic Politics.* Berkeley: University of California Press, 1993.

GOODMAN, LOUIS W., and DAVID ERNEST APTER. *The Multinational Corporation and Social Change.* New York: Praeger, 1976.

LANVIN, BRUNO. *Trading in a New World Order: The Impact of Telecommunications and Data Services on International Trade and Services.* Boulder, CO: Westview Press, 1993.

MADELEY, JOHN. *Trade and the Poor: The Impact of International Trade on Developing Countries.* New York: St. Martin's Press, 1993.

MAGDOFF, HARRY. *The Age of Imperialism.* New York: Monthly Review Press, 1969.

NANDA, VED, et al. *World Debt and the Human Condition: Structural Adjustment and the Right to Development.* Westport, CT: Greenwood Press, 1993.

POLYCHRONIOU, CHRONIS. *Perspectives and Issues in International Political Economy.* Westport, CT: Greenwood Press, 1992.

PORTER, TONY. *States, Markets, and Regimes in Global Finance.* New York: St. Martin's Press, 1993.

RILEY, STEPHEN P. *The Politics of Global Debt.* New York: St. Martin's Press, 1993.

SAID, ABDUL AZIZ, and LUIZ SIMMONS, eds. *The New Sovereigns: Multinational Corporations as World Powers.* Englewood Cliffs, NJ: Prentice Hall, 1975.

SERVAN-SCHRIEBER, JEAN-JACQUES. *The American Challenge.* New York: Atheneum, 1968.

TUSSIE, DIANA, and DAVID GLOVER. *The Developing Countries in World Trade: Policies and Bargaining Strategies.* Boulder, CO: Lynne Rienner, 1993.

VERNON, RAYMOND, and DEBORA L. SPAR. *Beyond Globalism: Remaking American Foreign Economic Policy.* New York: Free Press, 1989.

WALLERSTEIN, EMMANUEL. *The Capitalist World Economy.* Cambridge, UK: Cambridge University Press, 1980.

Chapter 14

ETHNICITY, TERRORISM, AND NONVIOLENCE

The nation-state is no longer regarded as the highest form of human organization. Since World War II there have been many experiments in supranationalism, and as the turn of the century approaches one can discern a trend toward regional economic integration; also, recently a limited integration of security functions at the global level has been achieved through the UN Security Council. Curiously, simultaneous with this trend has been the emergence of a growing disenchantment from "below" with the political institutions of the nation-state; an emphasis on ethnic, cultural, and political identity has reasserted itself and occasionally exploded in many parts of the world. These developments demand new explanations of the interactions between nations and nations, nations and states, and states and states in which ethnic nations play key roles.

ETHNICITY[1]

The reasons for the conspicuous rise in ethnic politics are not always apparent. Ethnic movements have developed in environments that seemed unlikely spawning grounds for secession and violence. Though contemporary social science has discovered many useful things about political development, it may have masked to some extent the fact that a nation-state is at heart an intuitive expression of a

[1] This section is adapted from A. A. Said and L. R. Simmons, *Ethnicity in an International Context* (New Brunswick, NJ: Transaction Books, 1976).

people's perception of proper social and political organization. That such perceptions can and do change despite the social cohesion believed to be supplied by good communication networks and economic integration is one profitable inference to be drawn from the resurgence of ethnic activity.

As we argued earlier, the state, as an organizational expression of the historical preoccupation with physical security, has been progressively undermined by the development and proliferation of conventional and nuclear weapons—simply put, dangers cannot be kept outside borders. The state remains, therefore, an essentially territorial form of organization in a century where security is as much determined by technology as by geography. No longer fully credible as the sole guarantor of individual security, recognition and acceptance of the state's authority is undergoing a historic transformation. Antistatist politics as manifested in ethnic disassociation is one aspect of this transition.

Liberal theories of development have never been enthusiastic about the idea of ethnic diversity. Coexistence at the global level was seen to require a tolerance of diversity among political systems, but the ideal nation-state was imagined to be socially homogeneous. Quite often, state builders encouraged if not insisted on the detribalization of national politics, because the dominant approach to development emphasized the necessity of rationalizing economic and political systems to achieve economic growth.

The future of ethnic conflict is, of course, closely tied to the future of the multiethnic state. A sample of 132 states shows that only 12 (9.1%) can be considered ethnically homogeneous. Twenty-five states (18.9%) are comprised of an ethnic nation that represents more than 90 percent of the aggregate population, and in another 25 states the largest ethnic nation accounts for possibly 75–89 percent of the population. However, in 31 states (23.5% of the total) the significant ethnic group constitutes only 50–74 percent of the population, and in 39 states (29.5%) the largest group does not account for half the state's population. It is estimated that in 53 states (or 40.2%), the population includes five or more significant ethnic nations.

Never before have issues of human rights and cultural self-determination attracted so much popularity and scholarly attention. What are the human rights of these ethnic nations? What should be the position of the analyst and practitioner in response to secessionist movements? Should the prerogatives of the sovereign state swallow the rights of the ethnic nation? Can the two be reconciled? Despite one's position on this dispute, the ethnic and the emerging neoethnic groups will not disappear from world politics. As actors in the global system, they are indications that our perceptions of the dynamics of world politics, specifically, the causes of war and peace, may lag behind the consciousness of the individuals and nations we study. The ethnic nation cannot (yet) compete with the state in nuclear warheads and warships, but it continues to exercise formidable influence over the primary political identity of countless individuals. It is from the power of this identity that revolutions have been born.

Ethnicity Versus States

A revived sense of ethnic identity has grown in the last few decades, and ethnic politics has emerged as a significant factor in the global system. In recent years the antagonism of indigenous ethnic communities in the Commonwealth of Independent States (the former Soviet Union) and the new states of former Yugoslavia, Iraq, China, Ireland, Sudan, Lebanon, and Sri Lanka (to name only a few) have wrought important changes in the relations among states. Ethnic conflicts and the transformation of ethnic discontent into ethnic nationalism worldwide have placed their mark on domestic and global politics.

There are perhaps as many as 862 ethnic groups living within the nation-states of the world: 239 in sub-Saharan Africa, 95 in the countries surrounding the Mediterranean, 93 in the Far East, 128 in the islands of the Pacific, 218 in North America, and 89 in Central and South America.[2] What future impact will they have if the overall effectiveness and cohesion of the nation-state as a form of economic and political association are further called into question?

The modern nation-state is struggling to overcome the internal contradictions between ethnicity and the state. These contradictions become fully visible when loyalty to the state and loyalty to one's ethnic identity conflict. The state can be defined in terms of territory, population, and government, and an entity is generally recognized as a state when it exerts political control over a specific geographical area. Control is accompanied by international recognition in the transactions among states; loss of control is invariably a precursor of loss of recognition. The state is a device, one way of organizing human affairs. But ethnicity is a conscious expression of people's shared sense of "peoplehood," a sense of "interdependence of fate."

We are entering a new era where state-nationalism as it has been known for the past few hundred years is undergoing serious stress. It may seem contradictory to talk of the decline of the nation-state in an era characterized by references to rising nationalism, but history contains many such paradoxes. In our era, the secessions of the Ukraine, Azerbaijan, Armenia, Bosnia, and many other nations mark a fundamental shift in world politics.

The proliferation of new states in recent years has obscured the absurdity of describing both the People's Republic of China and the Bahamas as nation-states. The real global system consists of no more than twenty or thirty national and transnational actors that have any significant impact, and the top ten actors have more than half of the world's human and natural resources. The nation-state as a unit of analysis includes differences of degree so vast as to constitute differences in kind. Ethnic groups, in contrast, are more clearly defined and therefore more truly comparable in nature than states.

In many instances, the human need for a more proximate and deeper sense of community is gradually dissolving the bonds of geography that have united

[2] George Peter Murdock, *Ethnographic Atlas* (Pittsburgh, PA: University of Pittsburgh Press, 1967).

diverse groups within states. An alternative community is found within the ethnic group or communal group—groups that find their interests coinciding in a political context other than that of a nation-state. Such a community may on occasion even rejoice at the defeat of its state, because defeat for the state could result in conditions favorable to group interests. In such a situation, the internal struggle within the state may have an analogue in external politics as domestic disputes lead to foreign policy disputes.

The present phenomenon of ethnic conflict cannot be adequately understood using the traditional concepts of international relations. Concepts such as balance of power or bipolarity are not particularly useful. As Andrew Greeley has observed:

> The conflicts that have occupied most men over the past two or three decades and which have led to the most horrendous outpouring of blood have had precious little to do with this ideological division. . . . In a world of the jet engine, nuclear energy, the computer, and the regionalized organization, the principal conflicts are not ideological but tribal. Those differences among men which were supposed to be swept away by science and technology and political revolution are destructive as ever.[3]

Roots of Ethnic Conflict

The modern experience of national integration has not been an unqualified success, and the contemporary resurgence of ethnicity is in part an unanticipated byproduct of efforts to coercively assimilate diverse peoples into a civil society. Social and political mobilization, buzzwords of the 1960s, did not create new modern nations that neatly coincided with the political scope of the state. Rather, increased contact, exposure, and communication among groups in a modernizing society often served to magnify cultural differences, produce conflict, and induce political disassociation. Nor did economic development—an increase in material goods and services—immunize societies from ethnic conflict. The concomitants of economic growth, such as urbanization, secularization, and industrialization, fostered competition among ethnic groups over limited opportunities and resources. This trend should be understood as an effect of contemporary social changes because such groups often enjoyed stable and mutually beneficial relations during earlier centuries.

For example, this pattern is often overlooked in analyzing ethnic conflict in Africa. It is suggested that "tribalism" is inherent to politics in Africa and, in the short term, largely indelible. This assumption, however, obscures the fact that Africa's precolonial past reflects relatively harmonious trade and coexistence between most "tribes" and that ethnicity first became an issue when colonial governments forced people to come to the towns to earn money to pay their taxes. Faced with competition for scarce employment in an alien environment, people fell back on ethnic social networks to cope and survive. This trend was further

[3] Andrew Greeley, "The Rediscovery of Diversity," *Antioch Review,* Fall 1971, p. 343.

aggravated during the decolonization period as politicians drew on ethnicity to forge constituencies.

Anthropologists have contributed much current thought on ethnic conflict, and we will briefly consider a few key concepts they have developed. The first concept is that of culture, which the French scholar Claude Lévi-Strauss defined as "the complex whole which includes knowledge, belief, art, morals, custom, and other capabilities and habits by man as a member of society."[4] An ethnic group is a culture, and yet it may belong to a larger culture; it is what Frederick Barth called an *atomic group.* Atomic groups are "biologically self-perpetuating, their members share fundamental cultural values, realized in overt unity in cultural form; they make up a field of communication and interaction and their membership identifies itself and is identified by others."[5] Barth goes on to argue that ethnicity is often most important among the various elements of personal identity, includes a distinct set of values and social priorities, and often has a determinant influence on how people conceive of and act in the world.

Stable ethnic relations do not require isolation or limited contact between groups. Again, history has many examples of pacific patterns of contact among groups. Required is a sense of cultural and social boundaries; that is, some aspects of group identity—whether land, language, religion, or something else—are not called into question by the outsiders with whom contact is frequent. For this condition to be met, interaction among groups requires tacit rules that define what is negotiable and what is not, and such rules may take many decades or even centuries to evolve. When these tacit limits are acknowledged by others, it is possible for ethnic groups to interact both cooperatively and competitively without serious conflict. However, when the nonnegotiable is questioned, whether in terms of ownership of land, access to resources, or the right to worship, conflict is a likely result. As argued earlier, such conflicts have occurred frequently during the social changes associated with "development."

Ethnicity and Development

While there is nothing inevitable about ethnic conflict, neither can we be sure that nation-state builders will discover the precise formula to absorb dissident ethnic elements. Thus the ethnicity is an irreducible dilemma for the state, one that under specific conditions can emerge as a truculent divisive force. Social stress, such as economic scarcity or political or cultural repression, can exacerbate these tendencies, but even an absence of these tensions (were it possible) would not mean the disappearance of so fundamental an identity group.

Milton Gordon has reminded us that the term *ethnicity* has been used to embrace the unities of race, religion, and national origin. However, the common

[4] Claude Lévi-Strauss, *Structural Anthropology* (Garden City, NY: Anchor Books, 1963), p. 19.

[5] Frederick Barth, ed., *Ethnic Groups and Boundaries* (Boston: Little, Brown, 1969), p. 10.

denominator of these categories is a "common social-psychological referent" that acts to create a consciousness of peoplehood. Can one really expect an individual or group to give up or reformulate values, attitudes, and norms that are so deeply rooted? As Gordon states:

> Common to all these objective bases . . . is the social-psychological element of a special sense of both ancestral and future-oriented identification with the group. These are the "people" of my ancestors, therefore they are my people, and they will be the people of my children and their children . . . in a very special way which history has decreed. I share a sense of indissolvable and intimate identity with this group and not that one within the larger society and the world.[6]

Clifford Geertz has elaborated upon the distinction between "us" and "them" inherent in such an outlook, which he refers to as communalism.[7] Geertz further identifies several ascriptive characteristics around which much ethnic conflict has revolved:

1. *Assumed Blood Ties.* Two examples here are the "hill tribes" of Southeast Asia and the Kurds.

2. *Race.* In recent times, the countries most known for racial issues have been the United States and South Africa. In the latter case, a complex and invidious system of racial classification, known as apartheid, became the central question of politics and will remain so until its last traces disappear. However, European countries have, through immigration, developed their own racial problems, which continue to grow in intensity and political salience.

3. *Language.* Belgium has seen a succession of governments fall over issues related to the fundamental conflict between the Dutch-speaking Flemings and the French-speaking Walloons. After more than a century and a half of such conflict, the issue continues to color all other political questions in the country and to determine the evolution of the state. Canada is another example of a country divided on linguistic lines. For years there has been a movement for secession in the province of Quebec, and it has created a series of constitutional crises. Efforts to give the francophones special conditions in the Canadian federation have created a (predictable) backlash in English-speaking provinces.

4. *Religion.* There are numerous examples of conflict between religious communities, though it is not always clear whether the fundamental issue is one of belief. In terms of scale, the conflict between Hindus and Muslims that led to the partition of India and the creation of Pakistan may have been the largest. India is the stage for several others, including further tensions between Hindus and Muslims over religious sites and the persistent and very violent Sikh separatist

[6] Milton Gordon, *Assimilation in American Life; The Role of Race, Religion, and National Origin* (New York: Oxford University Press, 1964), p. 29.

[7] Clifford Geertz, "The Integration Revolution," in *Old Societies and New States,* ed. Clifford Geertz (New York: Free Press, 1963).

movement that was responsible for the assassination of Prime Minister Indira Gandhi. Another example of protracted and violent conflict, at least nominally religious, is the turmoil in Northern Ireland in which Protestants and Catholics have feuded, and continue to do so, over the self-determination of that territory. Finally, we can mention the persistent tensions between Christians and Muslims in African countries such as Sudan and Nigeria, where the historical influences of missionaries, Jihad ("holy struggle"), and modernization have combined to produce protracted and, at times, violent conflict.

5. *Custom.* Examples are the Bengalis in India and the Javanese in Indonesia.

Whether we are dealing with the extermination of Brazilian Indians or the contemporary ethnic conflicts in parts of Africa, Ireland, or India, we are naturally attracted to the anomaly of the late twentieth century—the impulse for Western modernization and the accelerating consciousness for self-determination among varieties of linguistic, religious, and geographical ethnic nations. The question that such a conflict poses for a humane observer may be phrased in this manner: Although I believe that states must assimilate ethnic nations Y and Z in order to provide the modern economic, health, and social services that they deserve as citizens of the twenty-first century, what if nations Y and Z resist encroachment on their independence? What rights, if any, do they have under a given scheme for modernization? What limitation, if any, should be placed on the central authority in their attempts to force secessionist ethnic nations to adapt to the political economy of the state?

Each of us could suggest a different solution that placed more or less emphasis on the fruits of modernization or the political or cultural expression of ethnic identity, but finally we must confront the root question of how we shall balance our commitment to human rights with the contemporary experience of "state building"—often a bitter by-product of civil war. Then again, our view of the controversy may be considerably influenced by the state we are living in at a particular point in history. States racked by ethnic conflicts are probably less inclined to view secession and civil war as expressions of some transcendent human struggle than states that experience an acceptable level of ethnic conflict that does not approach disassociation.

Yet another problem is posed when a state or international agency, attempting to intervene in behalf of an ethnic minority, confronts the dilemma posed by Conor Cruise O'Brien:

> We tell, let us say, the Tutsi that the right he fancies he possesses to dominate the Hutu is not a real right. He replies in effect that as far as his culture is concerned it is right. We tell him it is not a right, because it is contrary to democracy, an ideology to which our ancestors became converted in the nineteenth century. He says his ancestors did not become so converted; are we claiming that our ancestors were superior to his? Now, that is a forked question, and we have to be very careful how we answer it. If we say, "No, no, of course not my dear fellow," he can say in reply: By what right then are we telling him that he must act according to the acquired convic-

> tion of our ancestors who are admittedly no better than his own. If, on the other hand, we say, yes, our people represent a more advanced stage of civilization than his do, he may reply that this is exactly his own position in relation to the Hutu.[8]

The response of the state to disaffected ethnic minorities has not been generous by most Western standards. The Tibetans with the Chinese and the Kurds with Iraq are indispensable reference points for predicting the state response to ethnic conflict and the politics of disassociation. Self-determination movements are invariably viewed as threats to the survival of the state. States threatened by such acts of disassociation have most often treated the leaders of these movements as traitors and have interned them without regard for even their own concepts of due process.

States can usually be expected to lend covert or overt assistance to other states confronting ethnic dissidents unless, of course, manipulation of ethnic dissidence is perceived as a potential foreign policy ploy of one state to disrupt the internal affairs of another. Basque nationalism furnishes a good example of covert aid, Chinese foreign policy in Myanmar of the overt variety. The Basque region is on the border of Spain and France. Although the French deny providing assistance to the Spanish government, since 1970 France has increased the expulsion of Basque political refugees. Basques, on either side of the border, note that improved French-Spanish relations that culminated in the French sale of armaments to Spain have contributed to growing collaboration of the governments on the Basque problem. In contrast, General Ne Luin of Myanmar has alleged that China has furnished sanctuary to Kachin dissidents and has contributed to the credibility of reports linking China to other secessionist movements within Myanmar.

Ethnicity and Foreign Policy

It should by now be increasingly evident that ethnic conflict in Ethiopia can make itself felt in the diplomatic struggle in the Middle East or that Basque terrorism that ignores the French-Spanish border can create problems between two states, but there is another dimension to the study of ethnic conflict that demands a brief inquiry. The state now shares the stage with other actors, such as multinational corporations, transnational subcultures, and, of course, ethnic groups. Quite often these ethnic groups, dissatisfied with political and social conditions at home, have begun to pirate international passenger flights, assassinate diplomats in foreign lands, and even extort ransom from multinational giants such as Ford Motor Company. Kidnappings of business executives and diplomats have become a familiar feature in contemporary world politics.

The mobility of ethnic groups in the global environment and the highly integrated state of our technology makes disruption of world services an easy mark. This vulnerability naturally calls forth a response by states, manifesting itself in

[8] Conor Cruise O'Brien, "On the Rights of Minorities," *Commentary*, 55, No. 6 (June 1973): 46.

new conventions and bilateral treaties with procedures for extradition and perhaps even international accords. This is only one local consequence of ethnic conflict for politics among states. Another is the manipulation of ethnic conflict in one state by another state. The Indian Parliament has acknowledged that hundreds of Nagas have been trained by the Chinese, armed, and returned to northeastern India. The previously mentioned alleged Chinese activities within Myanmar are another example.

It is also becoming increasingly evident that these rebellious secessionist-ethnic groups will traffic in contraband in order to finance guerrilla activities or to maintain their bases of political and cultural sovereignty within a state. This trafficking raises a fundamental question about the processes through which foreign policy takes shape. Governments still continue to pursue—with only slight deviation—practices formed in the nineteenth-century crucible of diplomacy. These procedures call for direct transactions among governments who exercise political control over a geographical area. In an age of political consciousness characterized by "retribalization," this is a short-sighted posture. Difficult as the task may be, foreign policy must communicate with different ethnic groups within a single state if it wishes to achieve its objectives. Such communication will require differentiating messages on a scale that would have been impractical a century ago. It might also require political contacts with dissident ethnic groups, occasionally at the expense of political relations with the constituted central government, depending on the objectives to be achieved.

Neo-Ethnic Groups

Ethnicity is not just an anachronism of feudal and preindustrial society. It demonstrates remarkable persistence even in postindustrial countries such as the United States, where behavior resembling "tribalism" is reasserting itself in societies considered both modern and technocratic. As we approach the twenty-first century, many people seem to have wearied of the millennial visions promised by the ideologies of the nineteenth century. We venture to suggest that no new universal secular ideology has presented or is likely to present itself, but that a popular radicalism, a neo-ethnic response to the depersonalization and rationalization of postindustrial society, is becoming more widespread in the wealthier countries.

Such a politics of neo-ethnicism is investing itself in styles, politics, and social organization in the United States, particularly, and it will have a wide impact on approaches to national development and integration. Neo-ethnicism as a system is a transition from the national consciousness of the nation-state to more communal forms of identity and organization characterized by cultural patriotism and ethnic nationalism. The result is a redefinition of national consciousness, which some have described in its extreme form as a process of retribalization. It reflects an exhaustion with the cumulative preoccupations of national and world institutions, which seem too big, too remote, and in some cases too oppressive, and a preference for the study of personal and parochial problems, which seem more immediately relevant. It is expressed in a variety of ideologies, among a variety of classes.

In conclusion, it appears that the intensification of ethnic consciousness and the subsequent fragmentation, rather than political consolidation and social integration, may well be a function of modernization. The concept of development, long considered to be an increase of GNP and PQL (physical quality of life), or a rise in production and consumption, is now redefined by many in terms of "liberation" from externally imposed values, socioeconomic-political inequities, or suppression of cultural expressions. Finally, such trends suggest that the energies and attentions of governments may become so absorbed by ethnic divisions and associated problems that the quality of both foreign and domestic policies will be negatively affected.

TERRORISM

Terrorism is the use of violence by states and by nonstate actors (described here as terrorist groups) for political purposes. Our concern here is not with state terrorism, much of which belongs in our discussion of war (Chapter 9), but with terrorism practiced by nonstate actors. This type of terrorism can be understood as a function of the present distribution of power and level of integration of social, economic, political, and communications systems, just as the balance of power was a function of an earlier, different geopolitical system. The growth of terrorism is related both to the changing nature of international relations and to the transnational politics of the twenty-first century.

Terrorism as a System

It is useful to distinguish terrorism as a system from terrorism as a technique. As a technique, terrorism is employed by pirates, common criminals, national liberation movements, and governments. Accordingly, it does not lend itself to meaningful analysis, because in one instance and from one perspective it is an act of cold-blooded, senseless murder, and from another an act of liberation.

A productive analysis of terrorism must assume that terrorism is a system. The identification of acts of terrorism must be made on an empirical basis in every situation. As a system, it is useful to analyze terrorism in a four-part framework: (1) the level of integration of political, economic, social, and communications systems; (2) the distribution of power in the system; (3) the capacity of the system to oppress terrorism; and (4) the capacity of the system to respond to the perceived needs of terrorists.

Terrorists have emerged as volatile actors in world politics who enjoy several advantages over their inevitable adversary, the nation-state. The disturbing message of terrorists gives them access to "air time," where their objectives and aspirations are easily comprehended, reduced, and transmitted by the world's media. In contrast, the objectives and aspirations of the state are often perceived as confused, conflicting, uncertain, and difficult to reduce to unequivocal messages. The terrorist's capability to communicate specific demands and ideas almost always exceeds the capabilities of the state except in time of war, which is often a moment of atypical consensus within the state.

Goals and Objectives of Terrorists

The capabilities of terrorists to achieve their objectives have, in some cases, begun to approximate the effectiveness of the state. The terrorist's success has either been a function of straining the patience and morale of a target society, as the Irish Republican Army (IRA) has done with the British public, or affecting the consciousness of the world community, as with the Popular Front for the Liberation of Palestine (PFLP). Terrorists' capabilities are a product of extrinsic factors, not the intrinsic strength of a popular movement, as in the case of a national war of liberation. The combination of high media visibility and a capability based upon extrinsic politics has made the terrorists a more believable and potent adversary. The introduction and proliferation of weapons of war have permitted the terrorists to acquire sophisticated armament, surface-to-air missiles, and, in time, nuclear weapons.

While the terrorists' capabilities flow from extrinsic considerations, the objectives of terrorist groups in several parts of the world cannot be separated from the political environment where they have developed or the sociopsychological characteristics of those conscripted to serve their objectives. In the first case, terrorist groups in Turkey, Sri Lanka, and Lebanon have defined their operations in terms of the right of self-determination. Indeed, this putative right of self-determination has provided the legitimizing ideology for many of these groups. Yet the position of the terrorist as an "unprivileged belligerent" under the Geneva Convention of 1949 has become a code word for secession and the politics of disassociation—an anathema to the integration of many states. As long as states refuse to yield sovereignty to "nations" within their political jurisdiction, the grievances of many of their so-called terrorist groups will not be abated. The tension between the nation and the state—the source of a preponderance of the terrorist activity in world politics today—insures the longevity of many terrorist groups and the proliferation of others.

The emergence of terrorist groups as actors is less a function of their capability and more a response to the vulnerability of the global system. The highly integrated institutions in the global system are vulnerable to minor disruptions that can produce widespread damage or fear. An integrated system provides the logistical and functional requirements that contribute to the vitality of terrorist groups. Terrorism is not a peculiar pathology. The demand for self-determination and the struggle against internal political oppression or external exploitation form the basis for terrorist groups.

The contemporary practice of terrorism has raised many new questions for the interaction of states. How will states react to other states that permit their territories to be used as sanctuaries? Will states stage the equivalent of terrorist raids of their own, as in the case of Israel in Tunisia and the United States in Libya? Is there a role for international law in the conflict between the terrorist and the state, or will each state deal with the terrorists by entering into bilateral treaties of extradition and trying captured persons as criminals under its domestic law? Should acts of terrorism be considered political crimes and immune from prosecution?

The plans of terrorists are not desultory acts of tactical violence. Terrorism reveals strategy and tactics. The strategy of terrorism is contingent upon the environment where terrorists operate—whether urban or rural, regional or international. The tactics used by terrorists in a preindustrial society differ from those employed in industrial or postindustrial societies. The target and audience of terrorism is determined by the capability and objectives of the terrorists at any given time. Terrorists that are relatively weak attack a symbolic target—persons or objects rather than the seat of power. However, as terrorism becomes a revolutionary movement, the targets become less symbolic and more pragmatic.

Terrorism has often been initiated as a means of self-defense by the weak and exploited and may well persist as long as the global system lacks effective machinery to regulate the power of the more important actors—states and corporations. Seen from the status quo point of view, terrorists commit political crimes through hijacking, murder, and kidnapping, but revisionists view many acts of powerful states and wealthy MNCs as equally unjust. In fact, war by one state on another can be an act of terrorism, and so can certain profit-making policies of MNCs.

The inability of international law and such international conventions as the human rights covenants to assist those who assert their rights to human dignity, survival, and self-determination insures the persistence of terrorism. In this sense, terrorism is a symptom of a deeper problem in the international system. There are few if any channels through which the weak can seek redress against injustice perpetrated by the strong. Though sympathy for the concerns of terrorists is radically reduced by revulsion at their methods, the spread of terrorism is a testimony to how prevalent a perception of oppression and disempowerment is among minorities in many different lands.

Legal Control of Terrorism

A question that has preoccupied lawyers is "Because there is no agreed-upon legal definition of terrorism, should acts of terrorism be regarded as political crimes or merely common criminal offenses?" We can, in fact, distinguish three stages in the development of international legal concern with terrorism. During the first stage, which followed World War I, concern focused on the legal definition of terrorism. The second stage, extending over the 1930s, was characterized by attempts to regulate terrorism at the international level. The third and present stage centers upon the efforts carried on within the United Nations to deal with new forms of terrorism such as air piracy (Conventions of The Hague, 1970, and Montreal, 1971; The Convention of the Prevention and Punishment of Crimes Against Internationally Protected Person, Including Diplomatic Agents [signed in New York 1973]; and The International Convention Against the Taking of Hostage [signed in New York 1979]).

The problem of differentiating between terrorism and political crimes has not been resolved. The first attempt to define terrorism in a court of law was undertaken by German courts in 1929, in a case of extradition. The signing of extradition treaties that differentiated between political crimes and terrorism underscored the need for a clearer definition of terrorism. The Unification of Penal Law in 1935 developed a definition of terrorism, which remains in use today, as an act in which the perpetrator has created "a common danger or a state of terror that might incite a change or raise an obstacle to the functioning of public bodies or a disturbance in international relations."[9]

In 1937 the Convention of the Prevention and Repression of Terrorism instituted the first attempt to control terrorism. The convention stipulated that each of the contracting states is obligated to consider acts of terrorism in its criminal legislation. Regulations within the convention dealt with extradition and preserved a state's right to "try its own citizen even when he has committed a crime in another nation."[10]

The UN General Assembly voted in 1972 to establish a 35-member committee to study the problems posed by terrorism. This action followed a long and intensive discussion caused by the presentation by the United States of a general draft for a Convention on Terrorism. The draft attempted to prevent the spread of violence across borders to states not party to internal or external conflicts. The measure has been postponed repeatedly by the General Assembly. In December 1985 the General Assembly adopted without a vote the Resolution on Measures to Prevent International Terrorism, which appeals to all states to become parties to the conventions related to various aspects of international terrorism. It also urges (in paragraph 9) all states to

> contribute to the progressive elimination of the causes underlying international terrorism and to pay special attention to situations, including colonialism, racism and situations involving mass and flagrant violations of human rights and fundamental freedoms and those involving alien occupation, that may give rise to international terrorism and may endanger international peace and security.

Present legal concern with terrorism is confined to definition for the purpose of extradition and for the purpose of containment of terrorist acts. Many extradition treaties in force today have differentiated between terrorism and political crimes. Containment is of primary importance along with a means of enforcement.

NONVIOLENCE

Nonviolence is an alternative strategy to terrorism. The term *nonviolence* is invariably used to describe pacifism, a lifestyle, a set of beliefs, an instrument of power, and a method of resolving conflict. Our discussion refers to nonviolence as a

[9] Tran-Tram, "Crimes of Terrorism and International Criminal Law," in M. Cherif Bassiouni and Ved P. Nanda, eds., *A Treatise on International Criminal Law* (Springfield, IL: Thomas, 1973), p. 495.

[10] Bogdan Zlataric, "History of International Terrorism and Its Legal Control," in M. Cherif Bassiouni, *International Terrorism and Political Crimes* (Springfield, IL: Thomas, 1974, c1975), p. 484.

means of affecting change and resolving conflict. There are important questions about nonviolence that deserve the attention of students of international relations. Can nonviolence be used as a tool to empower an ethnic or minority group in a society to realize self-determination? What part does the level of commitment of nonviolent activists play in the success or failure of a particular movement? Can nonviolence provide a framework for promoting development? Can nonviolence serve as a communications process?

Nonviolence motivates people to act justly and ethically and to demand just and ethical action, particularly by those in power, without resort to physical coercion or combat. The first premise is never to participate in anything that is immoral. Plato sets forth this principle in the *Apology* (also in the first book of the *Republic,* the *Euthyphro, Crito,* and *Phaedo*), exemplifying it in Socrates's refusal to take part in unjust action. There is an injunction to act morally and not to be silent in the face of injustice; yet each person must develop her/his own morality from within, though each owes a duty to assist others and the community at large in that development by sharing, or dialoguing one's own views.[11]

Nonviolence is action based upon principle, yet undertaken in the tactical way that best serves to make the moral point effectively. Tactics and strategy are important to consider in deciding what to do. The key here is the relation of ends to means. There is no separation. The effect of an act together with its intention determines its character. The means used, through their effect, determine what the actual end is. Unjust means cannot bring about just ends. The means must also be just: Considering all the effects and side effects, the means must be appropriate to the ends, or they are not means to that end. This is the heart of the idea of nonviolence.

Nonviolence as proposed by Henry David Thoreau and Ralph Waldo Emerson and used by Mahatma Gandhi and Martin Luther King, Jr., interprets the preceding to mean that violence is always wrong and should never be undertaken for any purpose. Just what constitutes violence is a complex question. Clearly, killing people and inflicting serious injuries are violent. Other physical, economical, social, political, and psychological actions may be also, depending upon their intent and effect. The ultimate aim is to achieve justice and moral interaction among people without creating violence. Ideally, all human interactions should take place on the basis of mutual respect and understanding in which all parties see themselves as members of a community of soul (or of mind), regardless of whether they are members of the same community in the usual political and sociological senses.

The Relationship Between Principle and Practice

Nonviolent action is always intended to have an effect. Occasionally the action itself may directly or indirectly cause the desired end, as when a demonstration

[11] Our colleague Stephen Sachs, Indiana University and Purdue University, Indianapolis, has developed this theme elaborately.

convinces political leaders to change their course of action. Most often nonviolent action, when successful, is a catalyst in building moral and political support for changing social and political policy, as was the case with the civil rights movement in the United States in the 1960s with lunch counter sit-ins and demonstrations. Sometimes nonviolent action is easy enough to carry out, as in signing a petition in a popular cause in a democratic society. When it is most essential, nonviolent action requires people to have the courage and solidarity to take considerable risks. Socrates made his moral point effectively by his willingness to die for his principles. Gandhi's march to attempt, peacefully, to occupy the salt works in India was powerfully effective because so many persons had the courage to just keep marching in file to the entrance, where the guards beat them down with clubs. The U.S. civil rights movement made powerful gains through its risk taking. When, in Birmingham, peaceful marchers, kneeling and singing hymns, were attacked by police wielding clubs and unleashing police dogs, the moral point of the marchers was forcefully made to the millions who saw the event on television and perceived the justice of the marchers and the injustice of the authorities.

Tactically nonviolent action is often provocative. It is taken to place the opposition, often the authorities, in a double bind. If the nonviolent act is allowed, it makes its point, and the movement gains strength. If the authorities resist, particularly where they resort to violent means, the relative justice of the actors and injustice of their opponents is magnified, bringing considerable political gain to the activists.

Nonviolence requires courage. But courage is not foolhardiness, and action that is intentionally or recklessly destructive of one's self or supporters is harmful and thus inherently violent and unjust. Courage, the will to act, must be balanced by moderation, which Plato calls temperance. To be just, one must be reasonable and act reasonably. Being reasonable involves a number of qualities, including taking the time to understand and evaluate a situation carefully before acting. This way, action will take into account all of the elements of the situation and be appropriate to them. Interestingly, law, which aims at justice, has often been called reason. The idea of the "reasonable man" is essential in law (Oliver Wendell Holmes's discussion of the concept of the reasonable man in his essay "The Common Law"). To be reasonable means to act with a certain restraint, attempting to settle issues by negotiation and simple means before resorting to coercive means, or any means that exceed the needs of the situation. Abraham Lincoln's attempt to resist secession of the southern states gently, upon his becoming president, is an important example. He ordered the federal agencies to carry out the law and operate federal services as well as possible in the South without the use of coercion, leaving it to the South to initiate military action. Similarly, Lincoln's restraint of his generals as military governors and administrators of justice under martial law demonstrates an important element of reasonability. Fanaticism, as exemplified by Iran's Ayatollah Khomeini's relentless and suicidal war with Iraq, is an absence of reason and is inherently unjust and violent. In fact, most of the most destructive acts in history resulted from fanatical, often self-righteous, pursuit of narrowly conceived principles.

Nonviolent action is moral action, and its ultimate success depends upon the moral consciousness of the members of the community. A well-calculated act will reach people where they are, mobilize their support, and ideally not only mobilize their support in terms of their present consciousness, but also raise their consciousness. Many factors are involved in the effect of any action, but perhaps the biggest factor is how open people are to a particular action and to the general principle or movement to which it relates. How will an action be perceived? Martin Luther King, Jr., and other civil rights activists were successful in gaining much public support with numerous marches in the South. Unfortunately, when King led a march in Cicero, Illinois, against the opposition of the National Guard, much of the public blamed the marchers and the civil rights movement for the violence. In important regards the march was not successful. Yet in others it was. One needs to carefully consider where people are at the time and what effect a given course of action may have. From that essential standpoint, it is not enough just to act on principle. The greatest concern is the long run and the impact an act may eventually have in moving consciousness forward.

Nonviolence as a Power Technique

As previously stated, nonviolence has been used as a technique of power. Similar to other techniques of power—conventional war or guerrilla war—nonviolence has its own requirements for effectiveness that need to be adhered to in order to produce the maximum impact of the technique. Nonviolence as a power technique is about nonviolent struggle that can lead to both justice and peace. It is a means of wielding power, a strategy designed to fight a violent opponent willing and well equipped to wield military force. Nonviolence strategy is also designed for use against opponents who cannot be defeated by violence.[12]

Nonviolent strategy conducts and resolves conflicts by the use of psychological, economic, and political weapons. The history of nonviolence has yielded three principles of nonviolent struggle: first, symbolic forms of nonviolent protest (such as vigils, marches, and flying of flags); second, noncooperation (including social boycotts, economic boycotts, labor strikes, and many forms of political noncooperation, ranging from repudiation of legitimacy to civil disobedience and mutiny); and third, nonviolent intervention, ranging from hunger strikes through establishment of self-reliant institutions, nonviolent occupations and blockades, and establishment of a rival parallel government.

Nonviolent strategy has a long history with varying degrees of success. Success sometimes has come through changing the minds and attitudes of the opponents, but that outcome is rare. More often, partial success has been achieved through accommodation (gaining and giving up part of one's objectives), as in most labor strikes. Nonviolent strategy has also demonstrated its capacity to produce nonviolent coercion of the opponent (so that no alternative remains but to

[12] The concept of nonviolence as a power technique is developed by Gene Sharp in *The Politics of Nonviolent Action* (Three Volumes) (Boston: Porter Sargent, 1973).

capitulate). At times, the opponents' regime has even disintegrated in the face of massive repudiation and paralyzing noncooperation, as was the case in the downfall of the Marcos regime in the Philippines in the 1980s. Nonviolent strategy has been used in recent years in many parts of the world, including Mexico, Chile, Korea, South Africa, Israeli-occupied territory, Sudan, various parts of the former Soviet Union, Poland, Hungary, Myanmar, Brazil, and China.

Historically, nonviolent strategy has wielded significant power in conflicts when applied skillfully and has often been met with serious repression by the opponents. That response is a recognition of its power. In fact, the brutalities of repression against nonviolent resisters trigger a process of "political jujitsu" that increases the resistance, sows problems in the opponents' own camp, and mobilizes third parties in favor of the nonviolent resisters.

RECOMMENDED READINGS

ALEXANDER, YONAH, and JOHN M. GLEASON. *Behavioral and Quantitative Perspectives on Terrorism.* New York: Pergamon, 1981.

BOZEMAN, ADDA. *Politics and Culture in International History.* Princeton, NJ: Princeton University Press, 1960.

BRASS, PAUL R. *Ethnicity and Nationalism: Theory and Comparison.* Newbury Park, CA: Sage, 1991.

BURGER, JULIAN. *Report from the Frontier: The State of the World's Indigenous Peoples.* London: Zed Books, 1987.

CHOMSKY, NOAM. *The Culture of Terrorism.* Boston: South End Press, 1988.

ENLOE, CYNTHIA H. *Bananas, Beaches, and Bases: Making Feminist Sense of International Politics.* Berkeley: University of California Press, 1990.

GANDHI, MOHANDAS K. *Autobiography: The Story of My Experiments with Truth.* New York: Dover, 1983.

GLAZER, NATHAN, and DANIEL MOYNIHAN. *Ethnicity: Theory and Experience.* Cambridge, MA: Harvard University Press, 1975.

GREGG, RICHARD B. *The Power of Nonviolence.* Philadelphia: Lippincott, 1934.

MOYNIHAN, DANIEL P. *Pandaemonium: Ethnicity in International Politics.* Oxford, London: Oxford University Press, 1993.

ROTHMAN, JAY. *From Confrontation to Cooperation: Resolving Ethnic and Regional Conflict.* Newbury Park, CA: Sage, 1992.

SAID, ABDUL AZIZ, and L. R. SIMMONS, eds. *Ethnicity in an International Context.* New Brunswick, NJ: Transaction Books, 1976.

SCHAFFERT, RICHARD W. *Media Coverage and Political Terrorists: A Quantitative Analysis.* New York: Praeger, 1992.

SCHLAGHECK, DONNA M. *International Terrorism: An Introduction to Concepts and Actors.* Lexington, MA: Lexington Books, 1988.

SHARP, GENE. *Gandhi as a Political Strategist: With Essays on Ethics and Politics.* Boston: P. Sargent, 1979.

YOUNG, CRAWFORD. *The Rising Tide of Cultural Pluralism: The Nation-State at Bay?* Madison: University of Wisconsin Press, 1993.

Chapter 15

HUMAN RIGHTS

Human rights may be difficult to define but they are impossible to ignore. We may quibble about a form of government, but torture, hunger, and political imprisonment are the same by any other name. Violations of human rights are not a monopoly of a single government or a group of states. They are global.

Human rights are concerned with the dignity of the individual—the level of self-esteem that is secure and self-accepting. The Universal Declaration of Human Rights (1948), the European Convention for the Protection of Human Rights and Fundamental Freedoms (1950), the International Covenant on Economic, Social, and Cultural Rights (1966), and the International Covenant on Civil and Political Rights (1966) are part of the process of enlarging the dignity, freedom, opportunity for creativity, and welfare of individuals and the development of an environment and appropriate institutions to promote these goals.

Though the pursuit of human dignity is universal, it is defined by the culture of a people. Politics is a cultural activity and reflects tradition and environment. The global debate on human rights assumes that, in spite of the differences that characterize the diversity of cultures, political conduct can be conceptualized by certain common norms and attitudes. In the modern global system, Westerners have concentrated on discovering common denominators rooted in the Judeo-Christian tradition from which a calculus of human rights would emerge. This emphasis on Western common denominators has posited a parochial view of human rights, neglecting the traditional cultures and present conditions of the Global South.

In the West, the increasing totality of the nation-state, the changing nature of its security functions, and the integration and standardization required by complex technology underscore the issue of human rights. The expanded role of the state narrows individuality, the preoccupation with national security undermines the civil rights of the person, and technification obscures self-definition.

In the Global South, the institutions that performed the traditional functions of social and political organizations have declined, and the new structures patterned after the Western or Marxist models have not been established firmly. The need to satisfy and promote human rights persists, but this function is only partially incorporated into the present political system. This situation, however, cannot last because dignity seems to be a nonnegotiable human need.

The increasing complexity of Western society, the urge for modernization in the Global South, and the disparity in growth between rich and poor states have ascribed a higher priority to efficiency than to human dignity. In the process, violations of fundamental human rights have become widespread.

INTERNATIONAL CONCERN FOR HUMAN RIGHTS

The Congress of Vienna in 1815 demonstrated international concern for human rights for the first time in the modern era. The congress dealt with religious freedom as well as civil and political rights and heard petitions by individuals and groups for international protection of those rights. Additionally, participants in the congress agreed in principle to abolish slavery. This agreement was followed by a number of antislavery acts and treaties: the Berlin Conference on Africa in 1885, the Brussels Conference of 1890, the Saint Germain Treaty of 1919, and the Geneva Conference of 1926. Great Britain's Abolition Act of 1833 ended slavery in the British Empire. Russia, France, Prussia, Austria, and Great Britain signed the Treaty of London in 1841 to abolish slavery. In 1845, France and Great Britain agreed to cooperate to end slave trading.

The Hague peace conferences of 1899 and 1907 introduced the notion of the right of individuals to appeal to the Court of Appeal (although the proposition was not ratified). The Central American Peace Conference of 1907 provided for the right of aliens to appeal to the courts where they resided. The problem of minorities' rights, however, was emphasized at the expense of other human rights such as those of women and children.

During the first two decades of the twentieth century, World War I, the efforts of peace groups, the impact of the Fourteen Points of President Woodrow Wilson, and the Bolshevik Revolution underscored the principle of international agreement to regulate the sovereignty of states. The Peace Conference at Versailles in 1919 demonstrated its concern for the protection of minorities. Several treaties were concluded, with the new states stressing minorities' rights, including the right to life, liberty, and freedom of religion; the right to the nationality of the state of residence; complete equality with other nationals of the same state; and the exercise of civil and political rights.

Minorities' rights were placed under a system of international guarantees, with the Council of the League of Nations acting as guarantor. These rights were obligations of international interest and could not be modified without the assent of a majority of the Council. Violations were to be referred to the Permanent Court of Justice. The court's judgments, however, had no binding force. Rights of individuals were not covered by the system of minorities' rights, and only states could seek redress for violations of rights.

The International Labor Organization (ILO), in particular, has made important contributions to the development of human rights. One of the oldest international organizations, it has established conventions on the right to organize and bargain collectively, abolition of forced labor, and ending discrimination (in employment and occupation). The ILO has been a pacesetter for other specialized agencies.

In the 1940s, the shock and horror felt by people around the world upon learning of the atrocities committed in World War II, including attempted genocide, contributed to international efforts to create some sort of legal structure to enforce human rights, even though this of necessity implied some scrutiny of states' internal affairs.

The Dumbarton Oaks proposal of 1944 for the establishment of the United Nations asserted as one of the purposes of the organization to "promote respect for human rights and fundamental freedoms." Thus, unlike the Covenant of the League of Nations, which does not refer to rights of individuals, the UN Charter underscores the principle of human rights.

The Charter, however, fails to define human rights in specific terms and does not provide for adequate legal machinery to assure the effective implementation of its provisions. The role of the United Nations is further curtailed by Article 2(7) of the Charter, which upholds the concept of state sovereignty, preventing control or intervention by the UN in domestic matters of states. In 1946 the Security Council of the United Nations established the Commission on Human Rights and charged it with the duty of drafting an international declaration on the rights of individuals. The Universal Declaration of Human Rights was adopted by the General Assembly in 1948.

The Universal Declaration of Human Rights is an informal instrument appended to the Charter of the United Nations. Its purpose is to explain the contents of the human rights provision of the Charter and thus to be a preliminary formulation of the fundamental freedoms that require recognition internationally through a series of binding covenants. It consists of thirty short articles, dealing with civil and political freedoms, as well as economic, social, and cultural rights. Its scope is broad. It is in a certain sense an act of faith in a better future for humanity. In an effort to conciliate clashing ideologies of member states, the terms defining each right have been kept general and noncommittal.

The adoption of the Universal Declaration of Human Rights with its definition of standards of fundamental freedoms lacked an international obligation binding on UN members to assure that their own legislation afforded protection of rights enumerated in the declaration. The declaration is, in fact, only a statement of general moral principles; it invokes moral values, setting forth a common standard of achievement among the states of the world. More particularly, it is not a treaty and does not have binding international force.

The adoption of the Universal Declaration of Human Rights necessitated a further differentiation between rights and freedoms that had to be defined with legal accuracy and others that were described in general terms. This was accomplished in the drafting of two separate covenants, isolating political and civil liberties from economic, social, and cultural rights. The covenant dealing with the latter rights imposed on member states the duty to submit reports on their progress in the protection of human rights. The covenant on political and civil rights stimulated extensive debates as it contemplated the creation of a nine-member human rights committee that would receive complaints of violations submitted by any member state against any other signatory member.

A proposal to grant individuals the right to petition an international body for relief against a state's violation of their human rights was abandoned for fear that the covenants may become political instruments rather than effective procedures in the protection of the fundamental freedoms of individuals. Accordingly, the United Nations has consistently refused to reach any agreement that would institutionalize strong measures of international control for the protection of individual freedoms. Finally, in 1966, the UN General Assembly unanimously approved the two human rights covenants. Although the covenants are binding only upon states that have ratified them, the Universal Declaration, the two major covenants, and a variety of related covenants that have since been concluded have established a set of international norms of human rights law. Though the machinery for the enforcement of these norms is partial and weak, the current "human rights regime" has arguably made significant contributions to the protection of human rights and thus prevented many violations. In 1994 the United Nations created the office of High Commissioner of Human Rights, thus adding weight to the United Nations' commitment to human rights concerns.

Beyond international organizations, two regional organizations, the Council of Europe and the Organization of American States, have addressed themselves to human rights. The West European states have been most sensitive to the development of institutions to promote human rights. The statute of the Council of Europe of 1949 asserts that human rights and fundamental freedoms are the basis of the emerging European system. The signatory states affirmed "their devotion to the spiritual and moral values which are the common heritage of their peoples and the true source of individual freedom, political liberty and the rule of law." Acceptance of the provisions on human rights is a condition for membership in the Council of Europe.

The European Convention on Human Rights of 1950, entered into force in 1953, was the first attempt to give specific legal content to human rights in an international agreement. The European Commission of Human Rights, created in 1953, and its associated bodies, the European Court of Human Rights and the Committee of Ministers, represent important progress in the area of human rights.

The commission, the court, and the Committee of Ministers review the decisions of national tribunals but do not perform the functions of an appeal court. The deliberations of the court are secret, but the final findings are pronounced in open session. The decision of the court is not binding, and the convention does not confer upon the Council the power to enforce the judgment of the court.

The Inter-American System of Human Rights is another regional model of concern for human rights. In the Declaration of Mexico of 1945, the American republics asserted the need to harmonize the rights of individuals with the interests of the community. The declaration called on the Inter-American Judicial Council to develop a draft on the International Rights and Duties of Man. The Bogotá conference of 1948 produced the American Declaration of the Rights and Duties of Man. More than a decade later the Santiago Conference of 1959 produced the Inter-American Convention on Human Rights, which provided for the establishment of the Inter-American Commission on Human Rights and of the Court of Human Rights, which came into existence in 1960.

As of this writing, eight states have accepted the compulsory jurisdiction of the Inter-American Court of Human Rights. In 1988 and 1989, the first contentious cases resulting in rulings by the court against a government that had accepted its compulsory jurisdiction occurred. The government of Honduras has not yet expressed any inclination to disregard or reject the rulings of the court in these cases. If the rulings are successfully implemented, as is expected, these cases will create a very useful precedent for future efforts to enforce human rights agreements.

Finally, nongovernmental organizations (NGOs) such as Amnesty International, World Watch, and the Minority Group perform important investigative and communicative functions in the area of human rights. Nongovernmental organizations maintain a consultative status with the United Nations and its specialized agencies and international conferences. The contributions of NGOs, including fact-finding, monitoring, and reporting human rights violations on the national and international level, are impressive. There are today approximately a thousand nongovernmental human rights organizations throughout the world. These agencies create a flow of information as well as exert pressure through lobbying in national states and international forums.

THE FIRST GLOBAL CONFERENCE ON HUMAN RIGHTS

The first Global Conference on Human Rights met in Vienna from June 14 to 25, 1993. It took place twenty-five years after the first international conference on human rights in Tehran and following four formal preparatory committee meetings and regional meetings in Tunisia, Costa Rica, and Thailand. More than 1,500 NGOs from all regions of the world attended the conference, culminating their work to influence its agenda and outcomes. One hundred sixty-seven governments adopted, by consensus, the Vienna Declaration and Program of Action.

This final document lays out consensus language by the world's governments on principles in the human rights arena and recommends implementation of an action program in some key areas.

The Vienna Declaration calls for the integration of women's rights into the mainstream of the UN's human rights activities and programs and endorses a number of specific mechanisms proposed by NGOs. Women's groups were clearly the most organized constituency in the preparation for the conference, and their success is reflected in the advances that are detailed in the final document. There was strong endorsement for children's rights, the rights of the disabled, and the need for human rights education. The rights of indigenous peoples were given support with some important new initiatives, but the document falls short of recognizing their right to self-determination. The Vienna Declaration calls on the General Assembly to take up as matter of priority consideration of the question of the establishment of a High Commissioner for Human Rights: a proposal that was strongly supported by a wide cross section of NGOs. The other important proposal, the establishment of an international penal court, was referred back to the Law Commission and, thus, failed to receive a clear endorsement.

The issue of the universality of human rights had been one of the most contentious during preparations for the conference, with some governments, particularly from Asia, claiming that cultural and religious particularities and the issue of national sovereignty should be given greater consideration. The Vienna Declaration strongly affirms the universality of human rights, but the language on cultural and religious particularities is weak.

The other contentious issue was the indivisibility of civil and political rights vis-à-vis economic, social, and cultural rights. The declaration affirms the relatedness of these sets of rights and repeatedly links human rights with democracy and development. The right to development was for the first time recognized as a universal and inalienable right, implementation of which requires effective national policies and equitable economic relations.

HUMAN RIGHTS: CULTURAL AND IDEOLOGICAL PERSPECTIVES

Western Liberalism

The fundamental problem of political life—the tension between the rights and liabilities of the individual and the duties and powers of government—has characterized the development of the state. Since ancient Greece, the Western practice has drawn on both Platonic and Sophistic philosophy. For the Platonists, the individual beyond a political community (*polis*) had no rights; it was through the *polis* that individuals gained the spiritual and political attributes that made them human rather than barbaric. Therefore, concern for the whole of the political community preceded the claims of any individual. This type of political community was organic, because the individual functioned merely as a part of an organic whole and gained significance only in reference to that whole.

The Sophists based the state upon a contract acknowledging that the individual had natural rights apart from the political community. The state arose only when individuals saw that it would benefit them to surrender their purely selfish interests in order to better secure their existence. For the Sophists, the community was predicated upon a philosophy of nominalism: The members did have an identity beyond the political community. The rationale of the state was not to achieve an organic harmony and a common good, but rather to maximize the interests of the individual members of the state.

The Platonic-Sophistic dichotomy was reproduced with greater sophistication by the Nominalists of the seventeenth century and the Organicists of the nineteenth century. The Nominalists saw the political community held together by an intricate balance of power that gave rise to a harmony of interests and became the basis of laissez-faire economics and liberal politics. The interests of the individual and the community were so conceived as to coincide.

The Organicists asserted that human values and perception are structured by objective categories that one brings into the world at birth. Accordingly, the individual has a categorical identity—as a member of a class, nation, and race—that ultimately determines one's actions.

Socialists: Marxists and Neo-Marxists

Marxism is an elaboration of the concept of humanism that was developed during the Renaissance asserting the basic dignity and worth of the individual and emphasizing a person's capacity for self-realization through reason. Karl Marx emphasized economic rights, affirming that the collapse of the capitalist system was inevitable and that the proletariat (the working class) would seize the means of production and establish a new socialist system. This socialist system would, then, work toward the attainment of communism under which all would share equally the benefits of the new society. The exploited proletarian class would construct a new classless society where all individuals would be treated equally and justly.

The rapid expansion and even more rapid collapse of Marxist political systems have given rise to very diverse views on the subject of Marxist humanism. In the erstwhile Marxist societies (led by the former Soviet Union), a more "traditional" approach to the subject of Marxism focused its attention on class struggle and the liberation of the working class. The class struggle was promoted as the force that molds the consciousness of the working class and allows the working class to free itself from the oppression of the exploitative classes. As one traditional Marxist, Ladislav Shtoll, wrote, "It will not be amiss to recall Engels's *The Condition of the Working Class in England* where it is stressed that the workers can maintain their human dignity, their human countenance, only if their whole life is filled with a burning hatred for the exploiter class."[1] The traditional Marxists contended that there can be no genuine humanism under the capitalist system because of the oppressed condition of the working class. Under the capitalist sys-

[1] Ladislav Shtoll, "The Class Struggle and Humanism," *World Marxist Review,* 1, no. 3 (1958): 28.

tem, the worker is viewed only in terms of market value, not as a human being with a myriad of needs and cares. Thus, under such a system, the basis for a humanistic society could never be constructed. As another traditional Marxist writer phrased it, "The problems of humanism . . . are, in the final analysis, reduced to the need for a just organization of society."[2]

While traditional Marxists stressed the class struggle and the monolithic unity of the communist movement, other Marxists were beginning to explore new routes to social change. These "neo-Marxists" were devoted to developing a more humane socialism independent of the dominant centers of Marxist thought in Moscow and Beijing. The neo-Marxists were opposed to the harsh and repressive Stalinist system and demanded autonomy for each national movement. The slogan of the neo-Marxists has been "Socialism with a human face."

The Global South

Existential conditions in the Global South differ from the West. Increased institutionalization of the national state has accentuated the confrontation between the Western individual and the state. In the West, human rights tensions derive from the frustrating efforts to fit the contemporary environment into the state. Tensions in the Global South represent these nations' equally frustrating effort to fit the state into their traditional institutions. Human rights concerns in the Global South center more on poverty, hunger, disease, illiteracy, low productivity, mass unemployment, and glaring disparities in the distribution of benefits.

The "nation-state" and a progressive (as opposed to a static) vision of reality have inspired explorations, and sometimes produced friction, in the relationships between traditional cultural patterns and the structures of government. The Global South is in a marked intellectual and political/institutional discontinuity with the old. The family and the community are no longer adequate as organizing principles and as safeguards for certain basic human rights. Nothing has replaced them, except perhaps anger and sometimes ugly cynicism.

The nation-state model has required Global South governments to enter into competition with traditional authority. This, in turn, has prompted the attempt to introduce new values, interests, and goals in an effort to supplant traditional ones. While the old has been destroyed, the new has not yet appeared. The reasons are technical as well as ideological. The new states have no commonly accepted values; hence, their new national structures are fragile. Political systems in the Global South have tended to merge, under the influence of one-party systems and militarism, with an ever-widening public sector. Hardly any Global South government has been able to institutionalize itself firmly to establish liberal or popular institutions, or to relax its vigil against subversion, imagined or real. The central structures of government are modern in form only, not in substance.

States of the Global South have patterned their political systems after Western or Marxist models and, consequently, suffer constant confrontation between individual rights and liabilities on the one hand and state duties and powers on

[2]Roger Garaudy, *Marxist Humanism* (Paris: Edition Sociale, 1957), p. 88.

the other. The Western liberal emphasis upon "freedom from restraint" is not well established.

Common Human Rights?

There are many views of human rights, but hardly a clear focus. Human rights in Western liberalism and socialism-Marxism are expressed in demands for the redress of grievances and satisfaction of new needs, whereas in the past they represented a desire to be left alone. The Greco-Roman and Judeo-Christian traditions asserted both rights and duties, as expounded in the "natural law" arguments of the times.

Thus in Western liberalism and socialism-Marxism we see a movement away from the person's duties to the state, through the individual's pleas to be left alone, and toward demands by individuals that the state perform more duties. As each stage develops, the number of individual rights expands while the province of individual duties narrows. On the other hand, the demand for the expansion of the duties of the state is satisfied only through the enlargement of state powers. These contradictory aspects run deep in the present human rights debate in Western liberalism and socialism-Marxism. This contradiction has placed the state in a cross fire between individuals and groups demanding equal rights. The essential contradiction is that government intervention to meet demands of an individual or a group diminishes the rights of other individuals or groups in exact proportion to its success. The trend will persist until there is a change in the allocation of power.

We must also recognize the connection between the type and number of rights and the nature of the environment. In Western liberalism and socialism-Marxism there has been a definite shift from an abstract concept of universal rights toward a concrete concept of essential rights. The shift is indicative of societal conditions that must be taken into consideration in the dialogue on human rights. Europe and North America are in a stage of development substantially different from much of the Global South.

HUMAN RIGHTS: COLD WAR AND POST–COLD WAR

The end of the Cold War lifts the "semantic fog" of ideology that obscured many of the real forces that have been reshaping the international scene for some time. While the most obvious of these forces are ethnic nationalism, the pressure of human numbers and activities on the physical limits of our planet, and the disquieting situation facing the Global South, the Cold War left a tragic and cruel legacy in the area of human rights. It left a world divided over four areas of conflict: (1) a conflict of civil and political rights versus economic, social, and cultural rights; (2) a conflict among "liberty, equality, and fraternity"; (3) a conflict between two versions of the modern democratic state; and (4) a new conflict between the rich and the poor.

While the concepts of human rights and democracy have become accepted norms of aspirations for every society, at least on the global and national public level, definitions of those concepts are seriously challenged. The very language and meaning of human rights and democracy are becoming lost in the deep shifts of economic, social, and political structures of the world that do not reflect the emerging postmodern, post–Cold War, post-Industrial-Revolution society.

We are in the midst of a global "tectonic shift," a loss of "paradigmatic" guidelines, a "shaking of the foundations."[3] It may be that Norberto Bobbio is correct: *The Era of Rights*[4] may not be over. But it is no less possible that we are in the beginning of a search for *global stability and order,* or that we are launched on a "Sustainable Development Decade."[5] We may be entering a "New World Order" where the powerful technologies of *1984* and *Brave New World*[6] are at the disposal of the rich and powerful few to manipulate the great majority of the people of the world, and in which the "growing global gap" (GGG) between the rich and the poor is written off as "inevitable." This risk means that the various foundations and assumptions of democracy and human rights need to be reformulated.

The modern democratic state came into existence in the nineteenth century in Western Europe, America, and the British dominions, largely as the effect of the French Revolution and the industrial revolution on the absolutist nation-state of the sixteenth and seventeenth centuries.[7] Two of the most basic characteristics of the modern democratic state, rooted in the industrial revolution, were—and still are—(1) consumerism equals happiness and economic growth, and (2) the "dribble down" theory of democracy, cultural "enlightenment," and social and economic development. The first model of the modern democratic state was—and still is—a capitalist, mercantilist, middle-class system and society, emphasizing civil and political rights, arguing that cultural, economic, and social rights will come later, that they will have to await their proper time.

The socialist revolutions brought a new model (especially with the Russian and Chinese, then the Cuban, examples), an alternative model of a new modern democratic state competing with the capitalist model. While the capitalist model emphasized individual, competitive, middle-class political and civil rights, the latter model emphasized socialist democracy seeking to redress the balance and promote equality—especially economic equality.

These two models of the modern democratic state—the capitalist, liberal state and the one-party, socialist state—sought to advance human rights in their

[3]This phrase, the title of a book by Paul Tillich about the experience of World War II, is still a good phrase, and much more global than when the book was written.

[4]Norberto Bobbio, *A Era dos Direitos,* translated from the Italian into Portuguese.

[5]The "Decade of Sustainable Development" is a phrase that was legitimized by the Brundtland Commission in *The World Commission on Environment and Development on Our Common Future* (New York: Oxford University Press, 1987) and was given more exposure at the United Nations Conference on Environment and Development in Rio de Janeiro in 1992.

[6]Aldous Huxley, *Brave New World* (New York: Harper, 1946).

[7]A. D. Lindsay, *The Modern Democratic State* (1943), p. 1. Lindsay (who became Lord Lindsay of Birker) was the articulator of the Labor Party in Great Britain. The book was published again in 1962—Galaxy series, Oxford University Press, New York.

different ways, addressing different problems with different priorities. Though these two distinct versions were both products of the Industrial Revolution, they created two radically different models of the modern democratic state—two versions of modern democracy. Both models are incomplete. One often emphasizes political and civil rights, arguing that if these juridical rights are established and enforced, the other rights (economic, social, and cultural) will "naturally" happen in society, and cannot be enforced by law in any way. The other advances the primacy of economic rights over political rights.

These two approaches to democracy, as exemplified by the best-known and by far most powerful states, the United States and the former Soviet Union, finally canceled out each other and spent their energy and wealth in weapon production and ideological clashes, with tremendous waste, failing to expand democracy or promote justice in either society.[8] Neither one had been able to achieve its own nominal goals to impose in one way or another its own way of life on the rest of the world. Today they are both facing ideological, as well as economic and political, bankruptcy. They consumed each other in an ideological and militaristic Cold War, which weakened them financially and technologically at the cost of the welfare of their own people.

We are now in a "postmodern world," which no longer is dominated by industrial technology, but by electronic technology. We are increasingly dominated by monopolies of information and analysis, more than by military power, concentrated wealth, or the new global élites. The old debates of the era of industrial technology have been superseded by new technology and the global society that is now appearing. The new debate is between laissez-faire or liberal capitalism and social democracy or socialism. Now, neoliberalism, or neocorporatism,[9] is the dominant theory, largely in the absence of new analyses and new theories.

[8]There is an already-old argument among historians as to who "caused" the Cold War—whether the capitalists or the socialists were the aggressors. Great debate during a great dinner party—but in the meantime, there is enough "blame" in both camps, and there are much more urgent issues!

[9]Some attempts of "compared definitions" are necessary because the language of politics is sensitive to cultural and historical changes—especially in moments of fluidity like our own time. It is more important to understand the evolving concepts than to freeze or create new dogmas in such a situation. Today, we are (or should be!) very much in the "mode" of trying to describe a set of new realities than we are in the "mode" of ideological conflict. To that extent, it is necessary to be free and to let others allow concepts and perceptions to evolve. We have inherited a language of theory of politics and society that itself betrayed reality, but today we have an opportunity to develop a new language, though it will take some time to do so. Here are some of the old concepts that are subject to reinterpretation in the light of the "New Revolution":

"Liberalism," in the United States, is considered as a mildly reformist, paternalistic government that often seeks to intervene in favor of more equality within the "pluralist" (competitive) capitalist system.

"Liberalism" in continental Western Europe, Latin America, and much of the United Kingdom is laissez-faire capitalism, the state as a guardian of social order and a protectorate over the "free-market system."

"Neoliberalism" in continental Western Europe and Latin America is laissez-faire capitalism, with an alliance with some of the governments or states, integrating itself in the "global economy." In many areas of the United States and in the United Kingdom the phrase "neoliberalism" is being supplanted by "neocorporatism."

"Trilateralism" includes elements of neoliberalism and neocorporatism.

"Corporatism," originally from the Mediterranean medieval system, was a "club" of the élites

We are beginning to get a glimpse of the electronic-age new world order.

The basic conflict between the two approaches to democracy, incited by their deep mutual distrust, spilled over from the beginning into the forums of the United Nations. In the area of human rights, the conflict was between civil and political rights, on the one hand, and economic, social, and cultural rights on the other. The argument was between the juridical approach (middle-class, individualistic, and liberal) and the economic approach (one-party, revolutionary, class-war). The United Nations was one of the first victims in the struggle to develop and implement the Universal Declaration of Human Rights.

The socialist camp advocated class conflict, the dictatorship of a vanguard party, and revolution, and finally sought to create the new "socialist person," creating the basis of a new culture of security and equality for all before political liberty could be established. Of course, the establishment of the new class of managerial bureaucrats (from Soviet roots) impeded the functioning of the "transmission belt theory" (Marxist phrase for internal party two-way communication). In the name of equality and dignity, an oversized, arbitrary, usually insensitive bureaucracy became the major obstacle to freedom and a sense of community.

During the Cold War, the vision of the French revolutionaries was swept away, and an imaginary conflict among "liberty, equality, and fraternity"—which emphasized the conflict between liberty and equality and ignored fraternity—took root in both Cold War camps.

The Cold War undercut the efforts to promote full democracy, full humanism, and full human rights. Further, the Cold War undermined development in the Global South. The expansion of full democratization and full humanization was undercut in the two systems, in different ways. The Cold War took precedence, and the result was the failure of the different models of development.

The two superpowers competed for global hegemony, undercutting efforts to strengthen the already-weak international system (the United Nations, the Organization of American States, the World Bank, and the IMF). This competition also led to neglect of human rights and human-rights protection systems.

The two superpowers of the Cold War devalued the concept of democracy.

---

of the powerful "corporations" that—usually informally—made the major decisions and plans of the society, using the state apparatus as a tool, not as a decision-making system but as a representative of the whole society.

"Neocorporatism" is the emerging alliance between *some* transnational corporations and banks, *some* national corporations and banks, and *some* governments or states. Neocorporatism is new in the sense that some of the states or governments have become major partners of the élite or club of the global economy, whereas in "old" corporatism the state was a junior partner, and it was more national than global. There is still a question whether some of the major financial actors (banks, corporations) will be allied with a state or whether they will seek to be free from all national regulation.

"Social democracy," or a semiregulated welfare state, can be considered as a society with a mixed economy, with some state planning and some free-market dynamics.

See Hugo Assman, *Clamor dos Pobres e "Racionalidade" Economica* (Buenos Aires: Edicoes Paulinas, 1985). Assman has given a basic outline of the various contemporaneous schools of thought of global economic and political order.

Neither one had been able to realize its own nominal goals, not having benefitted from initiating either model. The two former superpowers had conflicting but incomplete and inadequate visions of democracy and human rights, but a person can imagine that the two visions could be complementary rather than conflicting.

The driving power in the global community today is economic and technological power, as manifested by the North American, Japanese, and Western European models, which are all tainted with racism, cultural arrogance, and imperialism. Today, after the Cold War, there is a great vacuum in the center of the discussion of the theories on human rights and democracy. The world lacks a new democratic paradigm, a new set of global core values, and an integrated view of all human rights. At present, nations face a double threat: one, the global competition to survive; the other, neocorporatism, the tendency to seek today's economic superpower status, to become technological and economic Japan, Inc., or U.S.A., Inc.

Now neoliberalism and neocorporatism are the dominant views—largely in the absence of new analyses and new theories. It is too early to be able to describe the new, post–Cold War, postmodern, pre-electronic-age profile. We do not have even an adequate language to discuss what is happening, not to mention what is going to happen in the next twenty years!

The French Revolution began with its three great themes—liberty, equality, and fraternity—seeking to bring them into balance, well aware that liberty without equality would lead to tyranny, that equality without liberty would finally suffocate itself, and that only community would make the other two live together creatively. The history of the struggle for human rights has been characterized by a lack of attention to the issue of fraternity, or community, thus causing the tension between liberty and equality.

The United Nations in the Universal Declaration of Human Rights sought to make the five categories of human rights (political, civil, economic, social, and cultural) interdependent, interrelated, and equally important, but the United States and the former Soviet Union undermined the development of a world community.

Faced with new technologies and the postindustrial modernization processes, human rights theorists and activists have become concerned that the modern, technologically competent, wealthy state can be a new form of oppression, and there is now a search to counterbalance the power of the neocorporatist state (an alliance between the state and the big banks and corporations). The discussion today focuses on strengthening the civil society.

There is a great distance between human rights principles and their application. There are three great opportunities to relate theory with the practice of human rights in the world today:

First, there is the possibility of integrating and invigorating human rights, ecology, and environmental development movements in the NGOs, of putting together the Earth Charter of the environmentalists with the Universal Declaration of Human Rights.

Second, the increasing awareness of widespread poverty, affecting to some degree every nation in the world and probably more than half of the people in the world, is leading to a new focus on human rights. The greatest and most widespread violation of human rights today is poverty. We cannot imagine anything that is more cruel, vicious, or obscene than letting small babies and children die of hunger in the midst of material abundance. There is a rising tide of literature in Latin America, at least, on the rights of the poor, and there is no doubt that there will be more of this debate in the United States in the years to come.

Third, the world community is becoming painfully aware that the isolated cultural islands that we used to think of as nation-states are increasingly obsolescent. During the "liberal" years, global awareness and sensitivity to other cultures were often considered as optional exercises. Today, "multiculturalism" is both a present reality and one that must be understood and practiced more widely.

We need to develop the essential, global core values and processes that may enable us to dialogue among the many peoples of the world, and upon which we can develop common, cooperative global programs. The vision of the Universal Declaration of Human Rights—together with the Earth Charter—will move a step forward when there is an integrated mentality that makes human beings the primary goal of social endeavor, but with due respect for nature. Perhaps the greatest Western thinkers in this area are Teilhard de Chardin and St. Francis.

It must be argued that full democracy must embrace all three of the components of the motto of the French Revolution and all five of the components of the Universal Declaration of Human Rights. Without all of these components, democracy will be skewed. We have a sense (from the English, American, and French revolutions) of freedom from political tyranny and the virtues of individual freedoms. We have a sense (from the former U.S.S.R., the People's Republic of China, Cuba, and several African nations) that economic equality can provide security in education and health. There are many versions of the fraternity model—but no one has yet been able to put all three together in a dynamic profile. Perhaps it can be done only by one nation or a few—perhaps it can only be a global achievement!

The struggle of the centuries for humankind has been for liberation, peace, and justice. We have finally reached an understanding of modern democracy, based on the dreams and principles of the United Nations and the imperfect and incomplete democratic visions and experiences of the English, Americans, French, Russians, Chinese, and Cubans (among many others). Now the industrial society that bred much of our thought has been overtaken by events. And we are finding it difficult to retool intellectually and develop new concepts. We find it even more difficult when we have to invent the new tools on the road!

The agelong division between the rich and the poor is not improving. Postmodern technology and the inherited fears and existing concentrations of wealth and power are exacerbating the growing gap between the rich and the poor. We can see already the tendencies in the postindustrial era: more poverty, greater wealth among the rich, more repression of the poor, growth of the global luxury class (expanded tourism, fortress subdivisions and condominiums, and the rising tide of defensiveness, dependence, and timidity in the corporate middle class).

The world community is still struggling to encompass all three components of liberty, equality, and fraternity, for all persons of all genders and all ages to embrace interrelatedness and interdependence, and to give equal importance to the five categories of the Universal Declaration of Human Rights. The failure of the two competing views of human rights and democracy—the capitalist and the socialist visions—showed that civil, economic, social, cultural, and political rights are interrelated, interdependent, and equally important. Human rights are indivisible. The two models have failed, and it remains to be seen if the world can become a community or will slip into chaos.[10]

TOWARD GLOBAL HUMAN RIGHTS

The common bonding culture of the world today—such as it is—is the product of the acculturation of non-Western élites that occurred as a result of the political and economic vitality of the West. The common language of the world, then, is largely Western in form and content and the result of what must be described as political, economic, and cultural conquest of the peoples of the Third World, or the Global South.

This "conquest" has its own style for each of the three major subcultures of the West, the Europeans, the Russians, and the Americans, but all have generally assumed their own superiority in contact with non-Western cultures and have usually entered into such contacts on the back of power.

Such an experience of cultural contact in a context of unequal political and economic relations has naturally colored the cultural exchange. Whereas it left the West feeling more superior and more insensitive, it left the non-Western cultures defensive and unsure of themselves.

With the passage of the last fifty years the internal conflicts of the West and the assimilation and diffusion of Western technology by the Global South have redressed the balance somewhat. Among other adjustments, there is a slowly-growing tide of greater self-confidence and a rediscovery of the inherent worth of their own cultures among many non-Western peoples.

The mounting problems of the world have induced at least the beginnings of a new humility in the West, and also the beginnings of a still-embryonic sense of interdependence in all sectors of the world. Though it is commonplace to say it, only through global cooperation can the world survive and become human.

As discussed earlier, such cooperation is only possible if there is a greater fund of common values. Common values can no longer be imposed by the West or anyone else—they must be invented and developed through the consensus-

[10]An elaborate discussion of this topic is in Brady Tyson and Abdul Aziz Said, "Human Rights: A Forgotten Victim of the Cold War," *Human Rights Quarterly*, Vol. 15, no. 3, August 1993.

making process. Such a process today demands respect by and for all cultures and also demands more—not less—participation of all peoples.

We need to move beyond the capitalist, socialist, and industrial-technology visions of human rights and democracy. These visions project a parochial view of human rights that excludes the cultural realities and present existential conditions of non-Western cultures of the Global South, resting on the premise of an industrial society that has been overtaken by events. The traditional debate about democracy and human rights assumes that in spite of differences that characterize the diversity of cultures, political systems can be validated by criteria derived from capitalist and socialist experience.

The development of a world conception of human rights is undermined by the lack of agreement on sources of human rights, including the very foundation of international law. The uncertainty about the content of the doctrines of human rights—including the lack of a process of evolutionary consensus on global core values—poses additional obstacles. In fact, the very conception of the organization of society differs from one culture to another. The West emphasizes political rights; socialists, Marxists, and neo-Marxists favor economic rights; and much of the Global South values obligations. The Western tradition posits freedom and individualism in order to avoid the outcome of a despotic system; socialists emphasize social justice; and the Global South maintains cultural traditions that often support a coercive system. The West emphasizes individual interests; socialists choose collective interests; and élites of the Global South value the good of community. These cultural differences are exploited by élites who often equate the good of the country with élite interests. Even in the areas where natural rights indisputably transcend cultural values, as in the right to survival, the vested interests of élites serve as the basis for disagreement in the exercise of human rights. Such political use of those rights increases the possibility of the perversion of the concept.

There are many roads to humanistic cultural pluralism, many potential systems of communitarian, free, creative life, and many potential languages, arts, music, drama, and literature that are compatible with humanistic ethics. There is no doubt that every community needs some "cultural revolution" to remove the things that dehumanize society or inhibit human development. However, only as the primacy of the cultural community as the principal source of human realization is made clear, will creativity have a chance to replace conformity and cooperation a chance to replace competition.

A retreat to a cultural ghetto by any group is not only a denial of the rich diversity of the modern cultural experience, but also a rejection of responsibility for future generations. The inexorable dynamics of modern history rules out pretensions by any one group or cultural tradition of establishing a world hegemony. In the new age of interdependence, the whole world needs the whole world. World order becomes a historical process whereby human beings choose and create their future within the context of their environment to achieve a humanist and creative society.

RECOMMENDED READINGS

AMNESTY INTERNATIONAL. *Report on Torture.* New York: Farrar, Straus and Giroux, 1993.

BROWNLIE, IAN, ed. *Basic Documents on Human Rights.* 3rd ed. New York: Oxford University Press, 1992.

CLAUDE, RICHARD. *Comparative Human Rights.* Baltimore: Johns Hopkins University Press, 1976.

FALK, RICHARD. *Human Rights and State Sovereignty.* New York: Holmes & Meier, 1981.

NEWSOM, DAVID D. *The Diplomacy of Human Rights.* Lanham, MD: University Press of America, 1986.

SAID, ABDUL AZIZ, ed. *Human Rights and World Order.* New Brunswick, NJ: Transaction Books, 1978.

SCOBLE, HARRY M., and LAURIE S. WISEBURG. *Access to Justice: Human Rights Struggles in South East Asia.* London: Zed Books, 1985.

SHUE, HENRY. *Basic Rights: Subsistence, Affluence, and U.S. Foreign Policy.* Princeton, NJ: Princeton University Press, 1980.

SPEIVACK, NEAL, and ANN FLORINI. *Food on the Table: Seeking Global Solutions to Chronic Hunger.* New York: United Nations Association of the United States of America, 1986.

STROVER, ERIC, and ELANA O. NIGHTINGALE. *The Breaking of Bodies and Minds: Torture, Psychiatric Abuse and the Health Professions.* New York: Freeman, 1985.

SWIDLER, ARLENE. *Human Rights in Religious Traditions.* New York: Pilgrim Press, 1982.

UNITED STATES DEPARTMENT OF STATE. *Country Reports on Human Rights Practices for 1993.* Washington, DC: U.S. Government Printing Office.

VAN DYKE, VERNON. *Human Rights, the U.S. and W77orld Community.* New York: Oxford University Press, 1970.

VASAK, KAREL, and PHILIP ALSTON, eds. *The International Dimensions of Human Rights.* Westport, CT: Greenwood Press, 1982.

VINDENT, R. J. *Foreign Policy and Human Rights: Issues and Responses.* Cambridge, UK: Cambridge University Press, 1986.

WEISBORD, MARVIN R., et al. *Discovering Common Ground: How Future Search Conferences Bring People Together to Achieve Breakthrough Innovation, Empowerment, Shared Vision, and Collaborative Action.* San Francisco: Berret-Koehler, 1992.

Conclusion

TOWARD COOPERATIVE GLOBAL POLITICS

A NEW FRAME OF REFERENCE

As the new millennium approaches, it is not clear whether the world is coming together—or falling apart. Our morning newspaper may trumpet the worldwide triumph of consumption-based capitalism or the emergence of Western-style democracy in unexpected places. But when we turn on the evening news, it appears that religious or ethnic fanaticism, rampant nationalism, or the raw ambition of some regional dictator is creating chaos rather than anything remotely like "order" of any kind. Which is it: chaos or a new world order?

World chaos, in an increasingly interdependent and crowded world, is an invitation to disaster, with the great accumulation of nuclear, chemical, and biological arms in many nations (including the United States and Russia), creeping famines and pestilence in the world, and adventurist political and military leaders.

Yet, the existing world order is detrimental to the great majority of the poor and the weak. The existing system—the present distribution of power is really "disorder"—favors the rich who are getting richer and the powerful who are getting more powerful.

It might be helpful if we acknowledged that the collapse of Soviet-style socialism lifts the "semantic fog" of ideology that obscured many of the real forces that have been reshaping the international scene for some time. Among these forces is "nationalism." At the beginning of the twentieth century, the world was basically organized into European-style empires or spheres of influence that ignored underlying ethnic aspirations for self-expression. The Soviet empire turns out to have been the last gasp of a dying worldview, rather than the beginning of a new one. The demise of the Soviet empire in 1989 is the end of a long process that witnessed the passing of similar hegemonies whose metropolitan centers at one time included England, France, Belgium, Holland, Spain, Portugal, Germany, Austria-Hungary, Turkey, Japan, and—with respect to the Philippines, Cuba, Panama, and Puerto Rico—the United States.

These empires, for the most part, have devolved into constituent parts, sometimes founded on common ethnicity or religion, sometimes not. The number of independent "nation-states" more than tripled during the postwar period, becoming, in the process, the "norm" of the global system. The dominant ethical value in international discourse was sovereignty; the violation of this norm, aggression. The Soviets, of course, defined aggression differently than did the Americans. Where the old imperial lines drawn on the maps coincided with "natural" ethnic communities, the decolonization process served stability and order; where it did not, it caused wars.

As the ideological fog of the Cold War lifts, the enduring organizing power of ethnicity and religious belief as the central reservoir of meaning for human communities is thrown into the bold relief it has long deserved. The artificial boundaries drawn by European explorers are legacies more often perceived as forces for division or civil war than for unification—as in the former Soviet Union, Ethiopia, and former Yugoslavia. An important point to stress is that the motivating force behind what is generally termed factional or sectarian violence is no different, in principle, from that which motivates the aspirations for self-governance within nations whose existence is sanctioned by diplomatic recognition. The status quo's "tribalism" is the revolutionary's "nationalism." The motive behind terrorism in Ulster or Sri Lanka is, for those who carry it out, no different from the "patriotic" drive for independence that only a century ago forged modern Italy and Germany out of constituent entities that shared an ethnic heritage. This same impulse allowed Brazil, Algeria—and the United States—to throw off a hated imperial yoke.

Despite the emergence of so many new nations, it is important to note that the relative status of nations and regions has been relatively stable. At the beginning of the twentieth century the list of major powers included the United States, Great Britain, France, Germany, Austria-Hungary, Italy, Russia, and Japan. China and Brazil were accepted as future major powers. As the end of the century approaches, if we substitute the European Union for the European powers—acknowledging that relative rankings have altered somewhat—the names on this list have changed not at all. China and Brazil are still future major powers. If we step back a thousand years, Europe, the Islamic Crescent, and China's sphere of influence already dominated human history. If we grant that Japan and the emerging Pacific Basin still acknowledge China as their cultural home, only the Middle East, as a region, has experienced a fundamental decline in its global influence—a decline that understandably motivates present resentment in the form of Islamic fundamentalism.

The emerging "new world order" is as much a redefinition of what is important as it is the discovery of new forces at work. While most experts on international relations will readily acknowledge the continuing power of national and ethnic identity as a major shaping force within the global system, many will argue that there are some fundamentally new forces at work. But this is as much a matter of perception as it is descriptive of the underlying reality. Take, for example, the rise of the ecological ethic and green politics. The negative ecological consequences of industrialization are not new. They go back to the earliest phases of the Industrial Revolution in the eighteenth century. And criticism of the rape of the environment goes back almost as far. The fine system of national parks in the United States is the result of green politics at work in the late nineteenth and early twentieth centuries.

What is new is the growing organizational and political power of the critics. More of us accept the tenets of the Gaia hypothesis than in the past. What is beginning to shift are our values—and our knowledge of just how damaging our behavior has been all along. As a species, we've actually traveled this road before. Some 10,000 years ago, when agriculture was invented—probably in what is now western Turkey—neolithic "farmers" at first planted nothing. The first 300 years or so of the agricultural revolution consisted of a breakthrough in the systematic gathering of the natural produce of the Earth. This innovation resulted in the creation of the world's first true villages and a sudden, rapid rise in population. But systematic exploitation without returning seed to the land led to mass starvation. The survivors learned that we must return to the Earth what we take from it.

The modern industrial revolution started about 300 years ago. Again, we are systematically reaping what we have not sown. Once again, our numbers have exploded. And, once again, we face mass starvation. The present poverty in the Global South and in parts of industrial societies is also the by-product of economic and political structures and belief systems grounded in uncontrolled materialism. The ecological ethic is not new, nor is it necessarily a modern discovery. The question is "Will we come to our senses in time?" Take the case of technology itself—often portrayed as a "new" independent force for change. Has the relative speed and scale of technological change really become more salient? Of course. Is it really new? Of course not. Roman engineering reshaped the world order of the ancient world, and tens of thousands of Romans died of poisoning caused by drinking water flowing through the "high technology" of lead pipes.

What is changing is not so much the basic forces shaping events; they have been here all along. What has changed is how we feel about them and the relative weight we assign to them. More of us refuse to accept that 13 to 18 million human beings, most of them children, die each year as a result of hunger, while our planet has enough resources and know-how to provide enough for every person on Earth. This new attitude has an important consequence. The new frame of reference of world problems is an artifact of the minds and hearts of people. It is not something that is happening to us, or that we are discovering through observation. We are creating it.

THE FIRST GLOBAL CIVILIZATION

The Cold War political order has dissolved faster than visions of a new order to replace it are being developed. For all its unpleasantness, the bipolar Cold War at least offered predictability and stability for half a century. The current fluid situation offers both the potential for evolution into a stable, peaceful relationship at a much lower level of tension and armaments, and the risk of devolution into instability like that of pre-1914 Europe. The end of the Cold War may usher in another specter of balkanization among nations, competing with and fearing one another. The new concentration of power on the world level—globalization and privatization—may leave us in an even more desperate situation.

The likelihood of a good outcome will be greater if nations are guided by a vision of a more stable, peaceful political order. But it is not enough for each nation to have its own vision of a better future. Unless the vision is shared by nations whose independent actions must be coordinated to bring it into being, their actions in pursuit of their own visions are not likely to produce a result that is desired by any of them. Today, such a vision does not seem to exist.

We are not going to get a viable global order by bringing the poor of the world up to the ever-ascending material standard of living of the industrialized countries. Even if this were a feasible goal, the planet would not stand it. And the crisis we face will probably not be resolved by the industrial societies descending to the Global South's poor standard of living. We certainly are not in a stable situation so long as these disparities remain between those who are living quite well and those that are barely living.

We have moved from a humanity that lived its collective life as fragments of the whole into a new context of humanity as a whole. We are living in the first global political community. As we stated earlier, the first global industries are emerging, and, along with them, the foundations for a global economic system. We have entered the first truly global civilization since the days of the Roman Empire.

World politics is shifting from a horizontal axis of right versus left or West versus East to a vertical axis of economic materialist values versus ecological, feminist, and spiritual values. These issues for the near future focus on who controls the system of technology and who controls the system of beliefs. At present the material beliefs underlying the world economy prevail. On the surface, policy seems to be the critical issue. That is an illusion. The belief system is the issue. Likewise, on the surface, equity seems to be the issue. The real issue is the belief system. We are driven to contribute to the starvation of the Global South because of unconscious belief systems.

In the currently dominant world economy, we have some assumptions that are being challenged by a majority of people of the globe. The first is that it is perfectly appropriate that the rich should use whatever they want if they can pay for it. Second, there is an assumption that it is appropriate to resolve social issues—issues that may affect other peoples around the globe and future generations—

by economic rationality. In other words, it is ultimately economic reasoning that guides our development policy. There is an assumption—the *consumption ethic*—that somehow we are better off if we consume more and more. All the economic indicators we use are essentially indicators of resource consumption. They go under different names, and they may look a little different. But when we come right down to it and see the correlation between resource consumption and indicators such as GNP, we have built a premise that increased consumption is increased economic growth, and it is the desired positive direction of development.

The culture of the industrialized nations dominates the globe with that type of thinking. Implicit to a great extent is the assumption that all of the world's religion-based culture are predicated on illusion because they cannot be supported by materialistic science, which is the best knowledge the world can have. All of the cultures of the world are overrun by this ideal. They all have to become materialistically and economically westernized if they want to play the game. In development, human needs, human rights, and the quality of human interactions are all sacrificed in pursuit of the elusive goal of economic development. The development policies in industrialized countries are based on these premises too.[1]

There is an increasingly disquieting situation facing the Global South. It was not very long ago that we spoke confidently of the Global South moving through a process of development analogous to that through which the West had moved. It was widely accepted that the Global South was experiencing a takeoff, like an airplane moving down a runway, gradually gathering speed, and eventually reaching a self-sustaining velocity, where it is able to make its own way under its own power. It just seemed to be taking a little longer than expected for the assistance, the foreign aid, the investments, and that sort of thing from the West to have their intended effect.

We are facing a situation where there is no realistic prospect that a large number of countries of what we call the Global South are in fact going to approach anything like sustainable development or modernization in the Western sense. There are a variety of reasons for this situation. Population pressures on the land, people having to leave rural areas as a consequence, growing urban agglomeration, massive unemployment, urban unrest—these are only a few of the reasons. The result is political instability—governments and populations under siege. Additionally, increasing energy costs have hit the Global South very hard. The annual energy bill now facing the Global South is considerably larger than the entire aggregate flow of assistance to the Global South. Finally, the kind of environmental limits that we have now begun to recognize as part of the physical makeup of the planet simply will not permit a replication of Western patterns of development.

[1]For an insightful study of transition see Willis Harman, *Global Mind Change* (Indianapolis: Knowledge Systems, Inc., 1988).

COOPERATIVE POLITICS

The illusion of independence has been replaced by the paradox of interdependence. Interdependence provides increased points of leverage for the rich and powerful, but it also raises the costs of exercising that influence and reduces the freedom of action of the privileged. There is a particular irony here for the industrialized countries in that interdependence implies global issues, necessitating a global response, but interdependence also circumscribes the exercise of global power. The uninformed or careless use of power—particularly military power—in such circumstances can easily be self-defeating.

All of this suggests the utility of a nontraditional approach to national security—an approach that is beginning to receive attention. This strategy calls for a state to strengthen mutual dependencies and cooperative linkages between itself and other states—that is, to exploit existing tendencies toward interdependence. Security from this perspective is achieved less by placing a potential adversary state at a power disadvantage than by circumscribing its freedom and incentive for hostile actions. But, as previously noted, such ties constrain the actions of all states involved. Consequently, adoption of an interdependence strategy carries with it an implied willingness to downgrade sovereign freedom of action as a defining characteristic of national security. A fully developed interdependent system, however, carries the promise of security that is durable—not the elusive kind with which we have been familiar. This statement is true because from an interdependence perspective, world politics assumes non–zero-sum characteristics. Enhanced security for one state requires improved security for all. Hence, the concept of common security postulates the existence of common interests that, if served, result in increased security for all states. The maintenance of the system as a whole thus becomes a priority goal of national policy.

A mere handful of states can no longer control what goes on in the world. Hegemony has become a historical curiosity. The superpowers have been deposed, the victims of their own technological breakthroughs. The only workable instrument for the ratification of interstate decisions in the emerging world order will be a broad consensus of peoples and governments.

Consensus—the distinctive political tool in relations among equals—has already gone far to replace armed force as the preferred instrument of national policy. "Realists" may object to the naïveté, the instability, or the shortsightedness of some manifestations of the consensus, but it would be sheer folly to challenge either its existence or its power. The process of consensus is so new a method of reaching binding international decisions, that mistakes and contradictions in its application are inevitable. But we have little choice: The emerging global order will either learn to live with mass opinion or it will not survive. Trial and error—seasoned by patience—will teach the elements of an operational code to govern the new process, and consensus will become a more efficient and predictable instrument.

Consensus does not demand a radical transformation of the global system.

Most of the old ways of thinking and acting in world politics will be useful in the future. Negotiation, persuasion, accommodation, and even certain forms of coercion will remain as standard features of interstate life. The loss of the ability to force a verdict by war will do little more than impose one more limitation on the practice of statecraft—a more fundamental inhibition than any the system has accepted up to this point, it is true, but nevertheless one that will leave room for vigor, imagination, and skill in framing and executing national policy.

The process of consensus, however, underscores the obsolescence of the competitive model of world politics that has long served as the basis of international economic and political structures. It is a model predicated upon the assumption that competition among nations, all pursuing their own self-interest, will, through Adam Smith's "invisible hand," miraculously lead to the increasing betterment of everyone. Consensus introduces a cooperative model of world politics that focuses on the benefits of international stability in the global system. No one country can achieve it by itself. In fact, everyone has to make sacrifices. The cooperative model departs from the zero-sum competitive power-politics model where one nation gains and the other loses, and moves toward common action resulting in mutual benefits.

In economics, the competitive model has functioned well to explain the provision and distribution of private goods. It served the very important function of guiding the stimulation of economic expansion and development. The problem is that the model simply failed to explain voluntary cooperation to provide public goods, as opposed to private goods. Public goods are those that are shared and enjoyed by a large number of people. Two key characteristics distinguish public goods from private goods. The first characteristic is that, in general, they cannot be provided by any single individual or small group of individuals. A major, concerted effort by a large number of people is needed. The second key characteristic of public goods is what is referred to as nonexcludibility, that is, each person can benefit from the public good even if that person does not contribute to the provision of the good (as with public television programming).[2]

In other words, there is a self-interested temptation for each person to take a free ride on the efforts of others: to simply sit back, let other people provide the public goods, and enjoy it without having contributed to it. Of course, if everybody always did that, we would not have any public goods. The important point to note here is that, because of these two key characteristics of public goods, the unrestrained pursuit of individual (or corporate or national) self-interest cannot in general provide public goods.

Public goods cover a wide area. Some obvious ones are an ecologically sound environment, international management of food and energy resources, national defense and the avoidance of Armageddon, and morality. Public goods require the correction of the aggregate negative side effects of the unrestrained

[2]For a thoughtful study of cooperative relations, see Thomas Arthur Cotton, "Public Man: A Model of Rational Cooperation," a Ph.D. dissertation submitted to the Department of Engineering-Economic Systems, Stanford University, Stanford, CA, 1978.

pursuit of self-interest. In other words, the avoidance of what we might call public bads is a public good. This is a key area in which international cooperation is going to be necessary. Carbon dioxide pollution that contributes to global ("greenhouse") warming, mass hunger, energy shortages, arms transfers, and ocean pollution are problems that no single country can solve. Each country is tempted to say, "Well, my contribution to this problem is minimal, so I'll go ahead with my polluting activity and let other people work to clean up the environment." Of course, we are aware that major polluters are not limited to nations. Each person, each arms-merchant country, can always say, "Well, I might as well go ahead and sell those weapons to such and such a country, because if we don't sell them, another nation will."

Morality (ethical rules to guide our conduct) is something that everyone benefits from and that no individual can provide alone. It requires continued cooperation by everyone holding that ethical system in order to maintain it. Yet, in general, everyone has a temptation to let everyone else behave ethically and to exploit that behavior by taking advantage of the other people.

So, the class of public goods clearly covers a wide range of important examples. Voluntary cooperation to provide public goods, it seems, cannot be explained by simple self-interested behavior. It requires some minimal ethical assumption. Ethics can be seen as motivated not by pure altruism, but by a more enlightened self-interest, based upon a more inclusive conception of the self (or of the community), in an increasingly interdependent and interconnected world. An ethical assumption to begin with is the existence of a norm of fairness, a norm that requires an individual to bear a share of the cost that is borne by those who are also cooperating in an action, rather than simply taking a free ride, as self-interest would dictate.

What are some of the characteristics of cooperation based on fairness that would be relevant to global cooperative politics? In the first place, to have cooperation of that sort requires the identification and acceptance of shared objectives that can only be reached through cooperative efforts. Second, each of the potential cooperators has to have an expectation of personal benefit from this cooperative effort. They are not obligated by fairness to contribute to an enterprise from which they expect to get nothing back. A third important aspect of voluntary cooperation based on fairness is that there must be a fair distribution of the benefits and costs of cooperation. Questions of international social justice cannot be avoided.

We simply cannot expect a person or a group—a minority group, for example, or a nation that feels it is being exploited—to be willing to make any significant sacrifice of their own self-interest to benefit their perceived exploiter.

Let us emphasize that fairness is an ethical norm, and at times it requires that we set aside simple self-interest in order to adhere to the norm. However, the norm of fairness does not require unilateral self-sacrifice. It is not a norm of pure altruism. Fair individuals are obligated to contribute to a cooperative effort only if they can expect to receive benefits from the like contributions of others. This is a key characteristic of the underlying concept of reciprocity, the obligation to return the favor, or, in other words, the obligation not to take advantage of someone who has done you a favor. For example, fairness would not require unilateral disarmament, although it would obligate one not to take advantage of disarmament by another nation. Similarly, fairness does not require contribution to a futile enterprise. We really have to have an expectation of receiving benefits from the cooperation of others.

Because of the mutual expectation of benefits, cooperation based on fairness requires mutual trust. Since no one party can force any of the others to cooperate, and since each one has a selfish temptation not to cooperate, each must trust the others not to take advantage of both the opportunity and the temptation to cheat. Cooperation, then, requires mutual expectation of a willingness to sacrifice short-term self-interests for the common good.

Cooperation based on fairness involves some risk because there is a need to rely on mutual trust. The more confidence one has in the trustworthiness of the other cooperators, the less this risk will be. The role of fairness in the game is to obligate cooperators not to take advantage of each other in a risky situation. It is sometimes necessary to build a basis for trust by starting with relatively low-loss, low-risk cooperative ventures and working up to bigger, higher-payoff, but higher-risk enterprises.

A related problem is the double standard of morality often used. People often have one standard of ethics with regard to their in-group, however that is defined, and a different standard of ethics with regard to their perceived out-group. This may be one of the greatest challenges in building international cooperation, because people tend to draw their in-group lines, at the farthest extent, at their own national borders.

Though having shared objectives that benefit everyone is a necessary precondition for cooperation, it is not sufficient. There is a crucial role for leadership in converting shared objectives and a shared norm of fairness into effective cooperation. Leadership is needed to establish the mechanisms for cooperation and to insure that efforts will be coordinated and that they will succeed. Leadership also has an important part in the formulation of common objectives in the first place. Mechanisms for cooperation must be established that determine the fair allocation of benefits and burdens, and that identify the roles and responsibilities of the various actors in the cooperative enterprise. Another role of leadership is to promote the development of solidarity. Solidarity is necessary for the underlying norm of fair reciprocity to be effective. Leadership has the role of setting an example of sacrifice of immediate self-interest in furtherance of common goals.

PREMISES FOR A NEW WORLD ORDER

World events and trends will continue to underline the precariousness of a national security strategy based on separateness in an increasingly interconnected and interdependent world. Moving beyond such strategies will require basic reformulations of our dominant worldview. To make the world safe for *humanity,* we must accord to each other and to the Earth the exalted place previously reserved in our thinking for such things as states, ideologies, and economic growth.

The emerging view expands the dominant Western perspective to incorporate traditional cultures. This broader view means freeing people from the dominance of economic logic over their lives, as well as freeing cultures from being driven off the globe by economically-based institutions. There is a great deal more emphasis on humane values. They are assumed to have some sort of reality, and economic values are assumed to be subservient to others—less fundamental in that they are, after all, only models or constructs whose primary usefulness is the extent to which they accurately express and aggregate the human values. Economic institutions, technology, and analyses then are viewed as a means to an end, not as ends in themselves. Technology and economic growth are not the end goals in this view. Rather, the goals of a society must relate to the culturally based goals of its people.

The materialist worldview implicit in the institutions of modern industrial nations is not a promising base on which to construct a viable new world order. A suitable new world order should enhance the four pillars of our existence: the natural environment in which we live, our planet; the human environment, that is, us; the political environment, that is, our institutions and the way we organize ourselves; and finally, the cultural environment, the way we live our lives.

Our natural environment is the basis of our existence, and the key value is ecological balance. If we lose our ecological balance we lose everything. Our human environment is the source of human life. Our basic needs include survival and material well-being, identity, something that gives meaning to life, and freedom. The key value in the human environment is human dignity. Our political environment refers to our belief systems and institutions. The key value in the political environment is coexistence. A viable political environment is one that is able to sustain pluralism, a thousand and one beliefs and institutions. It is where capitalism, socialism, tribalism, and communalism can supplement one another. Finally our cultural environment refers to our lifestyles and the way we deal with ourselves. The key value in the cultural environment is diversity. Tolerance becomes the governing principle of human cultural expressions. Culture becomes a resource because culture provides for deep-rooted human needs.[3]

The four key values of a new world order require change through developing more effective laws and through restructuring or establishing responsive governmental and nongovernmental organizations. Different actors, different power configurations, and plausible alternatives to the present system are needed. We need also a consciousness of transition processes. Change occurs most effectively through evolving consensus.

A new world order represents a shift in our perspectives and worldview from the nation-state to one world; from balance of power to justice; from national interest to human interest; from the rights of states to human rights; from inde-

[3]Johan Galtung discusses some of these concepts in "Solidarity in a Global Perspective," an unpublished presentation at The Ethnical Platform, New York City, January 25, 1987.

pendence and sovereignty of states to interdependence; from economic growth as a central value to transformation; from materialism to human progress through spiritual evolution; from an environment to be exploited to an environment that has rights of its own; and from coercion and war to collaboration and nonviolence.

Such a vision of a new world order requires a new system of diplomacy. We need to change the diplomatic method, and quite consciously so. The new diplomacy has a more hopeful view of what can be done than the traditional one. It is more concerned with social change than with merely preserving the international order as it exists and protecting national interests. The practitioners of the new diplomacy should be more problem solvers than philosophers, and they must possess some inherent distrust of overall theories and plans. But they must also possess a surer sense of values than there is in a game plan.

The new diplomacy must operate on a world vision other than the old diplomacy. The old diplomacy saw world politics as a struggle of nation-states to survive and to protect their national interests. The best that the old diplomacy hopes for is to oil the inevitable changes that occur, thus avoiding the destruction of (Western) civilization. The new diplomacy sees world politics as a struggle for world peace in the broadest sense that peace is more than the absence of war, but also is the presence of justice and freedom for all.

Peace is not seen as an abstract goal to be pursued; peace is a dynamic process of doing and being. Peace is a process. Peace includes both the absence of direct physical violence and war, and the elimination of structural violence. The latter refers to the consequences of social, political, cultural, economic, and civil structures—institutions and processes that lower the material and spiritual quality of human life and degrade the natural environment. Success in this struggle for world peace is dependent upon transcending in the critical areas the provincialism of the nation-states and making more real a world community.

The new diplomacy assumes that all peoples desire and are capable of self-government, that all peoples will find their own form of protecting their own dignity and freedom if they are allowed to do so, and that only in a world of freedom and social justice are the freedom and social justice of all really secure. To deny others and ourselves the legitimacy of caring for other people is to deny part of our own humanity. Likewise, to deny governments as agencies of society the legitimacy to promote humanist goals is to subject our corporate life to the ethic of the jungle, without a struggle.

The prizes to be won under the new diplomacy are novel and unprecedented, but they are worthwhile all the same. Success in the new diplomacy will go as it did in the old—to those who best learn and apply the rules. The penalty for failure may be a disaster; the reward for success may be a better life on this planet for everyone.

We are the heirs of an old order of violence. Our legacy would be much greater if we become the architects of a new world order founded upon human solidarity and the wholeness of planetary life.

RECOMMENDED READINGS

AXELROD, ROBERT. *The Evolution of Cooperation.* New York: Basic Books, 1984.

BOULDING, ELISE. *Building a Global Civic Culture: Education for an Interdependent World.* New York: Teachers College Press, 1988.

BROCK-UTNE, BRIGIT. *Feminist Perspectives on Peace and Peace Education.* New York: Pergamon Press, 1989.

CARTER, ASHTON B., ed. *A New Concept of Cooperative Security.* Washington, DC: Brookings Institute, 1992.

CHASE, JAMES, and MICHAEL CROMARTIE. *Might and Right After the Cold War: Can Foreign Policy Be Moral?* Washington, DC: Ethics and Public Policy Center, 1993.

EKINS, PAUL. *A New World Order: Grassroots Movements for Global Change.* London: Routledge, 1992.

GADDIS, JOHN. *The United States and the End of the Cold War: Implications, Reconsiderations, Provocations.* New York: Oxford University Press, 1992.

HOGAN, MICHAEL J. *The End of the Cold War: Its Meaning and Implications.* New York: Cambridge University Press, 1992.

LIPSCHUTZ, RONNIE D., and KEN CONCA. *The State and Social Power in Global Environmental Politics.* New York: Columbia University Press, 1993.

NORTH, ROBERT C. *War, Peace, Survival: Global Politics and Conceptual Synthesis.* Boulder, CO: Westview Press, 1990.

OYE, KENNETH A., ed. *Cooperation Under Anarchy.* Princeton, NJ: Princeton University Press, 1986.

SKOLNIKOFF, EUGENE B. *The Elusive Transformation: Science, Technology, and the Evolution of International Politics.* Princeton, NJ: Princeton University Press, 1993.

SNOW, DONALD M. *Distant Thunder: Third World Conflict and the New International Order.* New York: St. Martin's Press, 1993.

THOMPSON, SCOTT W., et al. *Approaches to Peace: An Intellectual Map.* Washington, DC: United States Institute of Peace, 1991.

WALKER, R. B. J. *One World, Many Worlds: Struggles for a Just World Peace.* Boulder, CO: Lynne Rienner, 1988.

WATSON, ADAM. *The Evolution of International Society: A Comparative Historical Analysis.* New York: Routledge, 1992.

ZIEGLER, DAVID W. *War, Peace, and International Politics.* 6th ed. New York: HarperCollins, 1993.

Authors' Postscript to the Fourth Edition

Throughout this book we have discussed values, politics, and the global predicament. We have emphasized that old attitudes, models, and practices are largely outmoded, and that new ones are necessary. The current global situation reflects elements of both old and new. We live in an era of transition, one whose scope and depth goes beyond anything yet witnessed in human history. We live in the midst of suffering and hope, and efforts to make new beginnings.

There is a striking parallel between the current global condition and the experience of an individual striving to overcome personal challenges in his/her life. With the individual, the first stage is a growing sense that something is not right. An introspective quest for more appropriate values follows, which may involve a systematic reexamination of old beliefs and habits, and a search for new ones. Once new value commitments are made, a constant effort is required to bring action into agreement with these values. From this perspective, we can discover, amidst the crises of contemporary global politics, a search for those values upon which a viable future for our planet can be built.

Some commentators have further suggested that humanity is currently at an adolescent stage of development. Adolescents are physically adults, but emotionally still very much like children. As a species, too, we have the physical and technical means to create a global civilization, yet we still tend to see the world in terms of limited group identities derived from the past. Just as adolescence can be a dangerous time, with new physical powers being tested and sometimes misused for childish ends, the current global era is characterized by agitation, violence, and upheaval as new technical capacities are employed to pursue traditional rivalries.

The issues facing us demand a new set of answers, arising from a new pattern of faith and belief. We feel strongly that those values must be spiritual in nature. As should be clear from the chapters of this book, we do not believe that everything in the universe, our world, or human nature is fully accessible to positivist science. Many aspects of our inner reality and life, including consciousness itself, remain mysterious, especially the age-old quest of the human spirit toward transcendence, a reaching toward an ultimate reality.

Throughout history, though admittedly for limited periods, various civilizations have demonstrated how spiritual values can engender social progress. At the same time, we would hasten to acknowledge that these same values have just as often been corrupted and manipulated to justify actions that represent their antitheses. This in itself, however, should not prevent an appreciation of the historic association between the emergence of a truly moral social order and widespread commitment to spiritual values.

Therefore we do not hesitate to take a position in regard to André Malraux's famous declaration that "the twenty-first century will either be religious or it won't"; that is, we either face the choice of moving in the direction of creativity or of becoming even less so than we are today. We prefer to use the term *spiritual* instead of *religious*. Although these terms are often used interchangeably, we see a distinction between them. The term *religion* refers to an institutional framework within which a specific theology is pursued, usually among a community of like-minded believers. *Spirituality*, on the other hand, transcends the boundaries of religion, suggesting broader human involvement that comes from the inner essence of a person. At the level of the individual, it refers to action borne of a commitment that is not necessarily informed by allegiance to a particular religion.

We agree with the definition of spirituality put forth by the Scottish Council of Churches (1977): "Spirituality is an attempt to grow in sensitivity to self, to others, to non-human creations and to God who is within and beyond this totality." Spirituality is a shift in consciousness that sees the whole of existence contained in the parts, and from the parts the whole is constructed. Spirituality filters out the superficial, the changing, and so the essential emerges. The term *holistic* expresses another metaphor for the spiritual: holding all directions in simultaneous connection—including both the horizontal and vertical directions. The horizontal connects one person with another, with all people, and with all things. Vertically, higher and lower levels of consciousness are joined. This creative organizing force of spirituality has historically been funneled into Indian, Chinese, Middle Eastern, and Mediterranean society through such well-known visionaries as Buddha, Krishna, Moses, Jesus, Lao Tzu, Muhammad, Saint Teresa, Rumi, and many others. In modern times, this creative force has found expression in Elizabeth Cady Stanton, Mahatma Gandhi, Martin Luther King, Jr., Dalai Lama, Desmond Tutu, Elie Weisel, and many others.

Spirituality starts from the individual—from our very essence. Yet politics also is inherently spiritual because our public life reflects our social values. The reconnection of politics to our highest and most worthy values is now the most important task in political life. World events and trends will continue to expose the precariousness of international relations based on separateness in an increasingly interconnected and interdependent world. Spirituality provides the possibility of experiencing and accepting human solidarity and, most importantly, the wholeness of human life: Spirituality is an experience of a sense of unity that overcomes the principle that divides humanity on the bases of religions, races, genders, and classes.

Just as we find that the naive materialism of the post-Renaissance centuries is no longer working, changes have begun in the direction of a more inclusive epistemology. As we enter the twenty-first century, we are recognizing that the deeper we delve into the fundamentals of science, the closer we are to the fundamentals of many of the traditional mysticisms. We are now coming to recognize the reality of "the sacred," which we define as any process that explicitly links us to the largest possible context to which we belong. Gregory Bateson, when once asked to define *sacrament*, said, "the recognition of the pattern which connects." *Buddha* translates literally as "the one who woke up," and refers not just to the historical personage but also to any human being in a state of full awareness, i.e., a person dedicated to the support of the total patterning and harmony of our world.

Reinvestment of "the sacred" means both the humanizing of that state of being and the consecration of the human. It is the recognition that sacred activity is not separate from immediate personal and interpersonal experience. Reinvestment of the sacred acknowledges the presence of both human responsibility and divine will in our activity.

First, second, and third worlds (also known, respectively, as the industrial north, communism, and the Global South) are now recognized as a single world. The oppressor and the oppressed are seen simply as people, experiencing life with its vicissitudes. Reason and intuition are seen as twin faces of truth. Planning and spontaneity converge to offer an expanded window of experience. Civilization and barbarism evolve into culture. Propositional, and anecdotal knowledge eventually become the essence of all knowledge.

When we develop the view that all being is one, that human consciousness comprises both analytical and intuitive modes, we begin to see the individual parts of reality as well as the whole of it. The complementary functioning of the rational and the intuitive is a measure of human creativity. When we reconcile the two, we come to terms with ourselves as a whole, and bridge the gap between appearance and reality, without which there can be no vision. Then we do not see one another as rivals; indeed, we discover that the whole world needs the whole world.

A new ethic must allow humanity to experience itself as complete, as we already are. It must value acceptance of the self as a whole, embracing the unconscious as well as conscious. The integration of the personality at the individual level becomes a metaphor for the integration of humanity at the species level.

We feel that inner commitment to a vision of humankind's place in the universe that gives priority to ethical thought and values over mere physical existence is a fundamental prerequisite for survival and, ultimately, prosperity on the planet. Furthermore, we accept the testimony of saints, mystics, and millions of ordinary people through the ages that there are inner/higher forces that can be drawn upon for inspiration, courage, and perseverance. It may be that only this kind of inner strength and creative energy can sustain us and enable us to, in Dietrich Bonhoffer's classic phrase, "say yes to the twentieth [and in our case twenty-first] century."

Religious traditions and spirituality, however, must be reborn if they are to respond to contemporary spiritual needs. Though most religious and ethical systems promote reciprocity and goodwill, their institutions and outlooks are too frequently identified with just those aspects of the past that contribute to current division and conflict. Put very simply, spiritual values for the present and future cannot be partisan; they must speak to the universal human need for transcendence, unity, and justice.

In conclusion, we affirm that achieving a unifying global consensus as the basis for a humane, ecologically viable, new global system is possible. The essence of such a vision must be *felt* as well as rationally argued, because it involves both the head and the heart. From this perspective, a new global system requires new political and social arrangements, a new (or renewed) vision of humankind's existential reality and purpose, and an unrelenting effort to make the former truly reflect the latter. This is an agenda for world politics worthy of what we see as the best in human nature and experience. We invite you to consider this perspective as you try to comprehend and find a place in our world.

Index